Movies and Meaning

Movies and Meaning
An Introduction to Film

Stephen Prince

Allyn and Bacon
Boston London Toronto Sydney Tokyo Singapore

Vice President, Humanities: Joseph Opiela
Editorial Assistant: Kate Tolini
Marketing Manager: Karon Bowers
Editorial Production Service: MARBERN HOUSE
Composition Buyer: Linda Cox
Manufacturing Buyer: Megan Cochran
Cover Administrator: Linda Knowles

Copyright © 1997 by Allyn & Bacon
A Viacom Company
Needham Heights, MA 02194

Library of Congress Cataloging-in-Publication Data

Prince, Stephen, 1955-
    Movies and meaning : an introduction to film / by Stephen
Prince.
        p.   cm.
    ISBN 0-02-396806-0 (alk. paper)
    1. Motion pictures.   I. Title.
PN1994.P676   1995
791.43--dc20   95-43380
                                                  CIP

Printed in the United States of America
10 9 8 7 6 5 4 3 2 1   01 00 99 98 97 96

For My Parents

Contents

Preface   xi

1 The Camera and Film Structure   1

The Concept of Structure   3

Structure and the Camera   8

Structural Design and Creative Choice   31

The Camera and Viewer Perception   36

Summary   41

Suggested Readings   42

2 Elements of Mise-en-scene: Cinematography   43

Components of Mise-en-scene   45

The Essentials of Cinematography   47

Summary   67

Suggested Readings   68

3 Elements of Mise-en-scene: Production Design and Performance Style   69

From Art Director to Production Designer   70

Basic Tools of Production Design   71

The Design Concept   80

Production Design and the Viewer's Response   82

Acting   85

Summary   102

Suggested Readings   103

4 Editing: Making the Cut   104

What Is Editing?   105

The Principles of Continuity Editing   121

Alternatives to Continuity Editing   131

Summary   149

Suggested Readings   150

5 Principles of Sound Design   151

Sound Design   153

The Codes of Sound Design   156

Types of Sound   168

Summary   182

Suggested Readings   183

6 The Nature of Narrative in Film   184

The Turn to Narrative in Early Film History   186

The Significance of Narrative   190

Elements of Narrative   190

The Viewer's Contribution to Narrative   209

Summary   212

Suggested Readings   213

7 Modes of Screen Reality   214

Basic Modes of Screen Reality   216

Genres and Screen Reality   242

Summary   252

Suggested Readings   253

8 Hollywood International   254

The Global Dominance of Hollywood   256

International Influence of Hollywood Style   267

Summary   278

Suggested Readings   278

9 The Cinema in an International Frame   279

The International Auteur Cinema   280

Cinema and Society: The New Wave Phenomenon   299

Summary   315

Suggested Readings   316

10   Film Criticism and Interpretation   317

Why Criticism Exists   318

The Task of the Critic   320

Modes of Criticism   321

Creating Criticism   329

Summary   338

Suggested Readings   340

11   Models of Film Theory   341

Realist Models of the Film Experience   343

Auteurist Models   347

Psychoanalytic Models   351

Ideological Models   354

Feminist Models   362

Cognitive Models   366

Summary   371

Suggested Readings   372

Glossary   374

Index   385

Guide to Color Plates   46

Preface

This book is designed to give students an in-depth introduction to the motion picture medium. Virtually everyone reading the book knows about the pleasures that movies can offer, the ways they can thrill, amuse, sadden, and excite the emotions. But, however strong their love for movies, most viewers lack a detailed knowledge of the medium. This book assumes no prior knowledge of film on the part of the reader. The text is organized around three basic questions: how movies express meanings, how viewers understand those meanings, and how cinema functions globally as both an art and a business.

Most introductory film textbooks concentrate on the first question and tend to minimize or disregard the other two questions. A special feature of this book is the attention given to the ways viewers respond to the elements of film structure and the attention given to cinema as a global business as well as an art. To fully understand the medium of cinema, students need to know what filmmakers do with the tools of their craft, how viewers respond to the audiovisual designs those tools create, and how cinema functions as both an art *and* a business.

Each of the textbook's three guiding questions opens up a series of topics. The first question—how do movies express meaning? —asks what filmmakers do and how they do it. The basic tools of filmmaking include cinematography, production design, the actor's performance, editing, sound design, and narrative structure. Each of these areas contributes to the overall design of a film, and, by manipulating these tools, filmmakers are able to express a range of meanings.

The second question—how do viewers understand films?—asks about what viewers do when watching movies. How do viewers interpret the effects filmmakers create? How do filmmakers anticipate and build on the likely ways viewers will react to certain kinds of stories and audiovisual designs? What makes movies understandable to viewers in the first place? How can filmmakers facilitate the viewer's ability to understand and interpret the images on screen?

To talk only about what filmmakers do to create meaning on screen is to leave out a crucial part of the picture. One also needs to know what viewers do with the movies they watch because, without viewers, there are no meanings in film. The medium of cinema depends on a contract between filmmaker and viewer. Together, they co-create the film experience.

Accordingly, the text examines how filmmakers create images and sounds and also looks closely at the mechanisms and processes by which viewers make sense of those images and sounds on screen. Where appropriate, the chapters discuss the viewer's *interpretive* contribution to the screen experience, the ways that viewers actively look for patterns in the images and sounds on screen and link them in ways that have meaning for them. The viewer's interpretive contribution refers to the ways viewers actively process and interpret audiovisual information in cinema. Viewers do this by applying to the screen aspects of their real-life visual, personal, and social experiences as well as their knowledge of motion picture conventions and style.

The third question—how does cinema operate as an international medium?—asks about the dual capacity in which cinema functions as both an art and a business on a global scale. To pretend that the cinema is mainly an art or medium of creative expression distorts the understanding of its nature, because it is also a business. In some ways, it is more fundamentally a business than an art. The way it operates as a business in a global context influences the production of certain kinds and styles of film. Cinema is an international medium, operating in a global economy and with films created by directors representing a diverse range of countries and cultures.

The focus throughout the text is on narrative filmmaking and on fictional narrative in particular, since these include the most popular forms of filmmaking, those seen by the largest audiences, and are what most people mean when they talk about "the movies." Throughout the text, boxes extend the major topics of discussion into more specialized areas and supplement film examples with brief profiles of major directors. The reader will gain a more comprehensive understanding of the medium of cinema by exploring these boxes. Each chapter ends with a few suggested readings to direct the interested reader's attention to more intensive discussions of issues raised in the chapter. Boldface terms throughout the text designate items defined in the glossary.

About the Photographs

Photographic illustrations in the chapters utilize production stills and frame enlargements. Production stills are made by an on-set photographer during the course of a film's production, and they only *approximate* the actual shots and compositions of the film. To exactly reproduce the actual images viewers see when watching a film, frame enlargements must be used. All photographs in the text that are frame enlargements are labelled as such. The reader will note that, in general, the production stills look sharper and richer than the frame enlargements, which tend to be softer and grayer. But for the purposes of teaching, where an exact reference to a film's images is necessary, frame enlargements are required, and they are used here in that context. The reader seeing a frame enlargement can be confident that, with respect to all matters of camera perspective, she or he is seeing the exact frame as it appears in the film.

About the Text

Chapters 1 through 6 focus closely on the basic elements of creative design in motion pictures—the camera, cinematography, production design, the actor's performance, editing, sound, and narrative. Chapter 1 explains the concept of film structure and how camera position, angle, lens, and movement may be used to achieve a variety of visual designs and meanings in cinema. Chapter 2 extends this discussion of the camera by exploring cinematography, one of the components of mise-en-scene, a term that designates the collective contributions of cinematography, production design, and performance style. Chapter 2 studies how filmmakers use light and color to achieve effects on screen and how viewers interpret those effects.

Chapter 3 examines the areas of production design (this includes costume design, set design, and use of mattes and miniature models) and acting, considered in terms of the unique characteristics of film acting and how the performer becomes part of a film's total visual design or mise-en-scene.

Chapter 4 examines film editing. What is editing, what are the principles of continuity editing (the most commonly used system in filmmaking), and what are some alternatives to continuity editing? How do viewers draw inferences and interpretations across shots?

Chapter 5 discusses an often-overlooked filmmaking tool—sound design. How do filmmakers design their soundtracks, how do they manipulate sound, and how does sound combine with images in ways that enrich those images? How do viewers interpret sound in relation to images?

Chapter 6 examines the nature of narrative in film. What is film narrative, what are its elements, how do filmmakers organize those elements, and how do viewers contribute to the narrative experience?

These six chapters closely examine the basic tools of the filmmaker's art and how viewers respond to the audiovisual designs those tools create. The focus of Chapters 7 through 11 expands to cover larger issues of cinematic design, of art and business in a global context, and of film criticism and theory.

Chapter 7 looks at how films construct different types of "reality" on screen. The representation of screen reality—the ways movies persuade viewers that what they are seeing is "real"—varies considerably across different categories of film and involves differing kinds of manipulations by filmmakers and assumptions by viewers. Four basic types of screen reality are explored.

Chapters 8 and 9 examine motion pictures in a world context. Chapter 8 studies the impact of popular American commercial filmmaking upon world markets and the ways the American industry is organized to compete aggressively in overseas markets. It also traces the connections between blockbuster films—so important in today's industry—and the world market. Chapter 9 examines explicit international alternatives to the Hollywood model of popular commercial moviemaking. These alternatives are discussed in terms of *auteur* directors and national, new-wave film styles.

Chapters 10 and 11 discuss film criticism, interpretation, and film theory. These areas are the logical end-point of an introduction to film. Chapter 10 explores the nature of film criticism, what it is and what it does, and how film critics create that criticism. Chapter 11 examines theories about the nature of cinema, surveys the most important theories, and discusses their strengths and weaknesses.

When the reader has finished *Movies and Meaning,* he or she will have a comprehensive understanding of three major, central issues of film study: (1) how filmmakers achieve their effects; (2) how viewers make sense out of what they see on screen; and (3) how cinema operates as both an art and a business in a global context. Above all, it is the author's hope that students will finish this book wiser about the cinema and with greater affection for it, an affection strengthened by knowledge of its secrets.

Acknowledgments

Writing a book of this size and scope presents numerous challenges. The chief issue is to find the right approach for an introduction to a medium as extensive as the cinema and that now encompasses a century of creative development. The approach adopted here is accessible for the reader and easy to understand while honoring the complexity of the medium. Without oversimplifying the medium or the issues involved in cinema study, considerable effort has been spent to make the writing style appropriate for the general reader.

For their valuable assistance in helping me find the right blend of topics, concepts, relevant film examples, and style of presentation, I must thank my careful editors who helped guide this text toward completion. The project really began at the prompting of Kevin Davis at Macmillan who was very enthusiastic about producing a new film textbook and urged me forward despite my initial hesitation over what seemed a daunting task. I must also thank Macmillan's excellent development editor, Linda Montgomery.

At Allyn and Bacon, Joe Opiela helped steer the text toward completion. Joe was an especially good interpreter of the readers' reports. He made valuable suggestions for bringing the text into line with their recommendations. His support is greatly appreciated.

The photo program is a key feature of this text. My thanks go to Terry Geeskin of the Museum of Modern Art's Film Stills Archive and to the staff at Jerry Ohlinger's Movie Material Store.

Most of the photos in this text are frame enlargements from the actual films under study. Edd Sewell kindly taught me how to use a darkroom. My thanks to Gerry Scheeler for the loan of lights and camera equipment and thanks also to Carl Plantinga and Richard Dillard for their support. A special thanks to Eric Poe Miller and Grant Corley for designing the figures used in the text.

Quotations from Pauline Kael's review of *Last Tango in Paris,* originally published in *The New Yorker,* are used with permission of E. P. Dutton, publisher. Quotations from *"Dead Again* or A-Live Again: Postmodern or Postmortem?" are used with permission of University of Texas Press, publisher. A special thanks to the essay's authors, Marcia Landy and Lucy Fischer, for their kind permission to reprint portions of their essay.

As always, Bob Denton, my department chair, came through with whatever resources or support I requested. His help and friendship have been a great boost to
my scholarship over the past six years.

Thanks, also, to Teresa Darvalics for her valuable manuscript assistance and
to Elizabeth Thomas for her help and for everything else. Finally, special thanks to
Marjorie Payne, my editorial and production editor, for a close and careful reading of
the manuscript and for the outstanding visual design she gave the book. She took exceptionally good care of the author's work.

Movies and Meaning

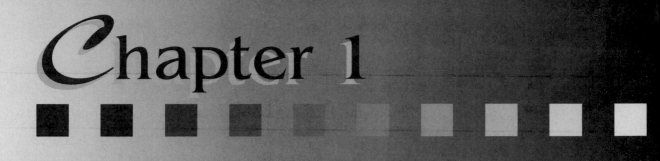

Chapter 1

The Camera and Film Structure

Chapter Objectives

After reading this chapter, you should be able to

- explain the nature of film structure and its relation to the ways movies express meaning
- describe the relation between film structure and the cinema's properties of time and space
- distinguish the three basic camera positions and their expressive functions
- describe how camera position can clarify the meaning of an actor's facial expression and gestures
- distinguish the three basic camera angles and describe the ways they influence viewer response

- differentiate telephoto, wide angle, and zoom lenses and explain their optical effects
- explain the three basic categories of camera movement and their expressive functions
- explain how a film's structural design is shaped by a filmmaker's choices about how to use the tools of style
- describe the relation between the camera's view of things and human perception
- explain how the camera creates images that both correspond with, and transform, the viewer's visual experience

Key Terms and Concepts

structure
running time
feature films
story time
internal structural time
frame
composition
wide screen
letterboxed
panned-and-scanned
camera position
long shot

medium shot
close-up
establishing shot
normal lens
telephoto lenses
wide-angle lenses
angle of view
depth of field
zoom lens
motion parallax
motion perspective
pan and tilt shots

dolly or tracking shots
boom or crane shots
suspense
surprise
subjective shot
rack focusing
production values
shutter
persistence of vision
flicker fusion
phi phenomena
beta movement

The shark in *Jaws* (1975) and the dinosaurs in *Jurassic Park* (1993) thrill movie-goers throughout the world. What excites viewers about these films, though, is much more than the sum of their special effects. These films thrill because they are made to do so. Without always being aware of it, viewers respond to the design of a film's creative elements—camerawork, lighting, sound, editing. These are elements of film structure. To understand how movies express meaning, one must begin by understanding their structural design.

This chapter explains the concept of film structure, the camera's role as an element of structure, and the relation between the camera's method of seeing and the viewer's perception. Through their structural design, films correspond with, and transform, the visual and social skills and experiences viewers bring to the medium.

☐ THE CONCEPT OF STRUCTURE

To understand how movies express meaning, and how filmmakers work, one must become familiar with the concept of **structure.** A convenient way to illustrate this concept is to make a distinction between structure and content. Consider the average newspaper movie review. It provides a description of a film's story and a paragraph or two about the characters and the actors who play them. In addition, the reviewer might mention the theme or themes of the film. These descriptions of story, character, and theme address the content of the movie.

Now, instead of thinking about content, one could ask about those things that help create the story, give shape to the characters, and illustrate and visualize the themes. These are questions about structure. Structure (which might also be called *style* or *technique*) depends upon manipulations of the camera, lights and color, production design, performance style, editing, sound, and narrative. These elements of structure, and the particular ways they are used by a filmmaker, create the audiovisual design of a film. Without structure, there can be no content and no film. Structure, then, refers to the audiovisual design of a film and the particular tools and techniques used to create that design.

The Role of the Director

Who creates a film's structure? A wide range of creative personnel design picture and sound on any given production. These include cinematographers, editors, sound designers, production designers, and many other important collaborators. Although filmmaking is a collaborative enterprise, one individual has overall artistic authority, and this is usually the director. The director coordinates and organizes the artistic inputs of other members of the production team, who generally subordinate their

---

Batman (Warner Bros., 1989)
Distinctive structural features of *Batman* include the title character's striking costume along with dark lighting and stylized set design. Together these help establish the film's grim, urban fantasy world of crime and superhero adventure.

JFK (Warner Bros., 1991) Director Oliver Stone confers with actor Kevin Costner during filming of *JFK*. Stone has established a distinctive film style, but collaboration with artists and performers is essential to the making of any film. Directors can realize their vision only by cooperating with, and depending on, the talents of other production personnel.

artistic tastes or preferences to a director's stated wishes or vision. The director, in turn, answers to the producer who generally has administrative control over a production (e.g., making sure the production stays on schedule and within budget).

In practice, great variety exists in the working methods of directors. Some directors, such as Robert Altman (*Ready-to-Wear*, 1994; *The Player*, 1992), welcome input from other production team members in a spirit of shared, collective artistry. Other directors, such as Alfred Hitchcock or Charles Chaplin, tend to be more autocratic and commanding in their creative approaches. Some directors, such as Stanley Kubrick (*Full Metal Jacket*, 1987), take an active role in the editing of their pictures. Most directors place special emphasis upon the quality of the script, believing a polished script to be essential to making a good film. Two of Clint Eastwood's best films as director, *Unforgiven* (1993) and *The Bridges of Madison County* (1995), feature exquisitely written scripts. Whatever particular working method a director may employ, on most films, the director is the key artist overseeing and organizing the film's audiovisual structure and the contributions of other production personnel.

Structure, Time, Space

The elements of cinematic structure, organized by directors and their production teams, help shape distinctive properties of time and space in a film. A convenient way of thinking about the arts is to consider the properties of time and/or space that they possess. Music, for example, is primarily an art of time. Its effects arise through the arrangement and sequence of tones in a musical composition that has some duration or length. Movies, by contrast, are an art of time as well as space.

Structure and Time

The time component of movies has several aspects. **Running time** designates the duration of the film, that is, the amount of time it takes a viewer to watch the film from beginning to end. Most commercially released films are called **feature films,** which means that they typically run between 90 to 120 minutes. Some films, however, are much longer. The Russian production of *War and Peace* (1968) runs for 7.5 hours.

Story time designates the amount of time covered by the narrative, and this can vary considerably from film to film. In Fred Zinnemann's Western, *High Noon* (1952), the story spans 1.5 hours, roughly equivalent to the running time of the film itself. Story time, on the other hand, can span many epochs and centuries, as in Stanley Kubrick's *2001: A Space Odyssey* (1968), which goes from the dawn of the apes well into the age of space travel. Filmmakers may also organize story time through the use of flashbacks so that it becomes fragmented, doubling back on itself, as in Orson Welles' *Citizen Kane* (1941), in which the story of Charles Foster Kane is told largely through the recollections of friends and associates who knew him.

Internal structural time, a third distinct aspect of cinematic time, arises from the structural manipulations of film form or technique. If a filmmaker edits a sequence so that the lengths of shots progressively decrease, or become shorter, the tempo of the sequence will accelerate. A rapid camera movement will accelerate the internal structural time of a shot. Regardless of the shot's actual duration on screen, it will seem to move faster.

In *Dances With Wolves* (1990), the editing imposes a slow pace upon the story by letting many shots linger on screen for several seconds. Director Kevin Costner thought a slow pace suited this stately epic about an era when horse and wagon were major modes of transportation. By contrast, the pacing of contemporary urban action films such as *Die Hard with a Vengeance* (1995) races at breakneck speed, rarely pausing long enough for an audience to catch its breath.

Dances With Wolves (Orion Pictures, 1990) and **Die Hard** (Twentieth Century Fox, 1988)
The slow pace and long running time (nearly 3 hours) of *Dances With Wolves* help establish the film's epic focus on the final years of the Sioux. Snappy editing and a fast pace would be as ill suited to this material as a leisurely pace would be for contemporary action films such as the *Die Hard* series

FRAME SIZE AND ASPECT RATIO

Apocalypse Now
(United Artists, 1979)
The full, widescreen frame showing the helicopter attack in *Apocalypse Now* and its panned-and-scanned counterpart. Note how cramped and tight the composition is in the panned-and-scanned version compared with the spaciousness of the full framing. The full frame image has an epic quality that the other version cannot possess. Frame enlargements.

Different frame sizes affect the spatial properties of cinema. In the classical Hollywood period of the 1930s and 1940s, frame size remained fairly standard, with an aspect ratio (width to height) of 1.33:1. Since the 1950s, however, **widescreen** ratios have been popular. Today, viewers see films projected in ratios of 1.85:1 or 2.35:1. These ratios are much wider, more rectangular, than the classical Hollywood ratio, which was nearly square-shaped. Obviously, a filmmaker's compositions will differ depending on the aspect ratio employed. Widescreen ratios, for example, permit compositions to utilize the horizontal axis of the frame more effectively than they do the vertical axis, as these illustrations demonstrate.

Aspect ratios are not freely interchangeable among media. A widescreen ratio of 2.35:1, designated for viewing on a big theater screen, translates very poorly to home video. The television monitor has a ratio of 4:3, nearly square. Accordingly, the widescreen film must be reformatted for its video release. It will either be **letterboxed** or **panned-and-scanned.** If letterboxed, frame bars mask the top and bottom of the television monitor, producing a wider-ratio picture area in the center of the screen (and without eliminating anything from the top and bottom of the image). Viewers of a letterboxed video get to see proper, or nearly-proper, screen ratio, but the tradeoff is a pathetically shrunken image that lacks the majesty and power of its big screen counterpart.

Panning-and-scanning produces a video image that fills the television monitor but in an incorrect aspect ratio. A panned-and-scanned format reproduces only part of the widescreen frame because the entire frame cannot fit on the television screen except through letterboxing. A technician handling the video transfer decides where the center of interest lies in a widescreen shot, and only that portion is transferred to video. The viewer gets to see a full-size image on the TV monitor, but it is one that represents only a portion of the original widescreen frame.

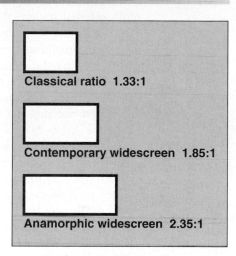

Classical ratio 1.33:1

Contemporary widescreen 1.85:1

Anamorphic widescreen 2.35:1

Figure 1: Aspect ratios

Once Upon a Time in the West
(Paramount Pictures, 1969)
Anamorphic widescreen images are created by squeezing a wide angle of view onto the film, then unsqueezing the image during projections to fill a theater's wide screen. These frames from *Once Upon a Time in the West* show the squeezed image as it appears on the strip of film and how it appears once it is unsqueezed during projection. Anamorphic widescreen films must be either letterboxed or panned-and-scanned for transfer to video. Frame enlargements.

Internal structural time is distinct from a film's running time or story time. A film's internal structural time never unfolds at a constant rate. It is a dynamic property, not a fixed one. Filmmakers modulate internal structural time to maintain viewer interest by changing camera positions, the lengths of shots, color and lighting design, and by altering the volume and density of the soundtrack.

Viewers of narrative films perceive internal structural time as a series of story events held in dynamic relations of tension and release. Viewers often describe films as being fast or slow moving, and many viewers today prefer a fast pace. Although internal structural time results from a filmmaker's manipulations of cinema structure, viewers experience this type of time subjectively, and their responses often vary greatly. One viewer loves the dramatic intensity and emotional lyricism of *The Bridges of Madison County* (1995), while another finds the film simply too slow and, therefore, boring.

Filmmakers exercise great control over the internal structural time of their films and, by doing so, hope to affect the viewer's subjective judgment of the viewing experience. Viewers' subjective judgments, however, remain their own, and, as subsequent chapters will show, in this way viewers become co-creators of the meaning and experience of every film.

Structure and Space

Cinema is an art of time *and* space. The spatial properties of cinema refer, first of all, to the arrangement of objects within the **frame.** The term *frame* refers to the dimensions of the projected area on screen. Objects can be arranged within this area in terms of height, width, and apparent depth. The arrangement of objects within these dimensions is the art of **composition.** Composition is a function of the elements of the camera that are studied in this chapter.

The spatial properties of the cinema, though, are more complex than the simple arrangement of objects within the frame. Cinema corresponds in key ways with the viewer's experience of physical space in daily life. These correspondences influence the responses of viewers to the events depicted on screen and are partly established through matters of camera placement and the appearance of depth and motion within the projected image. Cinematographers control the distribution of light on the set to accentuate the shape, texture, and positioning of objects and people. Because of this, the resulting film image can be made to appear entirely three-dimensional. Film editors may join shots so as to establish spatial constants on screen that hold regardless of changes in the camera's position or angle of view. A film's sound designer may use sound to communicate information about physical space. The spatial properties of cinema are multidimensional and may be expressed through many elements of structure. This chapter and succeeding ones explain these spatial properties and how filmmakers manipulate them.

■ STRUCTURE AND THE CAMERA

Structure refers to the audio visual design of a film and to its properties of time and space. What is the camera's contribution to this structure? Four fundamental features immediately stand out. The camera's position, angle, lens, and the camera's movement have a major impact upon the visual structure of every film.

Camera Position

The most basic way of classifying camera usage is in terms of **camera position.** This refers to the distance between the camera and the subject it is photographing. Obviously, the camera-to-subject distance is a continuum with an infinite series of points from very close to very far. In practice, however, the basic positions are usually classified as variations of three essential set-ups: the **long shot,** the **medium shot,** and the **close-up.** Each of these positions has its own distinct expressive functions in the cinema.

Filmmakers typically use the long shot to stress environment or setting. The long shot can also show a character's position in relationship to a given environment. In this respect, it is sometimes referred to as an **establishing shot** when it is used to open a film or to begin a scene. Many detective films, for example, begin with a long shot of the urban environment, often taken from a helicopter. In *Jurassic Park* (1993), long shots place attacking dinosaurs and their terrified human victims in the park's clearly established settings.

In contrast to the long shot, the medium shot brings viewers closer to the characters while still showing some of their environment. Sometimes medium shots are labelled according to the number of characters who are present within the frame. A

The Gold Rush (United Artists, 1925)
Charles Chaplin's composition for this shot in his *The Gold Rush* stresses the social isolation of the little tramp. The tramp stands alone in the foreground as compared with the merry couples in the background of the frame. In addition, the tramp's motionless figure contrasts with the movement of the dancers. Through composition, Chaplin describes the loneliness of the little tramp. Frame enlargement.

E.T.: The Extra-Terrestrial (Universal Studios, 1982)
This long shot from *E.T.: The Extra-Terrestrial* offers a spectacular contrast of moon and bicyclist. By contrasting the environment, in this case the treetops and the gigantic moon and the tiny size of bicycle and rider, the shot conveys a poetic image of the majesty and mystery of the universe.

Aliens (Twentieth Century Fox, 1986)
Medium shot compositions can stress the relationships among characters by arranging multiple characters in dramatic, striking ways within the frame. The colonial Marines wage a desperate battle in *Aliens* against a relentless alien life form. The two-shot framing stresses the group response by the Marines.
(Museum of Modern Art/Film Stills Archive)

one-shot, for example, would include a single character, whereas a two-shot, a three-shot, and a four-shot designate medium shots with larger numbers of people. In *Aliens* (1986), medium shots stress the armed response of a group of Marines to the alien threat by showing how the group itself responds.

The close-up, on the other hand, stresses characters or objects over the surrounding environment, usually for expressive or dramatic purposes. In this image from *Apocalypse Now* (1979), Captain Willard (Martin Sheen) confronts the renegade army of Colonel Kurtz. The close-up emphasizes Willard and his response, not the army itself, which remains in the background.

The fact that filmmakers can choose among different camera positions illustrates a basic difference between cinema and theater. In theater, the spectator views a play

Apocalypse Now (United Artists, 1979)
Captain Willard (Martin Sheen) in a close-up from *Apocalypse Now.* The close-up framing emphasizes Willard's presence and expression relative to the renegade army of Montagnards in the background of the shot. The close-up works in conjunction with the depth of field. The telephoto perspective controls focus to establish Willard as the optical subject of the shot rather than the army, which is out of focus.
(Museum of Modern Art/Film Stills Archive)

Red Psalm (1972)
Jancsó's long shot compositions emphasize groups in conflict. Government soldiers close in on the small band of protesting peasants in *Red Psalm*.

(Museum of Modern Art/Film Stills Archive)

from a single, fixed vantage point, a position in the auditorium usually from a distance. By contrast, in film, viewers watch a shifting series of perspectives on the action, and their ability to understand the story requires synthesizing the shifting points of view as the filmmaker moves from one camera position to another, from **shot** to shot.* How viewers synthesize changing camera positions is a major issue to be examined in the chapter on editing.

Most films involve some combination of long shots, medium shots, and close-ups. Some directors, though, may favor one camera position more than the others. The Hungarian filmmaker Miklós Jancsó tends to favor, almost exclusively, the long shot and medium shot positions. Jancsó rarely relies on close-ups. He also downplays editing almost entirely, constructing films 90 minutes and longer that are composed of as few as 25 shots. These shots may be sustained for several minutes before cutting, as the camera moves in and around characters and objects.

Jancsó's purpose in relying almost exclusively on the long shot and the medium shot is to stress group dynamics, to emphasize that political revolutions—the subject of many of his films—are about clashes among groups with different political interests. He is less interested in dealing with individual characters and therefore tends to discard the close-up in favor of the long shot because he wants to talk about groups, not individuals. Jancsó's style is unique, and it illustrates how a director, sensitive to the differing expressive potentials of camera positions, will match cinematic ideas with appropriate structures.

Camera Position, Gesture, and Expression

By varying the camera-to-subject distance, the filmmaker can manipulate the viewer's emotional involvement with the material in complex ways. The spectator's viewpoint, of course, is the camera's. What the camera sees is what the spectator sees. As the camera moves closer to a character, viewers are brought into that character's personal space in ways that can be expressive and emotional.

*A shot is the basic building block of a film. An unedited shot corresponds to the amount of film footage exposed by the camera from the time it is turned on until it is turned off. Individual shots are then sequenced and trimmed by the editor to create the finished film.

In social encounters, in movies as in real life, people define their relationships to others by sending clear signals, meaningful displays of posture, position, gesture, physical touch, eye contact, and vocal inflection. These signals express emotion and help define relationships as already existing, as potential, personal, intimate, impersonal, hostile, etc. These signals vary by culture, but all members of a society learn how to read the expressions and gestures coming from other people as a way of inferring what they are thinking or feeling. The camera captures and records this kind of information in the gestures and expressions of actors on screen. By varying camera placement, filmmakers can call attention to significant expressions and gestures and thereby help viewers understand the meaning of the relationships and situations depicted on screen.

This may be part of the enduring fascination motion pictures hold for their audiences. One of the basic pleasures of going to the movies is watching the people on the screen—studying their faces, and watching their expressions and gestures. When a filmmaker cuts to a close-up, the director can emphasize and clarify a character's reaction, as well as bring viewers into the action and the personal, emotional space of the character.

Clarifying Emotional Reactions with Camera Position   In George Cukor's *A Star Is Born* (1954), James Mason plays the tragic Hollywood actor, Norman Maine. With his acting career in ruins, the alcoholic Maine collapses into despair and considers suicide. He begins to cry.

The camera draws in to a medium close-up, and director Cukor keeps the shot on screen for what seems like a lifetime to the viewer. Cukor said, "To see that man break down was very moving. All the credit for that goes to James [Mason]. He did it all himself. What I did was to let him do it and let it go on and on, let the camera stay on him for an eternity."

A Star Is Born (Warner Bros., 1954)
Changing facial expressions in a single, extended shot from *A Star Is Born* convey the despair of Norman Maine (actor James Mason). As a photographic medium, the cinema is especially powerful in its ability to capture, and emphasize, the smallest details of human facial expression as signs of emotion. The face is one of cinema's most profound channels for emotional expression. Frame enlargements.

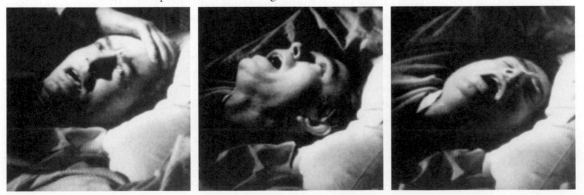

The Mask (New Line, 1994) Unreal faces in fantasy films can still have a special expressive power. Bulging eyes and gaping mouth accurately convey a fright response, though with unrealistic exaggeration. Frame enlargement.

The viewer grows uncomfortable, awaiting the cut, wishing to be released from this intimate glimpse of a man's private hell. The camera's position is close and unrelenting as the viewer watches a terribly private moment for an unbearably suspended time.

Facial expressions do not have to be realistic to retain their special expressive power. Close-up camera positions in *The Mask* (1994) emphasize the special magical face of the main character. The special effects-created facial expression *transforms* normal human reality but also *corresponds* in important ways with real facial cues. The bulging eyes and open mouth accurately convey the character's startled, alarmed response to a woman pointing a gun at him, but they do so with great exaggeration.

Chaplin's Use of Camera Position   Few filmmakers understand the emotional implications of camera position better than Charlie Chaplin understood them. Chaplin used a formula to guide his camera placements: long shot for comedy, close-up for tragedy. He had an instinctive grasp of the emotional implications of camera position.

He understood that the long or medium shot was best suited for comedy because it allowed viewers to see the relationship between Charlie the tramp and his environment. This was especially pertinent when he caused chaos and confusion, as he might when tackling a waiter carrying a tray of food or stepping on a board with a brick on one end, and causing it to catapult onto the head of a policeman. Laughter depended on seeing these relationships while having sufficient emotional distance from the character. The long shot gave viewers that emotional distance. By contrast, Chaplin knew that the close-up, by emphasizing a character's emotional reaction, could invite tears rather than laughter. Aiming for the heartstrings of his audience, Chaplin nevertheless used his close-ups sparingly, so they would have exceptional dramatic intensity.

The ending of *City Lights* (1931) illustrates this perfectly. Charlie has been courting a blind flower girl who believes that Charlie is a millionaire. Charlie happily plays along. At the end of the film, the flower girl regains her eyesight, chances upon Charlie, the disreputable tramp, and realizes he is her friend, a man she thought a millionaire.

The scene plays entirely in close-up, and, in the last shot of the film, Chaplin shows Charlie's most extraordinary expression, a mixture of hope, love, fear, embarrassment,

City Lights
(United Artists, 1931)
Chaplin's sublime expression in the final image of *City Lights*. Chaplin intuitively understood the emotional implications of camera position, and he reserved the close-up for special moments of pathos and sentiment. His extraordinary face, the tentative gesture of his hand, the rose it clutches—these emphasize his romantic yearning and his pained embarrassment at being revealed as a tramp and not a millionaire. Frame enlargement.

and humiliation, an expression the camera easily records and that is so sublime that words cannot do it justice. This is one of the most perfect close-ups in film history. It emphasizes the complex feelings between the characters, magnifies the emotions on screen, and intensifies them for the film's viewers.

Using Camera Position to Complicate Emotional Response

Directors can also use camera position to play against the viewer's desire for emotional involvement with the reactions of a character. Few filmmakers were better at this than Alfred Hitchcock. One of his signature shots is the high-angle long shot, which he uses at moments of dramatic intensity as a character faces a personal crisis or is placed in a situation of some danger.

In *Shadow of a Doubt* (1943), for example, young Charlie (Teresa Wright) loves and honors her older uncle (Joseph Cotton), but he is, in fact, a psychotic serial killer. When young Charlie discovers her uncle's true identity, she is emotionally shattered.

Shadow of a Doubt
(Universal Studios, 1943)
Hitchcock cranes up to a high-angle long shot as young Charlie (Teresa Wright) leaves the library knowing her uncle is a mass murderer. The composition pulls viewers away from Charlie during her moment of greatest emotional and moral crisis. Frame enlargement.

At this point, Hitchcock pulls the camera back so that the viewer is no longer in close physical proximity with her. He moves the camera away, to a higher and more distant position, pulling viewers away with it at the very moment they want to be physically close to her in her time of crisis. In essence, the movement of the camera plays against the viewer's emotional involvement in the scene.

The effects of camera position, then, are context-dependent, a matter of how a given position is related to the dramatic or emotional content of a shot or scene. By using camera position, filmmakers can enhance or inhibit the viewer's emotional involvement with a character or situation. Good filmmakers are intelligent in their choice of camera position, understanding when to cut in to close-up and when to pull back to long shot. Each position gives the viewer its own unique perspective on the action, and filmmakers understand that the effects of these positions can be enhanced by a careful choice of camera angle.

Camera Angle

Just as the camera's position varies throughout a scene or sequence, so, too, does its angle. Camera angles are classified as variations of three essential positions: low, medium (or eye level), and high.

The low and the high positions are usually measured as below or above the eye level of characters in the scene. A low-angle shot in *The Mask* shows the main character leering at a woman he has just frightened into a faint. The low camera position simulates her point of view as she lies on the ground.

Structuring Viewer Response

Like camera position, camera angle helps structure viewer responses. For example, in *Citizen Kane* (1941), director Orson Welles uses camera angle to evoke young Charlie Kane's boyhood feelings of bewilderment and powerlessness in his new foster home. Charlie's imposing guardian gives him a sled for a Christmas present. To magnify Charlie's feelings of powerlessness, Welles shoots the man towering above him, from the boy's point of view, using an extremely low camera angle that forces viewers to look up to this figure, much as young Charlie has to do.

The Mask (New Line, 1994) Camera angle can help visualize point of view. This low-angle shot from *The Mask* shows the main character leering at a woman he has just frightened into a faint. The low camera position simulates her point of view as she lies on the ground. Frame enlargement.

Ride the High Country
(MGM, 1962)
This low-angle shot from *Ride the High Country* increases the stature of aging gunfighters Gil Westrum (Randolph Scott) and Steve Judd (Joel McCrea) as they walk toward their last gunfight. By enlarging their stature, the low angle helps heroize the characters. Frame enlargement.

At the conclusion of Sam Peckinpah's Western, *Ride the High Country* (1962), the filmmaker suggests the heroic power of gunfighters Steve Judd and Gil Westrum as they walk to confront a band of outlaws by filming them with a low camera angle. As they walk toward the camera, the viewer looks up at them. The impression of strength that results is based on the viewer responding to the image in a way that is analogous to responses in real world situations where attractive and sympathetic figures might seem more imposing by virtue of their size or height.

Camera angle can also complicate emotional responses by playing against the visual relationships viewers want to have with characters, as Hitchcock does in his use of high angles during moments of extreme emotional crisis. In *Psycho* (1960), he uses one of these extreme high angles as a way of solving a dramatic and narrative problem. A first-time viewer believes that the psychopathic killer in the film is the deranged mother of motel owner Norman Bates. In the film's climax, Norman is revealed as the killer. Although the mother has been dead for many years, Norman has kept her alive in his mind by keeping her body in the house, dressing up like her, and speaking in her voice. Hitchcock's narrative problem was to keep the audience from realizing, midway through the film—when Norman moves her body from the upstairs bedroom to the basement—that the mother was dead.

Hitchcock attached his camera to the ceiling and filmed from directly overhead as Norman carried the corpse down to the cellar. The extreme high angle, coupled with the jostling movement as Norman goes down the stairs, prevents the audience from realizing he is carrying a corpse. The viewer is even fooled into thinking that the mother is kicking in protest.

Hitchcock's use of the high angle in this scene is an ingenious solution to his narrative problem. It also introduces a bizarre, distorting perspective into the scene and plays against the viewer's desired visual relationship with the characters. Because of all the questions the narrative has raised about this mysterious figure, viewers want to see Norman's mother clearly and up close, not from the odd angle Hitchcock uses. But, by delaying the desired response, Hitchcock builds considerable suspense, and the payoff at the end of the film—a close-up of the mother's skeletal face—is heart-stopping.

Other Angles

A significant variation from the three basic categories of camera angle is the **canted angle.** Filmmakers will sometimes use a tilted camera angle, leaning the camera to one side or the other, to make the world look off-kilter, often as a way of expressing a character's disoriented, disorganized frame of mind. Following an Allied attack on a submarine U-boat headquarters, director Wolfgang Peterson in *The Boat* (1981) uses a series of canted angles to record the dazed responses of the survivors. Similarly, during the climactic assault on the math professor's house in *Straw Dogs* (1971), Sam Peckinpah uses tilted camera positions to simulate the professor's terror and extreme anxiety. Throughout *Natural Born Killers* (1994), director Oliver Stone uses canted angles to intensify the film's disturbing, nightmarish vision of serial killers and the hideous world they inhabit.

Angle in Context

Although camera angles are capable of eliciting some of the kinds of emotional responses from viewers described here, it is important to remember that all of these responses are context-dependent. They depend on the emotional context and action of a given scene. Camera angles, in themselves, do not inherently express anything. They must be carefully matched by filmmakers to the material of the scene. In other contexts and other scenes, low, high, and canted angles may have other effects than those listed here.

Psycho (Paramount Pictures, 1960)
Hitchcock solves a narrative problem in *Psycho* by using this high camera angle. The bizarre, disturbing perspective conceals the fact that Norman's mother is dead as he carries her down to the fruit cellar. Frame enlargement.

ALFRED HITCHCOCK

Alfred Hitchcock was a consummate showman, entertainer, and serious artist who used film to explore dark currents of human thought and behavior. He thrived in the classical Hollywood studio system because his films were popular with audiences as well as enjoying considerable critical respect. As a result, Hitchcock became one of the most powerful Hollywood directors and one of the few known to the public by name.

Born into a Catholic family in London's East End in 1899, Hitchcock was a solitary boy possessed of an active imagination and fascinated by crime. Uncommonly anxious, he believed his many fears motivated his preference for making films about innocent people suddenly caught up in an unpredictable whirlpool of danger, madness, and intrigue. "I was terrified of the police, of the Jesuit Fathers, of physical punishment, of a lot of things. This is the root of my work."

In 1920, Hitchcock joined the British film industry as a scriptwriter and set and costume designer. In 1924 and 1925, he worked as an assistant director, and then director, in Germany on several British-German co-productions. He studied and absorbed the style of German Expressionism, and, in all

Vertigo (Paramount Pictures, 1958) James Stewart portrays a detective terrified of heights in *Vertigo*, Hitchcock's most passionate and poetic film. Stewart's pose here is a classic Hitchcock image of the individual haunted by the darkness in his own mind and beset by chaos in the outer world. Hitchcock's darkest films offer no places of safety. Frame enlargement.

of his subsequent films, he relied on expressionistically distorted images to suggest an unstable world.

Hitchcock rose to the peak of the British film industry with a cycle of elegant spy thrillers—*The Man Who Knew Too Much* (1934), *The Thirty-Nine Steps* (1935), and *The Lady Vanishes* (1938).

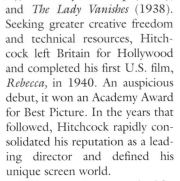

Seeking greater creative freedom and technical resources, Hitchcock left Britain for Hollywood and completed his first U.S. film, *Rebecca*, in 1940. An auspicious debut, it won an Academy Award for Best Picture. In the years that followed, Hitchcock rapidly consolidated his reputation as a leading director and defined his unique screen world.

Using suspense as a method for drawing the audience into the fictional screen world, Hitchcock concentrated on stories of crime, madness, and espionage in which ostensibly innocent characters confront their guilt and complicity in unsavory or villainous activities. In *Shadow of a Doubt*, a psychopathic serial killer (Joseph Cotton) visits his sister in a small California town, and his idealistic young niece discovers his secret and the many ties that bind her to him. In *Notorious* (1946), two American spies (Cary Grant and Ingrid Bergman) fall in love while manipulating and emotionally betraying one another. In

Japanese director Yasujiro Ozu, for example, uses low camera positions and angles extensively, but they are not correlated with any of the effects discussed here. To a large extent, they are motivated by the action of the films, which feature characters sitting on tatami mats and conversing (as is the custom in traditional Japanese homes). The camera gets closer to the ground to film them. One critic has suggested that these low

Strangers on a Train (1951), a charming psychopath (Robert Walker) proposes an exchange of murders to a celebrity tennis player. "You do mine, I do yours," he tells the shocked but intrigued athlete.

Hitchcock reached the height of his powers—and the zenith of his career—in the 1950s when he released a string of top-notch classics. In *Rear Window* (1954), a wheel-chair-bound photographer is intent on proving one of his neighbors is a murderer. With great suspense, Hitchcock explored the theme of voyeurism, applying it both to characters in the narrative and to audiences watching the film.

To Catch a Thief (1955) was a classy, witty Technicolor romp on the Riviera, and *The Man Who Knew Too Much* (1956) was a glossy, big-budget remake of his 1934 British hit. *Vertigo* (1958), a complex tale of detection, murder, and madness, was Hitchcock's most intensely personal, romantic, and poetic creation. Widely regarded as his masterpiece, it is hypnotic and dream-like, with a remarkable depth of feeling and an uncompromisingly bleak ending. Disappointed with its commercial performance, Hitchcock bounced back with *North by Northwest* (1959), a fast, witty, hugely entertaining summation of the espionage and chase thrillers he had perfected in his 1930s British career.

Hitchcock's next film, *Psycho* (1960), proved to be his most influential. This story of murder, madness, and perversion at a seedy roadside motel was a calculated exercise in audience manipulation in which Hitchcock wanted only to make his viewers scream. He succeeded brilliantly. In its coldness, its savage brutality and violence, and its merciless attitude toward the audience, *Psycho* anticipated, and introduced, the essential characteristics of modern horror films.

Hitchcock had one more hit in the 1960s—*The Birds* (1963)—and then began a period of decline. *Marnie* (1964), *Torn Curtain* (1966), and *Topaz* (1969) were critical and commercial disappointments. The industry and the modern audience were changing, and Hitchcock could not adapt. The old studio system was dead, and many of the stars (Grace Kelly, Cary Grant, James Stewart) who were essential to Hitchcock's films had retired or were too old for the parts he needed to fill. The brutality and cynicism of modern film, which Hitchcock had helped inaugurate with *Psycho*, swept by him. Hitchcock had relied for his best effects on suggestion and implication and was unable to relate to a world, and to a public, for whom extraordinary acts of violence were becoming increasingly commonplace.

Hitchcock achieved a brief popular comeback with *Frenzy* (1972), a hit about a British serial killer. Movie censorship had ceased, and Hitchcock included horrific and distasteful scenes of explicit violence, inadvertently, and, ironically, demonstrating how creatively beneficial Hollywood censorship had been for him. His last film, *Family Plot* (1976), was an entertaining but unremarkable thriller. Hitchcock's declining health prevented completion of additional films, and he died on April 29, 1980.

Hitchcock's genius for self-promotion (realized through his cameo appearances in his films and his witty introductions on his television show, which ran from 1955–1965) and his genius for frightening viewers made him one of the most popular and famous directors in screen history. But he was also a serious and sophisticated artist who made brilliant use of cinema as a vehicle for expressing the forces of darkness and chaos in human life.

positions and angles work to include the viewer in the world of the film, like a guest sitting on a tatami mat. To assess the function of camera position and angle, then, one must consider their potential for structuring emotional response in light of the expressive requirements of the scene. What are its dramatic, comedic, emotional, or cultural requirements, and how are these facilitated by camera position or angle?

Straw Dogs (ABC Pictures, 1971)

A. A tilted camera angle helps visualize the terror of a math professor (Dustin Hoffman) and his wife (Susan George) as a gang of thugs tries to break into their house. *Straw Dogs*. Frame enlargement.

Natural Born Killers (Warner Bros., 1994)

B. Unstable, tilted camera angles help establish the nightmarish, off-kilter world of serial killers in Oliver Stone's *Natural Born Killers*. Stone purposely created a wildly chaotic visual design to give the film a psychotic tone. Frame enlargement.

Invasion of the Body Snatchers (Allied Artists, 1956)

C. Sophisticated angular distortion in *Invasion of the Body Snatchers*. As Dr. Miles Bennell (Kevin McCarthy) leans forward to discover an alien seed pod, the camera's angle of view exactly matches his diagonal posture. As a result, the character seems to remain naturally upright in the frame while the greenhouse windows behind him tilt crazily. The resulting visual instability mirrors the narrative theme. Bennell remains human while the world around him is taken over by the alien body snatchers. Frame enlargement.

An Autumn Afternoon
(New Yorker Films, 1963)
Ozu's low camera positions are
motivated by the customary
seating in traditional Japanese
homes. To preserve eye level
framings, Ozu's camera assumes
a lower position. In this case,
cultural and dramatic
requirements motivate the
unusual camera position.

Camera Lens

Besides position and angle, a third factor defines the relationship between the camera
and what it photographs. This is the type of lens used in each shot. A filmmaker's
choice of lens can drastically affect the look of the image in terms of (1) the apparent
size of objects on screen and (2) the apparent relationships of depth and distance
between near and far objects. Camera positions are generally defined by the amount
of distance between the camera and what it is photographing, but, without knowing
something about the lenses employed, a viewer's judgments about camera position can
be misleading. Certain lenses, for example, may make the camera seem much closer to
what it is photographing than it really is. The lens is the device that gathers light and
brings it into the camera to a focused point on the film, thereby creating an image
which is recorded on the light-sensitive surface of the film, called the **emulsion.**

Focal Length and Depth of Field

When the lens is focused on a distant object, the distance between the film inside the
camera and the optical center of the lens is known as the **focal length.** The properties of different lenses are understood in relation to their respective focal lengths. A
focal length of 50 mm conventionally designates a **normal lens** for 35-mm film,
which is the film format used in commercial theaters. Lenses with focal lengths greater
than the normal range are **telephoto lenses** or long focal length lenses. Those with
focal lengths less than normal are **wide-angle lenses** or short focal length lenses.

The focal length of a lens is directly related to how much it sees, termed the **angle
of view.** At a shorter focal length, the angle of view increases, allowing filmmakers to
film a wider area. At longer focal lengths, the angle of view decreases, thereby limiting the shooting to a more narrow area.

Also varying with the focal length of the lens is the **depth of field,** the amount
of area from near to far that will remain in focus. A wide-angle lens can capture
much greater depth of field than a telephoto lens can. With the wide angle, the distance between near objects in focus and distant objects in focus can be very great.

Two portraits of the same subject, one taken a few yards away with a normal (55 mm) lens and the other at a much greater distance using a telephoto (205 mm) lens. Which composition is a function of camera position and which is a function of lens focal length?

By contrast, a telephoto lens will give filmmakers a shallow depth of field with only a limited area of separation between near and distant objects that are in focus.

Another important characteristic differentiating wide angle from telephoto lenses is the ability of telephoto lenses to make distant objects appear much closer. Filming a very distant object with a long lens can make that remote object appear much closer to the camera than it really is. In this respect, the effects of the telephoto lens can overwhelm the impression of true camera position. What might appear to be a close-up, in fact, could have been shot using a telephoto lens with the camera in a long shot position. In these two portraits of the wooden bridge, the bridge is the same size in each photo, but in one case the size is due to a close camera position while in the other it is due to the magnifying effects of a telephoto lens. Viewers will have developed an extremely sophisticated eye for cinema if they can tell when object size on the screen is due more to camera position or to the choice of lens.

In conclusion, wide angle lenses have a greater angle of view and depth of field than telephoto lenses. Telephoto lenses, on the other hand, magnify distant objects, making them appear closer than they are.

Zoom Lenses

In addition to normal, wide-angle, and telephoto lenses, a fourth category of lens is important in the cinema. This is the **zoom lens.** The zoom lens is a lens with a variable focal length, which permits it to shift from wide angle to telephoto settings within a single shot. This ability can create the appearance of camera movement, making it seem as if the camera is moving closer to or farther from its subject. In fact, however, the camera in a zoom shot remains stationary. Viewers with a sophisticated cinematic eye can discriminate zoom shots from true moving camera shots. In a moving camera shot, perspective changes; that is, the spatial relationship of the camera to the objects around it shifts as the camera moves. Consequently, the viewer's perspective—the camera—physically moves through space.

In a zoom shot, by contrast, perspective does not change. The size of the image merely increases or decreases. Zoom lenses magnify or, alternatively, shrink the size of the image and the objects it contains. Zooming in will magnify all objects evenly. Zooming out will shrink all objects evenly. This is what produces the impression of camera movement. As objects in the shot enlarge, the viewer has the impression of moving closer to them. The zoom shot provides simple magnification. The moving camera, by contrast, provides a series of changing spatial relationships produced by movement and known as **motion parallax** or **motion perspective.** The absence of motion perspective in a shot where the camera seems to be moving is a clear sign that the shot is a zoom and not a true moving camera shot.

Filmmakers sometimes use zoom lenses as alternatives to camera movement, especially if they are filming on a low budget and a quick schedule. Zoom lenses, though, can be used for sophisticated effects. In *McCabe and Mrs. Miller* (1971), the hero realizes a gang of gunmen has come to kill him. Director Robert Altman and cinematographer Vilmos Zsigmond employ a rapid zoom effect, moving quickly to an extreme telephoto position to convey the hero's sense of anxiety and the rush of excitement he feels. The optical effect produced by the rapid zoom captures these highly emotional reactions.

Using Lenses

Filmmakers often employ the telephoto lens to magnify distant objects when they are filming a scene on city streets in which several characters are walking along in conversation, surrounded by a crowd. A realistic impression depends upon the other pedestrians being unaware of the camera and actors. Filmmakers often place the camera at a very great distance and film using a telephoto lens that takes the distant actors and brings them into an apparent medium shot or close-up. The camera is so far away the other pedestrians don't notice it.

Viewers acquire greater cinematic sophistication when they become sensitive to the effects produced by different lenses used in the shots of a given scene. A filmmaker does not photograph all shots using the same lens. Just as camera positions and angles are routinely changed throughout a scene, so, too, are lenses. In a shot with extreme depth of field, where near and distant objects are in focus, the lens is likely to be a wide angle. If, on the other hand, depth of field looks very shallow, with a compression of distance so that a far-off object looks close, the lens used is likely to be a telephoto.

Some filmmakers are closely identified with certain types of lenses. Japanese director Akira Kurosawa, for example, favors telephoto lenses. Telephoto lenses distort movement toward or away from the camera because they magnify distant objects and compress depth of field. Kurosawa loves to film samurai galloping on horseback

Bullitt (Warner Bros., 1968) Extreme telephoto perspective in *Bullitt*. Steve McQueen is standing next to a busy freeway but the optical distortion imposed by the lens establishes a depth of field that includes only the actor. Nothing in the background can be distinguished. Furthermore, the camera is far away from the actor. The apparent medium shot position is an illusion created by the telephoto lens' ability to magnify distant objects. Frame enlargement.

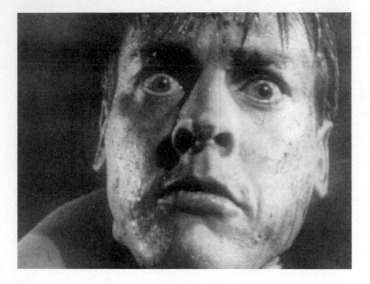

Invasion of the Body Snatchers
(Allied Artists, 1956)
Extreme wide-angle lens distortion in
Invasion of the Body Snatchers. Because
wide angle lenses enlarge depth of field,
they exaggerate the distances between
points or objects. Accordingly, the
contours of actor Kevin McCarthy's face
are stretched and bent in this very
dramatic fashion. The scene's action
motivates this distortion. Dr. Miles
Bennell (McCarthy) has just realized
that the woman he loves has been taken
over by an alien. The lens distortion
helps visualize his horrified response.
Frame enlargement.

toward the camera using a telephoto lens. Their movements are so distorted that they
seem to be riding in place. By contrast, Orson Welles often favored the wide-angle
lens. In *Touch of Evil,* his last American picture, made for Universal Studios in 1958,
Welles filmed his gargantuan detective hero, Hank Quinlan, with a series of extremely
wide angle lenses to exaggerate and enhance his huge and grotesque dimensions.

Evaluating Lens Choice

As with camera angle and position, evaluating a filmmaker's choice of lenses means
being sensitive both to structure—in this case, the visual properties of lenses—and to
the requirements of the scene or shot. Consider the moment in John Schlesinger's
Marathon Man (1976) when the evil Nazi dentist (Laurence Olivier) stabs the hero's
brother (Roy Scheider). This action is filmed with a telephoto lens so the stabbing is
brought close to the viewer while the city behind the characters remains out of focus.
Remember that the telephoto lens will tend to create a shallow depth of field. The

Marathon Man (Paramount
Pictures, 1976)
Telephoto lens perspective used
to isolate, emphasize, and
intensify a moment of violence.

plane of focus does not extend beyond the characters in this shot. It does not include the city behind them so the viewer's eye is not distracted during this confrontation. The lens, therefore, heightens and intensifies the act of violence by bringing it up close and by creating an exclusive visual focus upon it.

Because of this, it can be said that the director's choice of lens here is the appropriate one. By contrast, using a wide angle lens would increase depth of field so the city in the distance would be in focus, potentially distracting viewers from the foreground drama. The spectator's perspective on the action of a shot or scene, then, is crucially influenced by a filmmaker's choices of camera position, angle, and lens. A fourth important influence must now be explored—the effects of camera movement.

Camera Movement

Filmmakers are free to move their camera about. Indeed, this is one of the things that distinguishes cinema from theater. The camera's perspective changes from shot to shot, and it can shift and move within the shot. As with camera position and angle, which can vary along a wide range of possibilities, the camera can also move in virtually any fashion through space. To simplify things, this discussion will focus on three basic categories of camera movement: (1) **pan and tilt shots,** (2) **dolly** or **tracking shots,** and (3) **boom** or **crane shots.** All of these camera movements shift the boundaries of the frame. Moving the camera through space creates a fluid perspective on screen in which the boundaries of the frame are not fixed, as they are in a static shot.

Pan and Tilt

In a pan shot, the camera head rotates in a horizontal fashion from side to side on top of the tripod which remains stationary, producing a lateral movement on screen. By contrast, in a tilt shot the camera pivots vertically, up or down. If a filmmaker were shooting a skyscraper, he/she could start with a camera focused on the bottom of the building and then tilt slowly up to the top to reveal, perhaps, King Kong swatting at airplanes. Figures 1.1 and 1.2 illustrate the action of panning and tilting.

Figure 1.1: Pan   **Figure 1.2:** Tilt

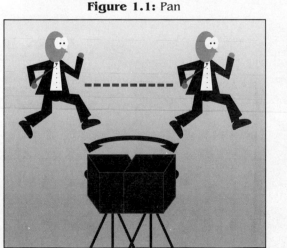

The Great Train Robbery
(Edison, 1903)
After holding up the train, the robbers run for their horses to escape. In the next moment, as they turn left and run down a hill, the camera operator will pan and tilt to follow the action. Frame enlargement.

Using Pans and Tilts

Both pans and tilts tend to establish linking movements, often used to connect objects or establish relationships between them, or call attention to new areas of the scene. Pans may also be used to readjust the frame to accommodate character movement. If a character crosses the room to open a door, the camera operator might pan to follow the movement. A very early example of this use of the pan occurs in *The Great Train Robbery* (1903). When the robbers make their daring escape from the train after holding it up, they go down an embankment and across a stream to reach their horses. As they do this, the camera operator pans left and tilts down to follow them. It is done a bit carelessly, however, and the robbers almost disappear from frame at one point before the camera picks them up again.

Easy Rider (Columbia Pictures, 1969)
Throughout *Easy Rider*, the tracking camera communicates the excitement and exhilaration of motorcycle travel. Notice the motion blur on the bridge in the background produced by its rapid movement relative to the camera. Frame enlargement.

As noted, the pan is usually employed as a linking device or to draw the spectator's attention to a new area of the frame. In most cases, the optical distance traveled in a pan is brief. Its physical design, however, permits the camera to rotate an entire 360 degrees on the mounting attached to its tripod. Nothing, therefore, except conventional usage, prevents filmmakers from executing a complete, circular, 360 degree panning shot. These tend to be rare, but they do occur. In *Easy Rider* (1969), when the heroes Wyatt (Peter Fonda) and Billy (Dennis Hopper) visit a hippie commune, the filmmakers stress the friendship and camaraderie that unite the commune members. In a scene where the hippies offer prayer for their harvest, cameraman Haskell Wexler uses a 360 degree pan across the faces of all the characters, who are grouped in a circle. Placed in the center of the circle, the camera slowly rotates a full 360 degrees, bringing into view each character's face and creating a symbolic image of unity and completeness.

Dolly, Tracking, and Boom

Unlike the pan and tilt, in dolly, tracking, and boom (or crane) shots, the camera— along with its tripod or base—physically travels through space. Because of this, these shots produce motion perspective, unlike pans and tilts. A dolly is simply a wheeled platform used for mounting the camera in a tracking shot. Sometimes these are called dolly shots because of this platform mount. In tracking, or dolly shots, the camera may move briefly toward or away from an object, such as a character's face, or may describe more extended, elaborate movements. In the latter case, a tracking shot may follow a character who is him/herself moving. As Rocky sprints along the streets of south Philadelphia to train for his big fight, the camera tracks with him (*Rocky,* 1976). The rapid track helps visualize Rocky's power and adds energy to the shot.

Tracking or dolly shots generally move in a direction parallel to the ground. By contrast, boom or crane shots move up or down through space. They take their name from the apparatus—boom or crane—on which the camera is mounted. A very famous boom shot occurs in *Gone With The Wind* (1939), when Scarlet O'Hara visits wounded confederate soldiers at the railroad station. The camera is initially very close to her, but then pulls back and booms up to a high angle view to show Scarlet

Figure 1.3: Tracking shot

surrounded by a huge field of the dead and dying. This change of perspective enlarges the viewer's angle of view and creates a powerful, dramatic effect.

Functions of Moving Camera Shots

Function 1: Expressing Movement   Filmmakers tend to use dolly, tracking, or boom shots for two purposes. The first, and perhaps most common, is to express a dynamic sense of movement that makes a shot or scene more sensuous and dramatically exciting. Japanese director Akira Kurosawa is a master of sensuous camera movements that add extraordinary dramatic and visual impact to his scenes. In films such as *Seven Samurai* (1954) and *Throne of Blood* (1957), where characters on foot or horse race through a dense forest, Kurosawa tracks the camera rapidly with them, darting in and out of trees, over streams, and under branches, plunging the viewer into dense foliage and expressing in the most visually convincing manner the sensation and experience of flight. Among American directors, Martin Scorsese (*Taxi Driver,* 1976; *The Age of Innocence,* 1993) and Brian DePalma (*The Untouchables,* 1987) are masters at using sweeping, sensuous camera movements to intensify the visual richness of their shots.

Expressing sustained movement.   Sometimes filmmakers are interested to see how long they can sustain a single camera movement within a shot as a way of dazzling the audience and setting themselves a technical challenge. In *Goodfellas* (1990), director Martin Scorsese uses a handheld camera in a single shot to follow the main character, a New York gangster, as he gets out of his car, crosses the street, enters the side door of a nightclub, winds through narrow hallways and a crowded kitchen, and walks into a ballroom filled with hundreds of people, including a stand-up comic in mid-routine.

The visual pleasures of the shot are what it's all about because the narrative information it conveys is minimal. Watching Scorsese pull off this sustained camera movement with its elaborate staging and choreography is extremely pleasant for viewers who recognize the challenge involved. Structure, not content, is the star here.

An earlier example of a sustained, sensuous, technically complex tracking shot is found in F. W. Murnau's *Sunrise* (1927), the first American film by this German director. Murnau is often credited with being the filmmaker who first unlocked the secrets of the moving camera. *Sunrise* is about a husband and wife, living on a farm, whose

Throne of Blood (Toho, 1957)
Kurosawa's tracking camera follows this samurai warrior on horseback as he gallops through a forest. Since the camera moves at the same speed as the horseman, the samurai remains in focus while the surrounding forest becomes a blur. Frame enlargement.

Goodfellas (Warner Bros., 1990)
Throughout *Goodfellas*, director Martin Scorsese uses the full range of cinematic techniques to
manipulate image and sound in striking ways. He mixes slow motion with normal speed, uses
freeze frames to stop the action, employs extended tracking shots, and, in this scene,
simultaneously tracks and zooms in opposite directions to create a strange, disorienting effect.

marriage is disrupted by a seductive woman who lures away the husband. As the husband walks into the foggy marsh to meet his lover, the camera follows in a single,
extended tracking shot. The husband crosses a bridge, turns to the right, goes past a
tree, rounds a corner, then turns back to the left, and crosses a fence, with the camera gliding hypnotically behind. Eventually, the camera tracks away from the man,
leaves him off frame, and moves on its own through branches and foliage to reveal
the man's lover waiting for his arrival.

Sunrise (Fox, 1927)
Changing visual orientations produced by the tracking camera within a single, extended shot.
Frame enlargements.

Because of the elaborate choreography of camera and character movement, and the frequent twists and turns and changing orientations, this tracking shot is among the most famous in screen history. It illustrates Murnau's extraordinary attention to the dynamics of movement and his recognition that the camera itself can become a main character in a film, participating in and commenting on the action.

Function 2: Symbolizing Thematic Ideas   In addition to using the camera to express a dynamic sense of movement, filmmakers also employ moving camera shots for more complex, frequently metaphoric or symbolic purposes. In such cases, the camera's movement—which is deliberate and metaphoric—enables filmmakers to visualize important thematic ideas. Camera motion correlates, as a visual design, with important issues in the film's narrative.

Some of the most unique and carefully conceived moving camera shots occur in the films of French director Jean-Luc Godard. Godard's films have an uncommon degree of self-consciousness in their use of technique and the manner by which they tell their stories. *Weekend* (1967) is Godard's dark, savagely funny satire of the barely-repressed violence of an absurd, Americanized consumer society. In the film, an amoral couple, Corrine and Roland, travel by car to Oinville where they plan to murder Corrine's mother so they might claim the family inheritance. On the way to Oinville, they are caught in a traffic jam. On a narrow country road, a long line of vehicles impedes their progress. Anxious to pass the bottleneck, Roland impatiently edges his car along the shoulder of the road and passes the other vehicles.

Godard films the sequence in a single, unbroken tracking shot that lasts over seven minutes. The camera tracks parallel to the road and the line-up of vehicles, keeping pace with Roland as he inches his way forward. The camera, however, frames the scene slightly to the rear, preventing viewers from seeing what lies ahead on the road.

The effect of this maddening and funny sequence depends on the duration of the shot—which lasts for an extraordinarily long time—as well as on the slow, methodical progress of the camera along what seems like an endless line of stalled vehicles.

Weekend (New Yorker Films, 1967)
Godard's tracking camera slowly travels the length of a line of stalled cars. The framing prevents a view of what lies ahead, deliberately frustrating the viewer. Finally, after several minutes, the camera reveals the cause of the accident. Frame enlargements.

The tracking shot here becomes a metaphor for the experience of being stuck in traffic and enables the filmmaker to subject the audience to that oppressive experience.

These examples of camera movement point toward an important conclusion. Whether a filmmaker uses it to convey the sensory experience of motion or to symbolically express thematic and narrative ideas, camera movement provides the filmmaker with an essential means of shaping and organizing the visual space of a scene. Camera movement imposes structure and meaning upon the composition of a shot.

Technology, Camera Movement, and Film Art

Technological developments in recent years have made camera movement especially easy for filmmakers to achieve. The design of the Steadicam, a gyroscopically stabilized camera mount which can be strapped to the camera operator's body and used to create a hand-held moving camera shot, has revolutionized the ease with which professional-looking camera movement can be obtained. In *Rocky* (1976), the capabilities of the Steadicam were first displayed in the sequence where Rocky runs up the steps of the Philadelphia Museum of Art. The camera operator tracks up with him, and the resulting hand-held shot has a completely fluid, smooth movement with no noticeable jostle.

Obviously, filmmakers in early years did not have the luxury of such devices. When viewing older films, therefore, one must be aware of the limited physical resources available in earlier periods. Sometimes, filmmakers had to struggle with clumsy or cumbersome equipment, and it is often their ingenuity at devising solutions to these technical problems that is a mark of their talent.

During production of *The Last Laugh* (1924), for example, F. W. Murnau experimented with many different ways of producing camera movement. The camera was attached to a ladder, to scaffolding, to a rubber-wheeled trolley, and to the stomach of cameraman Carl Freund while he rode a bicycle. So impressed was Hollywood with the work of Murnau and Freund in *The Last Laugh* that it sent a telegram to Ufa, the German studio that produced the film, inquiring about the special camera that had been used to take the shots, adding that in the United States there was apparently no such device. Robert Herlth, the set designer for *The Last Laugh* and several other Murnau films, remarked that what the Americans didn't know was that "we had discovered new methods with only the most primitive means at our disposal."

Technical sophistication, by itself, can be a misleading yardstick by which to measure the quality of films. Movie equipment today is so advanced that filmmakers of only moderate talent can produce images with a sophistication that the early masters— Renoir, Murnau, D. W. Griffith—could only dream of. Technology without intelligence, however, is just mechanics. It must be balanced by artistic vision and ingenuity.

☐ STRUCTURAL DESIGN AND CREATIVE CHOICE

A film's structural design is an expression of the creative choices made by filmmakers. The elements of film structure present filmmakers with a range of choices: where to position the camera, from what angle, which lens to use, whether to employ camera movement, how to light the set, how to choreograph the actors on screen, how to record the sound, and how to balance the dialogue, music, and sound effects. How a filmmaker confronts and resolves these choices defines the style or structure of a given film.

Structural Design in *The Man Who Knew Too Much*

A comparison of the same sequence in two different films by the same director will illustrate the importance of structural design. Alfred Hitchcock made two versions of *The Man Who Knew Too Much*. The first version, produced in 1934, was Hitchcock's first film for Gaumont British Productions. The second version was made for Paramount Pictures in Hollywood in 1956.

The story in the two versions is essentially the same. A group of spies who are planning to assassinate a political official during a performance at the Royal Albert Music Hall in London kidnap the child of a vacationing couple to prevent the couple from alerting authorities about the assassination plot. The climax of each film takes place at the Royal Albert Hall during the performance of the Storm Cloud Cantata. The mother, knowing that the fatal shot will be fired during the clash of the cymbals, awaits the moment with dread and confronts a moral dilemma: to tell the police about the plot and possibly lose her child, or to keep silent, save her child but implicate herself as an accessory to a murder plot.

Many of the same shots and camera angles are employed in the two sequences, but there is a considerable difference of structural design. Three areas of difference are especially important: differences in (1) shot number and scene length, (2) use of expressionist techniques, and (3) display of production values.

Shot Number and Scene Length

In terms of shot structure, the 1956 version is considerably more elaborate and has a more complex pattern of editing among the spectators, the musicians, the politicians, the

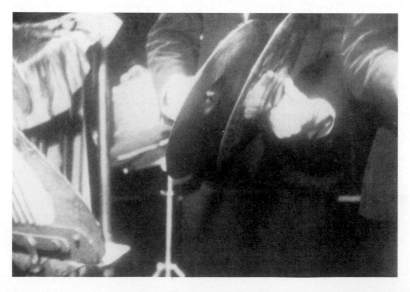

The Man Who Knew Too Much (Gaumont British Pictures, 1934)
In both versions, Hitchcock visually emphasizes the impending crash of the cymbals by showing them in close-up. Frame enlargement.

**The Man Who
Knew Too Much**
(Paramount Pictures, 1956)
In the 1956 version, Hitchcock
includes more numerous shots
of the cymbalist as well as four
shots of the musical score
for added suspense. Frame
enlargement.

assassin, and the mother in the music hall. In the 1934 version—from the opening shot
of the poster advertising the performance at the music hall to the clash of the cymbals
at the end of the scene—there are 81 shots, running 5 minutes and 46 seconds. In the
1956 version—from the opening shot of the poster to the clash of cymbals—it is almost
twice as long. There are 161 shots, running 11 minutes and 45 seconds. The second
version has twice as many shots and is double the length. This is mainly because of a
more elaborate pattern of editing the scenes among the characters at the music hall and
to Hitchcock's allowing a longer performance of the Storm Cloud Cantata.

Hitchcock remarked that, in order to achieve optimum suspense, the audience
should ideally know the precise point in the musical score when the cymbals will
clash—the moment when the killer will fire his gun. To approximate this in the second version, he includes five separate shots of the music score: first, as the killer
watches his accomplice reading the score in their box in the music hall; second, a shot
of the cymbalist's music stand; and finally three shots of the conductor's score—a
long shot, medium shot, and close-up—to increase dramatic emphasis. In contrast,
only one brief shot of the musical score is included in the first version.

Hitchcock includes these shots of the score to create **suspense,** which depends on
giving the audience crucial information. Hitchcock considered the opposite of suspense to be **surprise,** dependent upon withholding information from the audience.
The audience knows the shot will be fired when the cymbals clash, and suspense is created by delaying the moment. Hitchcock's more elaborately constructed 1956 version
heightens the suspense by using delay tactics, including additional shots of the spectators and of the orchestra performing the score. Because of these extra shots, it takes
much longer to get to the fateful clash in the second version than it does in the first.

Use of Expressionist Techniques
While the second version is more suspenseful than the first, the earlier version contains interesting visual effects that the 1956 version lacks. In the earlier version, the
mother visually searches during the performance for the assassin and his target. As she

looks about her, the camera pans to the left along the spectator boxes in the balcony, finally isolating a mysteriously darkened box in which a shadowy figure is moving. Then, within the same shot, the camera slowly pans back to the right, bringing the mother back into the frame, and continues panning, away from her now, to reveal a policeman standing in the aisle.

In the 1956 version, a static camera shoots the mother looking around the music hall. The mobile, elaborate panning shots that distinguish the earlier version are gone. There are, instead, simple cuts—from the mother glancing offscreen to shots of what she is supposed to be seeing. The result in the second version is a series of static frames, fewer mobile compositions.

In addition to the use of fluid compositions, the first version features explicitly *expressionist* devices that tend to be greatly minimized in the second. "Expressionist" images feature blatant visual distortions that are meant to represent a character's innermost thoughts or feelings. These feelings are made visible on screen through visual distortions. Hitchcock became familiar with expressionist techniques when he studied as a young filmmaker in Germany in the 1920s and observed such expressionist directors as F. W. Murnau working on their classic productions.

Virtually all of Hitchcock's films feature expressionist techniques, but the 1934 version of *The Man Who Knew Too Much* is more purely expressionistic than the 1956 version. In the earlier one, as the mother becomes increasingly agitated during the musical performance, she looks at the orchestra. In a **subjective shot,** representing her point of view, the orchestra becomes fuzzy and indistinct. To simulate her increasing agitation and nervousness, the camera operator adjusts the focus (called **rack focusing**) to blur the image of the orchestra. Her increasing anxiety is visualized in the loss of focus. She feels as if she is plunging into a dream world of fantasy and terror, becoming so anxious that she is about to faint.

The Man Who Knew Too Much (Gaumont British Pictures, 1934)
The 1934 version includes overt expressionist devices. The anxious mother scans the auditorium for signs of the killer. Hitchcock cuts to a subjective shot of the auditorium, representing her point of view, and then pulls the image out of focus to visualize her delirium of terror. Frame enlargements.

**The Man Who
Knew Too Much**
(Paramount Pictures, 1956)
In place of the fluid and
expressionistic camera
perspective of the earlier
version, the 1956 version
features largely static camera
perspectives and simple cuts
between the mother (Doris
Day) and what she sees. Frame
enlargement.

Hitchcock cuts twice to an out-of-focus shot of the orchestra to simulate the mother's anxious point of view. Following the second shot, he includes a disguised cut from the blurred image to the barrel of the assassin's gun as it pivots toward the camera. Nothing like this happens in the second version—no elaborate expressionist point-of-view shots from the mother's perspective. On the contrary, Hitchcock's techniques in the second version of the scene are more naturalistic and realistic rather than elaborate expressionist distortions.

Display of Production Values
In the second version, Hitchcock wanted to take advantage of the resources he could command as a major filmmaker in the Hollywood studios. He left Britain and came to Hollywood partly to gain access to the greater financial and artistic resources of the American studio system. Therefore, the second version, unlike the first, is filmed in Technicolor, an extremely vibrant and beautiful color process used throughout the 1950s. Robert Burks, who shot the 1956 version, was Hitchcock's regular cinematographer. Another close collaborator of Hitchcock's, Bernard Herrmann, the composer, is featured in the 1956 version. Herrmann created the musical score for this film, as well as for a number of other Hitchcock films of the 1950s and early 1960s. Herrmann plays the conductor at the Royal Albert Music Hall performance, and viewers see him prominently displayed in a number of medium shots and close-ups.

Working with these close collaborators, Hitchcock was clearly more ambitious in the scope he planned for this scene and in his desire to exhibit the production values now at his command. The increased number of shots in the second version—the music hall, the orchestra, and the audience—are designed to display these production values. **Production values** are those aspects of a film—set design, costuming, color, and special effects—that show the money invested. The Royal Albert Music Hall is given a great deal of visual attention and, consequently, appears to be larger and more imposing and spectacular in the 1956 film than it appears in the 1934 version.

In light of these differences of structural design, which version is better? The viewer watching both films will probably have a preference for one version over the other, but the answer to which one is better depends on a number of factors, including how one feels about the use of Technicolor versus black and white, naturalistic versus expressionist techniques, camera movement versus stationary shots, minimal versus maximal amounts of editing, and minimal versus maximal display of production values.

The structural design of each version has a different organization because of the way Hitchcock and his collaborators chose to exercise creative choice along the dimensions just examined. Neither version is clearly better than the other (although Hitchcock did prefer the later version). These are differences of *design,* not quality, and they result from the ways Hitchcock chose to use his tools of style. Again, some differences are partly attributable to Hitchcock's desire to exploit the technical resources of a major Hollywood studio, resources unavailable to him in the 1930s when he worked in Britain.

This comparison of the two Hitchcock films illustrates how structural design results from selective choices made by filmmakers and that there is no single way to film a scene. Instead, there are, potentially, many different ways to film every scene. These possibilities are gradually narrowed to a single approach as filmmakers decide how to organize the tools of filmmaking into a (hopefully) coherent structural design. Decisions about where to place the camera, whether to move it, and what type of lenses to use must be integrated with other decisions about lights, color, sets, costumes, editing, and sound in order to arrive at an organized, coherent, and expressive audio visual design.

■ THE CAMERA AND VIEWER PERCEPTION

The camera records screen action through a changing series of positions, angles, lenses, and movements. Does the camera's way of "seeing" approximate in any way to the viewer's customary habits of viewing the world? Is there a relationship between the appearance of images on the movie or television screen and the appearance of real-world objects and things in the mind's eye of the viewer? Obviously, both camera and human eye can see color, texture, movement, and the location of people and things in three-dimensional space. Motion pictures seem incredibly lifelike, and even impossible objects, such as the dinosaurs in *Jurassic Park* (1993), can be rendered with apparent photographic realism.

But the answer to the question of whether the camera's methods of seeing approximate the viewer's habits of perception is both a yes and a no. The camera can see selectively in ways the human eye cannot. Telephoto and wide-angle lens perspectives have no counterpart in human vision. The eye cannot magnify the size of distant objects, as a telephoto lens can, or increase the apparent distance between near and far objects, as a wide-angle lens can. A cinematographer who cranes up to a high-angle long shot employs a unique cinematic technique that the viewer's eye cannot duplicate, as does an editor who cuts among shots taken from different camera positions and angles, and with different lenses, to provide a shifting series of perspectives on the action. These are uniquely cinematic techniques that film viewers become familiar with and adept at interpreting by virtue of watching films.

Such techniques, used in conjunction with other elements of structure, such as costumes and set design, make possible the screen representation of imaginary worlds. Viewers have never seen living dinosaurs, but the creatures in *Jurassic Park* look

The Crow (MIramax, 1994)
Even in highly stylized films, facial expression establishes close correspondences with a viewer's real-life knowledge of human behavior and personality. Viewers of *The Crow* delight in the film's special effects fantasy world while studying the ghostly face of Eric (Brandon Lee) for clues to his feelings and motives. Frame enlargement.

extremely convincing and lifelike. Film viewers quickly learn that motion picture images and stories can define their own rules of representation and do so in ways that depart significantly from a viewer's own real-world experiences. The camera can be used to creatively and stylistically *transform* those experiences. Stylized films such as *The Crow* (1994) or *Batman* (1989) take viewers on imaginary journeys to worlds that differ remarkably from the one they inhabit in daily life. Viewers accept the unusual images, characters, and stories established in these films as a representational reality that is true on its own stylized terms.

But the camera and other elements of film structure do not simply alter and transform the viewer's experience of people, places, and physical environments. The camera's ability to stylistically transform these things co-exists with its tendency to establish clear and powerful correspondences with the viewer's real-world visual and social experience. Close-ups, for example, emphasize facial expressions. Social experience has taught viewers how to interpret these as signs of a person's thoughts, feelings, and intentions.

Eric, the murdered artist who returns to life seeking vengeance against his killers in *The Crow*, has superhuman powers and wears heavy, ghoulish make-up to accentuate his ghostly appearance. But his face is still the key to much of what happens in the narrative because it reveals his reasons for acting. Viewers study it for clues to his personality and emotions and interpret it by using skills that are routinely employed in everyday life. Moreover, although viewers understand that *The Crow* is primarily a revenge story that will follow the conventions of this kind of tale, they nevertheless relate these conventions to their extra-filmic knowledge of human behavior, and they measure the credibility of Eric's actions in the film with a socially derived understanding of motive, intent, and behavior. Eric may be a ghost with superpowers, but the anguish, the ruthlessness, as well as the tenderness he displays during his quest for vengeance, must correspond with the viewer's understanding of human behavior and feeling. Otherwise, the story and its flamboyant stylistic transformation of reality will lose credibility.

Among the most powerful correspondences the camera can establish with the viewer's experience are perceptual ones. On the movie screen, the viewer sees depth,

HOW MOVIES CREATE THE IMPRESSION OF MOTION ON SCREEN

On the motion picture screen, true movement does not exist. Viewers see only *apparent* motion. The movie projector throws on the screen a series of still photographs that are called *frames* and are contained on the strip of film running through the projector. (In this respect, *frame* has a double meaning. It refers to both the single image on a strip of film as well as the projected image seen on a screen.)

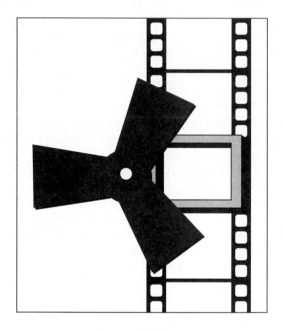

Figure 1: Intermittent motion
at 24 frames per second

As the strip of film runs through the projector, each frame is projected individually. A claw mechanism in the projector pulls each frame down in front of the light source, one by one. Each is therefore flashed separately on the screen. Inside the projector is a device called the **shutter,** which is like an on/off switch that alternately allows the light from the projector to reach the screen then cuts it off. It blocks the light from the projector for a fraction of a second while the next frame is pulled down into place. In the theater, viewers see a series of still frames projected on the screen, and they sit in alternating periods of light and dark without being aware of it.

Where, then, does the impression of movement and a continuously illuminated screen come from? It is because of several factors of perception. **Persistence of vision** (retinal afterimages) refers to the fact that the retina of the eye retains an image for a fraction of a second after the source is gone. These retinal afterimages explain why viewers fail to perceive the periods of darkness between the appearance of each frame on screen and see, instead, what seems to be a continuous stream of light and picture.

The cinema exploits persistence of vision in conjunction with the phenomenon of **flicker fusion.** If a light source is switched on and off rapidly enough, a threshold is reached at which fusion, or a blending together, of the individual pulses of light will occur. This fusion occurs above a certain threshold, which is called the *critical fusion frequency.*

Twenty-four frames per second, the projection speed of sound film, is adequate to sustain retinal afterimages and to produce critical fusion frequency. At 24 frames per second, viewers cannot see the pulsing light that the projector is emitting. (A popular nickname for the movies is "flicks." This term dates from the silent era when slower projection speeds were used, enabling spectators to see the faint pulsing of the projector light, that is, the flicker effect. Hence the term *flicks.*)

Persistence of vision and flicker fusion, then, explain part of the illusion on which the mechanics of

cinema depend—the perception of a steady beam of light illuminating the screen. They do not, however, explain the perception of apparent movement. The illusion of motion on screen seems to be related to what perceptual psychologists have termed **phi phenomena.** This name was used by Max Wertheimer (the founder of Gestalt psychology) to refer collectively to a series of conditions under which spectators will perceive apparent motion when no real movement has occurred. One of these conditions, called **beta movement,** involves the perception of apparent motion from one point to another.

If a series of closely spaced light bulbs are illuminated in sequence at a rapid enough interval in a darkened room, a spectator will seem to see a single light source moving across the room rather than a series of lights illuminated in sequence. The term *beta movement* refers to this perception. If the intervals between a series of illuminated lights (for example, the positions of a horse frozen in mid-flight into a series of film frames) are small enough, then for the eye, real movement exists, and the viewer will see a single, travelling light (or a galloping horse on screen).

Many viewers today watch movies by renting videotapes and playing them back on television screens. The mechanics of image generation on television are differ-

ent from image generation in film, but the principle of beta movement still applies to explain why viewers see motion on the TV screen. The television image is created by the illumination of small red, blue, and green phosphorus dots. The screen is composed of 525 lines, each containing many phosphorus dots that are illuminated in sequence as the screen is scanned line by line. One television frame is equivalent to the complete scanning of all 525 lines and is composed of two "fields." Odd-numbered lines are scanned first (one field), then the even-numbered lines (one field). The TV image runs at 30 frames (60 fields) per second. This is above critical fusion threshold. (In addition, the viewer sees a continuously illuminated screen because the eye cannot resolve or perceive the very small spaces between the phosphorus dots that make up the unilluminated portions of the screen image.)

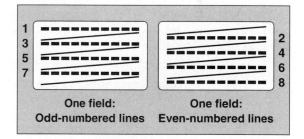

Figure 3: The video frame consists of two fields

In these ways, the most fundamental features of cinema—the appearance of continuous light and motion—are built on shared characteristics of perception common to all viewers. These features are automatic. Viewers do not have to make any effort to bring them into play. Seeing continuous light and motion on screen requires no special abilities or training. Building on these common features of perception, movies are accessible to everyone.

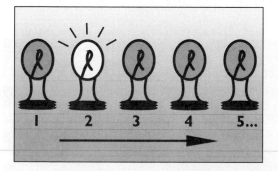

Figure 2: Successive events perceived as apparent motion

distance, and motion in ways that seem remarkably lifelike. A fully three-dimensional world seems to exist on the flat two-dimensional screen. When Eric flies through the darkened city as a crow, the viewer experiences the sensation of gliding through space because of the highly detailed and emphatic motion perspective that has been built inside the computer-generated flying shots. But movement and depth on screen are both visual illusions. Neither really exists.

The viewer's impressions of motion and three dimensions are among the most powerful effects the movies can create and are responsible for the medium's incredibly lifelike impact. The motion picture camera and projector create these illusions by building on features of visual perception shared by all viewers. The camera captures the same kind of information about light, shadow, color, texture, motion, and location in space that viewers routinely use in perceiving and responding to the real, three-dimensional world. Movies establish perceptual correspondences with the viewer's experience by building this information into the shots in ways that emphasize the three-dimensionality of the image appearing on the flat screen. This information in the film image tells viewers, at a perceptual level, that they are seeing three dimensions, not two, and movement where none truly exists. The appearance of movement and depth on screen are illusions created by cinema and are contingent on the camera's ability to establish perceptual correspondences with the viewer's experience of light, space, and motion in a real, three-dimensional world.

Cinema, then, both corresponds with and transforms the viewer's visual and social experience. This establishes a very complex relationship between movies and viewers. To understand pictures and sound, characters, and story in cinema, viewers use many of the same visual and social skills and sources of information that are used

---

Vertigo (Paramount Pictures, 1958)
The cinema may correspond with the viewer's real-world perceptual experiences, but it can also transform normal visual reality. To visualize the main character's fear of heights, Hitchcock in *Vertigo* combines a backward track with a forward zoom in this high-angle shot of a city street. Frame enlargement.

in everyday life. Filmmakers count on this and design their films in ways that invite the application and transfer of these skills to the movie screen.

Yet cinema also establishes its own peculiar laws. Gunfighters, mad scientists, and superheroes may populate Westerns, horror, and fantasy films but few viewers have such counterparts in their own off-screen experiences. Filmmakers can use the camera and film structure to make the unreal seem real. Viewers expect and take pleasure in cinema's abilities to both correspond with and transform their sense of the world.

Hitchcock's *Vertigo* (1958) has a main character who is afraid of heights. To visualize the character's dizziness, Hitchcock films a city street from an extremely high angle and combines a zoom in with a track out to suggest the feeling of falling through space. The resulting image departs from, and transforms, normal visual reality, and viewers accept this in the interest of style.

SUMMARY

Film structure or style results from the ways a filmmaker chooses to manipulate the camera, editing, light, sound, and color. This chapter has concentrated on the camera, specifically on the factors of position, angle, lens, and movement, and how these factors affect the way a viewer perceives the content of a shot or scene. By understanding the range of creative choices that confront filmmakers, and by appreciating their options in resolving those choices, one begins to understand a film's structural design. One cannot understand how films express meaning without knowing how filmmakers create structural design.

Camera positions are variations of three basic set-ups: the long shot, the medium shot, and the close-up. While long shots typically stress landscape or environment over character, close-ups usually emphasize character over environment. By varying the camera-to-subject distance, the filmmaker manipulates the viewer's emotional involvement with the scene or character in complex ways. Camera position can emphasize facial expressions as signs of a character's inner emotional life or can even work at cross-purposes with a viewer's desired relationship with a scene or character.

Camera angles are variations of low, medium (or eye level), or high angles. Like camera position, camera angle can be used to manipulate viewer responses. Camera angles can represent a character's point of view and emphasize a character's strength or, conversely, his or her insignificance. Angles can be consistent with, or play against, a viewer's desired relationship with a scene or character. As with camera position, though, the effects of camera angle are always dependent upon the emotional context and action of a given scene. By themselves, camera positions or angles do not inherently express anything.

Camera lenses supply distinctive optical characteristics to shots. Telephoto lenses reduce depth of field and angle of view, while wide-angle lenses enlarge these. Zoom lenses can substitute for camera movement, although they will not produce motion perspective as a moving camera does.

Camera movement includes pan and tilt shots, dolly or tracking shots, and boom or crane shots. Pans and tilts create linking movements, connecting objects or establishing relationships between them. Tracking and crane shots can add a dynamic sense of movement to a shot or express thematic ideas.

The camera, and the structural designs it helps create, both record and transform the outward appearance of things, the way they look. The cinema has a fundamental connection with the viewer's perceptual skills and experience. The viewer's impressions in film of continuous light, apparent motion, and spatial depth all derive from this fundamental connection. What makes the cinema such a rich imaginative experience is the way it builds upon and transforms this connection.

Style is best understood as a kind of creative response by filmmakers to the tendency of the motion picture camera to reproduce the surface appearance of the objects it photographs. By intervening stylistically—by choosing to use a wide-angle lens or a high camera angle—a filmmaker can creatively shape the material of the shot or scene while still taking advantage of the camera's ability to utilize important sources of information from the viewer's real-life visual and social experience.

SUGGESTED READINGS

David Breskin, ed., *Inner Views: Filmmakers in Conversation* (Winchester, MA: Faber and Faber, 1992).

David Cheshire, *The Book of Movie Photography* (New York: Alfred A. Kopf, 1979).

John P. Frisby, *Seeing: Illusion, Brain, and Mind* (New York: Oxford University Press, 1980).

Harry M. Geduld, ed., *Film Makers on Film Making* (Bloomington, IN: Indiana University Press, 1971).

E. H. Gombrich, *Art and Illusion* (Princeton, NJ: Princeton University Press, 1984).

Sidney Lumet, *Making Movies* (New York: Alfred A. Knopf, 1995)

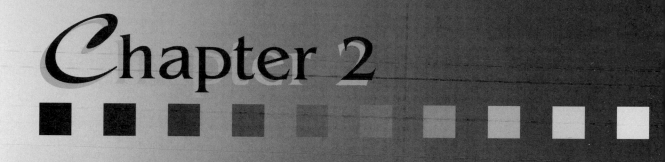

Chapter 2

Elements of Mise-en-scene: Cinematography

Chapter Objectives

After reading this chapter, you should be able to

- explain the concept of mise-en-scene and distinguish its components
- describe what the cinematographer contributes to mise-en-scene
- differentiate between realist and pictorial lighting designs
- describe the creative challenges of light source simulation
- explain why pictorial lighting designs work especially well for creating visual symbolism
- differentiate between hard and soft light and explain their expressive functions

- explain the differences between high- and low-key lighting set-ups
- explain the principles of lighting continuity
- explain the differences between lighting for color and lighting for black and white
- describe how color design establishes symbolic meaning, narrative organization, and psychological mood and tone
- explain how visual conventions help establish representational reality

Key Terms and Concepts

mise-en-scene
cinematography
production design
performance styles
wavelengths
hue
saturation
intensity
gray scale
primary color

additive color
subtractive color
practical lighting design
realistic lighting design
pictorial lighting design
rear projection
hard light
soft light
fall-off

contrast
high-key lighting
low-key lighting
key light
fill light
back light
flashing
conventions
film noir

Originally a French term referring to staging action in the theater, *mise-en-scene* denotes the overall look and visual design of a film. **Mise-en-scene** refers to all the elements that are placed in front of the camera to be photographed—sets, costumes, actors, props, light, and color. Unlike other elements of film structure, viewers tend to be highly aware of these.

Everyone who has seen Steven Spielberg's *E.T.* (1982) remembers E.T.'s childlike and vulnerable appearance. Martin Scorsese's recent adaptation of the Edith Wharton novel, *The Age of Innocence* (1993), stunned viewers with its elaborate historical recreation of sumptuously detailed period costumes and settings. Although viewers may not always be aware of the contributions of the sound designer or image editor, they remember a striking use of color or lavish costumes. This chapter examines the role of cinematography in film structure, basic approaches to lighting and color design, and how conventions of cinematography establish representational reality.

■ COMPONENTS OF MISE-EN-SCENE

The diverse elements of mise-en-scene fall into three categories. These are the categories of **cinematography, production design,** and **performance styles.** The first category, examined in this chapter, pertains to the use of light and color. The second category involves the design of the sets, locations, and all visual environments that are depicted on screen, and the third category deals with the actor's contribution to the film. Performance styles vary in different historical periods, and a filmmaker's use of actors can range from the strikingly realistic to the extremely stylized and pictorial.

The Importance of Collaboration

Although the actor's contribution to mise-en-scene is an important element of a film's visual design, the primary partnership or collaborative relationship that is relevant to mise-en-scene exists among the director, cinematographer, and production designer. Production designers and cinematographers translate into visual terms the vision of the director, and, in practice, they subordinate their own artistic inclinations to the director's wishes.

Although the cinematographer (also known as the director of photography) is the one who literally puts the director's vision on film, the production designer, who establishes a "look" for the film's sets and locales, remains an important co-creator of a film's visual style. During pre-production, the cinematographer and production designer consult with the director, discussing and defining the film's visual design. To accomplish this, these artists often use a common set of references, frequently drawn from such visual fields as architecture and painting, as well as other motion pictures.

To develop a visual style for their production, directors, cinematographers, and production designers often view movies together and study the visual achievements of other filmmakers. Director Steven Spielberg and cinematographer Allen Daviau watched and discussed a wide range of films to develop a basic style for *E.T.* These included *The Night of the Hunter* (1955), *Alien* (1979), *Apocalypse Now* (1979), and *Last Tango in Paris* (1972).

Visual references might also be supplied from painting. During pre-production of Robert Altman's *McCabe and Mrs. Miller* (1971), cinematographer Vilmos Zsigmond showed Altman a book of Andrew Wyeth's paintings, and they both agreed they would try to capture Wyeth's style of faded, soft, pastel images. Production designer Mel Bourne, whose credits include Woody Allen's *Annie Hall* (1977) and *Manhattan* (1979), and Adrian Lyne's *Indecent Proposal* (1993), characterizes the creative partnership necessary to plan the visual design of a film by stressing that the production designer and cinematographer should be working on the same wavelength which, in turn, comes from the director.

Color Plate 1. Lighting the crystal pyramid with a red light gives it a fiery glow that represents the lovers' passion in *Sliver* (1993). The red light contrasts with the cool blue of the surrounding scene. Frame enlargement.

Color Plate 2. Cinematographer Gordon Willis used amber light to create a unifying visual structure for the sprawling narrative of *The Godfather* (1972). Don Corleone (Marlon Brando) confers with a client who seeks the Godfather's help. In addition to using the amber motif, Willis dared to break a cardinal rule of film lighting in these low-key scenes: the actors' eyes are concealed by shadows. Conventional film lighting emphasizes illuminating the actors' eyes, but Willis thought his shadowy approach suited the film's gangster world.

Color Plate 3. Vibrant, warm color design typifies the first narrative segment of Spike Lee's *Malcolm X* (1992). The intense, bright colors of these early scenes contrast with the cool blues of the film's middle, the prison segment, and with the subdued earth tones of the concluding section dealing with Malcolm's career as a civil rights leader.

Color Plate 4. Color design extends and intensifies the dramatic and emotional context of a scene or film. Whereas Gordon Willis used amber to unify *The Godfather* narratives, cinematographer Vittorio Storaro used amber light to represent the intense romantic passion of the lovers (Marlon Brando, Maria Schneider) in *Last Tango in Paris* (1972). Frame enlargement.

Color Plate 5. Cinematographer Adam Greenberg uses hard, blue light to bring out the violence and savagery of *The Terminator* (1984). Color and lighting design extend the dramatic and emotional impact of the film's violent narrative. Frame enlargement.

Color Plate 6. While black and white film registers only shades of gray, color provides more abundant information about environments and objects. Because of their different hues, these red, yellow, purple, orange, and pink flowers separate naturally from one another. Their multiple colors provide a striking backdrop for the action in this scene from *Vertigo* (1958). Frame enlargement.

Color Plate 7. Color can add energy to the frame, intensifying the visual design of a shot or scene. The red roses behind Judy Garland create the dominant color effect in this shot from *A Star Is Born*, adding dynamic visual energy to the image. Frame enlargement.

Color Plate 8. Color can alter the representation of landscape. Color Westerns often look prettier than their black-and-white counterparts because color makes the West look more lush and vital. In *Shane* (1953), the bright purple of the distant mountains, the deep brown of the horse's coat and Shane's tanned fleshtones and buckskins provide a rich palette of color information. By contrast, black-and-white Western landscapes often tend toward a starker, harsher appearance. Frame Enlargement.

Color Plate 9. Cinematographers, production designers, and directors carefully organize the constituent colors in a shot or scene to create an overall mood or effect. Note the harmonious combination of greens and browns in this shot from *Out of Africa* (1985). By compressing foreground and background, the telephoto lens enhances the harmonious color design. Frame enlargement.

Color Plate 10. Color design can assume metaphoric functions, symbolizing a film's major theme. *Ride the High Country* (1962) protrays the declining skills and reputations of two aging gunfighters. The flaring colors of leaves in the autumn woods high in the mountains where the story is set, visualize the film's concerns with aging and death in the autumn of life. Frame enlargement.

Color Plate 11. Color design can suggest a character's psychological or emotional point of view. In *Vertigo* (1958), Kim Novak plays a mysterious woman with whom retired detective Scotty Ferguson (James Stewart) falls in love. In this scene, he watches her as she sits before the fire in his living room. Her bright red robe and the warm, glowing fire subtly embody the desire he feels for her. Note how his feelings are represented by and built into the color design of the scene. Frame enlargement.

Color Plate 12. Filmmakers can exaggerate or distort color to symbolize the inner truths of a scene's dramatic core. In *Vertigo*, Hitchcock uses flashing colored lights to portray ex-detective Scotty Ferguson's (James Stewart) descent into madness. The bizarre color effects lack subtlety, but they are an effective poetic means of conveying the character's mental breakdown. Frame enlargement.

Color Plate 13. Filmmakers frequently use special filters to create needed visual effects in combination with a scene's color design. In *Vertigo*, Hitchcock uses special diffusion filters to scatter light and color, thereby creating a ghostly effect suited to the story's apparent concerns with reincarnation and ghostly possession. Frame enlargement.

Color Plate 14. Color filters can shape a scene's color design to specific dramatic requirements. The amber filter used in this scene from *Out of Africa* creates a monochromatic effect and suggests the firelight that is supposed to be illuminating the characters' faces. Frame enlargement.

Color Plate 15. Many color films fade. The problem of color fading is a grave threat to the integrity of cinema because it effectively destroys the artistic achievements of earlier generations of directors, production designers, and cinematographers. The color dyes used in Technicolor "imbibition" films were extraordinarily saturated and stable, producing extremely rich and vibrant colors that tend to resist fading. Unfortunately, Technicolor closed its U.S. labs in 1974. While the Technicolor name persists, the authentic 3-strip process that gave cinema its greatest colors is now a relic of the past. Frame enlargement, *The Searchers* (1956).

Color Plate 16. Faded color in Joseph Losey's *The Go-Between* (1971). Note the strong pink and reddish cast to the image. The blue components are often the first to fade out, leaving many films with an unpleasantly monochromatic brown, pink, or red appearance. Color fading has been particularly devastating to non-Technicolor films of the 1950s–1970s. Frame enlargement.

▲ Color Plate 1.
Sliver (Paramount Pictures, 1993).

▲ Color Plate 2.
The Godfather (Paramount Pictures).

▲ Color Plate 3.
Malcolm X (Warner Bros., 1992).

◀ Color Plate 4.
Last Tango in Paris (United Artists, 1972).

▲ **Color Plate 5.**
The Terminator
(Hemdale, 1984).

▼ **Color Plate 7.**
A Star Is Born
(Warner Bros., 1954).

▲ **Color Plate 6.**
Vertigo (Paramount, 1958).

Color Plate 8. ▶
Shane (Paramount,
1953).

▲ Color Plate 9.
Out of Africa
(Universal, 1985).

▲ Color Plate 10.
Ride the High Country
(MGM, 1962).

◄
Color Plate 11.
Vertigo (Paramount, 1958).

►
Color Plate 12.
Vertigo (Paramount,
1958).

◀ **Color Plate 13.**
Vertigo (Paramount
Pictures, 1958).

▶ **Color Plate 14.**
Out of Africa
(Universal, 1985).

▲ **Color Plate 15.**
The Searchers
(Warner Bros., 1956).

▼ **Color Plate 16.**
The Go-Betweens (Columbia, 1971).

THE ESSENTIALS OF CINEMATOGRAPHY

The cinematographer, working with the director, plans the lighting and color design of a scene and the camera positions from which the scene will be photographed. Camera placement was examined in Chapter 1, so the discussion here focuses on lighting and color design.

Approaches to Lighting Design

As a cinematographer begins to map the lighting design for a scene, he or she can use two major strategies of lighting. These are realism and pictorialism. A cinematographer's lighting design will adhere more or less strongly to one or the other of these traditions.

Realism and Source Simulation

Every scene on screen implies a light source. If it is an exterior, daylight scene, the light source is, by implication, the sun. If it is an interior scene, then the table lamps, overhead ceiling lights, or street lights visible through windows become the implied source lights. These are "effect" lights because the cinematographer uses them to convey the effect that they are casting the visible light in the scene. This may or may not actually be true. If the table lamp in the set is rigged to be a real source of lighting for the camera, then it is called a **practical** since it is a visible light source on the set that actually works for exposure of the film.

In other cases, the actual lights for exposure may be off screen. The lighting design and the exposure setting on the camera are manipulated so that the viewer sees the table lamp as if it were casting the light visible on screen. Lights for effect, then, may be distinct from the lights for exposure. In the case of those lights termed *practicals,* the light source that creates the effect and the exposure is the same.

A lighting design that distributes light to simulate an explicit source on screen, whether it be the sun or a table lamp indoors, is a **realistic lighting design.** To obtain a realistic effect, a cinematographer balances competing considerations. Among these are depth of field (the amount of separation between sharply focused foreground and background objects) and how "hot" or brightly exposed the scene should appear to be.

Problems of Effects Lighting and Source Simulation

In the recent romantic thriller *Sliver* (1993), cinematographer Vilmos Zsigmond filmed a dialogue scene between Sharon Stone and William Baldwin set in a restaurant. The two were seated at a small intimate table illuminated by a candle in the center. This is the light for effect. Zsigmond worked to simulate the effect of the candle as the main source of light upon the actors' faces.

The creative challenge arose from the problems inherent in photographing candlelight. Candlelight is, of course, dim. Zsigmond could have opened his lens setting to a very wide aperture to provide the maximum amount of light for the film inside the camera. If he had, two things would have happened. First, depth of field would have been greatly diminished, and it was important—for the humorous effect of the scene—to see the reactions of other customers (in the background of the shot) to the sexual seduction between Stone and Baldwin. Depth of field, therefore, could not be sacrificed.

WHAT IS LIGHT AND COLOR?

Light and color are the tools of the cinematographer's art. In addition to planning camera set-ups and movements, the cinematographer organizes the lighting design of scenes and the placement of color gels to augment or enhance certain colors on screen.

Light is a form of radiant energy, a part of the total electromagnetic spectrum. Light is visible only at its source or as it is reflected off another object. Colors are visible when white light is broken down into its component **wavelengths.** Color arises when light of a given wavelength reaches the eye, whereupon it is interpreted as a color sensation by the brain. A rose appears red because it absorbs light of all visible wavelengths with the exception of red light, which it reflects back to the viewer. A bottle of green dishwashing liquid appears green because the liquid transmits only green light and acts as a filter to block out all other colors. Colored objects, then, appear to be colored, based on the light that they either reflect or transmit, depending on whether they are solid objects or transparent.

In the cinema, colors can be created on the set during filming by using these processes of reflectance and transmission. Lighting a blue object on the set will increase its ability to reflect blue back to the camera. Using a red gel or filter over a white light source will cause that source to transmit only red light.

Properties of Color

Three properties of color are important. **Hue** refers to the color itself. Red, blue, green, and yellow are hues. These four hues are unique. They do not resemble one another. By contrast, pink is not a unique hue. It is a derivative of red. **Saturation** refers to the strength of a color. Red is more highly saturated than pink. Consequently, a filmmaker interested in using a "strong" color should choose red rather than pink.

Intensity is the third property that describes the appearance of a color. Brightness is another way of understanding intensity. It refers to how much light a given colored object reflects. The viewer makes certain assumptions that influence the way colors are perceived. For example, the same piece of red cloth seen at high noon and then again at dusk will appear to be the same color, but its intensity will vary. Seen at high noon, it will appear to be much brighter than at dusk. This example illustrates how the viewer's perceptions of hue and intensity do not always correspond. In this case, it is because the viewer makes an assumption of color constancy while correcting for perceived variations in brightness.

The Gray Scale

Although the human eye ordinarily sees the world in color and color filmmaking takes advantage of this characteristic by manipulating and emphasizing various colors in meaningful ways, filmmakers may also work in black and white. Indeed, until the 1960s, black and white was a common format. Since the 1960s, black and white has been used more rarely but with powerful artistic effect. In *Schindler's List* (1993), about the Holocaust, Steven Spielberg wanted to avoid excessively pretty images, so he abandoned his usual palette of colors, reasoning that black and white cinematography would give his film a harsher and starker look, one more appropriate to its grim subject matter.

When filmmakers work in black and white, instead of organizing their mise-en-scene in terms of a color design, they have only the **gray scale** with which to work. Black and white film and television cameras see only degrees of brightness, ranging from white to black through intermediate shades of gray. This spectrum is known as the gray scale, and it determines which colors are used or avoided in costumes and sets during filming. Certain very different colors will appear to have the same degree of brightness. In black and white cinematography, this can create a problem. If two objects of different color have the same intensity or gray scale value, they will blend together on screen. Black and white film, registering only degrees of brightness, will not distinguish them.

In color film, hues will separate objects. Since there are no hues in black and white, cinematographers must separate objects by degrees of brightness. This can be done in two ways. One is to light the foreground, leav-

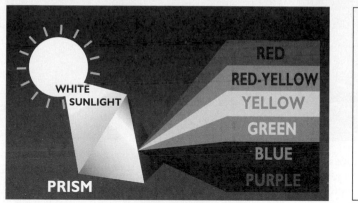

Figure 1: Prism

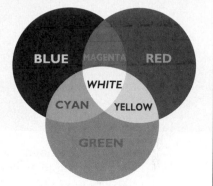

Figure 2: Additive mixing

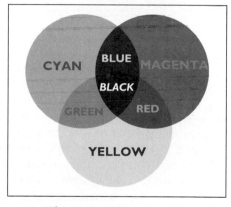

Figure 3: Subtractive mixing

ing the mid-ground somewhat dimmer and then adding brighter light to the background. Alternatively, separation of objects can be achieved by avoiding the use of colors that will be perceived by black and white film with the same degree of brightness. Cinematographer Laszlo Kovacs [*Easy Rider* (1969), *Ghostbusters* (1984)] points out that, in color, a brown head will separate naturally from a beige wall, but in black and white the two may run together. The cinematographer working in black and white has to keep in mind not how the human eye will perceive colors in a given scene, but rather how the black and white camera will read the brightness values of those colors.

Additive and Subtractive Color Mixing

Color film is based on principles of color mixing using only a few basic (**primary**) colors. The earliest color systems in film history were **additive.** By adding varying proportions of red, green, and blue light (achieved through the use of filters to convert the white projector light into these hues), a diverse range of colors could be produced on screen. Adding green and red, for example, will produce yellow. Additive systems in film, though, were clumsy and were soon replaced by **subtractive** color mixing. However, color television does use an additive system. Inside the television screen are a series of red, blue, and green dots that are illuminated at varying intensities and then mixed together

into the various wavelengths that the eye and brain perceive as color sensations.

Color motion picture film uses subtractive color mixing to remove various wavelengths from white light (which contains all of the wavelengths that can be resolved into separate colors). To do this, subtractive color filters are used. These are magenta, yellow, and cyan. These color filters subtract unwanted colors and transmit the desired color combinations. These color filters are contained as layers of dye in the strip of raw, unexposed film, and, as white light enters the camera, they filter and transmit only those few wavelengths needed for subtractive mixing.

Sliver (Paramount Pictures, 1993)
In these shots from *Sliver* a realistic lighting design required filming candlelight so that it
seemed to be casting the visible light on the screen. The candle appears very bright, but it is
not the real light source in the scene. The actual lights for exposure are off-camera. Frame
enlargements.

Second, going to a wide apertured setting would make the restaurant appear to be
flooded with light, to be very brightly lit but not by candlelight. (In fact, the restaurant
was flooded with light—for exposure, not for effect. These lights were off camera.)

At a wide apertured setting, therefore, the flame would not expose well. Because
of the other lights on set, it would not look hot enough for the viewer to believe that
it was the light source in the scene. To solve these problems, Zsigmond opened his
lens just wide enough to maintain adequate depth of field and supplemented the light
from the candle with a small electric bulb hidden behind it. As a result, the viewer
can see background customers in the shot (adequate depth of field), *and* the candle
in the foreground looks bright enough to be casting the illumination in the scene.

Cinematographer Michael Ballhaus devised a very creative approach to simulating light sources in Francis Ford Coppola's *Bram Stoker's Dracula* (1992). There
were no electric lights in Dracula's time—all light was supplied by candles, lanterns,
oil lamps, or torches. The light these instruments cast was flickering and unsteady. To
simulate this, Ballhaus placed his lights on flicker boxes that simulated a moving, flickering effect with an electric light source. Coppola's film is a gaudy, stylized, extravagant fantasy. Realism is not the sort of term that one would immediately apply to such
a film, but notice how, despite the fantastical nature of many of the film's visual
effects, realistic principles of light source simulation were followed in this film. Ballhaus and Coppola did not want any of the light sources on screen to have the steadi-
ness of electric lights.

Pictorialism

As discussed above, the goal of a realistic lighting design is to simulate a distribution
of light that is compatible with the implied source. An alternative—**pictorial lighting design**—stresses purely pictorial or visual values that may be unrelated to strict
concerns about source simulation. Realistic and pictorial approaches are not rigid categories, and many films may use both approaches. *Bram Stoker's Dracula* includes
scenes in which the lighting design is governed by extravagantly pictorial considera-

Bram Stoker's Dracula
(Columbia Pictures, 1992)
Pictorial lighting designs stress purely visual effects unconnected to issues of realism. In the next moment, Dracula's shadow will disengage itself from the vampire Prince and begin to strangle Jonathan Harker (Keanu Reeves). The effect is pictorial and poetic, but not realistic. Frame enlargement.

tions. When Dracula (Gary Oldman) meets with real estate representative Jonathan Harker (Keanu Reeves), who has journeyed by train and coach to the vampire's remote Transylvanian castle, Coppola and Ballhaus achieve one of their most striking pictorial effects.

Harker shows Dracula the portrait of Mina, the woman he is engaged to marry. Dracula realizes that she is the reincarnation of his own true love lost many centuries before. Because he wants to possess Mina as his own beloved, Dracula feels murderous rage toward Harker. As the two converse, Dracula's shadow, which had been cast upon the back wall, disengages itself from Dracula. The shadow advances on Harker and begins to strangle him.

The effect is not only visually striking but surprising and uncanny. Coppola and Ballhaus creatively violate the logic of shadow phenomena. In film, shadows are attached to or cast by the object to which they belong, but never do they behave independently of that object. Because of this, the positions of cast or attached shadows provide vital information about the shape and location in space of their objects. Coppola violates the perceptual regularities governing cast-shadow behavior, shocking viewers and directing their interpretations toward the supernatural. It is a purely pictorial (and physically impossible) moment in the scene.

The effect of the detached, independently motivated shadow was created by shooting part of the scene live and part of the scene with **rear projection.** Dracula's cast shadow upon the wall is not a true shadow at all but was created by a dancer working in sync with Dracula/Oldman's movements. The shadow created by the dancer was rear projected upon the wall behind Dracula and Harker. When the "shadow" disengages itself from Dracula, its object, the effect is created by the dancer's breaking sync with Oldman.

Pictorial Lighting for Thematic Symbolism Filmmakers often employ pictorial designs to visually symbolize the thematic content of a scene or film. Pictorial designs do this far more successfully and explicitly than realist designs because filmmakers can manipulate light and color in ways that are unfettered by concerns about realism and that can directly relate to the underlying social, psychological, or emotional themes of a scene. Pictorialism enables filmmakers to use light and color to visually embody the underlying significance of a given scene or film.

Cinematographer Vittorio Storaro's pictorial designs for Francis Ford Coppola's *Apocalypse Now* (1979) create a precise visual statement of the existential moral issues

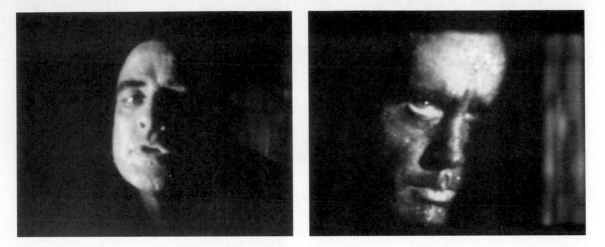

Apocalypse Now (United Artists, 1979)
Pictorial lighting for thematic symbolism: the faces of Kurtz (Marlon Brando) and Willard
(Martin Sheen). Cinematographer Vittorio Storaro's lighting design stresses the moral
conflict between the ongoing good and evil within each character and suggests an essential
moral equivalence between both men. Frame enlargements.

at the heart of the film. The Vietnam War drives a renegade American soldier, Kurtz
(Marlon Brando), insane, and the military brass send an assassin named Willard (Martin Sheen) upriver to Kurtz's compound to murder him. Most of the narrative takes
place during Willard's trip upriver and raises the question about what Willard will do
when he finally meets Kurtz. Will he kill him as he has been instructed, or, since both
men are equally murderous and bestial, will he join Kurtz instead?

To suggest the psychological and spiritual bond between the two characters,
Storaro employed a strikingly similar lighting design for each man. Kurtz is filmed
with his face half-in and half-out of shadow to convey the character's cruelty and
moral darkness and the inner struggle between good and evil that has driven him
insane. Part of his face is visible and the other half obscured by impenetrable darkness. After Willard kills Kurtz, the same lighting design is used to make him look like
Kurtz. Willard's face is partially eclipsed, half in the light, half in the shadow. The
lighting tells the viewer that Willard has become Kurtz. As the film now exists, however, the visual and thematic force of this pictorial statement is profoundly weakened.
After early test screenings indicated that the original ending did not work for audiences, Coppola added a different conclusion in which Willard rejects Kurtz's kingdom and leaves.

Coppola's original ending was more mysterious. In both the original and revised
endings, Willard kills Kurtz, but in Coppola's original, preferred version, Willard
remains behind on the steps of Kurtz's compound facing Kurtz's army, his face lit to
look like Kurtz. Coppola's preferred version ended here. He wanted the film to conclude with the question of whether Willard had become Kurtz, and Storaro's lighting clearly implied that he had. By changing this original ending and extending the

FRANCIS FORD COPPOLA

Along with Martin Scorsese, George Lucas, and Brian DePalma, Coppola belongs to a young generation of university-trained film students-turned-directors who established careers in the early 1970s. His earliest films (*Dementia 13*, 1963; *Finian's Rainbow,* 1968) are undistinguished and do not hint at the talent that suddenly burst forth in *The Godfather* (1972), the most successful example of epic narrative filmmaking produced by a major studio since *Gone With the Wind* (1939). Starring Marlon Brando and Al Pacino, *The Godfather* offers a richly romanticized and harshly brutal portrait of the rise to power of the Corleone crime family. Feeling he had oversentimentalized the Corleones in the first film, Coppola set out to destroy them in the harsher, bleaker sequel, *The Godfather, Part II* (1974), which many critics consider superior to its predecessor.

Between these two epics, Coppola made *The Conversation* (1974), an edgy, sophisticated portrait of the psychological disintegration of an electronics wizard and domestic spy (played by Gene Hackman). An extraordinarily stylized and ambiguous work, *The Conversation* avoids the formulaic features of the bigger-budgeted *Godfather* films.

These three films remain Coppola's greatest achievements as a director. His subsequent career is checkered with grandly conceived but incompletely realized ambitions. Seduced by a huge budget and ballooning ambitions, Coppola released *Apocalypse Now* (1979), a visually spectacular but conceptually muddled account of the Vietnam War. For much of its length it is undeniably hypnotic, but, after the precision and clarity of his previous three films, its diffuseness is disappointing.

His next films—*One From the Heart* (1982), *Rumble Fish* (1983), *The Cotton Club* (1984), *Peggy Sue Got Married* (1986), *Gardens of Stone* (1987), and *Tucker* (1988)—generally failed to connect with critics or public and often seemed more conventional than visionary. Part of Coppola's problem was a faltering economic base. He attempted to establish his own studio by creating Zoetrope Studios in 1980, but *Apocalypse Now* saddled him with huge debts, and the disastrous box-office performance of *One From the Heart* compounded his problems. The more conventional films that followed are partly a result of Coppola's efforts to extricate himself from a mountain of debt by crafting less audacious and more commercial products.

Coppola returned to epic form with *The Godfather, Part III* (1991), a compelling but uneven conclusion to the saga of Michael Corleone, and *Bram Stoker's Dracula* (1992), a controversial but genuinely visionary and flamboyant adaptation of the Stoker novel. The latter film is one of Coppola's most ambitious and artistically successful works.

Coppola remains a powerful force in contemporary American films. His up-and-down career is marked by an unresolved tension between grandiose artistic ambitions and the budgetary limitations and need for box-office success inherent in studio-financed productions. Unlike Woody Allen, who works successfully with limited resources, Coppola often requires huge budgets for his visions and has had difficulty accommodating the inevitable compromises such budgets entail.

The Godfather
(Paramount Pictures, 1972)
Coppola brilliantly integrated masterful storytelling, exquisite visual design, and grand artistic ambitions to produce *The Godfather,* an enduring modern classic. Marlon Brando's performance as Don Vito Corleone, the mafia Godfather, was so vivid and remarkable that it inspired a generation of mimics and comic impersonators.

narrative with images of Willard leaving, the integrity of Storaro's cinematography and lighting design was undermined, and the film as a whole was made thematically less coherent.

Types of Lighting Design: Hard and Soft Light

Once the cinematographer and director decide upon the overall balance of realist and pictorialist elements, they further specify their lighting design in terms of the proportions of **hard** and **soft light.**

Hard and soft light differ in terms of the properties of **fall-off** and **contrast.** Hard lighting features fast fall-off. The boundaries between the illuminated areas and the areas in darkness or shadow are sharply defined. The rate of fall-off, or change from light to dark, is very fast. This creates a high contrast between light and dark areas as they are distributed throughout the frame.

Another way of understanding contrast is in terms of shadow definition. High-contrast lighting produces strong shadow definition. (In everyday life, the characteristics of fall-off and contrast provide important information about the layout of the three-dimensional world.) The distribution of light and shadow, understood in terms of fall-off and contrast, conveys physical properties of depth, distance, and surface texture, expressed by the different ways light falls across objects in a room or scene. Motion picture images easily copy this source of everyday perceptual information, and filmmakers use this information to create a convincing impression of three-dimensional space on a flat, two-dimensional screen. By manipulating fall-off and contrast, cinematographers enhance the three-dimensional appearance of film images. Light organizes and defines space.

Soft lighting reduces sources of three-dimensional spatial information. Soft light is highly diffused or scattered, and it creates a flat appearance. Texture and depth cues

---

Bullitt (Warner Bros., 1968); **The Terminator** (Hemdale, 1984)
Soft light with low contrast and slow fall-off creates a "flat" look on Steve McQueen in this shot from *Bullitt*. Hard light with high contrast and fast fall-off accentuates the shape and texture of Arnold Schwarzenegger's face in *The Terminator*. Frame enlargements.

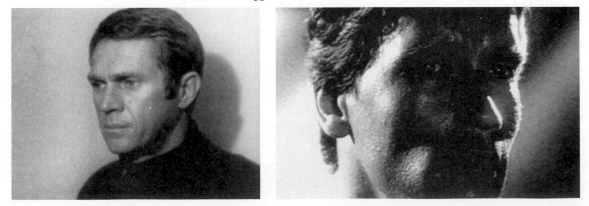

are reduced, although in color film the different hues will still provide information about the separation and distribution of objects. Consider the accompanying illustrations, one employing hard, high-contrast, fast fall-off lighting, the other soft light with low contrast and slow fall-off. The portrait employing the hard lighting design appears far more three-dimensional because the distribution of light more effectively conveys the physical characteristics of the performer and the surrounding environment.

Establishing Mood and Psychological Effect

Hard and soft lighting designs can have great impact upon the mood or emotional effect of a scene or sequence. In Charles Laughton's *The Night of the Hunter* (1955), the cinematographer employs an extravagantly pictorial, hard-lighting design. The images have extreme high contrast and very fast fall-off. The design is expressly psychological in tone. A demented preacher (Robert Mitchum) plots to murder his new bride because he wants to steal her money. The lighting design creates a chapel effect, giving the room a steepled appearance. The blades of light racing toward the ceiling comment on the preacher's religious mania and also on his sadistic violence. He will use a switchblade knife to murder his wife. The threat of violence is reproduced visually and amplified by the slashing blades of light pointing sharply toward the ceiling.

By contrast, in Steven Spielberg's *E.T.*, soft, highly diffused light eliminates shadows and creates a peaceful, soothing atmosphere in the bedroom of Elliott, the boy who befriends E.T. For the boy, the bedroom is a place of refuge and security, and the soft lighting establishes the appropriate atmosphere.

Establishing Time of Day

Hard and soft lighting effectively establish time of day in a scene. Here, as with other techniques, filmmakers manipulate elements of structure to make the world on screen

---

The Night of the Hunter (United Artists, 1955)
Hard lighting for psychological emphasis. Preacher Harry Powell, a religious psychopath, plots to murder his wife. The lighting makes the bedroom look like a chapel; but the slashing blades of light also evoke his sadistic, violent impulses. The complex currents of religion and violence that define Powell are effectively symbolized in this pictorial lighting design. Frame enlargements.

correspond with visual information that viewers are familiar with in daily life. Filmmakers use lighting design to establish the time a scene is occurring by mimicking the way sunlight changes during the course of a day. At noon, sunlight is hard and shadows are short. During the morning and at dusk, sunlight is more highly diffused and shadows are longer. Both bright exterior lights visible through windows of an indoor set and diffused light on the interior of the set will establish daytime, whereas night is indicated by using dark or dim exteriors and hard, contrasting illumination on the interior. In Peter Weir's *Fearless* (1993), cinematographer Allen Daviau used hard light to establish the late morning hour when a critical airline flight occurs. He positioned lights at a high angle to cast short shadows through the windows of the airplane set. The lighting arrangement realistically replicated qualities of light at this time of day.

Types of Lighting Design: High- and Low-Key Light

Hard and soft lighting designs can be achieved by using **high-key** and **low-key** lighting set-ups. The **key light** in the traditional three-point lighting employed in Hollywood films is the main source of illumination usually directed upon the face of the performer. The other two light sources are the **fill light** and the **back light.** The back light illuminates the rear portion of the set and/or the performer to establish a degree of separation between the actor and the rear of the set. Otherwise, the two would blend together. The fill light fills in undesirable areas of shadow that are created by the positioning of the key light and the back light.

Low-key lighting features a relatively bright key light compared with little fill light. This produces lots of shadows. In low-key lighting, most of the picture is underlit while other portions of the image area are adequately exposed. Typically, low-key lighting employs hard light in a high contrast, fast fall-off image. This style was popular in crime films throughout the 1940s and early 1950s. Many of these were called *films noir,* meaning dark film, a term designating the low-key lighting set-ups they employed as well as the moral darkness of their stories and characters.

Figure 3.1: Three-point lighting

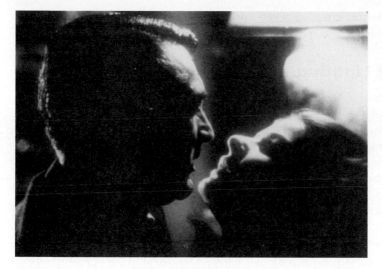

Notorious (RKO, 1946)
Low-key lighting selectively illuminates small areas of the frame and leaves the remaining areas deliberately underexposed. As a result, the characters in a low-key scene are surrounded by shadows. Devlin (Cary Grant), an American agent, embraces Alicia (Ingrid Bergman) before rescuing her from her murderous Nazi captors in Alfred Hitchcock's *Notorious*. The shadows add to the romanticism of the lovers' embrace as well as embody the sinister forces that surround Devlin and Alicia. Frame enlargement.

High-key lighting is the opposite of low-key lighting. High key employs similar, bright intensities of key and fill, producing an even level of illumination throughout the scene with low contrast and few shadow areas. While low-key set-ups are suited to the gloomy, sinister films noir, high-key styles brightened the tone of Hollywood's popular musicals. High-key styles assertively displayed the cheerful sets, colors, costumes, and dancing in such films as *Singing in the Rain* (1952), *An American in Paris* (1951), and *The Bandwagon* (1953). The MGM studio, in particular, favored high-

An American in Paris (MGM, 1951)
High-key lighting brightens the optimism of the musical and showcases its elaborate color, costuming, and set design. Gene Kelly and Leslie Caron perform the concluding seventeen-minute ballet in *An American in Paris*. The set design of this flower market scene intends to evoke the visual style of the French impressionist painter Manet.

key styles to showcase the sumptuous sets and costumes in their productions, musical and nonmusical alike.

Continuity of Lighting across Shots

Viewers watching a narrative motion picture generally want to believe in the plausibility and integrity of the world represented on screen. In other words, it should behave much as the viewer's own world does and obey the same kinds of physical laws of time and space, unless, as in adventure, fantasy, or science fiction, there is a clearly established reason for not doing so. Filmmakers manipulate cinematic style to represent *and* transform the viewer's sense of reality. Viewers, in turn, expect films to reference and correspond in key ways with their experience of the world, while granting filmmakers a great deal of freedom in the ways they do this. Stylistic manipulations operate within limits. These are partly dictated by the logical demands of the style itself. Sylvester Stallone's character Rambo can have superhuman abilities, but if these are too excessive, his adventures will lose all sense of danger and peril, and the films will lack suspense.

Stylistic manipulations are also limited by the viewer's demands for reference and correspondence in the represented screen world. In this respect, continuity principles impose fundamental limitations upon style in the interest of achieving reference and correspondence. In the areas of image editing and sound editing, principles of continuity are fundamental to narrative filmmaking. The same is true for lighting, irrespective of whether a filmmaker employs a realistic or pictorial design.

To establish the integrity and realism of the action occurring on screen, cinematographers must follow principles of continuity in their lighting designs. They are not free to drastically change light values from shot to shot. The shift from one shot to another should not introduce major changes in the light values that have been established for the scene. In the scene from *Sliver* that takes place in a candlelit restaurant, the overall light values must appear unchanged regardless of whether viewers see the action in long shot, medium shot, or close-up. A cinematographer, therefore, must take adequate measurements of the amount of light available within a scene and understand how to make small adjustments in that light depending on the camera's position. Close-ups, for example, are generally lit a little brighter than long or medium shots are, but viewers do not notice these small variations.

Filming on location can introduce complications in the way cinematographers plan for lighting continuity. When shooting out-of-doors, filmmakers must often supplement naturally available sunlight with artificial lights. The position of the sun in the sky overhead changes during the course of the day and so does the apparent hardness of the light. Light is hardest at noon. While filming *The Last of the Mohicans* (1993), cinematographer Dante Spinotti found that artificial electric lights offered several advantages during location shooting in the forest, where much of the film's action is set.

In designing a visual look for the film, Spinotti wanted to be faithful to the story's eighteenth-century period. At that time, there were no electric lights, so illumination in the forests would have been produced by sunlight during the day and by moonlight and firelight at night. To simulate the effect of powerful shafts of sunlight pour-

The Last of the Mohicans (Twentieth Century Fox, 1993)
Powerful electric lights illuminated the forests in *The Last of the Mohicans* and established continuity of lighting across shots. The artificial lights also provided convincing source simulation and permitted an expanded shooting schedule.

ing into the forest, Spinotti used a few, very large and powerful electric lights. These cast narrow beams of light and effectively simulated rays of sunshine penetrating the dark forest.

This use of artificial light accomplished two things. First, it established lighting continuity across shots regardless of the time of day or dusk when filming occurred. Second, using electrical lights that could be positioned at appropriate angles enabled filmmakers to compensate for changes in the sun's position. Using these lights also extended principle hours of cinematography beyond the noon hour when light was at its hardest and least diffused. Without the use of electrical lights, the film crew would have had only a few hours for a daylight shoot. Supplementing sunlight with the electrical lights permitted shooting well past the noon hour, even at dusk.

Continuity of Lighting within Shots

A cinematographer must plan for lighting continuity within shots, as well as across shots. Many shots involve camera movement. As soon as the camera begins to move, its relationship to the lights set up for the scene changes. Lights that provide adequate exposure and atmosphere for a camera in one position will not do so if the camera moves to another position on the set.

Camera movement necessitates several things. The cinematographer must plan for a lighting design that can accommodate the entire range of camera movement. Sometimes this requires adjusting the light level and the exposure level in the camera during the shot itself. In *Sliver*, the director wanted cinematographer Vilmos Zsigmond to design a lighting set-up that would permit the camera to move from one side to the other of a pair of conversing actors. A more traditional procedure would employ a cut from one over-the-shoulder set-up to the other. In this case, though, the director wanted to use camera movement instead of a cut.

Cinematographer Zsigmond designed two lighting set-ups, one for each over-the-shoulder position, and, as the camera moved, using dimmers, he dimmed one set of lights and brightened the other set. By slowly dimming the lights on one side of the actors and brightening them on the other side, Zsigmond was confident that the audience would not notice the change.

When filming Robert Altman's *Short Cuts* (1993), cinematographer Walt Lloyd confronted a scene in which a chauffeur drives a limousine in bright, hard sunlight, parks it by a house trailer, and goes into the trailer's dim interior. In one shot, the camera follows the chauffeur as he gets out of the car in the hard sunlight and walks over to the trailer, opens the screen door, and goes inside. To accommodate this drastic change in light levels from exterior to interior within the moving camera shot, Lloyd executed a wide range of "stop pulls," changes in the lens aperture setting that determines how much light the lens is letting into the camera. The stop pulls helped maintain light continuity as the action of the shot moved from the bright exterior to the dim interior.

These examples indicate one of the key requirements of a cinematographer's job—the ability to quickly and creatively solve artistic and practical challenges. Cinematographers must strategically fit the demands of a location shoot or a director's preferred visual design with available camera resources and the imperative for lighting continuity. This may entail supplementing natural light with artificial light, executing elaborate on-set lighting adjustments during the course of a shot, or re-adjusting exposure levels in the camera to compensate for changes in light level.

Lighting for Color

How does the use of color affect the cinematographer's lighting design? Color changes the way cinematographers set up a shot relative to filming in black and white. When shooting black and white, the cinematographer must be careful to avoid using colors such as red and green together that have the same degree of brightness and will be indistinguishable on the black and white film (which registers only brightness levels, not colors).

Working in black and white restricts the cinematographer's color palette to brightness values, ranging from white through gray to black. By contrast, the cinematographer who works in color has the opportunity to use it to add to the tone and atmosphere of the scene. By appropriately choosing film stocks with an understanding of their sensitivity to color, by employing color gelatins over the lights to intensify a dominant color motif within a scene, and by working closely with the production designer to establish the range of colors to be employed in sets and costumes, the cinematographer helps organize the color design of a given film.

Functions of Color Cinematography

Color design performs three basic functions in film. It establishes symbolic meaning, narrative organization, and psychological mood and tone.

Conveying Symbolic Meaning   Filmmakers often use color to establish a symbolic association or idea in the mind of the viewer that extends well beyond the character's emotions or story situation at that moment. At other times, filmmakers may establish a symbolic meaning that comments upon the character's feelings or actions in a scene but in a way that creates an additional, more intellectual perspective on the action.

Sliver features several love scenes between Sharon Stone, portraying Carly, a lonely woman who moves into a Manhattan high-rise apartment building, and Zeke, the manager of the building. At the conclusion of one of these scenes, cinematographer Vilmos Zsigmond used blue light to create a monochromatic tone to the nighttime scene. In the center of Zeke's apartment is a crystal pyramid that Carly pauses to examine. Zsigmond illuminated the crystal pyramid with a red light to give it a fiery glow, to make it a symbol of the lovers' passion, and to create an interesting visual contrast to the scene's predominantly blue design (see Color Plate 1).

Filmmakers can also establish symbolic meanings by desaturating color from the image. This can be done by **flashing** the film either in the camera before shooting or in the lab after shooting. Flashing involves exposing the undeveloped film to a small amount of light, which has the effect of softening contrast, illuminating the shadowed areas of the frame and washing out the color. Cinematographer Vilmos Zsigmond employed flashing on *Heaven's Gate* (1980), a period Western set in 1870, in order to give the images the faded, dusty look of old photographs.

These examples illustrate the manipulation of color for symbolic purposes. By intensifying certain colors or, alternatively, by desaturating them, color design can be used to evoke a specific set of associations in the mind of the viewer.

Establishing Narrative Organization   A second important function of color design in film is to help establish narrative organization. This is especially useful in films that have long running times and whose narratives cover many years. Such films include Francis Ford Coppola's *Godfather* epics, as well as Spike Lee's *Malcolm X* (1993).

Gordon Willis, the cinematographer on *The Godfather* (1972) and *The Godfather Part II* (1974), intentionally replicated the color structure of *The Godfather* in *Godfather II* in order to tie the two films together in a strong linear fashion. By using a golden, amber tone (that is, by adding a lot of yellow in the color design), Willis provided a unifying structure despite the changes in lighting and camerawork during the different time periods covered by the narrative. Throughout *Godfather I* and *Godfather II*, the unifying effects of this consistent color scheme prevail (see Color Plate 2).

The narrative of Spike Lee's *Malcolm X,* about the life of the charismatic black leader, is divided into three sections. The first traces his early life as a street hustler, the second his years in prison, and the third his rise in the Nation of Islam and career as a civil rights leader. Cinematographer Ernest Dickerson and production designer Wynn Thomas collaborated to create a color design that would organize the film's sprawling narrative by treating the three narrative sections in terms of separate color schemes (see Color Plate 3).

The first section of the film, dealing with Malcolm's life as a young man, is the most colorful, the most visually romantic, and the section that features the warmest colors. The sections dealing with Malcolm's time in prison contrast with the warmth of the earlier episodes by using a color scheme that stresses grays, blacks, and bluish grays. The lighting scheme is cool and hard, eliminating all diffusion.

The third section of the narrative, dealing with Malcolm's career as a civil rights leader and his relationship with the Nation of Islam, uses a color scheme intended by the filmmakers to be normal, natural, and earthy, emphasizing this clear-headed and enlightened portion of Malcolm's life. Accordingly, the color scheme in the last third of the film features browns, greens, and natural, earth tones. Dickerson wanted each of these color schemes to work on the viewer subliminally and to provide a way of visually characterizing the content of Malcolm's life during these periods.

Conveying Psychological Moods and Emotional Tones   Color design is most commonly used in film to augment and intensify the emotional mood and tone of a scene. Much has been written about the psychological and emotional effects of color schemes, and many cinematographers have strong preferences for and against certain colors, and they believe that the use or avoidance of individual colors can have precise effects on the emotional responses of viewers. In general, however, the emotional effects of color are strongly context dependent. Color can augment, intensify, sometimes contrast and undermine the dominant emotional tone and mood of a scene,

---

Under Fire (Orion Pictures, 1983)
Filmmakers tailor color design to a scene's specific dramatic requirements. Realistic designs furnish colors that are compatible with the physical locale portrayed on screen, even if this means that color must be diminished to achieve a realistic effect. Note how the dim lighting in this scene, set in an elevator, drains most of the color from the image. Strong, hard source lighting from above the performers (Gene Hackman and Joanna Cassidy) further bleeds color from the shot. A sophisticated color design must be adaptive to the changing dramatic requirements of a film's scenes. Frame enlargement.

but an individual color in itself can rarely supply emotional and psychological content that is otherwise missing in the scene.

In Spike Lee's *Mo' Better Blues* (1990), cinematographer Ernest Dickerson believed that a concept of hot versus cool could be an effective way of characterizing the jazz background of the film and of symbolizing the up-and-down life of the film's main character, Bleek (Denzel Washington). Dickerson employed this concept in a scene showing a confused Bleek who doesn't know which of his two lovers he is with. The camera positions alternately show Bleek first with one woman and then with the other.

To counterpoint the emotional pull that Bleek experiences between these two lovers, Dickerson used a hot and cold color scheme. He photographed one of the women, Indigo, in warm colors—oranges and reds. He shot the other woman, Clark, more ethereal in personality, in cool blues. As the dreamlike sequence progresses, Dickerson wanted the warm and cool lights to begin to vibrate and pull against each other, creating a visual tension that is an appropriate representation of Bleek's psychological and emotional confusion.

The colors work in the scene by creating a visual association with the emotional character of each woman. The characters' personalities are established through the narrative and the performances of the actors. These enable the viewer to arrive at an understanding of their emotional character. Dickerson supplied a color design that was pegged to this information and which effectively visualized it. In this way, the effects of the design are context dependent. They exist and make sense within a clearly established narrative and dramatic context. As a general rule, color design in film is context dependent. Rather than imposing extraneous meaning on a scene or film, color design extends, sharpens, heightens, or, conversely, minimizes, mitigates, or contrasts with the existing narrative, dramatic, or psychological material of a scene. Filmmakers integrate color design within the more general organization of a film's overall cinematic structure.

Color, emotion, and dramatic context. Bernardo Bertolucci's *Last Tango in Paris* (1972) and James Cameron's *The Terminator* (1984) illustrate the context-dependent nature of color design, the way that the psychological effects of color augment and intensify the dramatic context and design concept of a film.

In Bertolucci's *Last Tango,* cinematographer Vittorio Storaro employed a color design that heavily stressed amber light (see Color Plate 4). Storaro thought that amber, in the context of a film dealing with a passionate love affair, could effectively represent the lovers' passion. For Storaro in *Last Tango,* amber was the color of romantic desire, and he used it as an element of mise-en-scene throughout the film. However, for Gordon Willis in *The Godfather* films, amber functioned quite differently, not to signify passion but rather to provide an overall unifying narrative structure for the epic films. Willis used amber in diverse scenes regardless of their emotional content. In *Last Tango,* Stororo uses amber in scenes of romantic passion. In each case, the dramatic context and design concepts of the films define color usage. As these contexts vary, so can the use of the same color.

In James Cameron's *The Terminator,* a science fiction fantasy set in Los Angeles during two time periods, 1984 and 2029 A.D., cinematographer Adam Greenberg used hard, strong, blue light to photograph the terminator (played by Arnold Schwarzenegger) (see Color Plate 5). Greenberg found that the use of such lighting from a high angle effectively stressed the savagery of the terminator and made him seem less human. Greenberg also discovered that when he lit Schwarzenegger with strong light, the actor looked like a piece of sculpture. The high angle of the light increased the shadows on Schwarzenegger's physique and created a harder look. The harder the blue light on Schwarzenegger, the stronger and colder he looked. In *The Terminator,* color and lighting design strikingly supplement the dramatic context established by the film's violent narrative.

Visual Conventions and Representational Reality

Some light and color designs, if used extensively across many films, solidify as an established tradition and become enduring features of style. Through sheer repetition over time, they establish their own level of representational reality, both for other filmmakers and for audiences. Traditions of cinematographic design emerge, filmmakers quote from these in their own work, and what is "real" for an audience is sometimes a function of how films have in the past represented the world. Cinematography can profoundly influence the ways viewers and other filmmakers see the world.

The design of images and narratives often use **conventions,** sets of agreements shared by filmmakers and audiences about how acceptable representations should be constructed and about what will be accepted as real and plausible. Conventions are patterns that become familiar through repetition over time. Audiences grow accustomed to seeing certain types of characters, situations, and images and come to regard these patterns as adequate representations of reality. Many lighting and color designs, as visual conventions, establish their own validity through sheer repetition.

During the decade of the 1940s, hard, low-key lighting was an established visual convention pervasive in Hollywood cinema. Dark, moody, shadowy compositions were firmly established in crime and detective films, especially the **films noir.** The term *noir* is from the French word meaning dark and designates the "dark film." Consider the following illustration from Robert Aldrich's *Kiss Me Deadly* (1956). In a dark, shadowy office lit only by a solitary table lamp, two thugs wait to ambush detective Mike Hammer. Hammer and his enemies are partially illuminated amid a surrounding sea of blackness. This low-key composition is highly typical of film noir lighting styles.

Contemporary cinematographers photographing films whose narratives are set during the 1940s consciously try to evoke this lighting style. In *Bugsy* (1991), dealing with gangster Ben Siegel's experiences in Hollywood in the 1940s, cinematographer Allen Daviau wanted to evoke the flavor and look of 1940s pictures. He employed more hard light on this film than he had ever done before because hard lighting was one of the staples of 1940s crime film cinematography. Barry Levinson, the director of *Bugsy,* wanted the dark areas of the compositions to be extremely dark, and, to comply, Daviau worked with more small pieces of hard light than he had on any previous film.

What is striking about this aesthetic choice, from the standpoint of visual conventions, is that to evoke a period style and setting for *Bugsy* the filmmakers chose to imitate the lighting style of 1940s Hollywood pictures. That lighting style has, therefore, established its own reality and its own validity. To visually represent the world

Kiss Me Deadly (United Artists, 1956)
Low-key lighting evokes the shadowy, criminal world of film noir. The darkness visible on screen is more than night. It expresses a widespread moral and spiritual corruption. Detective Mike Hammer (Ralph Meeker) turns on his table lamp but fails to see the pair of thugs waiting to assault him. Frame enlargement.

of 1940s crime on film means to evoke the lighting style that Hollywood employed in its films during those years. Cinematic reality becomes a perceived social reality.

Lighting Conventions and the Perception of Social Reality

Another contemporary production, Kenneth Branagh's *Dead Again* (1991), demonstrates the lasting power and durability of this lighting convention. *Dead Again* is a romantic thriller whose story is set in two time periods, the 1990s and the 1940s. To establish a visual style for each period, cinematographer Matt Leonetti consciously evoked the dominant film lighting styles of each period.

Dead Again (Paramount Pictures, 1991)
Lighting conventions influence a viewer's perception of social reality. To establish different historical periods in *Dead Again,* cinematographer Matthew Leonetti followed the dominant Hollywood lighting designs of those periods. Hard-light and low-key set-ups give actress Emma Thompson a 1940s look, whereas soft lights and slow fall-off give her a contemporary, 1990s appearance. Frame enlargements.

For the 1940s, Leonetti chose to use hard-light and low-key set-ups. For the 1990s section of the story, Leonetti adopted a softer, more diffused lighting design because that is what many cinematographers today prefer. Contemporary films tend to use soft and diffused, rather than hard, light. The differences of lighting design in these illustrations are between hard, low-key and soft, high-key compositions. They are also representational differences between the cinematography employed in 1940s Hollywood and in 1990s Hollywood. To depict differing social eras, Leonetti manipulated the lighting conventions established in films associated with those times.

In this way, visual conventions come to generate their own artistic and social realities. The use of period lighting style conventions in *Dead Again* distinguishes the two different settings of the narrative and establishes for the audience, in visual terms, competing mise-en-scenes correlated with the different narrative periods and the social realities they portray.

Visual Conventions and Design "Quotations"

An additional set of examples can help clarify the way in which visual conventions take on a life of their own. One of the more striking features associated with lighting styles of film noir in 1940s Hollywood is the use of Venetian blind shadows as a recurring visual motif. In this illustration from the 1941 production *High Sierra,* the Venetian blind shadows are visible as a series of black bars that cut across the image. For many cinematographers and audiences, this visual motif is highly evocative of Hollywood crime films of the 1940s.

This motif has subsequently taken on its own life and turned up in a series of diverse productions. Bernardo Bertolucci's Italian film *The Conformist* (1971) featured a striking visual design produced by close collaboration between Bertolucci, cinematographer Vittorio Storaro, and production designer Ferdinando Scarfiotti. In researching *The Conformist*'s 1941 period setting, Scarfiotti, Bertolucci, and Storaro watched numerous movies from that period. The Venetian blind shadow imagery in the Hollywood films of that period greatly impressed them, and one of the strongest design features of *The Conformist* is light streaming into a room through Venetian blinds, casting sharp shadows across walls and characters. Scarfiotti intended this imagery to be exaggerated. Although he borrowed the basic motif from Hollywood in the 1940s, he amplified it to overcome the commonplace and familiar nature of

High Sierra
(Warner Bros., 1941)
Venetian blind imagery is a key visual feature of Hollywood crime films of the 1940s. Frame enlargement.

The Conformist (1971)
Intensification and exaggeration of the Venetian blind motif. Production designer Ferdinando Scarfiotti wanted to stylize the motif in order to make a lasting impression on viewers. Frame enlargement.

American Gigolo (Paramount Pictures, 1980)
Venetian blind imagery. Director Paul Schrader and cinematographer John Bailey used this motif to pay homage to *The Conformist*, which, in turn, based its Venetian blind design on Hollywood crime films of the 1940s. Frame enlargement.

the imagery. By strengthening the shadow effect, it became surreal and made a lasting visual impression on the viewer. Without this exaggeration, Scarfiotti believed the visual idea would remain half dead. It would not take on its own compelling life.

Almost a decade later, Scarfiotti worked as production designer on Paul Schrader's *American Gigolo* (1980), starring Richard Gere. Once again, he employed an extremely strong, exaggerated Venetian blind pattern of shadows on the walls of the sets and faces of the characters. The film's director, Paul Schrader, and cinematographer John Bailey greatly admired *The Conformist* and wanted to duplicate some of that film's visual design. Schrader and Bailey watched and studied *The Conformist* repeatedly before undertaking *American Gigolo*.

In this pattern of borrowings and influences, a specific visual motif from Hollywood in the 1940s (Venetian blinds) was taken up in an Italian film production in the early 1970s (which depicts Italy in the 1940s during the Fascist era). Subsequently, this motif appeared in an American production of the early 1980s, which depicted the life of a male prostitute. The repetition of visual conventions establishes compelling artistic realities, not only for audiences, but also for the artists who make films and who borrow from and are influenced by the designs of their peers and predecessors. Memorably pictorial light or color designs establish powerful artistic traditions and influences and may be "quoted" or borrowed by filmmakers of a later generation.

SUMMARY

The cinematographer controls and designs the use of light and color in film and the planning and placement of camera set-ups. The cinematographer helps the director achieve a desired visual design for the film by using the camera to capture images that reflect the director's visual goals. Cinematographers employ both realistic and pictorial lighting designs. In the first approach, they simulate the effects of a real light source on screen, and, in the second, they aim for purely pictorial effects with little or no source simulation.

Either approach to lighting design will employ varying proportions of hard (high-contrast) and soft (low-contrast) light. Specific lighting set-ups tend to create a hard or soft look. Low-key lighting is hard. High-key lighting is soft. Hard and soft light can be used to establish mood, psychological effect, and even time of day. Like image and sound editing, lighting designs follow continuity principles. Light levels and angles must match across shots and even within shots when the moving camera is employed.

With respect to color design, a cinematographer lights objects on the set or uses colored gels over white lights to manipulate color hue, saturation, and intensity. Color can be used to separate and define objects in a composition, but, when shooting black and white, a cinematographer has to use grey scale values to organize a composition. Color cinematography establishes symbolic meanings, narrative organization, psychological moods, and emotional tones. In each of these functions, color is integrated into the overall dramatic context and design concept of a scene or film.

Light and color designs, once established, can become enduring features of style, repeated in many films. When this happens, those designs take on a high level of representational reality. Filmmakers are sensitive to this, and, if they need to express a particular social milieu, such as urban crime, or a certain time period, such as the 1940s, they may deliberately imitate famous lighting designs from older movies, recreating those settings or periods. When contemporary cinematographers have needed to evoke the era of gangsterism or the period of the 1940s, they often chose to use a low-key lighting design because that design—commonly found in Hollywood films of the 1940s dealing with these subjects—has become a convention. For filmmakers and audiences, the representational reality of the low-key design, when used in these contexts, is completely convincing.

SUGGESTED READINGS

John Alton, *Painting with Light* (Berkeley: University of California Press, 1995).

American Cinematographer, monthly journal of film and electronic production techniques published by ASC Holding Corp., Hollywood, CA.

Christopher Finch, *Special Effects: Creating Movie Magic* (New York: Abbeville, 1984).

J. Kris Malkiewicz, *Cinematography: A Guide for Film Makers and Film Teachers* (New York: Van Nostrand Reinhold, 1973).

Kris Malkiewicz, *Film Lighting: Talks with Hollywood's Cinematographers* (New York: Prentice-Hall, 1986).

Dennis Schaeffer and Larry Salvato, *Masters of Light: Conversations with Contemporary Cinematographers* (Berkeley and Los Angeles: University of California Press, 1984).

Leslie J. Wheeler, *Principles of Cinematography,* fourth edition (New York: Morgan and Morgan, 1969).

Chapter 3

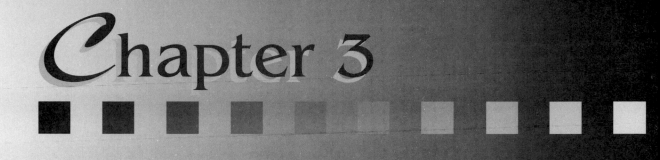

Elements of
Mise-en-scene:
Production Design and
Performance Style

Chapter Objectives

After reading this chapter, you should be able to

- explain what the production designer contributes to mise-en-scene

- describe costumes, sets, mattes, and miniatures, the basic tools of production design

- explain how production design creatively transforms real, existing locations

- explain how production design totally fabricates locales that are made to seem real

- describe how a design concept organizes a film's production design

- describe how production design in fantasy films incorporates elements of perceptual realism

- explain the special challenges of film acting that differentiate it from performance in theater

- list the basic types of film performers

- differentiate between method and technical approaches to performing

- describe four ways in which performance style functions as an element of mise-en-scene

- explain how performance style elicits interpretive and emotional responses from viewers

Key Terms and Concepts

production design
unit art director
supervising art director
costumes
sets
mattes
miniatures
pixels

design concept
forced perspective
coverage
stars
supporting players
extras
star persona

personality star
character star
method acting
technical acting
homage
typage
iconic coding

Mise-en-scene encompasses much more than the planning and execution of camerawork. Along with light and color, filmmakers use sets, props, costumes, and actors to achieve a film's total visual "look." This chapter examines the contributions of production design and performance style.

☐ FROM ART DIRECTOR TO PRODUCTION DESIGNER

The production designer is the individual who supervises the design of a film's visual environments. **Production design** designates the planning and creation of sets, costumes, mattes, and miniatures by the production designer in collaboration with the director. The production designer oversees the work of set decorators and designers, costume designers, and the prop crew. This array of artists and technicians creates costumes and sets using colors and concepts supplied by the production designer, who arrives at an overall visual organization through close consultation and collaboration with the director and cinematographer. As a result of these conferences, the production designer prepares a series of sketches that illustrate the overall design concept and organization of the film. Set and costume designers then work to produce settings and costumes that embody the concepts outlined in the production designer's sketches. During pre-production, the sketches are turned into storyboards and miniature models that are then used to plan, in advance, camera and lighting positions.

Although the title "production designer" is commonly employed in contemporary productions, during the studio era of the Hollywood period the title barely existed. During the 1930s and 1940s, each studio had an art department that employed illustrators, model builders, set decorators, prop men and prop women, and costume designers, all of whom worked under the production's **unit art director.** The head of the art department who oversaw all the films in production was the **supervising art director.** At MGM, this individual was Cedric Gibbons. At Twentieth Century Fox, it was Lyle Wheeler.

Producer David O. Selznick first employed the term *production designer* on *Gone With The Wind* (1939), as a tribute to the importance of William Cameron Menzies' design sketches. Menzies' sketches and storyboards provided the unifying visual structure that gave *Gone With The Wind* its stylistic coherence. This contribution was especially important because different directors worked on *Gone With The Wind*. The man who received screen credit as director was Victor Fleming, but during production Selznick changed directors several times, and it was Menzies' design concept that provided the film with its unifying visual structure.

Today the studios no longer operate art departments as they did in the 1930s and 1940s. Production occurs on a film by film, piecemeal, pick-me-up basis, as cast, technicians, and crew members are assembled only for the duration of a given production. In view of this, the supervising art director no longer exists. Today, the production designer has emerged as one of the key supervisors and co-creators of a film's overall visual style.

◻ BASIC TOOLS OF PRODUCTION DESIGN

Filmmakers design the visual environments of a film by using a set of basic tools that have remained essentially the same over many decades of filmmaking, although today they can be augmented by powerful special effects. These basic tools are *costumes, sets, mattes,* and *miniatures.* **Costumes,** of course, are the clothing worn by performers on the set in front of the camera. Period films use historical costuming whose style and fashions designate a particular time period. The sumptuousness of Martin Scorsese's recent production *The Age of Innocence* (1993) largely resides in the lavishly detailed costumes (and sets) that represent late-nineteenth-century New York society.

Sets are the physical locations in which the action occurs. These locations can be indoors in the studio (in which case an indoor location will sometimes masquerade as an outdoor location) or they can involve the use of "real," that is, non-studio-created, locales. **Mattes** are special paintings that are printed into the shot in the laboratory as a part of the background of a setting. Matte work can be exceptionally

Malcolm X (Warner Bros., 1993)
Skillful production design can vividly re-create historical eras. *Malcolm X* (Denzel Washington) speaks next door to the Apollo Theater in Harlem in the early 1960s. Note the period musicians featured on the marquee, the clothing styles, the antiquated microphone, and the storefront signs.

sophisticated and subtle, and, when done well, is virtually impossible for the casual viewer to detect. Digital mattes, created on the computer, are employed in many contemporary films.

Miniatures are small models that stand in for a portion of the set. Filmmakers often need miniatures when a very large set (such as the entire city of Gotham, in the case of the *Batman* films) is required for a scene but cannot be built on its true scale.

Costume Design

Costume design is a feature of all films, but it is in the period film and the fantasy film where the viewer is most strongly aware of the role that costume design plays in the overall mise-en-scene of the production. As with other areas of production design, filmmakers use specific design concepts to tailor costuming for individual characters in the film.

Production Design and Costuming in *Bram Stoker's Dracula*

Francis Ford Coppola's film *Bram Stoker's Dracula* (1992) used studio-bound set design and low-technology visual effects, processes, and techniques that were available to filmmakers in the earliest years of cinema. Coppola wanted to work in this low-tech way because of the period in which the film was set. Publication of Bram Stoker's novel occurred in 1897, and, for Coppola, this period symbolized the dawn of new technologies. The turn of the century brought the new medium of the motion

Bram Stoker's Dracula
(Columbia Pictures, 1992)
The imaginative design of
Dracula's suit of armor
contributes to the film's spooky
mise-en-scene. The helmet
appears batlike with horned ears
and menacing slits for eyes.
Frame enlargement.

pictures to the world, and Coppola wanted to evoke the period of early cinema by using a low-tech approach that avoided many of the most sophisticated computerized effects available to filmmakers today. To facilitate this approach, Coppola employed the work of several visual effects companies, Matte World and Visual Effects II among them.

For the design of nineteenth-century costumes and props, Coppola turned to Global Effects. These props include the rhino-headed bowie knife used by Quincy Morris to wound Dracula, Dr. Van Helsing's medical bag, and the doctor's book on vampires done in the style of a fifteenth-century pamphlet on that subject.

One of Global Effects' most important contributions to the film is the concept and design of the suit of armor worn by Prince Dracula when he first appears in the film as a fifteenth-century warrior. Costume designer Eiko Esioka initially conceptualized the armor's design. She wanted the costume to evoke the appearance of a human body stripped of skin. Global Effects president Chris Gilman liked this concept and decided to augment it with the use of a russet color to make it look like rusted metal. Looking at Dracula's armor, one does, indeed, see a human body stripped of its skin with the muscles visible. The original helmet design for the film, modeled on Japanese samurai warriors (Esioka is Japanese), was not deemed frightening enough, so another costume designer thought of making the helmet appear to resemble a bat with horn-like ears and slits for eyes. The result is a visually impressive, disturbing, and frightening visual concept that contributes, along with other details of setting and decor, to the film's eerie mise-en-scene.

Sets, Mattes, and Miniatures

The mise-en-scene of *Bram Stoker's Dracula* intends to evoke a highly stylized, fantasized, unreal time and place. The unreality of the film's world is achieved through the use of unauthentic locations, unreal sets and places that are created through the artifice of studio filmmaking. By choosing to work largely indoors on sets designed expressly to evoke the unreal world of the film, Coppola placed himself firmly within a tradition established early in the history of cinema by German expressionist filmmakers. In the

1920s these filmmakers chose to create their fantasy films using fabricated indoor sets because such sets gave them greater control over visual style and design than they could obtain by using real locations.

To illustrate the importance of the studio-designed set and matte work in the film, consider the following illustration from the brief sequence in the film's prologue when Prince Dracula returns from the battlefield to his castle to learn that his beloved, believing him dead, has thrown herself from the top of the castle. This is one of the most heavily stylized and powerful moments of the film. Little of what the viewer sees on screen, though, is real or actual. What appears on screen is not what actually existed in front of the camera.

The shot is a composite shot, pieced together from several components. In a long shot, Dracula rides away from the camera, down a hill surrounded by the impaled bodies of his victims. In the background, in the upper portion of the frame, the distant castle towards which he is riding looms ahead. Coppola thought of this shot as his "Spartacus matte" because the design of the image evokes a similar sequence in Stanley Kubrick's 1961 film *Spartacus,* in which action takes place on a road framed by the elevated bodies of crucifixion victims.

Coppola's shot was created in the following way. The crew shot the live-action component of the image—the horseman galloping down a path—on an indoor studio set. Effects artists then rear-projected this footage onto a glass screen containing the matte painting of Dracula's impaled victims. The skillful painting blended imperceptibly with the road on which the horseman was riding in the rear-projected image. The painting extended the landscape around Dracula in an expansive and imaginative way. To enhance the sense of reality possessed by this artificially created image, the filmmakers added a background light for the sun and a small lens flare to simulate what the camera might see when it was filming into the sun.

The transfer of live action into a rear-screen projection thrown upon a glass matte painting is consistent with the kind of low-tech approach Coppola wanted in the film. Viewers watching the sequence are subliminally aware that it is not real, authentic action that is occurring in front of the camera the way they see it on screen. However, because the blend of live action and matte painting is done so skillfully, this subliminal awareness actually adds to the atmosphere of fantasy, magic, and artifice, which are keys to the film's production design and its narrative about supernatural powers.

Coppola's low-tech approach, using glass matte painting and rear-screen projection, deliberately employs technologically out of date and traditional design tools and techniques. Today, by contrast, many filmmakers no longer employ traditional, handmade matte paintings and rear-screen projections. They now execute digital matte paintings in the computer. Light and color effects on a simulated landscape can be easily achieved by coloring **pixels** in the computer image. Once the digital matte has been painted by computer, it is added to the shot, again by computer, in a process called *compositing,* where computer-generated images are married to the live-action components of a shot. Digital matte techniques give effects artists far greater flexibility and creative power than the older method of painting a matte by hand did. Is there not enough light in the digitally composited image? Brighten some pixels. Are the colors too washed out? Give the pixels more hue saturation. The spectacular long

Do the Right Thing
(Universal Studios, 1989)
Visual transformation of a real location. By adding bright red to the wall behind these three men, the filmmakers provided visual stimulation for viewers and also commented symbolically on the atmosphere of racial tension that the film depicts. Frame enlargement.

shot in *True Lies* (1994) of a Swiss chateau nestled by a lake and the Alps was a digitally composited image employing a computer matte painting (the Alps).

Sets and Locales: Transforming a Real Location

Sophisticated production design can creatively re-organize authentic locations used as the backdrop for a film's narrative. In this way, production design stylizes and "dresses up" authentic, actual locations in order to integrate them into a film's unified mise-en-scene. Working on location does not have to necessitate a serious revision of the film's mise-en-scene as planned by the director, cinematographer, and production designer. Production designers can modify authentic locations to make them express a film's mise-en-scene.

Spike Lee's *Do the Right Thing* (1989) explores racial tensions that explode into violence on a hot summer day in a Brooklyn, New York, neighborhood. Wynn Thomas, the film's production designer, translated the ideas of heat and tension into a visual design for the film and transformed a real location into one that was suitable for the film's themes and visual concepts.

Thomas wanted to find a city block with few trees, to suggest the absence of shade and the inescapability of the summer heat. He also needed a block with several vacant lots because the story required a Korean grocery across from Sal's pizzeria, the central locale for much of the action. (Korean markets don't exist in the section of Brooklyn in which the film is set so the filmmakers needed the vacant lots to construct the market and the set for the pizzeria.) The location also needed vacant buildings so the filmmakers would not displace people from their homes during shooting. Once a street was found that met these criteria, the decayed brownstone exteriors of the existing buildings had to be refurbished. Their fronts were cleaned and repainted in keeping with the design concepts of the film. Thomas remarked that many viewers probably believed the filmmakers found the block exactly as it appears in the film. In fact, as noted above, the filmmakers transformed it and constructed several additional settings—the Korean market, Sal's pizzeria, and the radio station.

Because the action was confined largely to a single city block, Thomas worked to create sufficient color on screen to keep the audience interested. He began to see his own function on the film in terms of finding opportunities to add color to existing scenes. To evoke the oppressive summer heat, the underlying design emphasized warm browns and hot reds. One of the most memorable groups of characters were the three men who sit on the street corner under an umbrella and gossip about their

COMPUTER GENERATED IMAGES

Computer manipulation of images is an integral part of contemporary filmmaking. Because photographic information can be digitized, that is, turned into a mathematical language that computers can understand, filmmakers can now manipulate images with an unprecedented sophistication. For popular audiences, the most visible application of these abilities lies in special-effects work. The computer-generated dinosaurs of *Jurassic Park* (1993) and Forrest Gump's interactions with President Kennedy and other historical figures in *Forrest Gump* (1994) represent a new era and threshold of special-effects achievement.

One common application of digital imaging techniques is to create effects by erasing visual information from the frame. Digitally erasing the wires supporting Sylvester Stallone and the other actors who were hanging over cliffs in *Cliffhanger* (1994) added excitement by making the stunts seem far more dangerous than they were. Digital erasure eliminated a vital section of roadway in *Speed* (1994) and actor Gary Sinise's legs (he played a wounded Vietnam veteran) in *Forrest Gump*.

A more sophisticated application of digital techniques lies in building entire images inside the computer and then integrating these with live-action photography. Digital animators build a wireframe model of a dinosaur or other needed special-effects creature, animate the model, and then render it by adding three-dimensional information in the form of color, light,

Forest Gump (Paramount Pictures, 1994)
For the famous computer-generated shot of Forrest Gump's meeting with President Kennedy, actor Tom Hanks' photographic image was digitized and composited to the archival footage of Kennedy. The President's amused response to Gump, written by the film's screenwriters, required that his lip and mouth movements match the lines in the screenplay. Digital painting (accomplished by manipulating the brightness of individual pixels on and around Kennedy's mouth) supplied the illusion of Kennedy's speech. Frame enlargement.

neighborhood. Because the compositions were spare and basic—just three men in chairs sitting in front of a wall—Thomas thought that, if he painted the wall red, he could introduce a striking use of color into an otherwise static scene. When he suggested painting the wall to director Spike Lee, Lee immediately visualized it as a bright, fire engine red. The bright, red wall with its fiery coloring intensifies the film's mise-en-scene and its underlying concepts of heat, fire, and explosion.

Radical Transformation of a Real Location   To transform a real location and make it part of a film's mise-en-scene, filmmakers sometimes give it a reality on screen shadow, texture, and reflectance. By matching this information to the live-action components of the scene, the computer-generated image can be "glued" onto the live-action in a thoroughly convincing way.

When the dinosaurs hunt the children in the kitchens of *Jurrasic Park*, they are anchored in live-action space, via color, shadow, and reflectance information. The computer-generated dinosaurs cast shadows in the live-action space of the kitchen, and their images are reflected on the surfaces of steel tables and cabinets. When actress Mary Elizabeth Mastrantonio touches the shimmering, watery creature in *The Abyss* (1989), her touch spreads a rippling response across the creature's liquid face.

The creative challenge in producing convincing computer-generated imagery lies in matching the three-dimensional information common to both computer-generated and live-action environments. In this way, digital imaging corresponds with and transforms a viewer's understanding of three-dimensional space. This requires extremely detailed, painstaking work, but the results provide a spectacular degree of photographic realism to unreal images. Forrest Gump can meet and shake hands with President Kennedy, and Kennedy responds by speaking dialogue scripted by the film's writers. The moment is entirely fictional, but its photographic realism is extremely convincing.

The Mask (New Line, 1994)
Creating the fright response of Stanley Ipkiss (Jim Carrey) in *The Mask* required building a wireframe model in the computer of bulging eyes and tongue, adding light, color, and texture, animating the model, and then compositing it with the live-action image of Carrey. As with all such digital effects, the computer-generated information must match perfectly with the live-action components or the effect will lose credibility. Frame enlargement.

that it does not otherwise possess. Production design can radically transform the actual locale. The conclusion of *Terminator 2* (1991) is set in a steel works factory where the evil Terminator hunts his victims before eventually perishing in a vat of molten steel. The filmmakers faced an extraordinary challenge. The location was a steel mill that had been shut down since the mid-1980s and was about to be dismantled, but it had to appear to be an active factory with fiery, sparking furnaces. Although the actual mill used for the film was completely inoperative, the filmmakers employed lights and colored gels to make the factory spit fire and glow with molten heat.

Terminator 2 (Tri-Star Pictures, 1991)
Through some basic manipulations of light and color, an abandoned steel mill comes to fiery life in *Terminator 2*. Frame enlargement.

To create the illusion of the vats of molten steel in which the evil Terminator perishes, the filmmakers put extremely powerful lights inside the vats and used orange gels to give the lights a fiery glow. They then covered these with sheets of plastic, on which was placed a mixture of water, mineral oil, and white powder, to create the illusion of molten steel moving in the vat. They mechanically manipulated the lights to create a flickering effect to simulate the illusion of flame, and they augmented this effect with the use of heaters near the camera to create ripples in the atmosphere. These ripples simulated heat waves rising from the illusory molten steel. In the background, sparks dropped from sparklers to add atmosphere and realism to the scene. With these techniques, the dead factory came alive, and the molten steel on screen possessed a terrifying reality. Viewers did not realize that its true reality lay in some very basic manipulations of light and color.

Sets and Locales: Fabricating a "Real" Location

In *Do the Right Thing* and *Terminator 2,* the locations that viewers see on screen—a city block in Brooklyn, New York, and a steel mill—were filmed in the real locales, a steel mill and a city block in Brooklyn, New York. In many films, though, locations that may seem real and authentic are actually the work of clever reconstruction and reworking on a surrogate locale. In Oliver Stone's *Born on the Fourth of July* (1989), the sequences set in Vietnam and Mexico were filmed in the Philippines, and, more strikingly, the scenes set in Massapequa, Long Island, were filmed in Texas.

Born on the Fourth of July deals with the life of Ron Kovic, from his childhood home in Massapequa to his crippling wound in Vietnam and his difficult physical rehabilitation and psychological adjustment afterward. Shooting in Texas presented a number of problems. The Massapequa locations had to be reconstructed, and this involved building some exterior locales on indoor sets. The filmmakers fabricated the Kovic house and backyard, where Kovic talks with a fellow Vietnam veteran, indoors on artificially created sets. For the parade scenes on main street in Mass-apequa, the filmmakers imported spruce trees from Michigan to Texas because they are not indigenous to that state. The spruce trees on the street are artificial props used to evoke the reality of the represented location (as distinct from the real Texas location).

The Massepequa main street set was dressed and changed to reflect the different time periods of the film. Early in the narrative—during Kovic's childhood in 1956—a theater marquee seen in the background advertises the 1950s science fiction film *The Incredible Shrinking Man*. In 1969, when Kovic returns from Vietnam a wounded veteran, the camera pans the storefronts along the main street, revealing a psychedelic "head shop" next to the Marine Corps' recruiting center. To simulate different time periods, the production design crew repainted stores, boarded up others, and changed the signs and canopies on still others.

Radical Fabrication of a "Real" Location   How powerful can production design be in creating mise-en-scene? Production design can radically stylize locales to the point of totally fabricating a "real" locale. Viewers can be completely fooled about the reality of what they're seeing. Radically constructed by production design shops, locale becomes a totally plastic and manipulatable element of film structure.

The climax of *Bram Stoker's Dracula* is a chase in which Dr. Van Helsing and his friends pursue Count Dracula to his castle lair. The climax—with Dracula in a coach driven by his gypsy guards and chased by several riders on horseback—was filmed entirely on an indoor set designed to simulate a rocky mountain pass. The set itself was quite large—300 feet long and 150 feet wide. Because of its circular design, the 15 horses and riders continually ran in a circle, passing the same trees and boulders each time. Cinematographer Michael Ballhaus had to prevent the audience from noticing this and to create the sensation of a linear race—as opposed to a circular one. Ballhaus also had to simulate the appearance of riders who continually have the sun at their backs. He therefore employed four light sources to represent four different suns so that, across cuts and different camera positions, he could keep the riders' relationship to the "sun" relatively constant.

Bram Stoker's Dracula
(Columbia Pictures, 1992)
The climactic chase in *Bram Stoker's Dracula*. Swirling snow and motion blur provided by the tracking camera and telephoto lens prevent viewers from recognizing that this chase over a rocky mountain pass actually occurs on an indoor studio set. Frame enlargement.

Ballhaus used fog, snow, rapid tracking shots, and telephoto lenses to prevent the viewer from forming a clear impression of the rocks and trees on the set. The speed of the camera in pursuit of the galloping horses, the blowing snow and fog, and the rapid cutting all effectively prevent the viewer from noticing that this is an indoor set, as opposed to an exterior location, and that the actors and horses are, in fact, running in circles and retracing the same ground repeatedly. In this way, the set's production design integrates with other elements of film structure to create a unified mise-en-scene. Set design, camerawork, lighting and optical effects of fog and snow all work together to simulate what looks like a thrilling chase through Transylvania's Borgo Pass.

◻ THE DESIGN CONCEPT

In supervising the work of set decoration and costume design, production designers frequently employ a **design concept** that organizes the way the sets and costumes are built, dressed, and photographed. The design concept specifies the ideas, emotions, or images that production designers intend to evoke through the contribution of sets and costumes to a film's mise-en-scene.

Production design on Spike Lee's *She's Gotta Have It* (1986) and Martin Scorsese's *GoodFellas* (1990) employed especially detailed design concepts. *She's Gotta Have It* deals with the relationship between Nola Darling, a sexually active woman, and the three men with whom she is involved. Nola's liberal attitudes and sexual lifestyle make her an unconventional character, and the film studies the conflicts between Nola's desire for sexual freedom and the possessive attitudes of the various men in her life.

Nola's active sexuality is a central component of her identity, and Wynn Thomas, the film's production designer, incorporated her character into his design concept for her bed, which is the location where much of the film's narrative occurs. Thomas thought that the bed should be the most striking visual element in her apartment and that it should have, by virtue of its importance in Nola's life, the appearance of an altar. He, therefore, employed an Oriental fan design for the head of the bed and placed a series of candles along it. Nola lights these as if she were illuminating a sacred

She's Gotta Have It
(Island Pictures, 1986)
The design concept for Nola Darling's bed in *She's Gotta Have It*. The Oriental fan design of the bed makes it look like an altar while remaining simple in concept and execution. Frame enlargement.

Blade Runner (The Ladd Company, 1982)
Blade Runner's influential design concept followed the social realities depicted in script and novel. The visual clutter evokes a ghettoized urban future marked by social breakdown. The film's production design brilliantly visualizes the novel's themes of entropy and decay.
(Museum of Modern Art/Film Stills Archive)

altar. The overall design is simple, in keeping with the sort of thing Nola would be likely to do. The accompanying illustration shows how the altar-like design of the bed is incorporated into the mise-en-scene of the film.

For Martin Scorsese's *GoodFellas,* a saga about Italian-American gangsters from the 1950s to the 1990s, production designer Kristi Zea helped select props and costumes to evoke a very specific symbolic association. In a gaudy house in which the main gangster Henry Hill lives, she dressed Hill's wife (played by Lorraine Bracco) in a loud red and black pantsuit in a room filled with black lacquered furniture. For Zea—in the context of this film—red and black were hellish colors meant to suggest that these characters were on a path to self-destruction. This costume and set are only glimpsed for a moment on screen. However, a production designer's visual concept is often extremely detailed and precise, regardless of the amount of screen time given to the props and costumes.

Design Concept in *Blade Runner*

One last example of a design concept will illustrate how important and powerful an influence it is on the organization of a production. From the standpoint of production design, *Blade Runner* (1982) is one of the landmark films of recent years. Lawrence G. Paull, the film's production designer, consulted with the heads of production, the director, cinematographer, and other design artists, and based his design concept on the social realities evoked in the film's script and the novel from which it was derived.

Blade Runner is set in a futuristic society where all the people with money have relocated to pleasant off-world colonies, leaving the cities to choke in urban decay, architectural collapse, and overpopulation. The visual design of the film creates a world of clutter, a ghettoized alley environment in which transient, jobless, urban poor jostle in a mix of nationalities and languages while, far overhead, video monitors and electronic billboards carry corporate advertisements and media messages.

High-rise buildings of high-tech opulence co-exist with the crumbling alley environment, creating a striking mix of contrasting architectural and social styles and realities. Paull's production design is a stunning translation of the social realities of the story into extremely powerful visual environments.

☐ PRODUCTION DESIGN AND THE VIEWER'S RESPONSE

Production design, along with other components of film structure, can create highly artificial locations, effects, and images. The cluttered futuristic environments of *Blade Runner* and the gothic, ghostly lair of *Bram Stoker's Dracula* are clearly fictional realities that exist only on the movie screen. Viewers delight in these radical manipulations of character, place, and setting and embrace the movie magic that makes them possible.

Viewers expect the cinema to provide images, narratives, and spectacles that transform their sense of life and the world, but they also demand reference to life and correspondence with experience from motion pictures. These provide a grounding and a base for the sometimes elaborate transformations wrought by style. Production design, even at its most fantastical, can take the unreal and make it look real or, at least, credible and convincing. One powerful way of doing this is by building perceptual

---

Bram Stoker's Dracula (Columbia Pictures, 1992)
Production design may incorporate accurate three-dimensional visual information to lend credibility to unreal images or objects, especially when these are suggested by mattes or miniature models. The impression of enormous size and distance conveyed in this high-angle shot of Dracula's castle is achieved by using forced perspective in the model's construction and light and color to simulate aerial perspective (the tendency for the atmosphere to make distant objects look hazy and bluish). The model and the image are fake, but the three-dimensional visual cues employed make them appear real. Frame enlargement.

correspondences to real experience into even the most unreal and stylized of images. At the beginning of *Bram Stoker's Dracula,* real estate agent Jonathan Harker journeys by coach and train to visit Count Dracula in his castle, whereupon the vampire imprisons Harker in the castle and leaves for England. During these early scenes, the viewer sees the castle in a series of spectacular long shots.

The castle, of course, was nothing more than a miniature model. The model was only 6 feet high, one seventy-second the size of the imaginary castle it represented, and was constructed using **forced perspective.** Forced perspective is a deliberate distortion imposed by artists upon the linear perspective cues within a model or painting. According to the cues of linear perspective, parallel lines should recede or seem to come together as they move off into the distance. Of course, the degree of recession should be constant. In forced perspective, changes in the amount of recession are introduced. The lines converge or rush together much more rapidly in the represented far distance. This allows artists to suggest an enormous amount of depth on a flat surface or a small scale.

In addition to incorporating forced perspective to suggest the castle's immense size, the model's design also included information about aerial perspective. The castle model was built in three sections. Between each section were hung scrims—wire or mesh devices that decrease the intensity of light without diffusing it. Each of the scrims was illuminated with a blue, gelled light source. The scrims and colored lights created several of the components of aerial perspective. As the light diminished in intensity, it shifted toward the blue end of the spectrum on the remote portions of the model. The hazing component of aerial perspective was introduced by hanging tulle (the fabric used to make bridal veils). It acts as a diffusing material between the sections of the model.

These manipulations—the use of scrims, blue-colored lights, and diffusing material—accurately simulate the effects of aerial perspective and allow the viewer to perceive an enormous height (i.e., depth and distance) in the miniature model. The castle seems huge, ominous, and vast, especially when viewed in this high-angle camera position. Careful set design elicits a particular interpretive response from the viewer, making the unreal and fantastic image seem paradoxically quite real.

Production Design and Impossible Images

Another special effects example from *Bram Stoker's Dracula* provides a second illustration of the use of production design techniques to create impossible images. A spectacular effects scene shows Jonathan Harker journeying across Transylvania by train and coach. The train carries him through a tunnel toward the distant Carpathian mountains, enroute to Castle Dracula.

The tunnel was another miniature model, approximately 20 feet long, through which the camera traveled on a flatcar to simulate the point-of-view effect of the train drawing closer to the tunnel's opening. The design problem, here, was to persuade the viewer that the miniature tunnel and the miniature mountains beyond were the full-size tunnel and mountains they are meant to represent.

The design solution lay in manipulating the relationship among the camera, which is moving through the tunnel, the tunnel itself, and the miniature mountains

Jurassic Park (Universal, 1993)
Computer-generated dinosaurs in *Jurassic Park*. persuaded audiences to suspend disbelief, in part because of the extremely detailed and realistic light, color, texture, and motion cues that were built into the animation. Frame enlargement.

beyond in order to introduce accurate perceptual information about motion perspective. Motion perspective involves systematic changes in the apparent positions of objects as the viewer or camera physically moves from place to place. The filmmakers realized that if the camera, moving through the tunnel, seemed to be gaining too quickly on the miniature mountains, the viewer's eye would not be fooled, and the viewer would know immediately that he or she was looking at a miniature. Accordingly, to introduce proper motion perspective, the designers built a movable tunnel. As the camera on its flatcar passed through the tunnel, the tunnel itself simultaneously pulled back five feet from the background mountains. The visual displacement of the tunnel relative to the background mountains is correct from the standpoint of motion perspective. The sides of the tunnel seem to pass more rapidly than the rate of approach on the distant mountains.

Watching the film, the viewer is probably aware at an intellectual level that he or she is watching movie magic, an illusion created with sets and miniature models, but, because the viewer's eye is being given correct perspective information, the sequence has a strong realistic effect.

In conclusion, the apparent credibility achieved by sophisticated special-effects processes is based on giving the viewer much of the same kind of perceptual information that he or she would get if they could experience the real version of the on-screen scene.

When such information is present, viewers judge special effects to be convincing and plausible. Steven Spielberg's dinosaurs in *Jurassic Park* were created and animated in computers, then integrated (composited) with the live-action footage of the real actors. When the dinosaurs stalk the children through the kitchens, they seem real because they interact in perceptually valid ways with the live-action environment. Their reflections are mirrored in the steel surfaces of the tables behind which the children are hiding, and their shadows fall across the actors' faces. When such information is lacking, special-effects sequences often fail to grip the viewer, look flat, or seem ridiculously unpersuasive. The successful use of special effects can transform ordinary realities into completely imaginary and fantastic ones, and even the most fantastic of special-effects images can gain credibility by establishing a basis in perceptual realism. By building perceptual correspondences to real experiences into unreal, stylized images, production design helps satisfy the viewer's demand for reference and establishes the credibility of the unreal image.

☐ ACTING

Acting in Film and Theater

Acting and performance style are the third major component of mise-en-scene. What are the basic characteristics of acting in the cinema, and how does performance style become an element of mise-en-scene? Acting in the cinema is a uniquely difficult challenge. Although screen acting would seem to bear some similarity with performance in the theater, the differences between acting in the two media are more significant. Three major characteristics of the motion picture medium make the actor's task exceedingly difficult: out-of-continuity shooting, the amplification of gesture and expression by the camera and sound recording equipment, and the absence of an audience.

Shooting Out of Continuity

Motion pictures are filmed out of continuity. Scenes are not filmed sequentially as they appear in the finished film. The proper narrative sequencing of scenes as they appear in the finished film is achieved during the process of editing and does not indicate the order of shooting. The order in which scenes are filmed is determined by cost, and they are filmed in the most cost-effective manner possible. To save time and money, all scenes occurring in a given location or on a particular set may be filmed at one time, regardless of how they are distributed throughout the narrative. When the filming of all scenes in a given location or set has been completed, the production company then moves on to the next set or location—to film all the scenes that occur there. Proper narrative sequencing is then achieved in post-production editing.

Another way in which filming fails to observe proper continuity occurs during the shooting of individual scenes. Typically, the *master shot* is filmed first, and the performers run through the entire action of the scene from the master shot camera position. Then **coverage** is completed as the actors recreate bits of the action for inserts and close-ups. When filming coverage, an actor must be able to deliver all of his or her dialogue that will be recorded from a given camera position, regardless of when it may appear in the scene.

One of the most famous acting scenes in American films, the so-called Brother Charlie scene from *On the Waterfront* (1954), dramatically illustrates these challenges. Terry Malloy (Marlon Brando) and his brother Charlie (Rod Steiger) are part of the mob that controls the longshoreman's union on the New York dockyards. Sickened by its corruption, Terry wants to leave the mob, but his brother tries to persuade him to stay because he knows that if Terry leaves and becomes an informant—as the State prosecutor is urging him to—a mob contract will be issued on his life.

On the Waterfront (Columbia Pictures, 1954)
Rod Steiger and Marlon Brando in two camera set-ups from *On the Waterfront*. In the two-shot, both actors are present, and each can build a performance by playing off the other. In the close-up, however, Rod Steiger (*pictured*) had to deliver his lines while Brando was absent from the set. The angle of Steiger's eyes makes it seem as if he is looking at Brando, but he had to create his character in the scene under highly artificial conditions. Frame enlargements.

In the scene, a master shot of the two actors alternates with single close-ups of each. In the close-ups, actor Rod Steiger had to deliver all his dialogue in the scene that was to be recorded from this camera position, regardless of when the dialogue occurred. Complicating this task, as Steiger later reported, was the fact that Brando left the set on the days Steiger had to deliver these lines. Steiger played his scene and projected his emotions to an actor who was not there.

These conditions require that actors be able to recreate their character at any moment in the drama as required by the shooting schedule. In this respect, the performer in the theater has it a bit easier. He or she creates a character sequentially and chronologically in real time, from act one to the last act of the play.

Amplification of Gesture and Expression

A second condition of the motion picture medium that complicates the actor's contribution is the presence of the camera and sound recording equipment. On stage, the actor plays to an audience that is sitting some distance away in the auditorium. Gestures and vocal inflection, therefore, are generally played larger than life. By contrast, in film, the camera and sound equipment act as magnifying instruments, amplifying even the most insignificant of gestures and the smallest of vocal inflections. The film actor has to understand when a little is too much. He or she must know how every facial expression and vocal projection will appear when magnified on the giant motion picture screen so that they can precisely calibrate and control these reactions—to the smallest degree.

The acting styles of many famous motion picture stars would be totally inappropriate and ineffective on stage. The quavering, tremulous undertone in Judy Garland's voice is a subtlety of performance that precisely and powerfully conveys the

A Star Is Born
(Warner Bros., 1954)
Judy Garland's voice was an essential feature of her star personality. Quavering, tremulous, it conveyed the fragility and vulnerability of her screen personality. Brassy and loud, it conveyed her dynamic energy as a musical performer. In this respect, Garland was an extremely innovative performer. She relied on microphone and camera to amplify her star personality. Frame enlargement

vulnerability of her characters in movies such as *The Wizard of Oz* (1939) and *A Star Is Born* (1954). It is a characteristic captured by the motion picture medium in its ability to amplify voice and gesture. Humphrey Bogart's nervous facial tics and James Cagney's trademark shrug of the shoulders, repeated from film to film, helped establish the star presence of these performers. These tiny gestures would be lost if played to a theater auditorium.

Lack of a Live Audience

A third and final distinction between acting for film and theater involves the audience. On stage, performers can play to a live audience and can gauge their reactions according to the immediate feedback they get from them. The film performer does not have this luxury. He or she has to depend on the guidance of the director in shaping a performance.

Some motion picture actors periodically do stage work precisely because they value the immediate feedback of a live audience and consider this to be essential in developing their skills as an actor. By contrast, other performers prefer motion picture acting precisely because the audience is absent. Perhaps the most famous actor who can illustrate this point is Charlie Chaplin, who feared playing to live audiences. He preferred to perfect his performances in the relative seclusion of the motion picture studio before releasing them to audiences in theaters for viewing.

Categories of Film Performers

Motion picture actors tend to fall into three categories: stars, supporting players, and extras. The star is an indelible feature of motion pictures. Audiences go to the movies in large part because of the stars who appear in them, and this has been the case for decades. This is true not just for the American film industry, but for virtually every film industry in the world.

Stars are usually the best known actors who play the leading roles in a film. They command the largest salary, usually get top billing, and are foremost in the minds of viewers. **Supporting players,** as their name implies, have secondary and supporting roles in a production. **Extras** occupy the smallest amount of screen time; they are performers who appear incidentally and briefly, for example, pedestrians crossing a street or a crowd watching a baseball game.

Although stars typically get the most attention from viewers, many supporting players have established careers with considerable distinction and have created recognizable screen personalities. Supporting players such as Walter Brennan, for example, developed a distinct screen personality in films such as *Mr. Deeds Goes to Town* (1936), *Red River* (1948), and *Rio Bravo* (1959). Brennan frequently portrayed cantankerous old men and often came close to "stealing the show" from the established stars. Other supporting players, such as Danny Aiello and Robert Duvall in more recent years, have approximated star status. Duvall began his career with memorable supporting work in pictures such as *To Kill a Mockingbird* (1962) and *The Godfather* (1972) and has now, by virtue of his starring role in *Lonesome Dove* (1989), graduated to leading player status.

The Star Persona

The **star persona** is the collective screen personality that emerges over the course of a star's career from the motion pictures in which he or she appears. The star persona or on-screen personality is a collective creation generated by many films and is greater than any single performance in an individual film. One of the easiest ways of gauging whether a performer has become a star is to evaluate whether a star persona exists. Names such as John Wayne, Charlie Chaplin, Bette Davis, and Katharine Hepburn instantly call to mind a fixed, distinct screen personality that exists over and above, and that unifies, their individual film appearances.

Stars with long careers evidence interesting changes in their star personas. Often, if one examines the screen appearances of a star performer prior to their star status, one is struck by differences in the persona. Humphrey Bogart, for example, before he became a star, spent many years as a supporting player in Warner Bros. crime films.

The Shootist (Paramount Pictures, 1976)

After years of struggling in low-budget B Westerns, John Wayne achieved stardom in *Stagecoach* and during the next four decades projected a powerful masculine image characterized by physical strength, moral dignity, fair play, and stubborn independence. Directors John Ford and Howard Hawks appreciated Wayne's physical power on screen and considered it essential to the making of a good Western. Wayne's physical presence easily dominates the frame.

Casablanca, (Warner Bros., 1942); **The African Queen** (United Artists, 1951)
Evolution of a star performer. Two phases of Humphrey Bogart's career: the romantic
leading man (with Ingrid Bergman) in *Casablanca* and the player of grizzled, quirky,
neurotic characters, as with Katharine Hepburn in *The African Queen*.

In such pictures as *Angels with Dirty Faces* (1938) and *The Roaring Twenties* (1939),
Bogart portrayed a series of unsympathetic but interesting villains. The world-weary
romanticism of his star persona was not evident.

It was not until *High Sierra* in 1941 that Bogart, still playing a gangster in a
Warner Bros. picture, became a star in a role that allowed him to embody the kind of
bruised romantic idealism that he would go on to perfect in such enduring classics as
Casablanca (1942). In Bogart's later career, his star persona underwent another
change. In the late 1940s and early 1950s, Bogart stopped playing romantic leading
men and turned toward interesting character types in such pictures as *The Treasure of
the Sierra Madre* (1948), *The African Queen* (1951), and *The Caine Mutiny* (1954).
Gone were his romantic star qualities, and, in their place, was a series of neurotic,
quirky, and eccentric characters.

The career of Julia Roberts provides another illustration of the evolution of a star
persona and how this evolution is related to the creation of a film's mise-en-scene.
Roberts' star-making performance occurred in *Pretty Woman* (1990). Prior to *Pretty
Woman*, Roberts filmed *Mystic Pizza* (1988) and *Flatliners* (1990). Both of these
films are ensemble pictures in which Roberts is one supporting player among many.
Mystic Pizza deals with a friendship among three young women who work at a pizzeria in Mystic, Connecticut, and *Flatliners* is a supernatural thriller about medical students in contact with the afterlife. In neither film is Roberts, as an actor, given the
kind of visual presence and attention by the camera that she receives in *Pretty Woman*.
Consequently, her screen presence failed to establish itself in either picture with the
intensity that it did in *Pretty Woman*.

Pretty Woman
(Touchstone Pictures, 1990)
The making of a star performer.
Julia Roberts' role in *Pretty
Woman* established her as a
leading player. She was given
the camera (i.e., allowed to
command its attention) to a
much greater extent than in her
previous films and dominated
the film with charm and
glamour.

Personality Stars and Character Stars

Stars tend to fall into one of two categories. They are either **personality stars** or **character stars.** John Wayne, Judy Garland, Bette Davis, and Julia Roberts are all performers who have constructed an enduring screen personality that is greater than that represented by their appearance in any given film. John Wayne's screen personality is similar from film to film, as are the screen personalities of Barbra Streisand and Julia Roberts. Their stardom is a function of these screen personalities.

By contrast, the character star tends to play a greater range of roles, frequently changing visual and behavioral characteristics from role to role. Examples of character stars are Robert De Niro and Dustin Hoffman, but the supreme example is probably Meryl Streep, who, chameleon-like, changes accents, nationalities, and body language radically from one role to the next. She has appeared as an actress and country-western singer in *Postcards from the Edge* (1990), a distraught Australian mother accused of murdering her baby in *A Cry in the Dark* (1988), a Polish woman who has survived internment in the Nazi concentration camps in *Sophie's Choice* (1982), a Danish

Out of Africa
(Universal Studios, 1985).
The supreme character star:
Meryl Streep. As a performer,
Streep knows no limits. She is as
equally adept at comedy as at
drama, and there seems to be
no role she cannot play. Frame
enlargement.

author who establishes a life in Nairobi in *Out of Africa* (1985), and a white-water adventurer in *The River Wild* (1994).

Streep's ability to completely recreate herself from role to role is nothing short of amazing, and she is probably the purest example of a character star. More typical, perhaps, of the character star are performers such as Robert De Niro and Dustin Hoffman who—despite the wide range of characters they play—continue to project a fairly consistent personality from role to role. De Niro, for example, is known for his psychopaths in films such as *Taxi Driver* (1976) and *GoodFellas* (1990), while Dustin Hoffman tends to play more introverted, withdrawn characters who have trouble expressing themselves, as in *The Graduate* (1967), *Midnight Cowboy* (1969), *Hero* (1992), and *Rain Man* (1988).

Method and Technical Approaches to Performing

In creating a character, film actors tend to use either a *method* or a *technical approach* to acting. The so-called method approach grew out of acting teacher Lee Strasberg's workshops and exerted a powerful influence over a generation of actors in American motion pictures beginning in the 1950s. This generation included Marlon Brando, James Dean, Paul Newman, and others.

Method acting uses emotional recall to play a role. The actor, called upon to portray fear, anxiety, sadness, or other emotions, searches his or her own experience for moments when he or she personally experienced these emotions and tries to internally "reimagine" the situations that led to those feelings. The method actor searches for the relevant personal experiences that will enable him or her to feel the character.

Marlon Brando is one of the supreme exemplars of this approach. One of his greatest performances is in Bernardo Bertolucci's *Last Tango in Paris* (1972). During a long scene in the middle of the film, shot largely in a single take, Brando's character reminisces about his youth and his parents. Brando improvised the scene on camera and drew largely upon his own life to flesh out the memories of the character he was playing. The result is a performance of unrivaled emotional power that shocks and disturbs the viewer with its naked emotional candor.

Hombre (Twentieth Century Fox, 1967) Paul Newman belonged to a generation of method performers who emerged in American film in the 1950s. Trained at New York's Actor's Studio, Newman established classic rebel heroes in *The Hustler* (1961), *Hud* (1963), *Cool Hand Luke* (1967), and, more recently, has offered outstanding performances in *The Verdict* (1982), *The Color of Money* (1986), and *Nobody's Fool* (1994). Frame enlargement.

Last Tango in Paris
(United Artists, 1972).
In this single, lengthy shot, Marlon Brando used details from his own childhood to create his character in *Last Tango in Paris.* The raw emotional candor of his performance in this film remains unsurpassed in his career. Frame enlargement.

An alternative to method acting is **technical acting**, in which the actor thinks through the role and creates from a more detached, intellectual perspective, doing what seems right and appropriate for the scene instead of basing a character on personal, emotional memories. Many of the classic Hollywood actors of the 1930s and 1940s represent this approach, perhaps none better than James Cagney. In his autobiography, Cagney discussed one of his most famous scenes in *White Heat* (1948), where, as gangster Cody Jarret, he goes berserk in a prison cafeteria upon learning of his mother's death.

Cagney was asked whether he prepared himself in any special way for the extraordinary emotional and physical outburst he displays in the scene. Cagney politely replied that he didn't "psych himself up" in any special way and that he really didn't understand actors who felt the need to emotionally pump themselves up before a scene. Cagney said that he remembered seeing some lunatics in an asylum when he was a boy and tried to imitate the way they appeared. While Cagney seems to admit drawing on personal experience to play the scene, it is significant that he doesn't phrase it in emotional terms. He did not try to recall the emotions he felt as a boy seeing people in the

White Heat
(Warner Bros., 1948)
Exemplifying a technical approach to acting, James Cagney, as gangster Cody Jarrett in *White Heat,* goes berserk upon learning of his mother's death. The scene is a classic in the history of American screen performance. Frame enlargement.

asylum but merely tried to imitate some of the inmates' gestures and behavior patterns. He created the role from the outside in, rather than from the inside out.

Method actors, such as Brando, Dean, and Newman who arrived on the motion picture scene in the 1950s, brought with them a revolutionary new approach to screen performance, and the characters they played had an emotional rawness and candor that was, until then, unprecedented. Prior to their arrival, most Hollywood acting tended to be technical and without much psychologizing about a character's motivations and personality. Most performers on screen today tend to use a combination of the two approaches.

The Performer as an Element of Mise-en-scene

Now that the fundamentals of motion picture acting are clear, it is time to examine how performance style becomes an element of mise-en-scene. Filmmakers can transform performance style into an element of mise-en-scene in film in several ways: by emphasizing the unique body language of the performer; by regulating the intensity of performance style; by transforming the performer into a visual "type"; and, finally, by relating the performer to additional structural elements in the scene.

Emphasizing Unique Body Language

Filmmakers often capitalize on the unique body language of an established star so that it becomes a part of the visual design of the film. John Wayne's peculiar manner of walking, which involved an unusual combination of shuffling and striding across a room, became a justly famous part of his screen persona by virtue of its repetition in film after film over decades.

In 1976, near the end of his long and illustrious career, John Wayne appeared in *The Shootist,* a film with strong biographical elements in which he played an aging

---

The Shootist (Paramount Pictures, 1976)
John Wayne's unique body language became an essential element of the mise-en-scene in his films. In *The Shootist,* Wayne's famous walk dominates his entrance to the saloon in the film's climax.

gunfighter dying of cancer, much as Wayne, the actor, was to do shortly afterward. At the climax of the film, Wayne's character, gunman J. B. Books, agrees to meet three gunfighters for a shoot-out in the town saloon. Wayne enters the saloon, and the film's director, Don Siegel, highlights his walk by giving it an extraordinary screen emphasis and amount of screen time.

Presenting Wayne's entrance in medium long shot, Siegel has Wayne traverse the length of the saloon from the front door in the background to the bar in the foreground. Without cutting, Siegel allows the moment to play itself out in medium long shot, enabling the viewer to study and appreciate the intricacies of John Wayne's walk one more time (and in what was to be his last film). By emphasizing the unique body language of its star, the visual design of *The Shootist* tailors its mise-en-scene to fit the dimensions of John Wayne's star image, blending Wayne's screen persona and the character of J. B. Books into a seamless whole.

Charlie Chaplin is another example of a performer whose films are centered on his unique and expressive body language. Chaplin's famous exit at the conclusion of his pictures showed him walking away from the camera with his back to it, waddling in his famous splay-footed fashion and twirling his cane. Chaplin's camerawork was extremely simple and functional. He avoided extravagant camera movements and fancy angles, preferring, instead, to use the camera as a passive observer of his own pantomime performance, believing, correctly, that what he did in front of the camera was more important than how the camera itself might move to comment on the action of a scene. The mise-en-scene of his films centers on his body language and costume.

Regulating Intensity of Expression
A second way in which the performer becomes an element of mise-en-scene is through the way a film regulates intensity of performance expression. Acting styles range from minimal to maximal expressivity. French director Robert Bresson, for

---

Pickpocket (1959)
The blank expressions and emotionless playing style of performers in Robert Bresson's films help establish an extremely restrained mise-en-scene in which all elements of expression are carefully reduced and stripped to a minimum. Whereas most filmmakers work by piling on expressive details, Bresson works by cutting these back.

(Museum of Modern Art/Film Stills Archive)

example, prefers that his performers be empty vessels. He avoids using actors whose facial expressions and gestural styles project specific emotions. Bresson prefers that his actors be recessive, passive, and neutral in their facial and gestural styles.

Bresson's preference for relatively emotionless playing styles is a radical departure from the norms operative in the American tradition, which tend to emphasize performances that communicate a great deal of emotional information. Bresson's style, however, has influenced American filmmakers. The end of Bresson's *Pickpocket* (1959) shows the titular thief, in jail, finally acknowledging the grace a woman's love has brought into his life. By this acknowledgment, he achieves a kind of spiritual redemption. American director Paul Schrader was so impressed with this ending and its emotional restraint that he recreated it as an **homage** in two of his own films, *American Gigolo* (1980) and *Light Sleeper* (1992). (An homage is a reference in a film to another film or filmmaker.)

To gain a better sense of how performance styles based upon the display of minimal emotional information work on screen, compare the thief's expression at the conclusion of Bresson's *Pickpocket* with the expression on Chaplin's face in the concluding close-up of *City Lights* (1931) on page 14 in Chapter 1. Chaplin's performance style is based on communicating a great deal of emotional information about his character, and his expression at the end of *City Lights* is, consequently, much richer emotionally. Neither one is "better" than the other. Both are equally cinematic. It is on the issue of cinematic style, not quality, that they differ.

Maximalist Performance Styles

Many performers go to the opposite extreme of emotional excess, transgressing the boundaries of what seems naturalistic and plausible in a scene's dramatic circumstances. Akira Kurosawa's *Rashomon* (1950), is set in twelfth-century Japan and deals

---

Rashomon (1950)
Exaggerated, excessive performance styles may deliberately break with traditions of naturalism and realism. Toshiro Mifune and Machiko Kyo employ flamboyantly, extreme gestures and expressions in *Rashomon*.

(Museum of Modern Art/Film Stills Archive)

with a rape and murder, the circumstances of which are told differently by all of the witnesses. As they recall the rape, they assume extremely exaggerated and flamboyant acting styles. Actors in the film gesture wildly, cackle hysterically, and contort their faces into extreme emotional expressions.

Many viewers of the film are struck by what seems to be a flamboyantly melodramatic and excessive acting style. In part, this was precisely Kurosawa's intention. In *Rashomon* he wanted to recover some of the visual aesthetics and performance styles of the silent cinema. Acting in early silent films was coded in uniquely different terms from those that would become established during the sound period.

One scholar has termed early silent performance style "histrionic" because it was based on a series of precise and exaggerated gestures. The histrionic gesture for fear was to extend one arm, palm outward, and clutch the throat with the other hand. Shame was indicated by covering the face with one's hands or arms. This histrionic style of silent film melodrama was replaced in sound films by the verisimilar style, incorporating a more subtle and wider range of gestures based on concepts of realism and naturalism.

Through a film's modulation of the intensity of an actor's emotional expression, performance style can become a strong feature of mise-en-scene. Acceptable modulations range from the extremely minimal, as in the films of Bresson or the acting of Clint Eastwood, to the histrionically exaggerated, as in the films of Kurosawa or early silent cinema.

Typage

A third way in which performance style becomes an element of mise-en-scene is through the employment of **typage.** Here, performers and performances are visually stylized, often in extreme terms, to suggest that the character embodies a particular social or psychological type or category.

Social Typage   Social typage was a major feature of classic Soviet filmmaking in the 1920s. Directors such as Sergei Eisenstein cast performers whose physical characteristics could be made to suggest the more abstract characteristics of social class. In Eisenstein's *Potemkin* (1925), the sailors on board the battleship who mutiny against their oppressive officers are embodiments of working-class virtue. The actors portraying these sailors are beefy, muscular, and handsome. The actors portraying the ship's officers have unappealing physiques, alternately thin and wizened or obese. A master of visual caricature, Eisenstein correlated the appearance of actors, their face and body types, with more abstract ideas of social class.

In Sergio Leone's epic Western *Once Upon a Time in the West* (1969), the spread of corrupt business practices into the undeveloped American West is symbolized in the bone cancer that has twisted and crippled the body of the wealthy railroad baron, J. P. Morton (Gabriel Ferzetti). Morton's twisted body is given significant visual attention in the scenes where he appears. In Sylvester Stallone's *Rocky IV* (1985), a politically held belief that Soviet Communist society dehumanizes its citizens is expressed through the social typage of Rocky's Soviet opponent, Drago (Dolph Lundgren), who has a robot-like appearance and behaves as a merciless fighting machine.

A more recent and subtle kind of social typage can be found in the performance style of actor Kevin Costner. Costner's unpretentious film heroes are embodiments

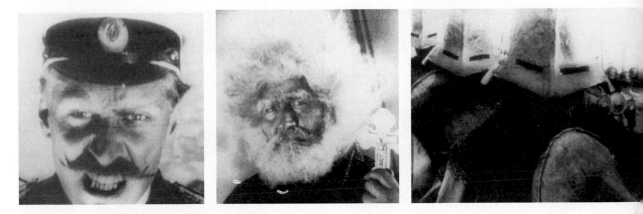

Potemkin (1925); **Alexander Nevsky** (1936)
Social typage in the films of Eisenstein. Opposing the mutiny in *Potemkin* are a snarling naval officer and a Russian priest, his hair flowing madly. In *Alexander Nevsky*, helmets give the evil Teutonic Knights a sinister and dehumanized appearance. Frame enlargements.

of the virtues of the common folk, and in films such as *Field of Dreams* (1989), *The Untouchables* (1987), and *JFK* (1991), Costner represents such ideals as small-town virtue, family bonds, and political idealism.

Psychological Typage Psychological typage can be seen in the *expressionist* style of filmmaking, which has its origin in the German cinema of the 1920s. Expressionist films such as *The Cabinet of Dr. Caligari* (1919) and *Nosferatu* (1922) present grotesque characters, pathological emotional states, and fantastic settings. The accompanying illustrations show the vampire Nosferatu emerging from the shadows, a rat-like skeleton, and the murderous Dr. Caligari who controls a sleepwalking serial killer named

Rocky IV
(United Artists, 1985)
In *Rocky IV*, the boxer is an explicit social type. Triumphing over a robotic Soviet opponent, Rocky wraps himself in the American flag to become an emblem of the renewal of the American warrior spirit and the winning of the Cold War during the Reagan era.
(Museum of Modern Art/Film Stills Archive)

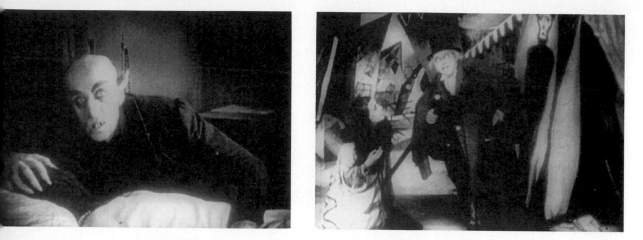

Nosferatu (1922); **The Cabinet of Dr. Caligari** (1919)
Contorted bodies, twisted psyches: the vampire killer in Nosferatu and the evil Dr. Caligari.
Frame enlargements.

Cesare. Their strange bodily contortions functioned as ways of typing or visualizing their inner abnormalities of mind or spirit.

The expressionist style entered the American cinema in the 1930s in the cycle of horror films made at Universal Pictures. Compare the character styles of Nosferatu and Caligari with this image from *Frankenstein* (1931) showing the Frankenstein monster enclosed within a visually and architecturally distorted set.

The Night of the Hunter (1955), a psychological thriller about good and evil focusing on a maniacal preacher's pursuit of two young children who know the hiding place of a fortune, drew upon expressionist pictorial and performance styles. Actor Robert Mitchum's extremely contorted face intentionally recalls the expressionist style of 1920s German cinema.

Frankenstein (Universal Studios, 1931); **The Night of the Hunter** (United Artists, 1955)
Contorted bodies, twisted psyches. German expressionism in this Hollywood horror film: *Frankenstein*. Frame enlargement. Robert Mitchum's facial contortions express his twisted and evil character in *The Night of the Hunter*. Frame enlargement.

Performance styles, then, can be manipulated to evoke ideas of social category or psychological condition. Soviet political typage evokes the idea of the virtue of the proletariat, while the visual typage operative in expressionist styles elicits the anxieties associated with the supernatural, madness, or psychological disturbance. Warren Beatty's production *Dick Tracy* (1990) illustrates a combination of psychological and social typage. The visual style of the film is borrowed from comic strips. The grotesquely exaggerated features of the gangsters, compared with Dick Tracy's clean-cut good looks and the virtuous appearance of his lover Tess Trueheart, are a powerful shorthand for visually expressing the social Darwinian view that criminals are mentally deformed and sick and that the law-abiding are virtuous and emotionally sound.

Visual Mediation of Performance

A final way in which performance style becomes an element of mise-en-scene is by a film's connecting the performer to additional visual elements within the frame. A viewer's understanding of performance is influenced or mediated by these additional visual elements. In the expressionist style of early German films, low-key lighting enclosed grotesque characters in a surrounding sea of darkness. The lighting mediates the message—by augmenting or adding to the performance styles used in those films.

The love scene in *Sliver* (1993) between Carly Norris and Zeke is first played in a warm, amber glow but, then, finishes in a cold, blue light. The passion of the lovers and their subsequent emotional distance is conveyed by the performances of Sharon Stone and William Baldwin, and it is augmented by the color design of the scene. The two are not separable. The viewer's emotional impression of the sequence is a product of both the performances and the color design. By being compatible with the psychological mood of the scene, the color design extends the emotional quality of the performances and the shift from passion to psychological distance in the characters.

Consider another example. In *Citizen Kane* (1941), the title character, newspaper owner Charles Foster Kane, announces to his employees that his newspaper will be guided by a series of principles. Among these are truthfulness in reporting and a commitment to look out for the interests of the poor. Kane announces these by leaning over his desk. As he does so, his face goes into the shadows. The scene is lit low key and occurs at night.

Citizen Kane (RKO, 1941)
Lighting and composition visually enhance an acting performance and make it an element of a film's total mise-en-scene. Charles Foster Kane reads his declaration of principles but steps into the shadows as he does so, enhancing the viewer's suspicion that he is insincere. Frame enlargement.

Because of the lighting, the viewer has an ambivalent response to Kane's declaration of principles. The viewer suspects that he doesn't really mean them. On the one hand, this conviction is based on an understanding of Kane as it has been developing through the narrative and also on Welles' masterful performance, portraying Kane's mercurial, opportunistic, and ever-changing personality. On the other hand, the viewer's ambivalence arises from the lighting design. The shadows that cover Kane's face as he reads the principles comment on his opportunism and deny his sincerity. Performance style and visual design become part of the unified whole called mise-en-scene.

Performance, Emotional Display, and the Viewer's Response

As with other areas of film structure, the performance component of mise-en-scene includes stylistic transformations of human behavior and feeling but also establishes clear references and correspondences with that behavior. Viewers evaluate performances by drawing comparisons with their real-world knowledge of human behavior and what seems to be a plausible, likely, or consistent response by a character in a scene's dramatic or comedic situation. These judgments are based on social knowledge and standards derived from real-life experience, as well as on the expectations of the genre or other storytelling conventions.

Experimental evidence indicates that people are extremely skilled at evaluating and identifying the emotions that can be conveyed through gesture and facial expression. Many of these emotions are context dependent. Certain gestures have certain meanings in given cultures. Other kinds of facial expressions, though, may cross cultures and may function as universal signs of human emotion (in particular, expressions associated with the emotions of fear, anger, happiness, sadness, surprise, and disgust). This universal aspect of facial expression gives the cinema enormous potential for communicating across cultures. A viewer can watch a movie from another country or culture and easily identify from the actors' facial expressions many of the emotions being conveyed in the scene. Facial expression in the cinema, and the camera's ability to emphasize it, is a major reason for the cinema's appeal throughout the world and across cultures.

The Interconnections Among Interpretive and Emotional Responses

Because facial expression and gesture invite comparisons with real-life emotions, situations, and circumstances, they elicit both interpretive and emotional responses by viewers. Watching a scene on screen, the viewer makes judgments about the character's emotions in relation to the scene or situation in the narrative. The viewer asks whether the reaction on screen is plausible, likely, convincing, and/or appropriate to the situation.

These are cognitive judgments that influence how viewers are likely to respond to the performance and the scene. If viewers decide that the actor's reaction is unlikely, disproportional, or otherwise unconvincing, their emotional responses may be inhibited or they may respond with ridicule to what is perceived as bad acting or bad screenwriting. These judgments influence the way viewers respond emotionally.

If viewers decide that the actor's emotional modeling in the scene is appropriate and convincing, given the narrative circumstances, they may go on to share in the character's emotions by way of empathy. Empathy is a willingness to understand a character's emotions and even, under the right circumstances, to feel similar emotions. It is based on complex allegiances with characters. Viewers engage in a complex set of evaluations about the moral and ethical acceptability of a character's screen behavior. This, in turn, influences their readiness to empathize with characters and situations.

In *The Silence of the Lambs* (1991), most viewers are probably frightened by the insane serial killer Hannibal Lecter, although they may also find him a compelling and fascinating figure. By contrast, the film's heroine, Clarice Starling, behaves in a way that most viewers probably deem exceptionally heroic, displaying extreme honesty and courage in her dealings with both Lecter and her male superiors at the FBI. As a result of the elaborate cognitive, emotional, and moral judgments they make about these characters, viewers have differing emotional responses toward them. They are frightened *of* Hannibal Lecter but are frightened *for* Clarice Starling when she is in a situation of danger.

The Silence of the Lambs (Orion Pictures, 1991)
Watching *The Silence of the Lambs,* viewers react to Clarice Starling (Jodie Foster) and serial killer Hannibal Lecter (Anthony Hopkins) by forming complex cognitive, emotional, and moral judgments about the characters. The elements of mise-en-scene assist viewers in forming these judgments.

The communication of emotion by actors on screen, then, is not a simple or straightforward process. It stimulates an intricate process of inference and evaluation, judgment and appraisal at cognitive and emotional levels by viewers. In films displaying high levels of craft and artistry, performance style becomes part of a unified mise-en-scene in evoking these reactions. Camera placement, color, composition, and other aspects of mise-en-scene work to emphasize the emotions displayed by performers. A director can cut to a closer camera position—the better to highlight a character's response and the actor's facial display at a crucial moment in the narrative—or a cinematographer and production designer can employ a palette of colors expressly designed to heighten the psychological mood or atmosphere of the scene. The design of a coherent mise-en-scene gives the filmmaker a uniquely powerful way of guiding the viewer toward a desired set of intellectual and emotional responses.

SUMMARY

A film's mise-en-scene refers to the design and manipulation of all the objects placed in front of the frame of the camera. These typically include sets, costumes, light, color, and the actor's performance. The three chief members of the filmmaking team who are responsible for mise-en-scene are the director, cinematographer, and the production designer. They form a close, three-way partnership to arrive at the visual concepts that will underlie and guide the visual design of the film.

Both cinematographer and production designer have the responsibility of helping the director to realize his or her vision for the film. The cinematographer does this by planning lighting and camera set-ups and assisting in the coordination of color as it will appear in the scene. Placing colored gelatins in front of the lights is one technique that is often used. The production designer assists the director, organizing a visual design for the environments of the film. Components of these environments include sets, costumes, mattes, and miniatures. The production designer, consulting with the cinematographer, helps organize the film's color design through the choices that are made about sets and costumes.

An organized and unified visual design, agreed upon by the director, cinematographer, and production designer, will facilitate a unified mise-en-scene in which all of the elements—costumes, sets, lights, color, and performance—work together to advance the narrative, to represent mood and atmosphere on screen, and to evoke appropriate interpretive and emotional responses by the viewer.

The creation of mise-en-scene illustrates how richly collaborative the process of filmmaking is, the final result being the work of collective judgments made by a variety of production team members about how to achieve a desired effect. An exceptional film requires a good script, strategic camera positioning, and sensitive image and sound editing. It also requires a sophisticated use of light, color, and architectural design. There are so many critical, creative responsibilities in a film production, so many collaborators in the process, and so many key points at which design and concept can break down, that it is easy to see why it is so difficult to make a good movie.

SUGGESTED READINGS

Beverly Heisner, *Hollywood Art: Art Direction in the Days of the Great Studios* (Jefferson, NC: McFarland, 1990).

Vincent LoBrutto, *By Design: Interviews with Film Production Designers* (Westport, CT: Praeger, 1992).

Sybil DelGaudio, *Dressing the Part: Sternberg, Dietrich, and Costume* (Madison, NJ: Fairleigh Dickinson University Press, 1992).

Jane M. Gaines and Charlotte Herzog, eds., *Fabrications: Costume and the Female Body* (New York: Routledge, 1990).

James Naremore, *Acting in the Cinema* (Berkeley and Los Angeles: University of California Press, 1988).

Roberta Pearson, *Eloquent Gestures: The Transformation of Performance Style in the Griffith Biograph Films* (Berkeley and Los Angeles: University of California Press, 1992).

Chapter 4

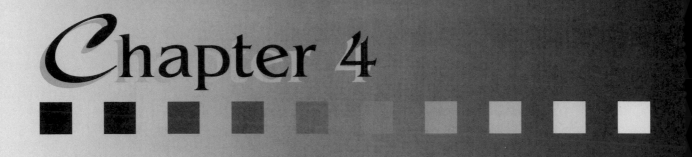

Editing: Making the Cut

Chapter Objectives

After reading this chapter, you should be able to

- define the role of editing in the production process
- explain the basic methods of joining shots
- explain how editing helps create continuity, dramatic focus, and tempo
- explain how editing controls the flow of narrative information
- describe the basic rules of continuity editing and the ways in which they establish continuity

- explain how continuity editing establishes a coherent and orderly physical world on screen
- explain how editing approaches that emphasize spatial fragmentation, space-time conflict, and associational montage work as alternatives to continuity editing
- describe how editing cues viewers to draw connections and interpretations across shots
- explain how editing establishes perceptual constancies across shot and scene transitions

Key Terms and Concepts

editing	wipe	matched cut
rough cut	montage	eyeline match
final cut	schema	shot-reverse-shot series
cut	parallel action	180-degree rule
rough cut	cross-cutting	jump-cutting
final cut	continuity editing	associational montage
dissolve	errors of continuity	long take
fade	master shot	sequence shot
iris		

E diting is regarded by many filmmakers as the single most important creative step in determining the look and shape of the finished film. A good editor can save a film that has been directed in a mediocre fashion, and poor editing can damage the work of even the finest director. This chapter looks closely at the role of editing in the production process, continuity editing codes (these are the rules of editing that are found in most commercial feature films), and alternatives to continuity editing.

☐ WHAT IS EDITING?

Editing is the work of splicing together shots to assemble the finished film. Editors select the best shots from the large amount of footage the director and cinematographer have provided, assemble them in order, and splice them together. In theory, the process of editing begins with the completion of filming or cinematography. In practice, however, the editor may begin consultations with the producer and director and may even begin cutting the film while principal filming is being completed. The amount of authority that the editor has may vary from production to production and, consequently, so may the editor's relationship with the director and producer. These factors determine when the editor may begin work and in what capacity on any given production. In general, the editor works in close collaboration with a film's director. Although they do not receive editing credit on screen, many directors, such as Steven Spielberg and Oliver Stone, exert enormous influence over the editing of their films.

Despite variations in the time at which an editor begins work on a film, the basics of editing remain constant. The first task is to assemble a **rough cut,** which is done by eliminating all of the unusable footage containing technical or performance errors. These may include out-of-focus shots or shots containing unstable camera movement, flubbed lines by an actor, inaudible sound recording, or improperly balanced color. Once all of this unusable footage has been removed, the editor then assembles the remaining footage in scene and sequence order. This rough assembly will be pruned, refined, and polished to yield the **final cut.** The final cut is the completed product of an editor's work. It includes the complete assembly and timings of all shots in the film's final, finished form. It is in the process of going from the rough cut to the final cut that the real art and magic in editing lies.

Methods of Joining Shots

In joining the shots into a rough and then a final cut, the film editor typically employs three basic types of visual transitions. These are methods of linking shots together, and they are used to signal changes in time or place in the story.

The most commonly used transition is the straight **cut,** which is the complete and instantaneous change of one image or shot to another. The cut is typically used to join shots in which there is no change of narrative time or place involved. A cut from a shot of Mel Gibson looking off-frame right to a shot of Danny Glover looking off-frame left tells the viewer that Gibson and Glover are looking at each other and that no changes in time or place have occurred in the story between the shots.

When changes of time or place do need to be specified, the editor has several techniques available. One is the dissolve. A **dissolve** is a shot used to indicate a slight change of time or place in the story. It is visible on screen in the following manner. One shot begins to fade out to black, but, before it is completely gone, the next shot begins to appear on top of it so that there is a moment of superimposition, when the two shots are visible simultaneously. If a film dissolved from a shot of Mel Gibson to a shot of Danny Glover, the viewer would know that some change in time or place in the story had occurred. The shot after the dissolve might be taking place several hours after the shot preceding it or it may be occurring in a new location.

A more substantial change of time or place is typically indicated by the use of a **fade,** in which the first shot fades completely to black. The darkness lasts on screen for a few moments and then the next shot begins to fade in. In a fade, there is no moment of superimposition. If a film faded from a shot of Gibson to Glover, the shot after the fade could be taking place several days or even weeks after the first.

By using these basic transitions, editors can establish important relations of time and place in the story. They are often used by filmmakers to bracket or segment sections of the storyline. These visual codes developed early in the history of film to enable filmmakers to organize their story material and to control time and space in

Running on Empty (Warner Bros., 1988); **Apocalypse Now** (United Artists, 1979)
Basic editing transitions help segment and organize the narrative. They may also create poetic
effects. In *Running on Empty,* the dissolve connects the faces of an estranged father and
daughter to suggest the deeper bond between them. In *Apocalypse Now,* a dissolve from the
face of Captain Willard (Martin Sheen) to fiery explosions in the Vietnam jungles suggests his
psychotic state of mind and his attraction to death and destruction. Frame enlargements.

ways that would allow them to tell more complicated stories. Without the ability to
establish that one chain of events is occurring at a much later time than a previous
scene by using a dissolve or fade, filmmakers would be greatly restricted in the complexity of the stories they could tell.

These transitional devices can also be used poetically, for the expressive visual
effects they make possible. In *Running on Empty* (1988), director Sidney Lumet and
editor Andrew Mondshein connect two scenes using a slow, lingering dissolve that
overlaps the faces of an estranged father and daughter. Each character is in a separate
location, but the dissolve connects their images in a way that suggests the love they
feel for one another despite their present alienation.

SIDNEY LUMET

Like Woody Allen, Sidney Lumet is a New York film-maker. The city provides Lumet with much more than a locale for his urban dramas of crime and corruption. Its milieu has shaped his intellectual and artistic sensibilities. By age four, he was a child actor in New York's Yiddish theater, and, at 26, he joined CBS television as an assistant director. Along with John Frankenheimer, Robert Mulligan, Martin Ritt, and Franklin Schaffner, Lumet belonged to an emerging group of television-trained film directors who began work in features in the 1950s.

His television training taught Lumet how to prepare and execute a production quickly and within a modest budget. His television and theater training also helped make him an extraordinary actor's director. Accordingly, Lumet's services are highly prized by film studio executives and by performers eager to work with a director whose films will showcase their abilities.

The son of left-wing Jewish parents, growing up in the politically turbulent 1930s, Lumet has frequently turned in his films to examinations of an individual's political conscience and its social or moral cost in a

Prince of the City (Warner Bros.-Orion, 1981)
Treat Williams portrays a corrupt cop desperately seeking redemption in *Prince of the City*. He finds it by informing on his friends and partners. Lumet's best work examines the ambiguities of heroism and the personal cost of acting on one's conscience within a corrupt system. Frame enlargement.

Other Optical Transitions

In addition to cuts, fades, and dissolves, editors use other optical transitions to sequence story information and create visual effects. The history of film is full of once-popular optical transitions, which, for one reason or another, have fallen out of favor.

A viewer who looks at films from the silent period, for example, may notice devices such as the **iris.** An iris is a circular pattern that appears on screen, gradually closing down over the image, as in an iris-out, to conclude a scene. To open a scene, an iris-in might be employed, in which case the image would appear inside a small circular opening that would gradually open up on the screen. Irises were used much like fades to signal the end of an important chapter in a story.

In Hollywood in the 1930s and 1940s, **wipes** were not uncommon. The wipe is visible as a solid line travelling across the screen, sometimes vertically, sometimes hor-

Wh

repressive or corrupt system. In *Serpico* (1973), *Prince of the City* (1981), and *Q & A* (1990), Lumet examines police corruption, the moral ambiguities of law enforcement, and the efforts of tainted cops and D.A.s to unravel convoluted networks of graft and influence peddling. Every film, but especially the epic *Prince of the City,* portrays the high personal cost of speaking out against the system and the moral price exacted from those who would inform against their friends. In the 1950s, Lumet had a close brush with the House Un-American Activities Committee, which was investigating left-wing political activity in Hollywood, and this sparked his enduring interest in the moral and social dynamics of informing.

Lumet has also incisively examined the legacy of leftist politics in American culture and society. *Daniel* (1983) contrasts the politically turbulent 1930s and 1960s with the quiescent and repressive 1950s. It portrays the personal and social trauma inflicted on the children of activist Jewish parents, arrested and accused of spying by the federal government and executed in the 1950s. Coming of age in the 1960s, the children must measure their parents' political ideology against the terrible cost paid for those ideas.

Running on Empty (1989) sympathetically portrays a pair of 1960s radicals living underground, on the run from the FBI, after bombing a university lab in protest against the Vietnam War. In the 1980s, they have nowhere to go. The ideas of the sixties are eclipsed, and they are stranded, running on empty.

Lumet alternates his deeply felt social dramas with purely commercial films, assignments he accepts to remain visible within the industry and to relax from the rigors of the more emotionally demanding works. *Murder on the Orient Express* (1974), *The Wiz* (1978), *The Morning After* (1986), and *Guilty as Sin* (1993) are well-crafted, if formulaic, entertainments. Lumet also specializes in adapting stage plays to cinema, a task facilitated by his expertise in both media. His works here include *The Fugitive Kind* (1960), *Long Day's Journey into Night* (1962), *The Seagull* (1968), *Equus* (1977), and *Deathtrap* (1982).

Lumet is a versatile, efficient, extremely intelligent filmmaker whose career vividly demonstrates the merits of small-scale, modestly budgeted filmmaking. Since he began directing in 1957, Lumet has made over forty films, an impressive body of work that has established a unique and essential voice in the American cinema.

izontally. As it moves, it pushes one shot off the screen to reveal another. Unlike fades and dissolves, which tend to be more gradual and subtle transitional devices, the wipe is an aggressive, highly visible device. Perhaps for this reason, Hollywood eventually stopped using it.

Functions of Editing

In turning a rough cut into a fine cut, the film editor employs optical transitions to create relationships of time between the shots in ways that correspond to the story's structure. In addition to this task—and after close consultation with a film's director—the editor routinely performs several other functions. These include the creation of (1) continuity, (2) dramatic focus, (3) tempo, rhythm, and mood, and (4) narration and point of view.

Stewart, as Jeffries, were laughing at his neighbor, even though this is not actually shown. This is one of the most powerful narrative effects that editing can create. It stimulates viewers to make associations and draw interpretations and connections from material presented in separate shots.

Establishing geographic consistency.   A second important principle of organization is employed in this sequence. The associations implied across shots establish geographic consistency in the world represented on screen. The physical layout of the apartment complex where Jeffries lives is established in a clear and coherent way even though viewers never see the whole complex in any single shot in the sequence.

As shot 11 (**l**) continues, Jeffries looks down, and his laughter and smile freeze. Shot 12 (**m**) shows in long shot Thorwald leaving his apartment carrying a suitcase, and then, in shot 13 (**n**), Jeffries looks off frame right at a more extreme angle than in shot 11. Shot 14 (**o**) is a long shot of the alley and the street beyond. After a beat, Thorwald appears and crosses the street. Notice how the more extreme angle at which Jeffries looks, in shot 13 (**n**) compared with shot 11 (**l**), serves to establish a different geographic location as seen by Jeffries—the alley and the street beyond it. These are positioned beside the edge of Thorwald's apartment building.

In keeping with the principle just discussed—the way that editing cues the viewer to make associations and draw interpretations across the cut—the extreme angle change of Jeffries' glance in shot 13 (**n**) provides a cue for the viewer to assemble the geographic layout of the apartment's courtyard, Thorwald's building, and the street in relation to each other. In each of Jeffries' reaction shots, Hitchcock has carefully coordinated the angles at which he glances (relative to the camera) with the implied positioning of objects, characters, and the apartment buildings themselves, across the courtyard. The relationship between the angles of Jeffries' glances and the physical positions of objects across the courtyard is so carefully and systematically worked out that a powerful illusion emerges: Jeffries as a spectator at his apartment window, watching a complete, coherent, and stable world outside that window. Using the angles of Jeffries' glances in the reaction shots of his face, viewers can easily identify the objects or characters he is looking at.

As the sequence continues, from shots 15–29 (**p–dd**), Jeffries continues to watch both Thorwald, carrying his suitcase, come and go and the activities of his other neighbors. The coordination of Jeffries' angled glances with the views outside his window and the repetition of previously established compositions and locales (shot pairs 13 (**n**) and 28 (**cc**), 14 (**o**) and 29 (**dd**), for example) reinforce the viewer's impression that the views of the apartments across the courtyard are part of a coherent and extended physical landscape. Viewers construct a general impression of the entire layout of the courtyard and its apartment buildings from the fragmentary close-ups the editing presents. Viewers go beyond the information in these individual shots to construct a comprehensive mental image of the courtyard into which the locale shown in each individual shot can be integrated.

Editing, schemas, and implied geographic consistency.   Perceptual psychologists refer to such a comprehensive mental image as a **schema.** Schemas are frameworks of perception or interpretation that help organize new information by specifying where that information is likely to fit within a larger pattern. Viewers use schemas to organize visual and narrative information as they watch a film. Using schemas, they take the information contained in separate shots and assign it to a larger pattern or structure. In terms of this sequence, that structure is the physical layout of Jeffries' apartment complex, about which viewers have formed a composite mental image (a schema) based on the projective geometry—the matching of Jeffries' angled glances with particular views of the courtyard—established by individual shots. By facilitating the viewer's creation of schemas pertaining to the layout of settings and locales, editing performs a powerful narrative function. It enables the viewer to form the impression of a coherent and stable physical world on screen, independent of changes in the camera's angle of view from shot to shot. This is an important point. By facilitating the viewer's ability to link shots together into meaningful patterns, and to infer larger relationships from the fragmentary content of individual shots, editing helps establish a strong basis for the viewer's ability to connect and relate story information in ways that are essential for narrative comprehension.

Establishing and altering a pattern of narrative disclosure. The next shots in the sequence maintain the pattern of narrative disclosure established thus far by the cutting. Jeffries continues to watch Thorwald, Thorwald's apartment, and the other neighbors, as the editing alternates, very precisely, between shots of Jeffries looking off frame and shots that represent what he sees across the courtyard. No shot includes both Jeffries *and* what he sees across the courtyard. Now, however, Hitchcock and Tomasini change their pattern of narrative disclosure. The final shot of the sequence fades in, showing a close-up of Jeffries asleep in his chair (**a**). (See photos, next page.) It is dawn, and the camera pans right, out his window (**b**), across the courtyard to Thorwald's apartment, where the viewer sees Thorwald leaving with a woman (**c**). The camera then pans left, back across the courtyard to Jeffries, who the viewer sees is still asleep (**e**). The image fades out.

This last fade concludes the extended sequence dramatizing Jeffries' growing suspicions of foul play following the mysterious scream. Notice the way that Hitchcock has systematically established a particular point-of-view structure in the sequence— alternating in separate shots between Jeffries' implied views across the courtyard and his reactions—only to change this structure at the conclusion of the sequence. Establishing and sustaining a clear pattern of editing and then abruptly changing it effectively underline the importance of narrative information. Modulations of style can emphasize the importance of key moments of narrative disclosure. At the end of the sequence, Hitchcock presents, in one shot, a view of both Jeffries and the events across the courtyard.

In terms of the flow of story information, this is a crucial reversal of strategy because, in this last shot, viewers are given information that Jeffries does not have, the only time in the film that this happens. Viewers see Thorwald leaving the apartment with a woman. It could be his wife, and Jeffries could be wrong about a murder. Knowing this, the viewer's willingness to trust Jeffries' judgment is undermined, and the viewer is forced to confront the moral problem of Jeffries' rear-window, Peeping Tom behavior. Jeffries becomes increasingly convinced that Thorwald has killed his wife, but viewers cannot share his conviction. Hitchcock emphasizes the importance of this disclosure and the doubts it generates by bracketing this last part of the sequence with another fade and by changing the visual design. Using the panning

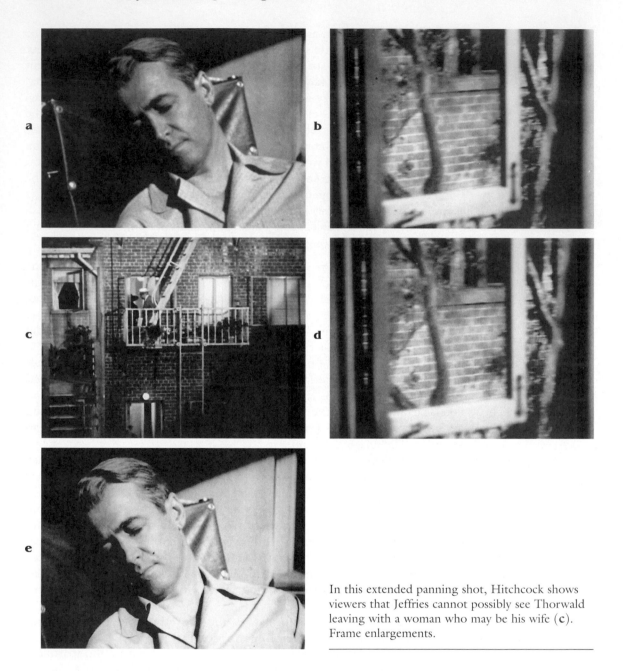

In this extended panning shot, Hitchcock shows viewers that Jeffries cannot possibly see Thorwald leaving with a woman who may be his wife (**c**). Frame enlargements.

camera movement—showing Jeffries asleep at the beginning and end of the shot— Hitchcock clearly establishes that Jeffries has not seen what the viewers have seen.

The editing of this sequence carefully regulates the flow of story information and point of view. The mood, tempo, dramatic focus, and continuity of the sequence are exceptionally strong. The sequence has no dialogue, and Hitchcock was especially proud of its purely visual design and of the ways that design could be manipulated in order to regulate and control the communication of narrative information. Hitchcock relies on the viewer's tendency to infer associated meanings between adjacent shots. He also relies on the viewer's ability to infer a comprehensive landscape from isolated details. By first establishing a sustained pattern of narrative disclosure, Hitchcock emphasizes key story information by dramatically changing that pattern of disclosure.

Controlling Narration Using Parallel Action   An editor's control over the presentation of narrative information rests on a fundamental building block of narrative filmmaking—the use of **parallel action,** in which a filmmaker uses editing to weave together several different lines of action that the viewer understands are occurring simultaneously. The sequence from *Rear Window,* where Jeffries' watches Thorwald's comings and goings during the night, manipulates multiple lines of action: Thorwald's trips to and from his apartment; the arrival home of the composer; the return home of Miss Torso; the comical response to the couple sleeping on their balcony in the rain; and Jeffries' surveillance of all this and his reactions to it. The editing references each of these lines of action to all of the others by establishing relationships of time and location. This function—referencing multiple lines of action occurring simultaneously—is the work of parallel action or parallel editing. Without the use of parallel editing; that is, editing that can interrelate multiple lines of action, filmmakers would be unable to present complex narratives involving the actions of numerous characters, story lines, and subplots.

One especially important form of parallel action is **cross-cutting.** In cross-cutting, the editor goes back and forth, typically with increasing speed, between two or more lines of action. *The Fugitive* (1993) opens with a spectacular train wreck during which the fugitive (Harrison Ford) escapes his jailers. The cross-cutting goes back and forth with increasing speed between shots of the oncoming train and the frenzied, panicked reactions of prisoners trapped inside a bus that has overturned across the tracks. By cross-cutting shots of increasingly shorter duration, the editor accelerates tempo and speed and increases the amount of tension.

Among the inferences viewers routinely draw across cuts are inferences of simultaneous action. The cross-cut shots of the train and the frantic prisoners give the viewer an unambiguous interpretation—the train is about to smash into the bus. When employing parallel action to construct complex narratives, filmmakers routinely assume that viewers will be making these inferences of simultaneity. Filmmakers guide viewers in drawing these inferences by composing and editing shots so as to create a strong flow of action across the cuts.

☐ THE PRINCIPLES OF CONTINUITY EDITING

As its name implies, **continuity editing** is a style of cutting that emphasizes smooth and continuously flowing action from shot to shot. Rather than noticing the abruptness of a cut in a popular movie, the viewer pays attention to story information and character relationships. Shots are joined so that the action flows smoothly over the cut in such a way that editing becomes subordinated to the flow of action and dialogue. The remarkable achievements of the continuity editing system are sometimes disparaged in discussions that describe the style as "transparent" or "invisible." In reality, continuity editing is a highly constructed and accomplished style. The impression of realism and naturalism results from a series of carefully applied editing rules.

A Continuous Flow of Action

The goal of continuity editing is to emphasize the apparent realism and naturalness of the story and to minimize the viewer's awareness of film technique and the presence of the camera. The remarkable achievement of continuity cutting lies in successfully meeting this goal. When viewers see a popular, commercial film in the theater, they rarely notice details of camera position and movement. Instead, they are swept up by the story and the characters. There is a major paradox here. As viewers watch a movie, they see a rapid succession of individual shots on screen, accompanied by an ever-changing series of camera positions and angles. What they *see*, therefore, is fragmentary and discontinuous. Film is put together out of hundreds of individual shots that are joined together. What they *experience*, however, is the impression of a smoothly flowing, unbroken stream of imagery in which the story and the characters come convincingly to life. How is this apparent contradiction between the reality of what viewers see and the impression of what they experience explained?

The answer is that filmmakers have discovered methods of connecting their shots that minimize the disruption of shot changes and maximize the extent to which action flows smoothly over these changes without any apparent break. In other words, continuity editing makes the impression of narrative wholeness and completeness possible. Continuity editing has also helped make cinema popular because it can be so easily understood. Continuity editing ensures ease of perception for the viewer. Films edited according to these principles do not pose difficult perceptual or interpretive challenges. Emphasizing story and characters, films can be edited so they will be easy to understand and will therefore appeal to wide segments of the market.

Here lie the true achievements of the continuity system. The system emphasizes visual coherence and continuity and ease of comprehension. These must be created in film. Because movies are made up of hundreds of fragmentary shots joined together, the potential for incoherence and discontinuity is always great, and filmmakers accordingly have to strive to achieve the opposite.

The Codes of Continuity Editing

The Hollywood classic *Casablanca* (1942) provides some representative sequences that display continuity editing codes in action. Among the most important codes of the continuity system are the following: the use of a master shot to organize the subsequent cutting within a scene, matching shots to the master, the shot-reverse-shot series with the eyeline match, and the 180-degree rule.

Casablanca is a wartime adventure film about heroic resistance against the Nazis, and it is also a lush, romantic melodrama. Rick (Humphrey Bogart), a nightclub owner, has come to Casablanca to get over a disastrous love affair with Ilsa Lund (Ingrid Bergman). Ilsa turns up unexpectedly one night in Rick's cafe and sets in motion the romantic fireworks that move the plot along to its exciting conclusion.

Matching to the Master Shot

In the first scene illustrated here, one of the attendants in Rick's nightclub awaits Rick's approval before admitting some customers into the room where roulette and gambling occur. Rick is filmed from behind, in the foreground. The door to his casino is visible in the background of the shot. This shot functions as the master shot position for this scene. The **master shot** shows the spatial layout of a scene, all of the characters' positions in relation to each other and to the set. The master shot is typically filmed first, with all of the action in a scene from beginning to end photographed from this position. Then directors bring in film inserts, close-ups, and medium shots that will be cut with the master shot to create the final edited scene. The master shot furnishes the basis for creating visual matches (matching visual elements in the frame from shot to shot) with other camera positions in a scene.

Rick glances up and sees his doorman pausing in the entrance with several guests (**a**). The doorman awaits Rick's approval or rejection of these guests before admitting them to the casino. Shot 2 (**b**) is an example of a **matched cut.** The two compositions—the master shot and the medium close-up of the doorman and guests—are matched in terms of the camera's angle of view, which is the same in each shot of the doorman and guests. The only difference is that the camera is closer in shot 2 (**b**). A second basis for creating the match lies in the positioning of the doorman and guests. They are oriented toward screen left, and their positions match in both shots. The match here is so strong that a casual viewer would not notice the cut.

The Eyeline Match

The doorman now glances off-frame left (**c**) (implying that he is looking at Rick who is off screen), and the film cuts to Rick, in shot 3 (**d**), looking off-frame right. Each looks in an opposing direction, one to the right, the other to the left, creating the impression that they are looking at each other. This match is known as the **eyeline match,** and it is an important code used to link the spaces in separate shots. The eyeline match establishes that two characters are indeed looking at each other and that the spaces they inhabit—although seen in different shots—are connected. Often in a scene, characters are interacting with each other but are presented in separate shots. The eyeline match helps create continuity between the separate images.

In organizing the cut to shot 3 (**d**), the master shot remains important. What else, besides the eyeline match, helps establish that these two characters are looking at each other? It is the information viewers remember from the master shot about the spatial layout of the room. From the master shot, viewers know that there is a direct line of sight from Rick's table to the door and that Rick and the doorman have an unobstructed view of each other. The angles of their glances match the information viewers were given in the master shot.

The Master Shot and Viewer Perception

An important principle of film perception and interpretation is apparent here. As viewers watch a movie, they are responding to more than the information that is on screen at any one moment. Viewers process

the shots on screen in relation to visual information that has come before. The master shot, in this context, helps furnish viewers with a map or visual schema of the room. This map of the visual layout of the room enables viewers to integrate fragmentary details, such as the composition of shot 2 (**b**). Viewers place this detail within their recollected sense of the overall layout of the room. The master shot makes this possible by establishing a schema for the overall layout of a scene. This makes it easy

for viewers to fit close-ups and other partial views of the action into the overall scene. The use of master shots helps the viewer interpret the action of a scene more easily.

The Shot-Reverse Shot-Series

Later in the scene, a Nazi supporter tries to enter Rick's casino. In shot 5 (**f**), the doorman and the German talk outside the room, where Rick shortly joins them in shot 6 (**g**). The cutting now goes into a brief **shot-reverse-shot series** (**g, h, i**) as Rick and the German exchange words. The camera is positioned over the shoulder of one character and, then, in the reverse-shot position, over the shoulder of the other character. This series of alternating compositions is a standard method for filming dialogue scenes. It creates something of a ping-pong effect as the composition continually shifts into reverse-shot positions. The cutting is typically coordinated with the flow of dialogue so that, as speakers change, so does the camera position. If the camera shifts into an extreme close-up isolating each character in a single shot, the eyeline match would be employed. In shot-reverse-shot cutting, editing follows the flow of dialogue, and the shifting camera positions mark the changes of speakers in the conversation. This gives a visual emphasis to the dialogue and facilitates the viewer's pick-up of story information.

The 180-Degree Rule

One of the most important codes of the continuity system, and the one that can be seen as the basic building block for creating continuity from shot to shot, is the **180-degree rule.** This rule is the foundation for establishing continuity of screen direction. The right-left coordinates of screen action remain consistent as long as all camera positions stay on the same side of the line of action. Crossing the line entails a change of screen direction.

Because filmmakers shift from shot to shot, changing camera positions and angles, screen direction is something that must be carefully established and maintained. Screen direction refers to the right and left orientations on screen. Right and left must remain constant across shot changes, but the potential for creating inconsistent right and left orientations from shot to shot is great. The 180-degree rule specifies how this may be prevented.

Within any given scene, a line of interest or action can be drawn between the major characters. The 180-degree rule councils filmmakers to keep their cameras on one side of this line from shot to shot within a scene. If a filmmaker were to cross the line by cutting to a camera position taken on the other side of the line, right and left orientation on screen would be reversed. If the line is crossed, characters on screen right would appear on screen left.

The 180-degree rule operates in the next scene in the film (**j–m**). Ugarte (Peter Lorre) comes into the casino to tell Rick that he has gotten some "letters of transit," which will guarantee their bearer safe passage from Casablanca, and he asks Rick to keep them for him. As Ugarte talks to Rick, they are seated at the table. The line of interest extends between them. Notice that the camera stays on the same side of the line in all of the subsequent shots. When both characters are in the shot, Ugarte is always on screen right and Rick is always on screen left, despite the changing camera positions. When a close-up isolates Rick, he is facing screen right, consistent with his position in the two-shot.

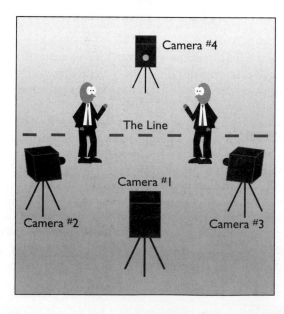

Figure 4.1: The 180° rule

Notice also that the line of interest is consistent with the line of interest established in the previous scene with the doorman and guests. Rick is sitting at his table with the chessboard and a glass of champagne, and the camera positions are on the same side of the table as they were in the earlier scene with the doorman and guests. In this sense, visual continuity has been maintained from scene to scene because a consistent line of interest is used as the basis of the 180-degree rule.

What would happen, however, if a filmmaker needed to cross the line and cut to a camera position on the other side of the room or set? There are various ways of doing this. A filmmaker may cut first to a series of camera positions on or near the line or may simply use a moving camera shot to cross the line within a shot. Whatever strategy is employed, the problems associated with maintaining or crossing the line raise the issue of visual change and perceptual constancy in the represented action on screen.

Camera Position and Perceptual Constants   Once relationships of direction and orientation are established on screen, filmmakers do not want to become slaves to them. It is important, therefore, to provide the viewer with a variety of changing visual perspectives on the action. The problem is to create this variety without confusing and disorienting the viewer, particularly when it is important to establish a coherent sense of a fixed visual landscape. The viewer must understand that although

Out of Africa (Universal Studios, 1985)
In *Out of Africa*, continuity of movement is maintained despite a change in its right-left orientation. The shot of Karen Blixen (Meryl Streep) riding toward the camera softens the right-left orientation and provides the transition necessary for maintaining continuity across the change in screen direction. Note also the motion blur produced by the panning camera in the first and last shots of the sequence. Because the camera is panning with the coach's movement, stationary pedestrians and buildings photograph with motion blur. Frame enlargements.

the camera's angle of view may change, the layout of the physical world on screen remains constant. In other words, if a character is shown standing at the bottom of a hill, the character must seem to remain there, unless shown moving elsewhere, regardless of whether a high-angle or a low-angle shot is employed and regardless of whether the camera photographs that character from the left or right side. The camera's relative positions, which may be constantly changing as the action unfolds on screen, are distinct from the perceptual constancies (e.g., up, down, left, right) that must prevail and not change in that represented action. The sheriff pursuing the prisoner must always be understood to be chasing his quarry regardless of the directions in which pursuer and pursued are shown moving on screen.

This relationship between the editing codes pertaining to screen direction and the constants of the physical world that are represented on screen is apparent in an early scene in *Out of Africa* (1985). Karen Blixen (Meryl Streep) arrives in Kenya and rides by coach from the train station to meet her new husband. Several shots show her riding in the coach, during which screen direction is reversed. This reversal, however, occurs in a way that is consistent with principles of continuity.

The first shot (**a**) showing Blixen travelling by coach is a telephoto long shot in which she appears, through crowds of pedestrians, riding toward screen left. The filmmakers then cut to a new camera position, framing her as she rides directly toward the camera. Consequently, this new framing (**b**), which is on the line of action (motion) established in the previous shot erases right-left coordinates. In this shot, movement occurs toward the camera, not to the right or left.

The next shot (**c**) shows Blixen riding toward screen right and represents a reversal of screen direction relative to the first shot. The editing, however, softens the reversal of direction by using as an intervening shot an image in which she rides directly toward the camera. By establishing a dominant line of action and then cutting to a camera position on that line, the filmmakers may then cross the line and reverse screen direction.

This method preserves screen continuity perfectly. Directional change occurs gradually, and the viewer understands that the layout of the physical world on screen has remained constant, despite changes in the camera's angles of view and the direction of motion on screen.

Errors of Continuity

Of course, the continuity system is not always perfect, and one of the pleasures of watching movies for viewers with sharp eyes is spotting errors of continuity. **Errors of continuity** are mismatched details in sequential scenes. Take, for example, Warner Bros.' 1938 production, *The Adventures of Robin Hood,* starring Errol Flynn as the title character and Basil Rathbone as the evil Sir Guy of Gisborn. In an early scene, the corrupt Prince John (Claude Rains) is scheming with Sir Guy. In the master shot, Prince John sits in the foreground on screen left and Sir Guy stands in the distant background on screen right with his back to the camera. As he begins to turn to face Prince John, the film cuts to a medium shot of Sir Guy. (The cut on movement is another of the basic codes of continuity editing in the Hollywood system. By cutting on movement—in this case, cutting to the medium shot position as Sir Guy turns—the cut itself can be disguised, and the action made to flow over the cut.) As Sir Guy begins to turn, he

Robin Hood: Prince of Thieves
(Warner Bros., 1991)
Because of the enormous complexity of assembling many hundreds of shots, virtually all films feature continuity errors. *Robin Hood: Prince of Thieves,* like any other film, has its share of minor continuity problems. Viewers with sharp eyes may find delight in spotting these.

starts toward the left. On the cut to a medium shot, however, he is turning to the right. By Hollywood standards, this is a fairly explicit continuity error, although, because of the amount of story information being communicated to viewers at this early point in the movie, it's doubtless that any of them noted the discrepancy.

The viewer with sharp eyes can spot continuity errors in virtually any movie. These arise because movie making proceeds on a shot-by-shot basis, with every-thing—from character positions and costumes to lights and props—re-created for each new shot. The possibilities of flubbing these re-creations, or mismatching these details, are enormous. The conditions of film production make it hard for filmmak-ers to avoid such errors. Consider, for example, Kevin Costner's *Robin Hood: Prince of Thieves* (1991). When Robin (Costner) and Azeem (Morgan Freeman) land on the shores of England, Azeem helps Robin up from the beach. In medium close-up, Robin holds out his right arm for assistance, and in the following shot viewers see Azeem helping Robin up by grasping his left arm.

The error arose because the action had to be created separately for each shot and was done so without properly matching continuity. In such cases, the editor's best hope is that the viewer will not notice the discrepancy, and, indeed, if the gaff is not glaring, viewers often fail to notice because they are busy absorbing story informa-tion and following the chain of events in the narrative.

Other kinds of continuity errors may develop because portions of a scene are shot at different, widely spaced intervals. For example, in *Cocktail* (1988), Tom Cruise passes a New York theater whose marquee advertises the film *Barfly* and, then, a few minutes later, when he passes that theater again, the marquee advertises *Casablanca*. As many readers undoubtedly know, some films seem exceptionally abundant with continuity problems. One such film was *Pretty Woman* (1990), whose continuity errors ranged from scenes in which Richard Gere's tie appears and disappears from shot to shot to other scenes in which his shoes and socks do the same thing, and still others, in which Julia Roberts takes a bite at breakfast from what is alternately a pancake and a croissant.

Facilitating Viewer Response

The editing codes just reviewed—cutting to match the master shot, the use of the 180-degree rule, and the shot-reverse-shot technique with the eyeline match—repre-sent some of the cornerstones of continuity editing. They work to emphasize natu-ralism and realism to the extent that it minimizes the amount of perceptual work that the viewer must do. This work is minimized because the positioning of characters, direction of movement, and angles of view are related across shots in an orderly way, enabling the perspective of each shot to link up in a coherent way with perspectives in other shots. Thus for the viewer a sense of a unified landscape is established stretch-ing across all the shots, each one of which is only a partial view.

Think of film viewing as an activity like a picture puzzle in which the overall pic-ture—Rick's casino or Jeffries' apartment complex, for example—emerges when all the pieces have been fit together. Each piece is a shot, and, if they fit together just right, the viewer easily sees the overall picture and not the pieces, just as with a puz-zle. In this way, continuity editing helps make the visual perspectives of each shot easy to interpret and movies themselves very easy to understand.

Continuity editing codes are so successful at simplifying the viewer's perceptual task that they can actually facilitate the comprehension of story information. Ample experimental evidence indicates that viewers understand story information more easily when continuity editing is used than when it is not. Rather than interfering with normal perception, continuity codes facilitate it. Clearly, this is one basis for the impression of realism and naturalism that results from films shot using the continuity approach. These editing codes mimic certain features of everyday visual experience in such a way that they pose few interpretational problems.

Hollywood filmmakers, who were never self-conscious about the techniques they used, were correct in deciding to use the continuity approach because, by simplifying the perceptual tasks presented to the viewer, such codes make films more accessible and attractive for audiences with diverse educational and cultural backgrounds. To the extent that continuity editing, then, poses few interpretational problems for viewers, it helps establish the enormous popular acceptance and emotional appeal of motion pictures. If continuity editing, which is the editing approach of popular cinema, were unnatural or difficult from the standpoint of visual perception, the movies would never have become the extraordinarily popular medium that they are. Continuity editing helps make movie narratives accessible and easily understood by viewers. The popularity of motion pictures is partly attributable to their ease of comprehension.

ALTERNATIVES TO CONTINUITY EDITING

As noted, popular movies are created according to continuity principles, but this is certainly not the only approach to film editing, and many filmmakers, and even some national cinemas, have used other methods of editing. Alternatives to continuity editing will be examined at two levels. The first involves microlevel alterations of codes in which filmmakers alter, in meaningful ways, specific types of editing transitions, such as cuts, fades, or dissolves. These alterations typically occur within a scene that has been constructed according to overall continuity principles. The second level of alternatives involves a greater departure from the continuity tradition. This level involves entire sequences or scenes in which the editing creates discontinuities of time or space.

Microlevel Alternatives

At the microlevel, filmmakers are free to alter and play with editing codes in uniquely creative ways. Many American films of the late 1960s and early 1970s experimented and innovated in a freewheeling way with scene and shot construction. Such films generally followed overall continuity principles, but freely altered individual editing codes.

One of the most stylistically innovative films of that period was *Bonnie and Clyde* (1967), edited by Dede Allen. Allen has reported that the film's director, Arthur Penn, kept telling her to make the story move more quickly, and, to do this, she broke a number of editing rules. For example, in some scenes she employed the technique of **jump-cutting,** a method of editing that produces discontinuity by leaving out portions of the action. The first scene of the film shows Bonnie (Faye Dunaway) in her bedroom. She paces restlessly about the room and lies down on the bed. Allen cuts

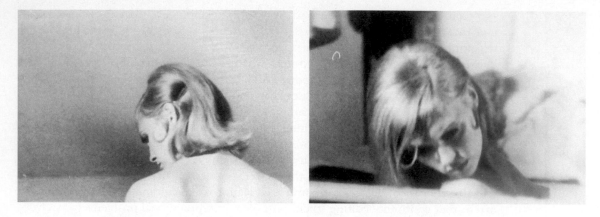

Bonnie and Clyde (Warner Bros., 1967)
This jump cut in *Bonnie and Clyde* shows Bonnie standing and looking down at her bed, then reclining on the bed. The intervening action is omitted. The result for the viewer is a small moment of perceptual disorientation. Frame enlargements.

from a shot of Bonnie walking over to her bed with her back to the camera to a shot in which she faces the camera and is already reclining on the bed. The cut between these two shots produces a jump, or discontinuity, in both her orientation relative to the camera and her position on the bed. This tiny break in the action creates a small acceleration in time, propelling the story forward a little faster than normal.

Another technique used for a similar purpose in *Bonnie and Clyde* changed the visual application of the fade. Under the continuity system, when a fade is employed, it signals a transition between scenes. The last shot of one scene fades out, and, then, after a moment, the first shot of the next scene fades in. As such, the fade is a slow device. It takes a second or two on screen for it to be fully executed. Director Penn and editor Allen, wanting to speed up the pace of the story, altered the conventional fade by replacing one-half of it with a cut. In *Bonnie and Clyde,* when the outlaw couple drives away from a store in a stolen car, the shot fades out, but, the next scene *cuts* in instead of *fading* in.

Allen said the following about this innovative technique: "I think a lot of people at the time thought it wasn't good editing. The first time Jack Warner saw a cut, he couldn't believe that we were going to fade out at the end of a scene and then cut in with the next or vice versa. The way that started was when I tried to fade on one side and the other side wasn't ready yet. We looked at it and Arthur liked it, and we began using it. It moved faster. It whooshed you into the next scene which Arthur thought was so important. A full fade has that black in the middle which brings things to a stop."

Another innovative film of the late 1960s, *Easy Rider* (1969), broke with tradition during scene transitions. Instead of dissolving or fading or simply cutting from one scene to the next, the filmmakers used a technique that can best be described as a form of flash cross-cutting. In conventional cross-cutting, filmmakers cut back and forth between two or more events in order to suggest that they are happening simultaneously. Cross-cutting is typically used within a scene to reference and compare two or more lines of action. As used in *Easy Rider,* the technique of flash cross-cutting is

ARTHUR PENN

Along with Sam Peckinpah, Arthur Penn is one of the great poets of screen violence. Unlike Peckinpah, though, who treated violence as an essential and instinctual component of human behavior, Penn places violent behavior within a clear social context and uses it to illuminate the political atmosphere of an era. *The Chase* (1966) presciently treats the United States as a gun culture and studies its festering climate of violence. In its horrific climax, the town sheriff (Marlon Brando) is savagely beaten and cannot prevent the public assassination of a small-time criminal under police custody. Here, as elsewhere in Penn's films, the killing of John F. Kennedy provides the model and resonant reference point for explorations of American social violence.

Penn trained as a television director and debuted as a feature filmmaker with an unusually psychological Western, *The Left-Handed Gun* (1958). *Mickey One* (1965) was a European-style, existential art film whose unconventional visual style and ambitious story was too far ahead of U.S. film culture upon its release. Penn applied the style of the French New Wave, primarily jump cuts and other unconventional edits and optical effects, to mainstream American film with *Bonnie and Clyde* (1967), a seminal work of modern cinema. Using slow motion and multi-camera filming for its scenes of violence, audaciously mixing high comedy and brutal violence, Penn's film captured the rebellious spirit of the times with its unconventional style and counter-cultural portrayal of *Bonnie and Clyde* as youthful heroes taking on the establishment. *Alice's Restaurant* (1969) and *Little Big Man* (1970) quickly followed, essential documents of late sixties film and society.

Penn faltered in the 1970s. With the eclipse of the social idealism and political excitement of the sixties,

Bonnie and Clyde (Warner Bros.-7 Arts, 1967) The slow-motion, bloody deaths of Bonnie and Clyde changed American cinema forever. Penn's gut-wrenching images established a new threshold of brutality on film, yet they seem almost tame by today's standards. Unlike later filmmakers interested in gore for its own sake, Penn used violence as a way of exploring the cultural climate of violence in American society. Frame enlargement.

and with Watergate the dominant metaphor of social corruption in the next decade, Penn was disillusioned and cut off from the social ferment that nourished his films. However, he managed a stunning artistic expression of a bleak cultural period. *Night Moves* (1975), a detective film, brilliantly captures the national darkness, despair, and confusion experienced in the wake of the assassinations of John and Robert Kennedy and Martin Luther King and the collapse of the sixties' social movements. It is, perhaps, Penn's best film.

Following *The Missouri Breaks* (1976), a big-budget Western teaming Brando with Jack Nicholson and widely regarded as a failure, Penn worked infrequently and without commercial impact. *Four Friends* (1981) was barely released; *Target* (1985) was an efficient demonstration of Penn's ability to make a plot-driven thriller; and *Dead of Winter* (1987) was an effective, if cold-blooded, psychological chiller that Penn directed as a favor to friends who would have otherwise been unable to get their script produced.

Penn's checkered film career demonstrates the essential interconnection of film and society. Penn thrived during a period of social turbulence when the film industry welcomed innovative, cutting-edge work and when he could connect his artistic visions to the political dramas unfolding around him. Disillusioned with the 1970s and disappointed with the special-effects-driven blockbuster fantasies that dominated American film from the latter half of that decade, Penn simply stopped working in film, except on an irregular basis, and has now turned his energies to a deepening involvement with the New York-based Actor's Studio. But Penn remains hopeful that the industry may again welcome his kind of film.

a method of scene transition in which the last shot of the first scene and the first shot of the next scene are intercut very rapidly, back and forth, so that, at the end of one scene and the beginning of the next, the viewer oscillates back and forth between the two at an extremely rapid pace.

Flash cross-cutting is a unique method of scene transition that, like the jump cut employed in *Bonnie and Clyde,* produces a noticeable break in continuity. These techniques call attention to themselves, and, for this reason, they are generally avoided in traditional continuity editing. The overall goal of continuity editing is to provide a smooth flow to the events of the narrative in such a way that the viewer is hardly aware of the visual technique and structure of the film. By contrast, the editing of *Bonnie and Clyde* and *Easy Rider* is extremely self-conscious and apparent.

One more example of a microlevel alteration of editing codes might be informative. The conventional method of executing a fade is to fade to black. Alternatively, filmmakers have sometimes chosen to fade to white. John Carpenter's production of *The Thing* (1982) employs a series of fades to white. Unlike the examples from *Bonnie and Clyde* and *Easy Rider,* however, in which the technical departure from a norm was essentially unrelated to the story's themes or content, the alteration in the Carpenter film has a clear bearing upon the content of the story. Carpenter's film takes place in Antarctica, in a white, frozen world of snow and ice. By fading to white, Carpenter references this frozen, sub-zero world at a visual level for the viewer. By fading to white, Carpenter returns visually to the emptiness of the snowy regions in which the story is set.

Scene- and Sequence-Level Alternatives

Spatial Fragmentation

The scene- or sequence-level alternative to continuity editing that is most commonly encountered by contemporary audiences involves the use of montage editing to create extreme spatial fragmentation. Continuity editing helps create a coherent visual space on screen with fixed, orderly physical coordinates by carefully matching angles and perspectives in close-ups and medium shots with those that were established in the master shot. By contrast, montage editing—used to create spatial fragmentation— tends to forego the use of a clear master shot, the matching of action to that master shot, and the systematic repetition of familiar camera set-ups. Take, for example, the boutique scene in Steve Martin's *L.A. Story* (1991). Steve Martin's character visits a hip boutique to get a new pair of pants in a scene that features extremely frantic, rapid cutting. The scene runs just under two minutes and is composed of 66 shots, many of which are less than a second in length.

These brief images fragment the spatial layout of the boutique by avoiding a repetition of familiar angles of view, showering the viewer with visual information at an extremely fast rate, and avoiding the use of a master shot. Instead of opening the scene with an establishing shot, the boutique is introduced with rapid close-ups of lights, signs, and merchandise.

Lacking an introductory master shot, the scene is built, instead, by accumulating details, bits and pieces of space and action, and, consequently, many shots fail to clearly match with the others, producing for the viewer a fragmentation of space and perception. The filmmaker's primary aim is to create a collage of discrete visual

Psycho (Paramount Pictures, 1960)
Rapid montage editing creates the sensation of a violent murder in *Psycho* by assembling flash cuts of murderer and victim. The violent pace of the editing intensifies the brutal nature of the scene. Frame enlargements.

impressions rather than a spatially ordered, coherent, and stable environment. The scene is organized, not in terms of visual or physical coherence, but according to an accumulative principle—the piling up of fragmentary details.

Although this kind of quick montage cutting is standard in contemporary films, there are clear historical precedents for it. In Alfred Hitchcock's *Psycho* (1960), the film's main character, Marion Crane (Janet Leigh), is murdered in her shower one-third of the way into the film. The murder itself lasts for forty seconds and is composed of 34 individual shots. These tend to fall into three categories: (1) shots of Marion struggling with her attacker, holding the killer's knife arm with her hand; (2) shots of Marion's face and hands as she writhes in the shower under the knife blows; and (3) shots of the killer stabbing toward the camera. By intercutting these three categories of shots at a rapid pace, Hitchcock and editor Tomasini create a scene of extraordinary violence, in which most of the actual violence is suggested since viewers almost never see the knife actually touching flesh. The impression of the murder is built up in the mind's eye by virtue of the rapid editing.

Space-Time Conflict and Discontinuity
A second category of sequence-level alternatives to continuity editing takes the principle of spatial fragmentation a step further. It stresses space *and* time conflicts and discontinuities. This category features spatial fragmentation as well as radical discontinuity in time.

In 1969, Sam Peckinpah's violent Western *The Wild Bunch* gave American cinema spectacular montages of unprecedented complexity, using principles of visual conflict, contrast, and discontinuity borrowed from the revolutionary Soviet film tradition of the 1920s. (It was this film tradition that first demonstrated the cinematic potential of montages based on principles of discontinuity.) Peckinpah's film opened and closed with elaborate gun battles that were edited to achieve maximum emotional impact and to render the spectacle of violent death with grace and beauty.

Four Modes of Fragmentation and Discontinuity   Peckinpah's montages exert four kinds of control over screen action. Events are slowed down, interrupted, paralleled, or returned to in ways that introduce elements of time and motion conflict. The opening scene of *The Wild Bunch* climaxes with a battle between the gang of outlaws—the wild bunch—and a posse of bounty hunters and lawmen. The posse ambushes the bunch, firing upon them from the rooftops of the town the outlaws had planned to rob. The wild bunch fires back at the posse, hitting two men on the rooftops.

The visual organization of the scene creates a series of parallel events presented by way of cross-cutting. The action goes back and forth between the bunch shooting at the posse and the posse on the rooftops returning fire (**a–h**). During the course of this action, two members of the posse on the roof are hit. As one falls toward the ground and the other falls toward the balustrade on the roof, the film introduces extreme elements of temporal and spatial discontinuity. The editing creates a false parallel between the two victims, false in terms of the impossible relationships of time that prevail between the two events. Victim one falls off the roof in slow motion (**i, m**) and victim two, hit later in the sequence (**k**), falls at normal speed, but both reach the end of their falls at precisely the same moment, as indicated by the matched cut in shots number 16 and 17 (**p, q**). A closer look at the editing shows clearly why these are impossible relationships of time. The fall of the first victim toward the street is interrupted four times during the course of the sequence. The first cut-away is represented by shot number 4 (**d**), the second cut-away is represented by shots 6, 7, and 8 (**f, g, h**), the third cut-away is represented by shots 10, 11, and 12 (**j, k, l**), and the fourth cut-away is represented by shots 14 and 15 (**n, o**).

Moreover, shots 9, 13, and 16 (**i, m, p**) are slow-motion images of the victim falling toward the ground. Time has been slowed down and extended by the cut-aways and slow-motion imagery. The event of the second victim falling toward the rooftop ledge is not presented using slow motion, but it is extended in time by two cut-aways, the first represented by shots 12 and 13 (**l, m**), and the second represented by shots 15 and 16 (**o, p**). Peckinpah's editing interrupts, slows down, parallels, and returns to multiple ongoing lines of action. Because of the use of multiple cut-aways and slow motion to extend the time of the first victim's fall, the simultaneous impact of the two victims in shots 16 and 17 (**p, q**) represents an impossible time-space relationship within the sequence. Peckinpah and his editors intercut normal speed and slow-motion speeds in the montage, extending a discontinuity of time and space. The first victim takes far too long to reach the ground to constitute a true parallel in time and space with the fall of the second victim, but each strikes ground and ledge at the same moment in the sequence. This doubles the force of their impact and provides a simultaneous resolution for these two lines of action that have been ongoing within the larger shoot-out.

These distortions of time and space show clearly how montage editing enables filmmakers not only to control the time-space relationships of their narrative, but to reorganize them in nonrealistic and discontinuous ways. The viewer of *The Wild Bunch* accepts these manipulations as permissible stylistic organizations of the action. The realism of the event, its continuity principles, have been replaced by an artistic and stylistic reorganization of the realities of time and space. The violent content of this scene is intensified by editing that "violently" shatters the continuity principles of normal time and space.

a

b

c

d

e

f

g

h

i

Slow
motion.

j

k

l

m
Slow
motion.

n

o

p
Slow
motion.

q

One final point to make about the use of montage to create spatial fragmentation and discontinuity is that these effects can also be achieved with great subtlety. The sequences examined from *The Wild Bunch, L.A. Story,* and *Psycho* involve extreme dislocations of time and/or space. However, filmmakers can also create subtle discontinuities that the viewer will readily accept as being consistent with a realistic style.

Director George Sluizer remade his 1988 French-Dutch production, *The Vanishing,* as an American picture in 1993. In the American remake, a murderer gives a young man a drugged cup of coffee, telling him that, if he drinks it, he will learn the fate of his girlfriend who disappeared without a trace three years previously. As Jeff (Keifer Sutherland) lifts the coffee to his mouth to drink, his gesture is slightly fragmented and elongated by being broken into a series of shots in which the action of each is slightly overlapped. As he raises the cup to his mouth, the action is presented in a medium shot, then in a medium close-up, then in close-up, then in extreme close-up, and, then, finally, back in medium shot.

With each new perspective, the action overlaps slightly with the end of the previous shot. Jeff's gesture is fragmented, but the principles of discontinuity have been introduced at a subtle level, one that does not undermine a realistic impression of time and space, unlike what is done in *The Wild Bunch.*

Modern Times (United Artists, 1936)

Associational editing invites viewers to draw intellectual connections between images. Chaplin compares factory workers and sheep in a famous association at the beginning of *Modern Times.* Frame enlargements.

SAM PECKINPAH

Peckinpah's films are widely identified with the explicit screen violence that they helped popularize, but his handling of violence is remarkably complex and ambiguous. Peckinpah stylized screen violence through slow motion and montage editing to give it a seductive aesthetic beauty while simultaneously emphasizing its physical brutality and moral and emotional horror. As a result, viewers are caught in a disquieting push-pull dynamic, alternately drawn to and repulsed by Peckinpah's imagery.

Ride the High Country (1962), Peckinpah's second feature, was a classically beautiful Western emphasizing an old-fashioned, straightforward heroism that would never again appear in his increasingly ironic and cynical films. His breakthrough film, *The Wild Bunch* (1969), used montage editing of a complexity unprecedented in the American cinema to portray the spectacularly violent end of a band of Western outlaws. The film's extreme violence made it wildly controversial and established Peckinpah as an authentically roguish voice in the American cinema and the most important director of Westerns after John Ford (*Stagecoach, 1939; Fort Apache*, 1948; *The Searchers*, 1956).

In the next five years, sustained by the social ferment of the late sixties, Peckinpah embarked on a brief but highly productive and influential period of filmmaking. He alternated between ultraviolent explorations of male brutality and corruption (*Straw Dogs*, 1971; *Bring Me the Head of Alfredo Garcia*, 1974) and gentle, funny, melancholy portraits of losers and out-

The Ballad of Cable Hogue
(Warner Bros., 1970)
In *The Ballad of Cable Hogue*, the former frontier hero is run over by an automobile and dies at the dawn of the modern era. Peckinpah loved outcasts, losers, and loners, and his best Westerns sadly contemplate the inability of these misfits to survive in a modernizing West. The car that runs over Cable kills not just Hogue but the old West that Peckinpah knew and loved. Frame enlargement.

siders in a vanishing West (*The Ballad of Cable Hogue, 1970; Junior Bonner*, 1972).

Pat Garrett and Billy the Kid (1973) was a grimly elegiac retelling of the legend and a meditation on the passing of the Old West. MGM re-cut the film against Peckinpah's wishes, deleting key sequences. Peckinpah had always had a tempestuous relationship with studio executives, but this was the beginning of the end for him. He made one more outstanding film (the weird *Alfredo Garcia*) and was then finished as a creative voice in the American cinema.

His few subsequent films (*The Killer Elite*, 1975; *Cross of Iron*, 1977; *Convoy*, 1978; *The Osterman Weekend*, 1983) lack a controlled design and show all too clearly Peckinpah's rapid and sad decline. Crippled by personal demons and paralyzed by a cynical disdain for modern corporate America, Peckinpah lost his ability to direct. Considered unemployable by the studios, and unable to work well when he did find employment, Peckinpah was largely inactive in his last years.

But the films he made during that spectacular burst of creativity from 1969–1974 profoundly influenced the representation of screen violence and dramatically demonstrated the creative possibilities of bringing bad or reprehensible characters to the center of a screen narrative. Peckinpah's is an authentically abrasive cinematic voice. His films morally challenge their viewers with tragic visions of the destructive effects of violence in human life.

Associational Montage

The third category of sequence-level alternatives to continuity editing is **associational montage.** In an associational montage, the arrangement of shots is intended by a filmmaker to cue a deliberate set of specific intellectual and sometimes emotional associations by the viewer. The shot combinations point toward a specific conclusion that the viewer is expected to reach or concept that the viewer is expected to hold. This category, like the others, also has its origins in the work of 1920s Soviet directors. For example, in *Strike* (1924), director Sergei Eisenstein wants to convey to the viewer the brutality of the Czarist government's decision to use troops to put down a workers' strike, and he cuts from shots of the troops attacking the workers to images of a cow being butchered in a slaughterhouse.

Familiar with Eisenstein's work, Charlie Chaplin, in his 1936 production *Modern Times,* employed a similar bit of associational editing: at the beginning of the film, he cuts from a shot of sheep being herded into a pen to a shot of workers leaving a subway and crossing the street to enter their factory. The viewer is asked to draw the appropriate conclusions based on the comparison of the two images.

This associational cutting in the Eisenstein and Chaplin films is not a true sequence-level associational montage because it is used only briefly within the body of an already-established scene. The principle of associational cutting is extended for an entire sequence in *Pat Garrett and Billy the Kid* (1973) so that director Sam Peckinpah can point out the irony in the fate of Sheriff Pat Garrett, killed by the same politicians who had hired him years earlier to hunt and kill the outlaw Billy the Kid.

The opening sequence of Peckinpah's film fractures time and space by intercutting two events: Garrett's murder in 1908 and an earlier meeting with Billy in 1880, shortly after Garrett was elected sheriff of Lincoln County, New Mexico. As the two scenes are intercut, events in the past (1880) and the present (1908) seem to interact with one another and to comment on each other. When Garrett meets the Kid in Old Fort Sumner in 1880, he finds Billy and his gang idly shooting the heads off chickens that they have buried in the sand. Garrett pulls out his rifle and takes part in the shooting. In the associational editing that follows, the film's viewer sees Billy

---

Pat Garrett and Billy the Kid (MGM, 1973)

Editing can fracture time and reorganize it in a symbolic and poetic way. In *Pat Garrett and Billy the Kid,* Billy fires his gun and, because of the editing, "hits" Garrett many years later as an old man. Frame enlargements.

in the past taking aim on the chickens, firing his gun, and, because of the sequencing of shots, seeming to hit Garrett who is shown as an old man in 1908. The intercutting of the two scenes makes the other members of Billy's gang also seem to hit Garrett, the old man, in the present.

The historical irony is clear. By killing the Kid, Garrett has unintentionally brought about a chain of events that ultimately leads to his own death many years later. By slowing down, interrupting, paralleling, and returning to events, Peckinpah's montage fractures time and reorganizes it in a symbolic and metaphorical way that brings out this historical irony for the viewer.

One of the most creative and imaginative sequences in *The Graduate* (1967) uses associational montage to show the hero, Benjamin (Dustin Hoffman), spending his days floating in his parent's backyard swimming pool and hanging around the house, and his nights making love with his next door neighbor, Mrs. Robinson (Anne Bancroft). The associative properties of the montage make a blur of time and place. The viewer knows that a great deal of time is passing—days, probably weeks—but can't say exactly how much. Most remarkably of all, different places and locations seem to blend into one another in a dreamlike way.

In the first shot of the montage (**a**), Ben gets out of the pool and puts on a white shirt and walks into his parent's house, pushing open the patio door. In shot 2 (**b-1**), Ben enters through a door wearing the white shirt, but he is now in Mrs. Robinson's bedroom. The strong match on action—Ben exiting screen left in the previous shot and entering screen right in the present shot—makes it seem as if he has walked into his parent's house where Mrs. Robinson is waiting in the bedroom.

Ben then sits with his head against the black headboard of a bed as Mrs. Robinson unbuttons his shirt (**b-2**). Shot 3 (**c-1**) is a close-up of Ben's head against a black background. The viewer assumes it to be the bed on which he was lying in the previous shot, especially because his facial expression matches in both shots. Ben then gets up, crosses the room, and closes the door, beyond which his parents are sitting at the dining room table (**c-2**). They glance at him as he closes the door. Ben recrosses the room and sits in a black chair in front of a television set (**c-3**).

Obviously, this is not the same room that the viewer saw him enter in the previous shot. Shot 4 (**d-1**) is a close-up of Ben's face against a black background, this time assumed to be the chair in front of the television. The camera then zooms out to reveal the bedroom with Mrs. Robinson dressing (**d-2**). She leaves. Once again, the viewer has been misled. The room in which Ben sits in shot 4 is not the same room where he was sitting in shot 3. Shot 5 (**e-1**) cuts to a close-up of Ben's face, once more against a black background. This time the viewer assumes it to be the bed on which he was lying in shot 4, but the camera zooms out to reveal that the background is a series of black cushions propped up in his bedroom in his parent's house (**e-2**). He glances out his window, puts on his swim trunks, and goes down the stairs. In shot 6 (not pictured), his mother watches him dive into the pool. Shot 7 is a close-up of Ben swimming under water. In shot 8 (**g**), he leaps up onto the inflatable raft, and shot 9 (**h**) is a matched cut on action as Ben is moving on top of Mrs. Robinson in bed.

Continuity principles, such as matches on action, have been followed in this sequence to create the overall, disorienting, dreamlike effect in which times and places are indistinct and melt into one another. This is a slower, more seductive representation of

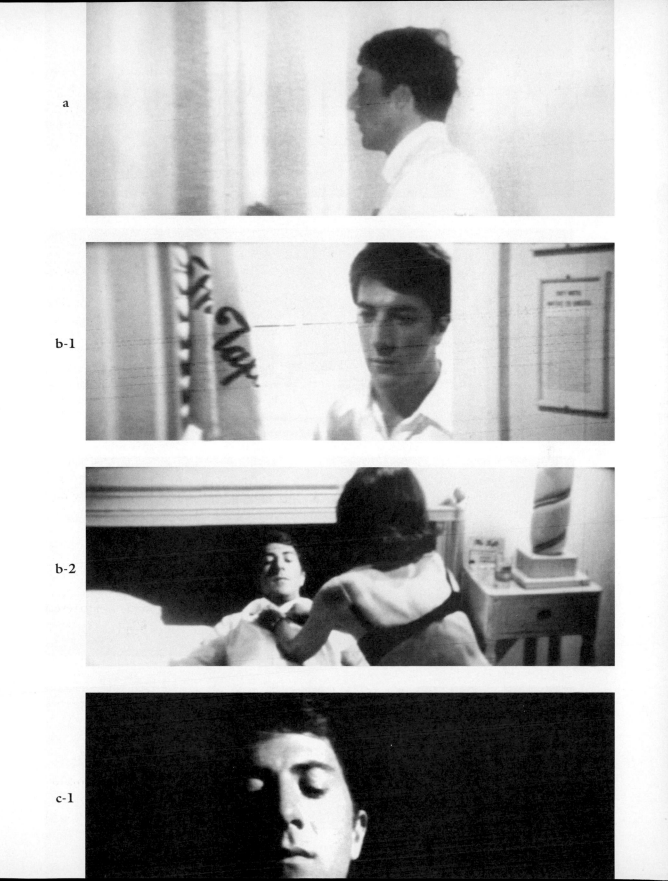

a

b-1

b-2

c-1

c-2

c-3

d-1

d-2

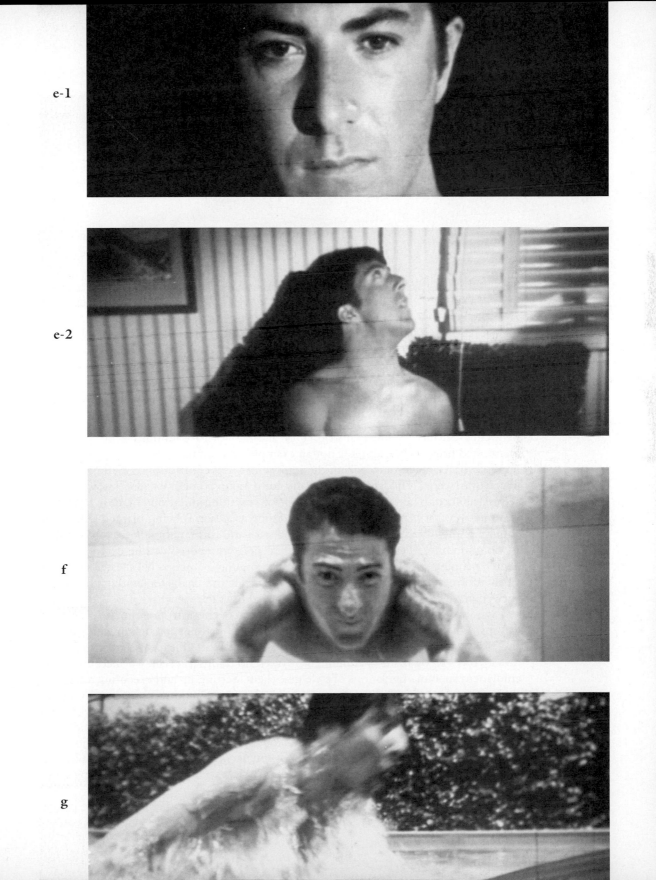

e-1

e-2

f

g

h

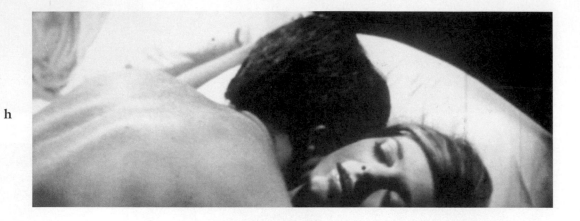

the breakdown of natural, "realistic" time than in the more violent, hard-edged montages of Peckinpah's films, but here, too, the viewer is invited to draw a clear series of associations across the cuts. In this case, the associations are psychological, having to do with Ben's alienated frame of mind. He is in a daze, disconnected from all of his environments, lonely and unhappy, sleepwalking through his life, barely conscious of his connection either to his parents or to Mrs. Robinson.

Sequence Shots   A fourth category of alternatives to continuity editing will be mentioned briefly, although it is not an example of montage proper. Instead, it is the opposite of montage, minimizing the importance and contribution of editing to the effect of a scene. This is the use of the **long take,** sometimes also known as the **sequence shot.** The term refers to a shot of very long duration. In *Easy Rider* the two motorcyclist heroes visit a hippy commune as a crop is being planted. All of the commune members gather to offer their thanks and to pray for a successful harvest. As noted in an earlier chapter, the prayer scene is composed of one extended 360-degree panning shot across the faces of the commune members. No master shot provides information about the overall positioning of the characters within the room. Viewers have to infer this as the camera pans across their faces.

Viewers sometimes wonder why the filmmakers chose to present the scene this way instead of using a more conventional continuity-driven approach in which inserts and close-ups are intercut with reference to a master shot. One answer to such a question involves recognizing that filmmakers often do things a certain way because of the enjoyment such manipulations of style give them. Setting up and executing a difficult shot can be an end in itself, offering its own pleasure, often sufficiently rewarding in itself. Certainly, a 360-degree panning shot can be a difficult shot to execute well, and it is one that viewers don't often see in films. Beyond this level of creative fulfillment, however, one should also point to the obvious symbolic dimensions of the shot. The complete circle formed by the camera's movements offers an image of unity, strength, and connectedness, which the filmmakers are using to characterize the hippy commune at this point in the narrative.

Long takes do not always have to be sequence shots. Sometimes a scene can be composed of several long takes. In Orson Welles' *Citizen Kane* (1941), Kane's parents strike a deal with a banker, Mr. Thatcher, in which the bank will act as Kane's guardian and assume control over his estate until he comes of age. The scene is largely presented in two long takes that, together, run for almost four minutes of screen time.

Both *Easy Rider* and *Citizen Kane* were films that broke with the standard rules of commercial filmmaking in their periods. Long takes and sequence shots, by minimizing editing, tend to impose a slower pace upon the narrative than does the quick cutting employed in *L.A. Story*. For this reason, these techniques are used less frequently in the commercial cinema. Studio executives worry about not "hooking" the audience and often prefer fast editing to an artistic use of a sequence shot or long take.

SUMMARY

Almost universally, filmmakers have regarded editing as the most important phase of production in terms of its ability to give the finished film a distinct shape, organization, and emotional power. There is, however, no one way to cut a scene or a film. Commercial filmmakers—crafting entertaining films for a diverse audience—value clarity of construction and immediacy of effect. The story has to be easily understood but emotionally compelling.

Continuity editing rules are the appropriate ones to follow. Continuity editing establishes a coherent and orderly physical world on screen, despite variations in camera placement and angle. The codes dealing with the maintenance of consistent directionality and the matching of visual elements from shot to shot help establish a stable physical world on screen. Continuity errors occur when mismatched visual elements violate the perceptual constants that a viewer looks for in the world represented on screen. If Julia Roberts is eating a croissant in one breakfast scene, she should not be eating a pancake in the next.

Realism is an elastic concept, however, and the physical and perceptual laws that continuity editing tries to honor can be subjected to distortion and manipulation. Understanding them as permissible expressions of style or artistry, viewers will accept many such manipulations. Editing enables filmmakers to create extreme distortions of time and space, some of which are inconsistent with strict continuity principles but may nevertheless be found in films that are major box-office successes. Although continuity principles furnish the basic pattern from which narrative motion pictures are constructed, the craft of editing is infinitely powerful in its ability to reorganize time and space, and many approaches to editing are permissible under the rubric of style.

Whatever approach a given filmmaker might use, if he or she is making a feature film and telling a story, the option of avoiding editing does not exist. Hitchcock, a director for whom editing was of great importance, once tried to do without it. In *Rope* (1948), he cut only when the camera physically ran out of film (approximately every ten minutes) and tried through elaborate means to hide the cuts when they did occur. The result is an interesting experiment but a sluggish film that lacks the dramatic rhythms and intensity that only editing can create. To be a filmmaker is to select, manipulate, sequence, and cut!

SUGGESTED READINGS

Ken Dancyger, *The Technique of Film and Video Editing* (Stoneham, MA: Focal Press, 1993).

Sergei Eisenstein, *Film Form* and *The Film Sense* (New York: Harcourt, Brace and World, 1949).

Vincent LoBrutto, *Selected Takes: Film Editors on Film Editing* (New York: Praeger, 1991).

Gabriella Oldham, *First Cut: Conversations with Film Editors* (Berkeley and Los Angeles: University of California Press, 1992).

Karel Reisz and Gavin Millar, *The Technique of Film Editing*, second edition (Boston: Focal Press, 1983).

Ralph Rosenblum, *When the Shooting Stops . . . the Cutting Begins: A Film Editor's Story* (New York: Viking Press, 1979).

Chapter 5

Principles of Sound Design

Chapter Objectives

After reading this chapter, you should be able to

- explain the nature of sound design, its expressive uses, and how it builds on the viewer's real-life acoustical skills and experience

- distinguish between realistic and synthetic sounds

- explain the fundamental differences between sound and image

- differentiate direct sound, reflected sound, and ambient sound

- explain six basic codes of sound design and their expressive uses

- explain how sound establishes continuity in film as well as intellectual and emotional effects

- describe how alterations of synchronous with nonsynchronous sound enable camera perspective to become very flexible

- explain the use and functions of dialogue in film

- describe sound-effects design and Foley techniques

- describe five steps for creating movie music

- explain five basic functions music performs in film

- understand how sound influences the content of images as well as viewers' interpretation of those images

Key Terms and Concepts

sound design
sound designer
realistic sound
synthetic sounds
direct sound
reflected sound
ambient sound
room tone

sound perspective
post-dubbing
synchronous sound
nonsynchronous sound
sound bridge
off-screen sound space
speech

voice-over narration
dialogue cutting point
Foley technique
spotting
temp track
cue sheet
leitmotif

Image editing employs standard rules and techniques that (1) provide editors with methods for organizing shots; (2) establish constancies of time and space between the story world on screen and viewers' experiences of their physical environment; and (3) are based on correspondence with the viewer's perceptual experience and have become familiar to viewers through constant repetition over many films. Like image editing, film sound has its own rules or codes of structural design. Sound editing, like image editing, is rule governed, and many visual techniques have equivalents in sound. One can speak of sound fades, sound cuts, sound dissolves, and sound perspective.

This apparent equivalence, though, can be misleading because sound performs a variety of unique functions in film. This chapter explains the concept of sound design, examines the basic principles of sound design, and discusses the three categories or types of sound in film: dialogue, effects, and music.

☐ SOUND DESIGN

Modern motion picture sound is extraordinarily sophisticated. Filmmakers today employ elaborate mixes of many different sound elements. On *Apocalypse Now* (1979), sound designer Walter Murch and his crew manipulated 160 tracks of recorded sounds that were mixed together to create the finished soundtrack. The complexity of modern film sound and its increasing importance in the artistic design of a film require a new creative member of the production team—the sound designer. **Sound design** is the expressive use of sound throughout a film in relation to its images and the contents of its narrative. The **sound designer** conceptualizes and executes this design. Walter Murch's brilliant work on *Apocalypse Now* elicited the credit "sound design" because of Murch's key contributions to the film's overall artistic effect. Since then, the term has come into general usage.

Sound design goes far beyond the routine technical challenges of getting audible sound and mixing effects and music with dialogue. Sound designers create a total sound environment for the film's images, an environment that not only supports the images but extends their meaning in dynamic ways. The sound design of a film builds a mix of *realistic sound* and *synthetic sound*. **Realistic sound** derives from actual sources, such as footsteps, the human voice, or automobile engines, although the sound designer may subject these to creative manipulation for expressive effect. For example, the sound design in *The Silence of the Lambs* (1991) made the serial killer Buffalo Bill especially sinister by accentuating the base tones in actor Ted Levine's voice. Unlike realistic sounds, **synthetic sounds** are invented and have no counterpart in actual life, but they easily link with images on screen and extend, in a totally convincing manner, the meaning of those images. The voice of Steven Spielberg's character E.T. synthesized a mix of multiple sounds including animals as well as people. In *Return of the Jedi* (1983), the sounds of the laser guns and the air motorcycles were created by electronically modifying and re-recording a mixture of sound sources.

The modern film audience is privileged to experience film soundtracks of unprecedented complexity and subtlety. Extremely sensitive audio equipment enables modern sound designers to create highly sophisticated manipulations of sound information. These manipulations are rule governed and exploit unique properties of sound that differentiate them from a film's image track.

Differences between Sound and Image

Sound designers orchestrate sound in relation to the images provided by the director and cinematographer, understanding that sound and images are uniquely different from one another. Two kinds of difference exist with respect to (1) what viewers notice about pictures and sound and (2) how sound and pictures structure time.

Perception of Image and Sound
Obviously, images are visible and can be seen and sound cannot. Like images, sound is cut and spliced, but it is done on magnetic tape. Image edits, whether cuts, fades, or dissolves, can be seen on screen. Sound splices are inaudible. Images can be touched. Sound cannot. It is less obvious that viewers notice images and, in important ways,

Apocalypse Now (United Artists, 1979)
To this shot of a spinning ceiling fan, sound designer Walter Murch added the sound of a helicopter propeller. This audiovisual combination places equal stress on image and sound components. Neither is dominant. Frame enlargement.

tend to be less explicitly aware of sound design. It also means that viewers think of cinema as an essentially visual medium, with sound as the back-up element, there only to support the images.

Because of this, viewers tend to interpret sound in reference to images. The information sound conveys is contextualized by viewers in terms of the image on screen. Viewers relate sounds to the images on screen and define them by those images. Often, though, it is sound that structures the image.

These interpretational habits persist even when they are inappropriate to the ways a film links image and sound. Walter Murch created one of the most memorable image-sound juxtapositions in *Apocalypse Now* by adding a helicopter sound to a shot of a spinning ceiling fan. Viewers hear a helicopter engine and propeller but see the spinning blades of the fan. In this striking contrast, sound and image are equally assertive, equally important, and they define each other through contrast. Viewers may think of the image here as being more important, but in actuality the helicopter sound contextualizes the image as much as it contextualizes the sound.

Sally Potter's *Orlando* (1993) portrays an Elizabethan-era youth who lives for hundreds of years during which time he changes into a woman. At the dawn of the industrial age, the heroine rides a horse through a field and stares with intense amazement off screen. On the soundtrack, viewers hear the roar of a passing train, but on screen all they see is some stream curl around the heroine's face. The sound here totally defines what viewers think they see and what they understand the character to be responding to.

This is the aesthetic paradox on which sound design rests—viewers notice images, even when sound is defining the content of those images and the way viewers interpret them. Sound design is an extremely powerful, but, for viewers, little-noticed element of film form.

Structuring Time

A second important difference between image and sound lies in the way sound can provide images with direction in time. Many shots, unless they contain explicit movement, are ambiguous with respect to time. They could be run forward or backward with little noticeable difference. A long shot of a forest or the exterior of a house is ambiguous in this way, but not a shot of traffic or joggers because the movement here provides direction in time. Viewers could tell whether the latter two images, but not necessarily the first two were run backwards.

Sound gives images that lack it a direction in time. With sound, viewers perceive such images as moving forward unambiguously. George Stevens' Western *Shane* (1953) clearly illustrates this principle. Stevens realized that a man dismounting a horse can look much more graceful than when he is climbing into the saddle. Accordingly, when the film's villain climbs into the saddle, the film editor used a shot of the character *dismounting* but played in reverse. The sound in the scene—a gurgling stream, wind, off-screen dialogue from other characters—gives the shot a clear forward momentum. Viewers aware of the trick can see that the shot is played backwards, but for most viewers—unaware of the editing magic at work—the sleight of hand passes unnoticed because of the way the shot is paired with sound that is clearly directional in time.

Sound gives images forward momentum or increases the momentum that the shots already possess. Sound temporalizes—adds directional time to—images. This is the principle that underlies all of the codes of sound continuity that will be discussed in this chapter. But creating continuity is only one of the achievements of sophisticated sound design, which, like image editing, is a rule-governed practice. What are the basic rules and procedures for manipulating sounds and for establishing relationships with images?

Shane
(Paramount Pictures, 1953)
Jack Palance, as the villainous gunfighter in *Shane* dismounts. Later in the scene, this same shot is presented again, in reverse, but viewers fail to notice the trickery because the ambient sound provides directional continuity and forward momentum. Frame enlargement.

☐ THE CODES OF SOUND DESIGN

The codes or rules of sound design construct an audio environment, a world of sound, that surrounds and modifies film images. Sound designers work with three types of sound—dialogue, effects, and music—and with three characteristics of sound in the audio environment—*direct sound, reflected sound,* and *ambient sound.*

Direct sound is sound that comes immediately from the source. It is spoken or recorded directly into the microphone and, therefore, usually conveys little environmental information. By contrast, **reflected sound** is sound that is first reflected off surrounding surfaces in the environment to produce a slight reverberation. It does not come directly to the microphone. Differing surfaces reflect sounds in differing ways, and these differences convey important information about the kind of physical environment in which the sound occurs. Hard surfaces such as glass or metal bounce sound quickly and efficiently whereas softer surfaces, such as carpeting or cushioned furniture, are less reflective. They absorb sound and, in extreme cases, may deaden sound.

Sound environments, then, can be characterized in terms of their sound-reflective or sound-deadening properties. Sound designers pay close attention to these features so that the audio environments they create for a film are not in glaring contradiction to the physical requirements of a scene or setting. Sound needs to reverberate in Edward Scissorhands' huge, vacant castle, but not on the western plains in *Dances With Wolves* (1990).

Notice that these characteristics of sound—its levels of directness and reverberation—communicate information about physical environments on screen, just as they do in actual life. Filmmakers build on these features to make film sound convey information about physical space in ways that establish clear correspondences with viewers' experiences of sound in everyday life.

Dances With Wolves
(Orion Pictures, 1990)
Audio environments created for film generally match the physical environments shown on screen. In this way, sound conveys essential information about space. Sound does not reverberate on the open plains in *Dances With Wolves.*

The third kind of sound in the audio environment is **ambient sound.** This term refers to generalized noises in the recording environment. If shooting takes place out of doors, ambient sounds may include the airplane traveling overhead, the cries of children playing in the distance, or the sound of wind in the trees. Ambient sound is found in all recording environments, even in an empty room. If a scene occurs in an empty room without any explicit sound, the soundtrack will not be dead or silent. Instead, it will carry room tone, the acoustical properties of the room itself, the imperceptible sounds that it makes. **Room tone** is a low level of ambient noise, and it indicates that the audio environment created by sound design is never silent or dead but always conveys some audio information.

These characteristics of sound in the audio environment are manipulated by sound designers to construct the finished soundtrack viewers hear when watching a movie. In creating that soundtrack, designers employ six essential codes of sound design: (1) the sound hierarchy; (2) sound perspective; (3) synchronous and nonsynchronous sound; (4) sound bridges; (5) off-screen sound space; and (6) sound montage.

The Sound Hierarchy

Because of the variety of sounds within the audio environment and the need to organize them to facilitate the viewer's understanding of story information, sound designers customarily treat them in terms of a hierarchy of importance. When filmmakers manipulate dialogue, sound effects, and music within a scene, the hierarchy of relationships typically emphasizes dialogue. Filmmakers generally consider dialogue the most important of the sound elements in a scene, and the volume of sound effects and music is usually kept at a softer level than dialogue.

Everyone has seen movies where an important character dies during a noisy battle. Often, the character makes a little speech before dying. When this occurs, the battle sounds invariably drop below the volume level of the character's dialogue. Then, once the character dies, the battle sounds rise again to their previous level. The hierarchy of sound relationships gives precedence to dialogue during otherwise noisy scenes. Prevailing assumptions stipulate that dialogue should always be clear, crisp, and understandable to the viewer.

Alternative Ways of Organizing Sound Types

The standard hierarchy is not employed in every film. Some filmmakers have deliberately avoided it. In the early 1970s, one major American filmmaker revolutionized sound recording techniques in ways that challenged the dominant place of the actor's voice in the hierarchy of sound. In *McCabe and Mrs. Miller* (1971), *California Split* (1974), *Nashville* (1975), and other works, director Robert Altman pioneered the use of multichannel, multitrack sound recording.

Rather than using a single boom mike (a microphone hung on a long pole suspended over a scene to record the voices of the actors), Altman employed radio mikes. Each actor was separately miked, and the recorded voice was transmitted to a recording receiver. Working with eight-track sound enabled Altman to simultaneously record the voices of up to seven actors.

In the sound mix, Altman then refused to grant any of the characters a predominant position in the sound environment. In some of the crowd scenes in *California*

ROBERT ALTMAN

Although Altman directed his first feature in the mid-1950s (*The Delinquents*, 1955), the 1970s saw him gain prominence as a leading American filmmaker. Unlike George Lucas, Steven Spielberg, or, in an earlier period, Alfred Hitchcock, Altman was never at home in the studio system. His career exhibits considerable friction and tension between the cynicism and European-style ambiguities of his films, with their offbeat audiovisual and narrative style, and the conventional norms of mainstream studio filmmaking.

With *M*A*S*H* (1970), Altman embarked on a series of revisionist genre films that displayed his own critical, questioning relationship with Hollywood norms. Ostensibly about the Korean War but really about Vietnam, *M*A*S*H* irreverently dissected war film clichés and became a counterculture hit. In short

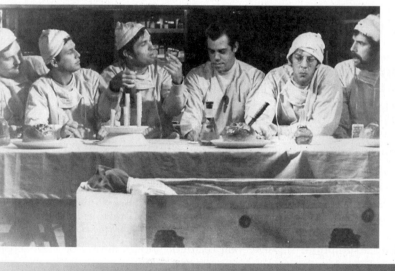

M*A*S*H (Twentieth Century Fox, 1970) Altman's films typically feature a large cast of performers, a dense sound mix with overlapping dialogue, and a loose, unstructured narrative. *M*A*S*H* is a dark comedy about Army surgeons during the Korean War, but everyone knew the film was really about Vietnam. The composition in this scene aludes to DaVinci's *Last Supper*.

Split, for example, many actors speak at once. The dialogue sounds multilayered and is full of overlapping speech. In addition, the radio mikes pick up ambient noises, like the rustle of clothing, which usually are not captured by more standard recording techniques. As a result, the audio environment in an Altman film is extremely rich and multidimensional, and the voice does not always predominate over other environmental sounds.

Alman's approach frustrated many critics because they were used to the standard sound hierarchy in which all voices were clearly modulated and balanced so that dialogue was never inaudible or obscured by competing sounds. His films of the early 1970s were extremely controversial, which indicates how important the standard sound hierarchy is in shaping not just film production but also critical responses to films.

order, Altman self-consciously revised the Western (*McCabe and Mrs. Miller,* 1971), the detective film (*The Long Goodbye,* 1973), and the gangster film (*Thieves Like Us,* 1974).

Founding the Lion's Gate production company in 1970, Altman began to explore multitrack sound recording in these films, but obtained mixed results until teaming with production mixer James Webb on *California Split* (1974). Henceforth, an uncommonly dense audio track distinguished Altman's work, featuring multiple, overlapping, layered effects and dialogue. In a clear departure from studio style, Altman's preferred sound design stressed complexity and ambiguity of speech and effects.

Altman reached his summit in the 1970s with *Nashville* (1975), a kaleidoscopic, multinarrative portrait of politics and country music that was an enormous critical success. Following this, Altman rapidly fell from grace in the studio system. His next films—*Buffalo Bill and the Indians* (1976), *A Wedding* (1978), *Quintet* (1979), and *A Perfect Couple* (1979)—were deemed excessively uncommercial by their studios and barely released. *Health* (1979) was shelved by its distributor.

Despite being given the assignment to direct *Popeye* (1980), Altman was now deemed unemployable by Hollywood. But instead of fading away or descending into bitterness, he simply continued working as an independent. For the next decade, he made mostly small-scale adaptations of theater plays (*Come Back to the Five and Dime, Jimmie Dean, Jimmie Dean,* 1982; *Streamers,* 1983; *Fool For Love,* 1985), but scored a triumphant return to prominent feature filmmaking with *The Player* (1992), a trenchant, caustic satire of a deal-driven, sequel-oriented Hollywood system. Ironically, the film was a hit inside Hollywood, which, oddly enough, welcomed Altman back. He followed *The Player* with another critical hit, *Short Cuts* (1993), an acidic, cynical adaptation of Raymond Carver short stories about Los Angeles. Altman was back on top. His next film, *Ready-to-Wear,* (1994), about the fashion industry, featured the cynical comedy, large, ensemble cast, and loose, wayward narrative that are essential Altman signatures.

Despite the wayward turns of his career, Altman's work has been consistently intelligent and stylistically experimental. His multitrack sound recording and kaleidoscopic, fragmented narratives are among his most recognizable features of style. In addition, Altman approaches each film as a collaboration among cast and crew. Minimizing directorial ego, he openly solicits ideas and input from others on the set and views his job as a facilitator and coordinator of the team's effort. Accordingly, his reputation among actors and crew is outstanding. Major stars eagerly accept cameo roles in his films because they want the experience of participating in the unique atmosphere of an Altman production.

Alternative Organizations of Sound Types in Early Cinema   Contemporary sound design has become extraordinarily sophisticated compared with the relative importance accorded sound in earlier periods. Some films from the early sound period feature alternative hierarchies of sound, different ways of organizing the three sound types. One occasionally finds an incomplete sound environment, a limited set of sounds in the audio space. (This term *audio space* is a bit imaginative, but, as will be seen when discussing sound perspective, sound does help create spatial relationships on screen, and it may reliably reflect the properties of physical space.)

In Sergei Eisenstein's first sound film, *Alexander Nevsky* (1936), about a Russian folk hero who repulsed a German invasion in the thirteenth century, music and dialogue tend to predominate in the sound structure of the film, with background ambient sound and sound effects used less extensively. Sometimes, in fact, ambient sound and sound effects are completely missing from scenes.

At the beginning of the movie, for example, a group of Mongol warriors visits Alexander Nevsky's fishing village. Viewers hear the sounds of their horses and armor as they arrive, but, on leaving, they make no sound at all. Their exit is completely silent. Later in the film, during the visually impressive sequence that details the burning of the city of Pskov and the slaughter of its inhabitants by the invading German army, viewers hear only music and dialogue without any sound effects. Even in close-up shots of the faces of screaming, crying children, viewers hear no screams.

During the climax of the film, the epic battle on a frozen lake between Nevsky's armies and the invading Germans, music and sound effects alternate one at a time. The music plays for a while and then stops, and viewers hear sound effects (swords clashing, men shouting). Then the sound effects stop, and the music begins again. These manipulations of sound may strike a modern moviegoer's ears as rather crude and unrealistic because of the peculiar manner in which effects and music have been edited so that they are never co-present and because of the lack of detail in the film's audio space, when compared with its often striking images.

Because the audio structure of a film is made up of discrete types of sound—music, dialogue, and effects—recorded in ways that suggest either direct sound, reflected sound, or ambient sound, most films establish a clear hierarchy of sound relationships that generally give the voice a privileged pride of place and surround the voice with music and important sound effects. However, as the examples of Robert Altman and Eisenstein's *Alexander Nevsky* indicate, not all films follow the conventional hierarchy in which voice, effects, and music are co-present but in carefully regulated volumes.

Sound Perspective

Because sounds may be recorded either directly or as they are reflected by an environment, filmmakers can use sound to communicate properties of physical space. Just as one can talk of visual perspective, therefore, one can talk of **sound perspective,** that is, sound that embodies the properties of the physical spaces seen on screen.

Alexander Nevsky (1936)
The soundtrack of *Alexander Nevsky* makes minimal use of sound effects and ambient sound even where images, such as this one showing a screaming child, suggest highly specific sounds. Frame enlargement.

Sound perspective in film is the use of sound to convey information about physical space. Sound perspective establishes correspondences with the viewer's acoustic perception of space in everyday life. Viewers can process and interpret this audio information about space in cinema just as they do in their real-world environments. As with visual correspondences, these audio correspondences facilitate the viewer's ability to understand a film's meaning and content.

Sound perspective often, but not always, correlates with visual perspective. If the action is presented in long shot, viewers also hear the sound as if from a distance. To establish this correlation, designers structure sound perspective in terms of the proportion of direct to reflected sound. On screen, as in everyday life, as the sound source gets more distant from the camera, the properties of reflected sound increase. As the sound source comes closer to the camera, the amount of reflected sound decreases. The use of reflected sound enables filmmakers to establish the location of a sound source within the visual space on screen.

If the action is presented to the viewer in close-up, direct sound should predominate over reflected sound. The sounds of actors' voices should be intimate and should sound as if they are spoken close to and directly into the microphone. Sound designer Walter Murch has stated that, with respect to sound perspective, he believes that he records not just sounds in the environment, but also the spaces between the listener and those sounds. In actual practice, however, microphone placement does not exactly parallel camera placement. Although the difference in camera placement between a close-up and a long shot may be very great, the difference in actual microphone placement may only be a matter of several feet.

Sound Perspective in Early Films

As with other attributes of film structure, filmmakers did not grasp the complexities of sound design all at once. The process of discovery was gradual. Sound came to the movies in the late 1920s, and filmmakers then had to figure out what could be done with it. Because of this and because early sound technology was quite limiting, soundtracks in many early films were less detailed and less reflective of the realities of sound space.

French director René Clair's *Under the Roofs of Paris* (1930), for example, is a mixture of pantomime, music, and some dialogue. Much of the film was shot silently, with a few talking sequences added later. At the beginning of the film, the camera booms down from the rooftops to the streets of Paris where a song salesman is performing a new tune for a group of onlookers. Viewers hear the song throughout the camera movement, and, as the camera draws closer, the song's volume increases. There is, however, no apparent change in reverberation.

At the end of the scene, the camera booms back up to the rooftops. This time the volume of the song does not decrease as much as it should given the amount of physical space the camera crosses. Again, there is no change in reverberation. The perspectives established by visual space and audio space do not correlate well. Because viewers hear direct sound during all of the camera's movements, there is an inconsistent rendering of sound space.

Pointing out this feature of *Under the Roofs of Paris* does not imply that René Clair is an inferior filmmaker because such is clearly not the case. Clair was one of the most important early practitioners of sound and a filmmaker whose career straddled the

Under the Roofs of Paris
(1930)
Correct sound perspective is not a feature of every film. The relationship of audio space and camera perspective often proves to be quite flexible. In *Under the Roofs of Paris,* as the camera travels from the rooftops to the street below, the appropriate changes in audio space do not occur. Frame enlargement.

silent and sound periods. Moreover, his work was a decided influence upon the American master Charlie Chaplin. Clair's film *A Nous La Liberté* (1931) was the inspiration for Chaplin's *Modern Times* (1936). The point here is to emphasize that these codes of sound design are learned applications of style that filmmakers gradually discovered as a way of creating credible audiovisual relationships on screen. The design difference between an early film such as *Under the Roofs of Paris* and a later film such as *Apocalypse Now* shows an extraordinary process of learning on the part of filmmakers.

Alternative Sound Perspectives

As with the hierarchy of sound relationships, filmmakers can play with sound perspective. French director Jacques Tati is one of the masters of sound cinema. Tati was a pantomime comedian whose films bear some relationships to silent comedies. Sound in Tati's films is unique. Dialogue is minimal, and the sound space is dominated by a multitude of carefully organized environmental sounds. Tati subjected his soundtracks to **post-dubbing.** After filming was done in the studio, he post-recorded the important sound effects and then manipulated their volume and reverberation to emphasize and change them in ways he could not have done had he recorded sound on the set during filming.

In Tati's masterpiece, *Playtime* (1967), he playfully distorts standard sound perspective. Early in the film, the main character, Mr. Hulot (played by Tati himself), is trying to keep an appointment with an official named Mr. Giffard. When Hulot tries to meet the official, he is instructed by the building's doorman to wait beside a bank of elevators while Mr. Giffard is paged. Hulot waits patiently, framed at screen left, while, on screen right, a vast, receding hallway extends into the distance. Hulot is seated around the edge of the wall, however, so he cannot look down this hallway. But the viewer can.

As Hulot waits, loud footsteps occur off screen. Because of their extraordinary volume, the viewer assumes the person these feet belong to must be very close by. However, a tiny figure appears in the distance at the end of the hallway. This is joke number one, reversing the expectation viewers developed based on the probable sound-space/image-space relation. The distant figure walks rapidly but advances slowly because of the length of the hallway. Due to the extraordinarily reflective and conductive properties of the glass, metal, and tile hallway, the footsteps remain loud and increase only slightly in volume as the man approaches. This is joke number two. The

Playtime (1967)
Director Jacques Tati satirizes sound perspective in this scene from *Playtime* by making sound perspective an unreliable indicator of visual space. The sound of Mr. Giffard's footsteps remains extremely loud and distinct despite the extraordinary amount of time it takes him to walk the length of this hallway. Frame enlargement.

third joke in the scene occurs as Tati, hearing the man but unable to see him, keeps trying to get up, assuming that he must be close given the loudness of his steps. The doorman, however, who can look down the hallway, keeps gesturing for Hulot to stay seated.

This scene is composed of a single shot, and the three distinct jokes that occur in it are all based on Tati's playful manipulation of the sound-space/image-space relation. In this case, sound perspective is an unreliable indicator of visual space and of the physical relations in the scene.

Tati's playful satire of sound perspective is, of course, meant to be a source of comedy. A noncomical alternative to classical sound perspective sometimes appears in contemporary films in which filmmakers reverse the relationship of sound and image perspective by filming actors in long shot but recording their dialogue in intimate terms. Peter Weir's *Dead Poets Society* (1989) deals with the relationship between an unconventional English teacher and his students in an elite prep school in 1959. One of the boys discusses with his friend his excitement over getting the lead role in the school play. The two boys stand on a pier next to the water and are filmed in extreme long shot. Their voices, however, have been miked in intimate terms so that they speak directly into the microphone without reflected sound. The audio space is close; the visual space is distant.

The scene reverses conventional sound perspective, with audio perspective inversely related to visual perspective. This reversal is a clear example of the cinema's transformational property, its ability to transform perceptual realities in ways viewers readily accept. The cinema records *and* transforms audiovisual information, and one must grasp both of these activities before one can have a comprehensive understanding of how films work.

Synchronous and NonSynchronous Sound

Filmmakers employ sound in both synchronous and nonsynchronous ways. **Synchronous sound** is matched with a clear source on screen. **Nonsynchronous sound** does not correspond with any visible source on screen. It is source-disconnected sound because, although viewers hear the sound, they cannot see its source.

In any given scene, sound designers employ both categories. Some sounds are connected to a source on screen, others are not. Synchronous sound occurs if viewers see Daniel Day-Lewis as Hawkeye in *The Last of the Mohicans* (1993) tell a British officer that he will not serve in the English army. If, by contrast, the camera stays on the British officer while Hawkeye speaks off screen, nonsynchronous sound is employed.

Switching between synchronous and nonsynchronous sound gives filmmakers enormous flexibility in the editing of their films. Not everything that is heard needs to be shown. This frees the camera from being a slave to dialogue or other sounds and enables it to reveal aspects of the scene independently of what viewers hear on the soundtrack. All a filmmaker need do is return periodically to image-sound synchronization in order to sustain the viewer's sense of important audiovisual relationships.

Sound Bridges

The distinction between synchronous and nonsynchronous sound is relevant to understanding how filmmakers use sound to establish continuity across shots. Because

The Last of the Mohicans (Twentieth Century Fox, 1993)
A sound bridge, composed of dialogue and ambient sound, links these different visual spaces provided by changing camera perspectives. The images contain no common elements, but the sound bridge establishes that they are parts of a single, extended locale. Frame enlargements.

sound gives images a clear direction and orientation in time—with sound, film images clearly move forward—sound can establish continuity of time across the shot changes in a scene. In the example from *The Last of the Mohicans,* viewers perceive continuity of time during the reaction shot of the British officer because they still hear other characters speaking. This enables viewers to know where in time to locate the shot of the officer. It also lets viewers know where in space to locate the shot. Because they can hear the other characters, viewers know the officer is close by.

Sound, then, can be used to establish continuity of time and space. Typically, this occurs through the use of a **sound bridge,** as in the example from *The Last of the Mohicans.* Dialogue or sound effects are laid across, or bridge, two or more shots or scenes, unifying them in time and/or space. In the early German sound film *The Blue Angel* (1930), as the schoolmaster (played by Emil Jannings) removes his handkerchief to blow his nose, the action cuts to a reaction shot of the schoolboys. While looking at them, viewers hear the sound of Jannings blowing his nose. Switching from synchronous to nonsynchronous sound, the image shifts from one containing the sound source to one that does not. Sound flows over the cut, establishing a continuity that links up the different images. In dialogue scenes using the shot-reverse-shot technique, passages of spoken dialogue will flow over the cuts to establish continuity across the shot changes.

Sound bridges, then, are characterized by a shift between synchronous and nonsynchronous sound in a way that establishes unities of action and time across the cut or scene transition. This is one of the most powerful and important uses of sound and clearly one of the most subliminal.

Alternative Sound Bridges

In contemporary films, filmmakers often employ a modified sound bridge in which the switch to nonsynchronous sound occurs before the cut, rather than after it. In recent films, sound cuts may precede the visual transition. In Mike Nichols' *The Graduate* (1967), a striking sequence expresses the social and emotional alienation of the young hero, Benjamin (played by Dustin Hoffman), when he dons a scuba suit and seeks refuge at the bottom of his parents' swimming pool. The camera films him alone

---

The Graduate (Avco-Embassy, 1967)
A creative noncorrespondence between image and sound in *The Graduate*. The sound bridge to the next scene begins well before the end of the final shot in this, the previous scene. As the camera pulls away from Benjamin (Dustin Hoffman) in the swimming pool, viewers hear him talking on the telephone in the next scene. Frame enlargement.

and isolated in the depths of the pool. As the camera tracks slowly away from him, viewers hear sound from the next scene (which occurs in a phone booth) for a few seconds before the cut. It is Benjamin talking on the telephone to invite Mrs. Robinson, his next-door neighbor, to meet him at a local hotel.

The sound of Benjamin on the phone, asynchronous with the shot of him in the pool, technically violates the time and space of the pool scene, but viewers accept this sound editing as a novel, interesting, and offbeat way of signaling the transition to the next scene. *The Graduate* was released in 1967. At the time this was a playful way of making the transition, although it has become more standard since.

Off-Screen Sound Space

Just as the distinction between synchronous and nonsynchronous sound is relevant for understanding principles of sound continuity, it also helps explain how sound can extend the viewer's perception of images. Nonsynchronous sound—sound occurring off screen—extends and enlarges the viewer's perception of the world represented on screen. That world is not co-extensive with the images on screen. Instead, through sound information, it extends into an indefinite, acoustically defined area of off-screen space. **Off-screen sound space** designates this area just beyond the frame line whose existence is defined through sound.

Nonsynchronous sound creates and defines off-screen space, extending the image beyond the borders of the frame. The viewer's perception of the extraordinary futuristic city in the science fiction film *Blade Runner* (1982) is created by more than the imaginative production design of Lawrence G. Paull. The city is acoustically defined. The sound design constructs the city as a pervasive, complex, audio presence extending into space well beyond the edges of the screen. The city is present acoustically even when it is not visible in the shots.

Extension of the frame into off-screen space is an essential technique in horror films where monsters lurk just out of sight. In Fritz Lang's *M* (1931), about the efforts of the police and the underworld to capture a child molester who murders his victims, off-screen sound is used to signal the presence of the murderer at moments when viewers cannot see him. As a little girl looks in a store window and then runs down the street, his rapid, frantic, off-screen whistling establishes his unseen presence and his desperate hunger for a new victim.

Bresson and Off-Screen Sound Space

Perhaps the most thorough and unique nonsynchronous approaches to off-screen sound space are found in the work of French director Robert Bresson. Bresson believed that images and sounds must not duplicate one another. He noted that "sound must never come to the help of an image, nor an image to the help of a sound," pointing out that when sound can replace an image, the image should either be cut or made less explicit in its dramatic or emotional content. Accordingly, Bresson's films are restrained stylistically, and the information conveyed by image and sound is carefully controlled and restricted. Bresson is acutely aware of what each channel can express, and he tries to avoid redundancy by creating images and sounds that say different things.

One of the ways he avoids redundancy is by using sound to create off-screen space, to imply the existence of things that he does not need to show. In *Pickpocket*

(1959), for example, an early sequence shows the thief trying to rob spectators at a race track. Bresson, though, never shows the track or any horses. Sound is used to establish the location and event and create the implied images. The image shows people watching something off screen, standing side by side, looking toward the camera while the soundtrack carries a race announcer's voice and the pounding of horses' hooves. These sounds create in the viewer's mind the images and impressions of a horse race. Having provided the sounds of a race, Bresson believes he does not need to show pictures. This would be redundant.

Off-screen sound is routinely used by filmmakers to extend the frame in ways that are consistent with visual information presented elsewhere in the scene or film. In *Blade Runner*, the city is a powerful acoustic presence, but it is also shown in spectacular long shots. By contrast, in the exceptional case of Bresson's cinema, sound is used to create images in the minds of viewers that are never shown on screen and which, Bresson believes, are richer than any screen image could be.

Sound Montage

Much contemporary multitrack sound design employs sound montage, the editing of sounds into highly intricate and complex patterns that create meaning and emotion through editing much as visual montages do. Viewers will accept sound montages as readily as they accept visual montages.

Apocalypse Now features one of the most creative sound montages of recent years during the opening scene as Captain Willard (Martin Sheen) lies on his bed in a Saigon hotel. Willard longs to be back in the jungle where he can safely satisfy his violent appetites in combat and by working as a paid assassin. As he lies in the hotel, Willard

Apocalypse Now (United Artists, 1979)
The beginning of *Apocalypse Now* shows Captain Willard (Martin Sheen) in a Saigon hotel room. A complex sound montage replaces Saigon's city sounds with jungle sounds to suggest Willard's desire to return to the jungle. Frame enlargement.

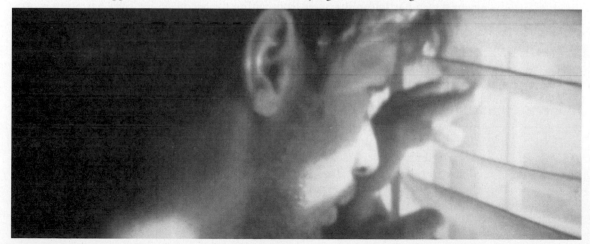

imagines himself in the jungle. The soundtrack carries an audio representation of this inner fantasy. Sound designer Walter Murch systematically replaced city sounds with a series of jungle sounds. Urban noises—a policeman's whistle, the engines of cars and motorcycles—give way on the soundtrack to the squawk of jungle birds, the buzzing of insects, and the cries of monkeys. Murch points out that these sound manipulations convey the idea that, although Willard's body is in Saigon, his mind is in the jungle.

Image editing arranges shots to express meanings not contained in any single shot taken in isolation. This scene from *Apocalypse Now* uses the same principle transposed to sound. The total arrangement of sounds expresses the reality of Willard's fantasy in a way that the individual sounds, taken in isolation, cannot. Montage works by assembling elements into a complex whole that is richer in meaning than each element taken in isolation. Since sound and picture are edited, they are easily assembled into montages. Today, multitrack recording and reproduction of sound, and elaborate mixing facilities, enable sound designers to create sound montages of unparalleled complexity.

These, then, are the most basic codes of sound design: the use of the soundtrack to establish a hierarchy of sound relationships, to create sound perspective, to create meaningful synchronous and asynchronous relationships with the image, to establish continuity, to prepare the viewer for a visual transition to the next scene, to establish off-screen space, and to establish intellectual and emotional associations through montage. All of these sound editing codes may be used with dialogue, sound effects, and music, the three basic types of motion picture sound.

☐ TYPES OF SOUND

Dialogue

Since the late 1920s when synchronous sound became a permanent feature of the movies, two primary kinds of dialogue have been employed in the cinema. **Speech** is dialogue delivered by characters on screen usually in conversation with one another. **Voice-over narration** is a monologue that accompanies images and scenes but is not delivered by a particular character from within the scene. Voice-over narration is provided by an all-seeing, all-knowing, detached narrator or by a character in the story usually from some later time than the time of the events portrayed on screen.

Voice-over Narration as an Element of Genre
While rarely used in commercial movies today, voice-over narration has been essential to certain kinds of genres. Film noir, for example, which developed in the mid-1940s and lasted until the middle of the 1950s, emphasized crime and detective stories, and many of these films—*Out of the Past* (1947), *Criss Cross* (1949), *The Killers* (1946)—told their stories through intricate flashbacks accompanied by voice-over narration. In voice-over, the tough private eye or the world-weary criminal delivered hard-boiled lines of dialogue. At the beginning of *Double Indemnity* (1944), with a bullet wound slowly leaking blood from his shoulder, a cynical insurance agent confesses his crime: "I killed Dietrichson—me, Walter Neff—insurance salesman—thirty-five years old, unmarried, no visible scars—'til awhile ago, that is."

Voice-over narration can be used for ironic or playful effects. In one of the most famous films noir, *Sunset Boulevard* (1950), the narrator turns out to be a dead man. The film opens with shots of a man's body floating in a swimming pool. The police arrive and remove the body as the narrator of the film, a screenwriter named Joe Gillis, tells how the murder occurred. It is not until the end of the movie that viewers realize the dead man is Joe Gillis. He even talks about how it feels as the police are pulling him out of the pool.

Of course, in the case of *Sunset Boulevard,* the narration is unreliable and misleading. Dead men don't talk. Director Billy Wilder, though, is playing against an established convention of voice-over narration, which is that the character doing the narration must survive the events of the story. In this case, he doesn't, and it enabled Wilder to pull off one of his darkest jokes.

Although voice-over narration is closely identified with the American films noir, it has also been used in documentary filmmaking, especially that subcategory of documentaries known as the *newsreel*. Newsreels routinely accompanied feature films, cartoons, and serials in the nation's movie theaters in earlier decades, and they typically employed the so-called "voice of God" narrator. Such a narrator was male, and he spoke with a deep, booming, authoritative voice.

Voice-over Narration and Point of View

Voice-over narration enables filmmakers to impose additional perspectives—moral, social, emotional, psychological—upon their images and the story being narrated. Film narration is almost always third person and is represented by the elements of structure as they are combined into an overall design. When voice-over narration is

---

Out of the Past (RKO, 1947)
Hard-boiled, tough guy dialogue, spoken as voice-over narration, coupled with dark, low-key lighting to establish the hard-edged, cynical atmosphere of classic film noir. Robert Mitchum (*left*), as the doomed Jeff Corey, provides the gripping narration in *Out of the Past*.

added to this design, interesting problems of point of view develop because a film can then have simultaneous first- and third-person narration. Which is the true perspective from which the story is told?

The "voice of God" newsreel narrator was satirized by Orson Welles in *Citizen Kane,* the life story of Charles Foster Kane, a rich newspaper man, who rose from humble beginnings. The film opens with Kane's death, and viewers are introduced to the character by a newsreel that newspaper reporters are watching in order to get some background for their stories about Kane's death. The newsreel is dominated by a "voice of God" narrator as director Welles expertly mimics the conventions of this kind of documentary.

Beyond the use of a fake newsreel, however, *Citizen Kane* offers a host of other voice-over narrators. The plot of the film is constructed as a series of flashbacks, each one narrated by the character doing the remembering, so that the portrait of Charles Foster Kane that emerges becomes kaleidoscopic. Kane's life is recalled by the millionaire banker, Walter P. Thatcher, who was given custody of Kane as a little boy; by Susan Alexander, Kane's second wife; by Jed Leland, the drama critic who worked briefly on Kane's newspapers; by Mr. Bernstein, Kane's chief editor and close friend; and by Raymond, Kane's personal valet.

Each of these characters narrates a section of the film, recalling events in ways that clash with the memories of the other narrators. For example, Jed Leland remembers the Charles Foster Kane who betrayed his ideas and principles, whereas Mr. Bernstein, whose memories are very fond, emphasizes those very principles, such as dedication to helping the poor and Kane's use of his newspaper to fight crime and to expose official graft and corruption.

In *Citizen Kane,* voice-over narration is used to frame the various flashbacks, and it colors them with a variety of psychological perspectives. *Citizen Kane,* in part, is a mystery film. The mystery is Kane's personality, which ultimately remains unknown and unknowable. It is difficult to reconcile all the different Kanes described in the memories of each of the narrators because each person's memories are so different. In this way, voice-over narration helps deepen, in emotional and psychological terms, the images of Kane revealed in the film. Moreover, it is difficult to reconcile

Citizen Kane (RKO, 1941) Jed Leland (Joseph Cotton), one of the principle narrators in *Citizen Kane* explains why Kane's first marriage failed. As he begins his speech, the image dissolves to the past to show the first Mrs. Kane at breakfast. The narrative voices are not easily reconciled. Leland describes events he couldn't possibly have witnessed. Frame enlargement.

the first- and third-person perspectives in the film. More than once, the camera shows events the narrator couldn't possibly have witnessed. In these cases it is difficult to say which narrative voice is correct. (And this is part of the mystery, too.)

Character Speech

The second primary category of dialogue in motion pictures is character speech. Motion pictures have drawn on a wide range of speech types. Shakespearean adaptations faithfully transpose the bard's language to the screen and frequently employ classically trained actors, such as Laurence Olivier, Ralph Richardson, John Gielgud, or Kenneth Branagh to deliver the lines.

At the other extreme from the poetry of Shakespeare lies the colloquialism of modern life. The dynamic impact of sound in the late 1920s and early 1930s was due largely to the electrifying presence of a new generation of screen actors. James Cagney, for example, brought his scrappy, high-voltage personality to a series of gritty, tough, urban dramas that allowed him to draw on his boyhood experiences growing up in the slums of New York's Upper East Side. The way Cagney moved and spoke electrified audiences because it was so different from the mannerisms and speech of stage-trained actors. In the Cagney classic *Angels with Dirty Faces* (1938), he plays a good-hearted crook named Rocky who greets his friends with the salutation, "Whadda ya hear? Whadda ya say?", rattled off in rapid-fire delivery. Cagney got this greeting from a pimp he had known when he was a youth.

By speaking to audiences in their own colloquial, familiar styles, movies are able to develop a deep and lasting rapport and to forge powerful emotional bonds with their audiences. In the 1950s, when Marlon Brando, playing an outlaw motorcyclist in *The Wild One,* was asked what he was rebelling against, he replied "Whadda ya' got?", and a young generation instantly understood his insolence and contempt for established society.

Angels with Dirty Faces (Warner Bros., 1938); **The Wild One** (Columbia Pictures, 1954)
The electrifying impact of rough, colloquial speech helped propel James Cagney and Marlon Brando to stardom. Playing a gangster in *Angels with Dirty Faces,* Cagney drew from the vocal patterns of the city streets where he grew up. As the outlaw motorcyclist in *The Wild One,* Marlon Brando's slurred, insolent speech conveyed his disgust with society.

Dialogue Editing

Whether it involves voice-over narration or speech, dialogue editing presents the film-maker with a series of challenges as well as creative opportunities. Editors first have to determine where to place the cuts to maintain continuity from shot to shot and dramatic emphasis. Obviously, there can be a lot of variation in how dialogue scenes are edited. A standard practice of cutting speech, however, involves locating a **dialogue cutting point.** The dialogue cutting point is that point at which the editor places the cut to ensure a smooth transition between speakers. Editors often link a shot of a character speaking to a shot of the listener who is about to begin speaking by placing the dialogue cut on the last syllable of the first speaker's final line.

This method ensures a smooth transition by producing a cut that is imperceptible for two reasons. First, the logic of the cutting appears to follow the rhythms and logic of the dialogue, with each shot change seemingly cued by changes in characters doing the talking. Second, the editing creates a subtle sound bridge, with the last syllable of the final line crossing the cut. In these ways, effective dialogue cutting helps produce continuity from shot to shot.

However, in editing dialogue a creative problem typically arises. When arranging shots into a sequence, the editor needs to maintain as much flexibility as possible in choosing different shots, visual details, camera positions, and camera angles. Editors do not want a scene's dialogue to force all of their choices of image. Nonsynchronous sound gives them an out. Editors will establish synchronous sound and then, once having established it, abandon it. Typically, the editing of dialogue involves a movement from synchronous to nonsynchronous sound and back again, in order to allow the camera and what it can show to remain as flexible as possible.

Sound Effects

Sound effects are the second principal type of sound in cinema. Many of the fundamentals involved in the editing of sound effects have already been touched upon in discussion of the codes of sound design. That prior discussion can be supplemented by noting that sound-effects work typically falls into one of two broad categories. *Effects design* involves the creative manipulation of sound sources. It is routinely used

---

Apocalypse Now (United Artists, 1979)
The sound of the machine gun in *Apocalypse Now* was actually a blend of multiple separate recordings expertly layered together to produce the psychological impression of a single, live source. Frame enlargement.

in contemporary film production. Often this manipulation is done electronically or by using digital computer technology and involves introducing changes in the sound wave characteristics of a given source. Sound designers such as Walter Murch oversee the creation of a total sound environment for the film, and this frequently involves techniques other than the direct recording of live sounds. In *Apocalypse Now,* during the scene in which panicky Americans machine-gun a group of Vietnamese in their boat, Murch realized that a direct, live recording of the machine gun would overwhelm the capabilities of the sound equipment. He therefore created the total sound by recording its components separately and then layering them in.

Furthermore, he wanted to manipulate the viewer's psychological and emotional response to the machine-gun sound. He wanted the viewer to feel that the sound was realistic even though it was not a real, live recording of a single source but a synthetic blend of multiple, separate recordings. In his work on sound design, Murch distinguishes the psychological components of sound from its actual, direct, live components. Only by manipulating the direct, live components does he reach the psychological dimension he is after.

Murch backed the microphone away from the gun to get a clean recording and then, later, added supplementary elements such as the clank of discharging metallic cartridges and the hiss of hot metal. By layering these additional features over the softer sound of the gun firing, Murch artificially created a convincing realism in ways that were compatible with his recording technology. Doing this involved "disassembling" the sound rather than capturing it live and direct on tape.

Besides effects design, the other major category of sound-effects work is the use of Foley techniques. **Foley technique** refers to the direct recording of live sound effects that are performed in synchronization with the picture after filming is completed. While the motion picture is projected in a sound recording studio, a Foley technician performs the effects. He or she may walk across a bare floor using hard shoes in synchronization with a character on screen to produce the needed effects of footsteps. The Foley technician may open or close a door or drop a tray of glasses on the floor to create these effects as needed in a given scene.

Foley techniques require considerable physical dexterity, often verging on the acrobatic, in the performers creating them. Foley techniques are a basic way of getting sound effects into a film. Unlike electronic-effects manipulation, Foley techniques are performed and recorded as live sound in the Foley studio. Foley techniques are often needed because many of today's films involve the use of radio microphones that are attached to individual actors in a scene. Unlike mikes on a boom overhead, radio mikes often fail to pick up natural sounds in the environment, and these may need to be dubbed later using Foley techniques.

Movie Music

Along with dialogue and effects, music is the third type of sound used in films. Music has always accompanied the presentation of films for audiences. During the silent period, film music was often, but not always, drawn from public domain, noncopyrighted classical selections or from the popular tunes of the era. Numerous catalogues offered filmmakers or musical directors a guide for selecting appropriate music depending upon the speed and tempo of the scene and its general emotional content. In addition, some original symphonic scores were composed for silent films.

The original score composed especially for motion pictures became standard practice in the sound period. While many different musical styles can be employed in film scoring—jazz (*Mo' Better Blues,* 1990), rock (*Bill and Ted's Excellent Adventure,* 1989), ragtime (*Ragtime,* 1981), symphonic orchestral (*Star Wars,* 1977)—music is typically used to follow action on screen and to illustrate a character's emotions.

Creating Movie Music

The production of movie music involves five distinct steps: spotting, preparation of a cue sheet, composing, performance and recording, and mixing. The first stage is **spotting,** during which the composer consults with the film's director and producer and views the final cut in order to determine where and when music might be needed. Spotting determines the locations in the film that require musical cues, where and how the music shall enter, and its general speed, tempo, and emotional color.

Much of this is left up to the composer, although detailed discussions with a film's director are not uncommon, especially when the director has strong preferences as to the style of scoring. Sometimes the director will impose a **temp track**—a temporary musical track derived from a score the director likes—onto the soundtrack of an edited scene, or even onto the entire film, and ask that the composer create something like the temp track. Not surprisingly, many composers find this stifling.

After the film has been spotted, the music editor then prepares a cue sheet. The **cue sheet** contains a detailed description of the action of each scene that requires music plus the exact timing—to the second—of that action. This enables the composer to

---

Platoon (Orion Pictures, 1986)
The score for *Platoon* deliberately avoids using conventional war-film music. Instead, composer Georges Delerue employed an already-existing classical composition—Samuel Barber's melancholy "Adagio for Strings"—and used it to emphasize the film's haunted, tragic tone.

work knowing the exact timing in minutes, seconds, and frames of each piece of action requiring music so that musical cues can catch the action and enter and end at previously determined points.

Once the cue sheet has been prepared, the third step is the actual composition of the score. This is done by the composer with a VCR and a videotape copy of the film. The videotape contains a digital time code that displays the reel number and the minutes, seconds, and frames in each reel for all of the action. Using the cue sheet and videotape the composer creates the score, carefully fitting the timing of music and action.

Computer programs known as "sequencers" enable the composer to lock the score onto the video's digital time code. Once this is done, any scene in the video can be played back, and the computer can call up the score, enabling the composer to check timings. Tempo adjustments—speeding up or slowing down the music—can also be made by computer to precisely match music with action. The sequencer can also generate a series of clicks that many composers use to establish a desired tempo for a given scene and that is then used as a guide for composition.

Digital technology has also altered the phase of composition in which the composer demonstrates the score for the director. Digital samplers enable composers to electronically simulate all needed instrumentation in their scores and to play the results for the director, who can hear a close approximation of the film's score-in-progress. Before the age of samplers, composers demonstrated their scores on the piano, which required that directors be able to understand how the piano performance would translate into full orchestration. The disadvantage of digital sampling is that demonstrations now give directors more input into scoring—an area that most are not qualified to handle—because, using a sampler's computer keyboard, anyone can easily manipulate the musical characteristics of a composition. Some directors, to their composer's dismay, find this an irresistible temptation.

Once the score has been composed, the next step is performance and recording of the score on a sound stage while a copy of the film is projected upon a large screen or video monitor. Timing of music to film action is facilitated by the use of clicks to establish tempo, "streamers" (lines imprinted on the film or video) that travel across the screen and mark the beginning and end of each cue, and a large analogue clock with a sweep-second hand. The performance of the score is often attended by the director and producer of the film.

The final stage in the creation of movie music is the process of mixing, which is the blending of the various sound tracks: effects, music, and dialogue. The mixing of movie music with dialogue and effects influences composers with regard to the kind of music they create. Because dialogue is considered the most important sound in a movie, music is typically mixed at a lower volume when it accompanies dialogue. Composers know this and work accordingly.

Hollywood composer Miklos Rosza pointed out that when music accompanies dialogue it should be simple, without a lot of ornamentation, because this will be lost in the mix when the music is buried beneath the dialogue. He also recommended that music in dialogue passages be scored with strings rather than brass instruments because he believed strings blend better with the human voice. Although there is much variation among composers in their approach to scoring, these remarks indicate something most would agree on—the film score is not autonomous. It must be written with the action of the film in mind and should be capable of blending with all other sound sources in the movie.

So much for the technical steps involved in producing movie music. What of its dramatic functions? Why is it used, and what does it accomplish in movies?

Functions of Movie Music

The great American concert hall composer, Aaron Copland, occasionally ventured into the world of filmmaking to compose scores for such pictures as *Of Mice and Men* (1940), *Our Town* (1940), *The Red Pony* (1949), and *The Heiress* (1949). Copland discussed the functions of movie music as he saw them, emphasizing five basic functions.

Setting the Scene   The first function of movie music is the creation of a convincing atmosphere of time and place. Movie music is used to characterize, musically, the locations, settings, and cultures where the story occurs. Often, this may involve the use of special instrumentation that reflects regional or ethnic musical characteristics. Jerry Goldsmith, one of today's most prolific and respected composers, employed pan flutes in his score for *Under Fire* (1983), a film dealing with the revolution in Nicaragua in 1979. By using an instrument that was not specifically tied to Nicaragua but was found in many peasant cultures in Central America, Goldsmith was able to create a musical score that tied the Nicaraguan revolution, musically, to its peasant origins, but in a way that included echoes of the peasant cultures of other Central American countries, much as the revolution itself did in the 1980s.

Sometimes the time and place that the movie composer wants to create is not one that exists in reality. For his celebrated score for the science fiction film *Planet of the Apes* (1968), Goldsmith relied on the use of unusual instruments, such as ram's horns and brass slide whistles, and unusual musical techniques, such as clicking the valves of woodwind instruments directly on the microphone. The result was a score that many people thought was electronic, although Goldsmith was quick to point out he did not use any electronic techniques. Instead, he used existing instruments but in an unusual manner to enlarge the sound possibilities of the orchestra. These new and unusual sounds were perfectly suited to the film's futuristic fantasy set in an alien and frightening world.

Under Fire
(Orion Pictures, 1983)
Movie music helps establish place and locale, often by employing regional or ethnic musical instruments or traditions. Jerry Goldsmith's score for *Under Fire* used pan flutes, associated with peasant cultures of Central America, to musically characterize the film's Nicaraguan setting. Frame enlargement.

Unfortunately, the scene-setting function of movie music sometimes draws upon and fosters cultural stereotypes. Dimitri Tiomkin, who composed the score for Howard Hawks' Western *Red River* (1948), needed music for a scene in which Indians attack a wagon train. He wrote music with a stereotypical tympani beat in order to suggest the idea that the Indians were about to attack. Tiomkin noted that this Indian music was quite artificial and without any real historical basis, but he also believed that, had he used authentic tribal music, the effect on the audience would have been less powerful because the music would have been unfamiliar. Tiomkin elected to use the musical stereotype because of its familiarity.

Adding Emotional Meaning   The second function of movie music, according to Aaron Copland, is to add psychological and emotional meaning to a scene or character. This is a function whose importance is stressed by all motion picture composers. Composer Hugo Friedhofer pointed out that music has the special ability of hinting at the unseen whereas images can only show what is visible. Music can extend the range of meaning of images by adding psychological or emotional qualities not possible in the pictures alone.

The tonal range of Western music, particularly the highly coloristic rendering used in the romantic period of the late nineteenth-century, has become the model for orchestral movie music because the emotional content of this musical style is familiar to audiences. Think of all the romantic melodramas in which the teary lovers are about to be parted and the violins are sawing away on the soundtrack, or the way the strings in John Williams' soaring score for *E.T.* capture the pathos of Eliot's goodbye to E.T. at the conclusion of that film.

E.T. (Universal Studios, 1982)
John Williams' expansive score for *E.T.* uses the highly coloristic tonality of Western romantic music to express the emotional content of the film, particularly the tender bond between Elliot (Henry Thomas) and *E.T.*.

Movie music emphasizes emotional effects on screen most often by direct symbolization—the music embodies and symbolizes an emotion appropriate to the screen action. An alternative approach is to employ contrast of image and music as a way of dramatizing emotion. This approach is employed less frequently than direct musical symbolization but can be quite effective.

Japanese director Akira Kurosawa loves to contrast music and image. In *Drunken Angel* (1948), the central character of the film, a small-time gangster, loses control of the local neighborhood he dominated. Furthermore, he is dying of tuberculosis. He wanders the streets shunned by shopkeepers, coughing his life out. To emphasize the character's despair, Kurosawa instructed his composer, Fumio Hayasaka, to accompany the action with a silly and mindless cuckoo waltz. Kurosawa knew that the mindless optimism of the waltz, by virtue of its extreme contrast with the character's situation, would underline and emphasize the gangster's despair and sadness.

Serving as Background Filler   The third essential function of movie music, according to Copland, is to serve as a neutral background filler, frequently in dialogue scenes. This use of movie music was more typical in older films than it is, perhaps, in contemporary filmmaking. During the Hollywood period in the 1930s and 1940s, films were distinguished by so-called wall-to-wall music. Music accompanied almost every scene, and it often assumed a kind of background filler function, just as Copland noted. Contemporary films tend to use music more sparingly, and composers such as Jerry Goldsmith believe that less music is better because, when used, it becomes more significant.

Creating Continuity   Copland emphasized as a fourth function the ways that movie music helps create continuity. Music, like dialogue and effects, can create a sound bridge across shots in ways that link and unify those shots. In montage scenes,

---

Citizen Kane (RKO, 1941)
Composer Bernard Herrmann provided a waltz and variations to link musically the different shots of *Citizen Kane's* famous breakfast montage. Frame enlargement.

for example, where many shots are edited together, music can supply a unifying structure for the montage. One of the best examples of this occurs in Bernard Herrmann's score for Orson Welles' *Citizen Kane*. A classic sequence shows Charles Foster Kane and his first wife Emily in a series of brief scenes, sharing breakfast over the years. Each encounter across the breakfast table registers further decay and disintegration in their marriage. Herrmann wrote a little waltz for the breakfast sequence and began a series of variations for each succeeding scene in the montage, with the music growing colder and more forbidding as the montage progressed, in order to comment on the increasing emotional alienation between Charles and Emily.

One of the most important ways that film music creates continuity is through the use of a *leitmotif* structure. A **leitmotif** is a kind of musical label that is assigned to a character, a place, an idea, or an emotion in a movie. Once assigned, a leitmotif can be repeated each time the character or idea or emotion reappears. This helps make the music recognizable to an audience, especially after stretches of the film in which no music has been heard, and it also helps characterize the character, place, idea, or emotion. The leitmotif can be presented with great invention and variation, restated in differing rhythms and colors. The use of leitmotif is one of the most common ways of scoring motion picture music. Leitmotif is derived from the operas of Richard Wagner, who used it as a way of helping his audience recognize and understand the characters and their emotional situations.

The Italian composer Ennio Morricone's score for Sergio Leone's *Once Upon a Time in the West* (1969) employs an explicit leitmotif structure. Each of the four major characters in the film has his or her own theme, and the themes reappear as the characters do throughout the film so that one can easily follow the story and its conflicts

---

Once Upon a Time in the West (Paramount Pictures, 1969)
Each character in *Once Upon a Time in the West* has his or her own highly distinctive musical theme. The film features an especially explicit leitmotif structure.

(Museum of Modern Art/Film Stills Archive)

simply by listening to the music. Almost every motion picture score is structured as a set of themes and variations, and this repetition of familiar musical material is a powerful means of creating continuity.

Music can also establish continuity in movies by creating pacing and tempo within scenes. As soon as music is added to a scene, the images take on a rhythm and pace they did not otherwise possess as relationships are established musically across the shots. Elmer Bernstein, composer of the score for the popular Western *The Magnificent Seven* (1960), has pointed out that his music for this film is actually faster than the action on screen. He wanted the music to help speed along an otherwise slow film. Bernstein's now-classic score adds immeasurably to the pacing of the movie, providing excitement in scenes that otherwise lack it.

Emphasizing Climaxes   Finally, Copland maintained that movie music emphasizes climaxes and concludes both scenes and the end of the film with finality. Music at the end of a film is typically dramatic, loud, and leaves one with a strong feeling of conclusion. Music in movies usually begins and ends on specific actions—doors opening and closing, cars pulling away, monsters jumping out of the dark. In these ways, musical cues alert the audience to the climaxes and the emotional high points of scenes. Danny Elfman's score for *Batman* (1989) is exceptionally accomplished in catching action and emphasizing climaxes.

Music need not always be used to heighten action. Sometimes, its absence can be very effective. In the police thriller *Bullitt* (1968), during the famous car chase, the music stops for the chase. As detective Steve McQueen begins to pursue a pair of suspected killers, the music begins in a tense and ominous fashion, but then, as the killers speed away and McQueen revs his car into high gear for the pursuit, the music stops and is replaced by revving engines, shifting gears, and squealing tires. Most movies rely on music as a way of making car chases more exciting, but the chase in *Bullitt* is historically important precisely for not doing that.

Contemporary Trends in Film Scoring

Movie music today performs these five basic functions, but the musical styles employed and the importance of music to the industry have changed since Copland's era. The use of romantic orchestral music to score films in the Hollywood period gave

Bullitt (Warner Bros., 1968) Sometimes no music at all can be more effective than a score. Most car chases in film feature loud music, but the classic chase in *Bullitt* creates excitement strictly through its sound effects. One mark of intelligent scoring is knowing when not to score. Frame enlargement.

way in the 1950s to more modern approaches. Elmer Bernstein composed a jazz-oriented score for *The Man with the Golden Arm* (1955), and Leonard Rosenman composed an atonal, 12-tone serial score for *The Cobweb* (1955). Folk and rock scores in the late 1960s distinguished *The Graduate* (1967) and *Easy Rider* (1969). At this time, the symphonic orchestral score fell out of style, but it made a triumphant comeback in the mid-1970s in the work of John Williams. His scores for the *Star Wars* films and Steven Spielberg's pictures re-established the symphony orchestra as an essential scoring resource.

Today, film music is a key part of the movie business. Studios often market films using contemporary music supplied by popular bands and singers and rely on sales of recorded film music as a supplementary source of income. (The parent corporations that own studios also own music publishing and recording businesses.) Because of this, studios are often interested in scores that can be marketed as popular songs. This trend goes back at least to David Raksin's score for *Laura* (1944) and could be found in the 1950s with films such as *High Noon* (1952), and in the 1960s in *The Magnificent Seven* (1968), *Breakfast at Tiffany's* (1961), and *Dr. Zhivago* (1965). Today, it is firmly established and is extremely common. The soundtrack of *Forrest Gump* (1994) was essentially a collection of popular tunes from the 1960s, while *Natural Born Killers* (1994) featured the work of popular 1990s performing groups.

The crafting of movie music as a series of pop hits has become a permanent fixture of the industry and has had a detrimental effect on the art of film scoring. The artistry of film scoring wants to create a fusion of music and image rather than detachable songs that can be marketed on their own and have only a marginal relationship with the images on screen. It was this development that effectively ended the long-time partnership between director Alfred Hitchcock and composer Bernard Herrmann. Herrmann had composed extraordinary music for the Hitchcock films *The Trouble with Harry* (1955), *The Man Who Knew Too Much* (1956), *The Wrong Man* (1956), *Vertigo* (1958), *North by Northwest* (1959), *Psycho* (1960), and *Marnie* (1964), and had served as a musical consultant on *The Birds* (1963). Herrmann composed a score for Hitchcock's next film, *Torn Curtain* (1966), which was grim and foreboding, but the producers at Universal wanted a pop song that could be hummed and played on the radio. Responding to their pressure, Hitchcock threw out Herrmann's score and substituted

Psycho
(Paramount Pictures, 1960)
Bernard Herrmann contributed brilliant scores for Alfred Hitchcock's pictures. The score for *Psycho,* for example, used only string instruments. The shrieking strings heightened the impact of the film's brutal violence. Frame enlargement.

Out of Africa (Universal Studios, 1985)
Composer John Barry has created some of the most notable original scores for contemporary film. In the 1960s, his brassy music for the James Bond movies helped ensure their popularity. More recently, his sweeping orchestral score for *Out of Africa* brilliantly expressed the film's lush, romantic qualities. Frame enlargement.

a more conventional composition in its place. Miffed at this treatment, Herrmann never worked with Hitchcock again.

Like Herrmann, most serious film composers regard the pop song approach as a compromise upon the integrity of their scores. Sometimes the application of pop songs is done in an almost schizophrenic fashion. *Robin Hood: Prince of Thieves* (1991), starring Kevin Costner, employed a score that used many period instruments, but, at the end of the film, over the final credits, a pop rock love ballad provided the exit music, roughly jolting moviegoers out of the medieval period of the movie.

The cross-marketing of movies and pop songs is now a firmly established feature of the industry. To some extent, film scoring suffers from this emphasis. Many films feature scores that, musically, have little to do with the action or emotions on screen. But despite this, the art of film scoring remains very much alive. Exciting, ambitious original scores by James Horner (*Field of Dreams,* 1989, *Glory,* 1989), John Barry (*Out of Africa,* 1985, *Dances With Wolves,* 1990), Danny Elfman (*Batman,* 1989, *Edward Scissorhands,* 1990), and others continue to make a distinguished contribution to modern movies.

SUMMARY

For most casual moviegoers, sound is often the least consciously noticed element of film structure, but its contribution to film cannot be overstated. The next time you watch a favorite movie on television, turn off the sound and see how impoverished the pictures become. Without sound, a movie loses much of its emotional impact.

Sound design creates a complex audio environment to accompany film images, establishing dynamic audiovisual relationships and shaping the viewer's interpretation of those images in subtle and almost subliminal ways. Sound design is orderly and rule-based, following a set of basic codes, some of which establish perceptual correspondences with the viewer's real-world audio experience.

Dialogue, music, and effects are controlled to establish a hierarchy of sound relationships with dialogue being given primary importance. Direct, reflected, and ambient sound levels are carefully related to camera position to create sound perspective. Editors alternate between establishing synchronous and nonsynchronous sound-image relations to keep camera perspective flexible and to maintain continuity. Sound editing establishes continuity across cuts, primarily by allowing sound to flow over the cut, as in the use of dialogue cutting points. Sound is also used to prepare viewers for visual transitions, as when a sound cut precedes a visual cut, and to establish off-screen space that extends the viewer's physical sense of the image. Finally, sound montages may establish intellectual and emotional associations that go beyond the content of the images.

Sound design works with three categories of sound: dialogue, music, and effects. Dialogue in film tends to be either voice-over narration or character speech. Sound effects are created using either Foley techniques or more elaborate electronic manipulations as part of a comprehensive sound design. Music in film tends to be composed within a late romantic style, whose musical conventions and range of coloring are familiar to most moviegoers. Movie music helps set the locale and atmosphere of time and place in the story, adds psychological and emotional meaning to a scene, provides background filler, establishes continuity, and calls attention to climaxes and conclusions of scenes.

SUGGESTED READINGS

Rick Altman, ed., *Sound Theory/Sound Practice* (New York: Routledge, 1992).

Michel Chion, *Audio-Vision,* edited and trans. Claudia Gorbman (New York: Columbia University Press, 1994).

Kathryn Kalinak, *Settling the Score: Music and the Classical Hollywood Film* (Madison: University of Wisconsin Press, 1992).

Fred Karlin, *Listening to Movies: The Film Lover's Guide to Film Music* (New York: Schirner Books, 1994).

Vincent LoBrutto, *Sound-on-Film: Interviews with Creators of Film Sound* (Westport, CT: Praeger, 1994).

Elizabeth Weis and John Belton, ed., *Film Sound: Theory and Practice* (New York: Columbia University Press, 1985).

Chapter 6

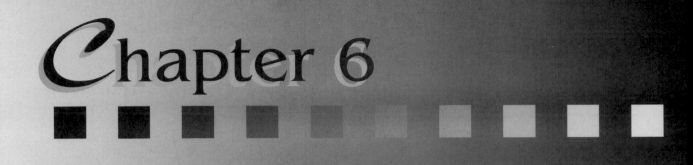

The Nature
of Narrative in Film

Chapter Objectives

After reading this chapter, you should be able to

- explain why the storytelling function came to film early in its history

- explain the relationship between narrative and the mass production of film

- describe the different criteria audiences use to evaluate fictional and nonfictional stories

- differentiate between story and plot and explain how filmmakers may creatively manipulate the story-plot distinction

- explain the basic principles of plot construction

- distinguish explicit causality from implicit causality and explain their different narrative effects

- explain why some filmmakers refuse to employ narrative causality

- describe the expressive uses of digressive subplots

- explain narrative point of view

- explain the viewer's perceptual and interpretive contribution to narrative

Key Terms and Concepts

story
plot
deviant plot structure
selection and omission of
   detail

explicit causality
narrative causality
implicit causality
digressive subplots
voice

point of view
real author
implied author
subjective shot

Commercial moviemakers use the elements of audiovisual design to construct narratives. They use the camera, light, color, production design, performance style, editing, and sound design as storytellers responding to an audience. Gathered at shopping mall cinemas and neighborhood movie theaters, audiences want movies that tell stories. Contemporary film production and distribution reinforce this preference, effectively segregating nonfiction from fiction films. Fictional movies are distributed on a mass national basis to chains of theaters and video stores where fans of Westerns, science fiction films, or other genres eagerly watch them. Nonfiction films, on the other hand, get more limited distribution. Distributors almost never show them theatrically on a national basis.

In light of these considerations, the importance of narrative for popular movies cannot be overestimated. What is narrative, and what are its structural elements in film? This chapter explains when and why narrative came to the movies, examines some of the basic elements of narrative structure, and concludes by examining what the viewer contributes to the experience of narrative.

◻ THE TURN TO NARRATIVE IN EARLY FILM HISTORY

The storytelling function came to film very early, but it was not there from the beginning. Public exhibition of projected motion pictures dates from 1895, when the photographic equipment manufacturers Auguste and Louis Lumière held a public screening of their short films. These tended to focus on documentary subjects: feeding a baby, workers knocking over a wall, a train coming into a station, or workers leaving a factory.

One film on the early program, *The Gardener Gets Watered* (1895), anticipated the use of film as a storytelling medium. In this short film, a gardener watering his lawn is tormented by a mischievous boy who kinks the hose, spraying the gardener's face when he looks at the nozzle and the boy straightens the hose. The gardener then retaliates by chasing and spanking the boy. The film shows a series of events with a clear beginning and a clear conclusion and, in this respect, anticipates a basic design of narrative.

The Emergence of Narrative Film

In the United States, an early exhibition context for the movies was the vaudeville stage where motion picture presentations appeared as one act among many, co-existing with slapstick comedians, singing performances, dramatic recitations, and animal shows. As early as 1902, however, narrative films, particularly comedies, began to appear on the vaudeville stage where they were greeted enthusiastically by the public.

Despite their early appearance, however, narrative films, whether comedies or dramas, co-existed with a vast amount of nonfiction film material. This included

The Gardener Gets Watered (1895)
Using film to tell stories followed soon after the invention of cinema. This early Lumière film, *The Gardener Gets Watered,* shows how quickly the storytelling impulse came to early filmmakers. Frame enlargement.

travelogues (films that present the viewer with images of beautiful, exotic, or far away places) and films focused on topical events such as a yacht race or political parades. By contrast, in motion picture theaters today, documentary film is virtually invisible, and as a percentage of studio production it is virtually nil.

What happened to change things? Why did narrative films become the clearly dominant category of production for the American industry? One reason is certainly the public's enthusiastic acceptance of early film narratives, whether comedies, dramas, chase films, slap-stick films, or trick films (films favoring such special optical effects as characters appearing and disappearing or moving in fast or slow motion).

But beyond this obvious public enthusiasm for narrative films lay a more subtle reason. By 1906, vaudeville started losing its place as the main forum for presenting motion pictures. Nickelodeons, storefront theaters where the public could see an entire program of films for 5 or 10 cents, appeared across the country in great numbers. Film historian Russell Merritt points out that by 1910 nickelodeons were attracting about 26 million Americans every week, which was a little less than 20 percent of the national population.

Narrative and Mass Production

The nickelodeon boom clearly indicated an explosion of popular interest in the movies, and it challenged producers to organize film production in a systematic way so that it could meet the growing popular demand. Using film to cover current events in documentaries presented a series of problems for early producers who wanted to maximize their output. The documentary filmmaker was a hostage to events. Production had to wait for the day or the month when an interesting yacht race or parade occurred. Meanwhile, the public was clamoring for films in the nickelodeons.

The advantage offered by narrative filmmaking is this—it enabled producers to systematize film production in an orderly fashion so that it could meet the rising public demand. Stories could draw on the scenic features of a given production company's locale. Production did not have to wait for the unpredictable current event. Instead, stories could be written as fast as films were needed.

The only limit on production in this respect was the imagination of the writers and the physical resources of the production companies. Historian Robert Allen has argued that the shift to narrative films can be explained in part by these advantages

The Birth of a Nation
(1915)
By 1915, cinema had reached artistic maturity and attained great narrative sophistication. *The Birth of a Nation* presented an epic (and intensely racist) narrative of unprecedented structural complexity. Frame enlargement.

D. W. GRIFFITH

In early film history, D. W. Griffith perfected (although he did not invent) the essential techniques of motion picture narrative. Griffith's understanding of the principles of film structure and the methods of cinematic storytelling was uncommonly sophisticated. Seen today, the camerawork and editing in his films seems thoroughly modern, even though the melodramatic stories appear dated.

Griffith was born in Kentucky in 1875, into a family ruined and impoverished by the Civil War and Reconstruction. Determined to become an actor and playwright, Griffith loved the theater and considered it to be a legitimate art. By contrast, he thought the movies were a bastard offspring, and he came to them reluctantly after failing to launch a successful theatri-

cal career. In 1908, Griffith made his first film at the Biograph Studio in New York, where he continued to work until 1913. In his Biograph films, Griffith developed an increasingly complex and expressive visual style that he used to put his stories across with maximum emotional impact. He perfected this style by directing a huge number of films. In 1910, for example, he directed 86 films and, in 1911, 70 films. Their subjects fell into categories that would define the basic Hollywood genres: gangster films, Westerns, biblical films, and war films.

At Biograph, Griffith strained against the narrative restrictions imposed by the one-reel format (one reel was approximately ten minutes). In 1911, he made *Enoch Arden* in two reels, and in 1913 he made the

The Birth of a Nation (1915); **Intolerance** (1916)
Griffith was a director of remarkable visual brilliance. In this moment of quiet intimacy from *The Birth of a Nation*, a soldier returning from the Civil War is greeted by his mother and sister. Their arms encircle and draw him into the house. The image is eloquent in its restraint and simplicity. Griffith was equally a master of epic compositions. Griffith's longshot stresses the colossal size of the Babylonian palace in *Intolerance*. Frame enlargements.

biblical epic *Judith of Bethulia,* his final Biograph film, in four reels. By moving to longer forms, Griffith was able to tell increasingly complex stories. After leaving Biograph, Griffith made two epics, *The Birth of a Nation* (1915) and *Intolerance* (1916), which masterfully wove together multiple plot lines and featured huge casts of characters. At silent speeds, each film ran approximately three hours.

Griffith's films are a virtual catalogue of modern motion picture technique. By using multiple camera positions and fluid editing, he divided a scene into its constituent shots, intercutting freely to create smooth continuity. Each shot was dramatically incomplete, recording just a fragment of the action and acquiring meaning in relation to the other shots that made up the scene. He drastically varied camera position and angle, freely incorporating low- and high-angle shots, as well as long shots, medium shots, and close-ups. In *Enoch Arden,* Griffith used a psychological image to show what a character was thinking. The camera draws close to the character's face, then Griffith cuts to a distant scene that represents the character's mental image.

Griffith skillfully placed his cameras to frame shots in highly expressive ways. In *The Birth of a Nation,* when the Little Colonel returns from the Civil War, he is greeted by his mother. Rather than showing the mother's face, Griffith discretely shows only her arms reaching out from inside the house to embrace him. This discrete framing, with its use of off-screen space, ironically intensifies the emotions of the reunion by emphasizing their private nature.

By 1915 and 1916, when Griffith completed his epics *The Birth of a Nation* and *Intolerance* he had perfected the essential building blocks of modern motion picture narrative: rapid changes of camera position and angle, close-ups used to intensify the drama and reveal emotion, complex editing used to divide a scene into a series of dramatically incomplete shots, camera movement used to extend the frame and to follow action, and cross-cutting of multiple storylines.

Unfortunately, Griffith's brilliant grasp of film structure accompanied racist and reactionary attitudes. Most notoriously, *The Birth of a Nation* portrayed the Civil War and Reconstruction as catastrophes that destroyed the happy plantation life of the South and, by freeing Southern slaves, unleashed a tide of black villainy against virtuous white aristocrats. In the film's climax, the Ku Klux Klan saves Southern honor and white virtue by restoring order throughout the South. Because of its virulent racism, *The Birth of a Nation* remains as inflammatory today as when it was first screened. Its explosive nature is evidence of Griffith's filmmaking skill. Its visual power and emotional manipulation of audiences make its racism all the more vicious and repugnant.

Griffith tried to rebut charges that he was a racist and calls for censoring the movies with *Intolerance,* a complex film weaving together a modern story of crime and gangsters with stories about the fall of Babylon, the massacre of the Huguenots in medieval France, and the crucifixion of Christ. Griffith drew an epic portrait of social intolerance by telling these stories simultaneously, cutting back and forth among them to create dramatic and emotional connections. Its elaborate narrative structure established *Intolerance* as a film far ahead of its time. Even today, it remains a challenging film.

Griffith continued to make several more outstanding films (*Broken Blossoms,* 1919; *True Heart Susie,* 1919; *Way Down East,* 1920; *Orphans of the Storm,* 1922), but during the 1920s his melodramatic stories seemed increasingly old fashioned, and, except for two productions, the coming of sound put an end to his career. His last picture was the undistinguished *The Struggle* (1931). Upon his death in 1948, at age 73, he was a lonely, forgotten man, who spent his last years living on the fringes of a Hollywood that had passed him by.

and points out that by 1907 comedies and dramas comprised 67 percent of all American film production. By 1909, production of fiction films had increased to an overwhelming 97 percent. Public interest and the needs of the expanding industry helped decisively shift film production into the narrative mold. In the next several years, the narrative sophistication of early film increased tremendously. The work of director D. W. Griffith, beginning in 1908, displayed a special narrative brilliance and an unprecedented sophistication of visual design.

☐ THE SIGNIFICANCE OF NARRATIVE

Stories are found in all cultures. In this respect, narrative is a universal human activity. Although some cultures, like the industrialized societies of the West, tell stories for entertainment as well as instruction, many other cultures use narrative as a primary means for socializing the young and transmitting important social values.

Because narrative is found in all cultures, many writers have suggested that it may be an essential method that human beings use to think about their world. Narrative may be a universal cultural expression also because it is a fundamental human way of thinking. To explain how things change, people tell stories. Not all narratives, though, are fiction.

Narratives can be fictional or nonfictional. Fictional narratives include novels or almost any popular movie in which the story is essentially imaginary. By contrast, historians frequently employ nonfictional narratives, presenting, for example, the Civil War as the story of Lincoln's efforts to keep the Union together and to ensure that the Southern slaves might be freed.

Narrative is a basic mode of explanation in history, but it can be found in a variety of other disciplines as well. In psychology, for example, Freudian psychoanalysis is essentially a narrative mode. The patient being treated by a psychoanalyst is invited to construct a story of his or her life. The analyst's work is to assist in assembling this narrative.

☐ ELEMENTS OF NARRATIVE

What are the basic elements of narrative as they are employed by motion pictures? Narratives have a temporal or time-based dimension in that they order events in sequence so that structure is imposed on the randomness of daily life. Furthermore, a narrative presupposes the existence of a narrator, either real or implied, a point of view from which the tale is told, and an audience for whom the tale is told. Fictional narratives, however, have an additional distinguishing characteristic, and this is an informal contract between narrator and audience that critic Peter Lamarque has called "the fictive stance."

Fictional and nonfictional narratives, then, have three fundamental sets of characteristics: (1) a contract between narrator and audience that determines how the audience evaluates the tale, (2) a story and plot sequencing events into a particular order that forms the narrative, and (3) a narrator and narrative point of view.

The Fictive Stance

Narrator and audience agree to confer the status of fiction upon the tale being told. The audience for a fictional narrative agrees not to give the contents of that narrative the same factual weight as it would a nonfictional account. This means that the fictional narrator is not limited by the need to be truthful and is not held accountable to truthfulness by the audience. Furthermore, the audience accepts the invitation to enter into a make-believe world. The audience agrees to a game with the narrator in which the contents of the story will be accepted as real at one level of make-believe even though the audience knows, at another level, that it is only a story.

Here is one of the great mysteries of narrative. Whether in literature or film, stories arouse powerful feelings in readers or viewers who know the contents of the story are not necessarily real. Emotional arousal is coupled with cognitive distance, and this is basic to the contract between the fictional storyteller and the audience. Film viewers know the story isn't necessarily true or real but decide to believe in it anyway for the duration of the film because it gives pleasure.

A story becomes fiction or nonfiction based on a complex series of transactions between narrator and audience. Does the audience adopt the fictive stance? Does it engage in make-believe? Does it suspend disbelief? Does it hold the narrator accountable for the truthfulness of the story?

Deciding Whether a Narrative Is Fiction

The contract between narrator and audience is very complex, and some stories and movies occupy grey areas. Are they fiction or nonfiction? How can one decide? With a movie such as *Star Wars* (1977), viewers clearly have a fictional story. The events in George Lucas' film do not exist in this world or in any easily imaginable world of the near future. By contrast, Leni Reifenstahl's Nazi production *Triumph of the Will*

Star Wars (Twentieth Century Fox, 1977)
Star Wars is a clearly fictional story. The setting is futuristic, the characters have no real-life counterparts, and the story events are entirely imaginary. Viewers of this film have no difficulty deciding whether to evaluate and experience it as fiction.

(Museum of Modern Art/Film Stills Archive)

Triumph of the Will (1936)
Leni Reifenstahl's *Triumph of the Will* seems to be a documentary record of Hitler's Nuremberg rallies, but the rallies were staged for the cameras, and Hitler is portrayed as a divine being. Is the film a documentary, or does it create a powerful historical fiction? Frame enlargement.

(1936) is a pseudo-documentary, a film that pretends to be a documentary while in fact creating a series of political fictions.

Reifenstahl filmed Hitler's Nuremberg rallies in 1934, a year after Hitler came to power. The rallies were intended to introduce him to the German people as well as to foreign leaders abroad. They were, however, staged for the cameras, and Reifenstahl carefully composed her images to establish clearly fictional associations between Hitler as a man and as a god. The opening of the film, for example, shows Hitler descending from the clouds in an airplane where he greets his ardent fans on earth, making a descent that gives him a divine aspect. The film occupies an uncertain middle ground, somewhere between fiction and nonfiction.

Audiences generally want to know whether the tale they are being told is truthful and to what degree, so they will know what stance to take regarding the story and its narrator. In the case of *Triumph of the Will*, the pretense of being a documentary, of being truthful, is obviously contradicted by the myth-making images that turn Hitler into a god. Similar problems arising from blurred boundaries between fact and fiction beset director Michael Moore in his documentary *Roger and Me* (1989), which deals with the shutdown of the General Motors plant in Flint, Michigan, and the ensuing impact on the city's economy. Criticism centered on the fact that Moore rearranged the actual chronology of events to make things that took place over a long period of time seem to unfold overnight.

JFK (Warner Bros., 1991)

Kevin Costner as District Attorney Jim Garrison in *JFK*. Oliver Stone's film created controversy because of its fluid mixture of real archival footage of the Kennedy years, faked footage made to look archival, and fictional characters who had no counterpart in the historical record. Director Stone meticulously sifted through the factual record surrounding the assassination, questioned the official findings that a lone assassin killed Kennedy, but often described his film as a myth. As a result, viewers could not tell where the film's factual ambitions turned into the fictions of myth or be sure the narrator knew where the differences lay. In comparison to a film such as *Star Wars*, the fictional status of this film is more ambiguous and harder to evaluate.

In his defense, Moore claimed that he was trying to portray the essential truth of the plant closings and the economic collapse of Flint and that he could not do this if he were confined to the real chronology of events. For some critics, this free-spirited way of portraying the plant closings violated the ethics of a documentary, which, they believed, meant being more objective and faithful to the actual record. The controversy surrounding *Roger and Me* grew from the fact that Moore violated the usual convention by which viewers evaluate nonfictional narratives.

More recently still, Oliver Stone's *JFK* (1991) seemed to want to play both ways with its audience, pretending to an exhaustive researching of the facts surrounding the assassination of President Kennedy while concocting an entirely speculative explanation for the assassination based on the unproved premise that Kennedy intended to withdraw American forces from Vietnam. Like these other films, *JFK* is an uncomfortable mixture of fact and fiction in ways that leave the audience unable to tell where the narrator believes the difference lies. Stone's blurring of the distinctions between myth and history was partly responsible for the film's controversy.

Most fictional narratives do not tend to invite this sort of criticism and confusion because they unambiguously evoke a fictive stance from the audience. The storyteller ordinarily is not held accountable for the truth of a clearly fictional story. Instead, the audience applies a different set of criteria. These have less to do with truth and veracity and more to do with the artistic structure and organization of the story. In other words, is it compelling, convincing, thrilling, entertaining, or amusing? The audience looks for a pleasurable stylistic design and execution. By creatively manipulating the elements of film structure—the camera, light, color, production design, performance style, editing, and sound—filmmakers achieve the stylish designs that give life to movie narratives and pleasure to audiences.

Story and Plot

Story and **plot** are fundamental characteristics of every narrative. Any given narrative points beyond itself to imply a set of events that are not directly portrayed. This larger set of events is the story. Plot, on the other hand, refers to the sequencing of directly shown events in a given film, book, or other narrative medium. Plot and story are not the same because books and movies may make use of flashbacks or other devices that change the actual order of narrative events.

To repeat, *plot* refers to the way in which narrative events are stylistically arranged and structured in the film, whereas *story* deals with the true chronological sequencing of all the classes of events that make up the narrative. Only a portion of those events may actually be shown in a film's plot. This distinction may seem abstract and difficult to grasp, but it can be a very useful tool for explaining narrative design.

Plot and Story in *Annie Hall*

Woody Allen's *Annie Hall* (1977) is about the relationship between a playwright, Alvy Singer (Woody Allen), and an aspiring singer, Annie Hall (Diane Keaton). The film's story deals with the meeting of Alvy and Annie, the growth of their love for each other, and the gradual dying of that love as the relationship breaks apart. At the end of the story, Alvy and Annie split up and lead separate lives.

Annie Hall (United Artists, 1977)
Story and plot do not correspond in *Annie Hall*. The plot scrambles story events in a
nonchronological way. In the plot, Annie and Alvy's tense date at the movies precedes their
loving, funny adventure with the lobsters even though, in chronological story time, the latter
comes first. Frame enlargements.

The story is clearly chronological, dealing with the growth and decay of a love
affair. The film's plot, however, imposes a structure on this story that breaks up and
rearranges the actual chronology of events. The plot jumps around in time to show
Alvy and Annie's affair at very different points in their relationship. In the first scene,
Alvy explains that he and Annie have broken up and that he's having a hard time coping with the separation because a year ago they were in love.

This admission cues a series of flashbacks showing Alvy's life as a child growing
up on Coney Island, his relationship with his parents, a few episodes from his ele-
mentary school years, and then, as an adult, a conversation he has with his friend Max.
Annie does not figure in any of this material despite the fact that these episodes are
cued by his recollection of their break-up.

Annie appears in the next scene. She meets Alvy outside a theater for a screening
of the French documentary *The Sorrow and the Pity* (1970). This scene apparently
occurs quite late in their affair because they are tense with each other and hostile.
Annie makes a reference to Alison, Alvy's first wife, and this cues a flashback to Alvy's
meeting Alison and to a subsequent scene between them indicating that that relationship, too, is doomed. The next scene returns to Annie and Alvy but this time at
a very early point in their relationship. It is a romantic moment, full of loving good
humor and joy. They are spending the weekend at a beach house and have a minor
disaster when several live lobsters escape the cooking pot and scatter across the
kitchen floor.

From this happy scene, the film goes next into Annie's past and shows a little
bit of her childhood in Chippewa Falls. Annie makes a reference to Alvy's second
wife, which cues another flashback to that relationship and its particular tensions.

The narrative then returns to Annie and Alvy at a point late in the relationship. They are in bed together, tense, angry, unable to make love. From this, the film cuts directly to the scene that shows their first meeting at a tennis club and then to a few scenes showing Alvy's early courtship of Annie.

Stylistic Design and Narrative

As this description makes clear, the narrative jumps around in time in *Annie Hall*. The editing of the film creates a kaleidoscope through which the viewer sees Annie and Alvy's affair. The story is broken into many different pieces, all arranged out of chronological order. Watching the film, the viewer mentally reconstructs the actual story from the mixed-up bits of the affair provided by the plot. The story is never directly depicted in its actual chronology. Instead, the plot imposes a fragmentary structure upon the story, inviting the viewer to reassemble implied material not actually seen, as well as the true chronology of events.

Admittedly, the structure of *Annie Hall* is a challenging and somewhat unusual one. In many films, there is little structural distinction between a film's plot and a film's story. Often, a plot presents the true chronology of a story from start to finish. The vast majority of commercially produced movies are told in a linear, chronological fashion.

However, many films do make use of flashbacks, occasionally a flashforward, and, less frequently, a movie such as *Annie Hall* will drastically rearrange the entire sequence of events. More recently, Quentin Tarantino's *Pulp Fiction* (1994) cleverly exploited the story/plot distinction by constructing a narrative composed of three relatively separate plots, each peopled by the same gallery of characters (primarily, two professional killers, played by John Travolta and Samuel L. Jackson, and a washed-up boxer, played by Bruce Willis). These characters and their separate plots cross paths at several strategic points in the film, most significantly when the boxer murders one of the hired guns (Travolta). Writer-director Tarantino stages this killing midway

Pulp Fiction
(Miramax, 1994)
John Travolta's hit man in *Pulp Fiction* is killed off midway through the film only to reappear in the concluding plot segment. Quentin Tarantino's film playfully exploits the story/plot distinction by rearranging its narrative events.

WOODY ALLEN

Born Allen Stewart Konigsberg in Brooklyn, 1935, Woody Allen adopted his now famous comic name when he began sending jokes to syndicated columnists while still in high school. The jokes and the name began appearing in national celebrity newspaper columns, giving Allen a measure of success very early in life, which he rapidly extended into a respected career as a writer for television comedy (*The Sid Caesar Show,* 1952) and as a stand-up comic and Broadway playwright *(Don't Drink the Water,* 1966; *Play It Again Sam,* 1969).

By the time he directed his first film, *Take the Money and Run* (1969), Allen had established himself as a successful comedy writer. Unlike many other leading American directors, Allen is a writer-director who first crafts a polished screenplay and only then takes a film project into production. The result is a body of work that is extremely literate, thoughtful, and intelligent and that subjects human relationships and moral issues to the kind of sustained comic examination that can be accomplished only by having outstanding scripts as the foundation of a production.

Annie Hall (1977) was Allen's breakthrough film. The sophistication of its cinematic structure, its blending of comedy and pathos, and its complex and bittersweet portrayal of a love affair placed it leagues apart from the earlier films—*Bananas* (1971), *Sleeper* (1973), *Love and Death* (1975)—which tended to be collections of slapstick gags and one-liners strung together along a thin narrative line. *Annie Hall* built on the enduring Allen comic persona—a bumbling nebbish neurotically tormented by life but whose anxieties brilliantly expose the moral dilemmas of modern society.

Characteristically, Allen demonstrated his versatility, and his controversial preference for drama over comedy, by following *Annie Hall* with a sober, psychological drama, *Interiors* (1978), in which he did not appear and which he intended as an homage to Swedish director Ingmar Bergman, whom Allen greatly admires.

Allen established an extraordinary directing career in the next two decades. Working swiftly and economically, he released one film every year, establishing an extensive and stylistically diverse body of work. His

through the film, during the second plot segment, then brings Travolta's character back in the third, concluding plot. The viewer realizes, with a jolt, that this last episode is occurring earlier in story-time than the second and watches Travolta with some sadness, knowing how that character will die. By manipulating plot and story, Tarantino cleverly shapes his narrative into a pleasurable artistic experience for the film's viewers and keeps them just a little off balance in their efforts to make sense of the narrative.

What Is Plot?

A plot is a highly organized structure composed of a nonarbitrary, nonaccidental sequencing of events. It involves a purposeful selection of details made according to the plot's particular laws of organization. These laws of organization determine how stories are constructed, and they will vary among story types or genres.

A Midsummer Night's Sex Comedy (Orion, 1982)
Woody Allen frequently appears as a performer in his own films. His fumbling, neurotic comic persona is instantly recognizable, whether it be in a period film such as *A Midsummer Night's Sex Comedy* or a contemporary comedy such as *Annie Hall* (1977), set in Allen's beloved New York City. The latter co-stars Diane Keaton, Allen's most inspired comic partner, and draws heavily from his life and experiences. Frame enlargement.

comic films—*Manhattan* (1979), *Hannah and Her Sisters* (1986), *Bullets over Broadway* (1994)—have been the most popular with critics and audiences.

Artistically more daring and offbeat films include the black-and-white study of a human chameleon (*Zelig*, 1983); a bitter exploration of movie stardom (*Stardust Memories*, 1980); an affirmative look at the dream world created by film and its power to alleviate the dullness and despair of life (*The Purple Rose of Cairo*, 1985); a loving, semiautobiographical homage to radio shows and Rockaway Beach, Long Island, in the 1940s (*Radio Days*, 1986); a probing psychological drama (*Another Woman*, 1988); and cynical, bitter portraits of marital conflict and human ruthlessness (*Husbands and Wives*, 1992; *Crimes and Misdemeanors*, 1990).

Creating a rich, artistically ambitious and consistently intelligent body of work, Allen demonstrates the virtues of inexpensive, small-scale filmmaking. He works regularly and often, with total artistic freedom, and he continually re-invents himself and his film style with each new production. By contrast, blockbuster directors, mired with huge budgets and difficult special-effects work, cannot be so artistically adventurous or provocative.

In genre films, such as horror films or Westerns, the laws of plot organization are extremely clear, and they are well understood by the audience. In a Western, for example, the conventions or rules that organize the plot are formulated at a highly explicit level. The audience expects not merely a violent narrative, but, more specifically, a plot that moves inexorably toward a climactic exchange of violence (the gunfight or shoot-out) that resolves plot conflicts in a decisive manner, one established as appropriate and necessary in the genre.

Plot construction can be consistent with an audience's expectations or it can deviate, sometimes significantly, from those expectations. Star John Travolta, playing a lead character in Quentin Tarantino's *Pulp Fiction*, is killed midway through the film in a surprising turn of events that is clearly not consistent with the audience's expectations. Given the importance of the character and the star playing him, a more normative plot structure would delay his death until the end of the film. Films such as

Pulp Fiction play off normative plot structures in imaginative ways. This can be an effective narrative technique because it places the audience in a fresh, unpredictable relationship with the principles of narrative structure operating in a given film. It can also be risky. Too much variation, or unwanted variation, can result in a plot structure viewers deem unsatisfying. This is particularly risky in highly formalized genre films such as Westerns, where viewers typically want repetition of familiar plot elements rather than extreme variation.

Deviant Plot Structure in *Red River*   **Deviant plot structure,** that is, a narrative whose design and organization fails to conform with viewer's expectations regarding what is proper or permissible, can clearly be seen in Howard Hawks' 1948 production *Red River,* which deals with the first cattle drive over the Chisolm Trail. Tom Dunson (John Wayne) leads his cattle on this perilous trek, assisted by his adopted son, Matthew Garth (Montgomery Cliff). During the drive, Dunson grows tyrannical and becomes a borderline psychopath obsessed with preventing cowboys from quitting the drive and threatening to hang those who do. Eventually, he becomes unbearable, and the men revolt. Matthew Garth takes the herd and leaves Dunson behind. Dunson swears revenge and tells Matt that he will kill him when they next meet.

The plot moves in traditional Western fashion toward an expected climactic gunfight. But it never occurs. Dunson catches up with Matt and confronts him, daring him to draw, even firing his gun in Matt's direction. Matt refuses to fire, however, and, instead of the anticipated gunfight, a comical fistfight develops that leads to a reconciliation of the two men. In the original screenplay by Borden Chase, Tom Dunson was killed by Matt, and the film concluded with Dunson's burial, thus ending the plot on a tragic note. Instead, and at the last moment, director Howard Hawks avoids the gunfight, adds some comedy, and ends with the characters as friends once more.

The ending of *Red River* is deviant from the genre because it so clearly violates one of the conventions of the Western. It seems less deviant from the standpoint of

Red River
(United Artists, 1948)
Deviant plot structures may twist in directions counter to an audience's expectations, especially if those expectations are shaped by the fairly rigid formulas of a genre. Instead of the anticipated gunfight, *Red River* concludes with a boisterous reconciliation between Dunson (John Wayne) and Garth (Montgomery Clift). Frame enlargement.

the director's other films, however, because in most of his work Hawks tends to prefer comedy and comradeship over tragedy. Nevertheless, the ending of this movie has always been controversial, with some viewers finding it to be a surprising and unacceptable last-minute turn of events.

Principles of Plot Construction

The plot of a narrative is a purposeful, nonarbitrary sequencing of events that follows laws of organization peculiar to the type of story being told. By organizing plot, filmmakers give narrative events a clear design. Unlike the events of one's daily life, which often appear to be somewhat unstructured, random, and in flux, events in a narrative have a clear shape and sequence. Filmmakers achieve this organization by employing three principles of plot construction: (1) selection and omission of detail, (2) causality, and (3) subplots.

The Principle of Selection and Omission   Narratives impose order through the careful arrangement of events, that is, through their **selection *and* omission of detail.** Not all events need be included in the plot. Many events in the story can be implied. In other words, plot construction includes the deliberate selection as well as the omission of detail. As a plot is constructed, some events are included and others are left out. In the case of mystery or suspense films, events may be deliberately withheld from the audience to be revealed at a later time. Withholding of detail is a highly effective narrative principle because it invites the audience's participation. The audience fills in the missing information to get a comprehensive sense of the story being told. Viewers enjoy mysteries, for example, because they try to figure things out before the detective does.

Microlevel selection and omission.   Details can be omitted from the plot at either the small or micro level of a film or at the large or macro level. Omission at the micro level typically occurs between shots as tiny bits of information are compressed or left out in the interest of speeding the story along in the most efficient manner. For example, if a character is leaving home to go to work, viewers don't need to see her exiting the front door, opening the car door, starting the engine, etc. All viewers need is a shot of her putting on a hat and coat and a bit of dialogue to establish the destination, and then a straight cut can speed the action to her office. This is a standard kind of narrative selection and omission that is fundamental to the making of any film.

A less routine kind of selection and omission at the microlevel occurs through the use of *jump-cutting* in which an editor will deliberately omit a bit of action that is perceptible to the viewer so that the event on screen seems to jump in a way that creates deliberate discontinuity. Neither of these types of microlevel omission need pose interpretational problems for a film's viewer.

Macrolevel selection and omission.   At the macro level, selection and omission of detail may pose serious interpretational challenges. Consider how it functions in Bernardo Bertolucci's *Last Tango in Paris* (1972). The film is a French-Italian co-production that deals with the emotional devastation of an American, Paul (Marlon Brando), living in Paris, whose wife has just committed suicide. Unlike Woody Allen's *Annie Hall,* in which the plot completely rearranged the chronology of story events, Bertolucci does not alter the chronology of events in *Last Tango.* However, he does omit key scenes and delays giving the viewer important information necessary to understand the story. At the beginning of the film, Paul appears in a state of extreme emotional distress, but the viewer doesn't know why. Walking beneath the tracks of an elevated train, Paul screams an obscenity into the roar of the express passing overhead, but the reason for his distress (namely, his wife's suicide) is not made clear until much later. After meeting his young lover, Paul next appears standing in a bathroom as a maid cleans a tub full of blood. He stands silently as she talks about how the police have questioned her about the suicide committed in the bathroom. At this point in the narrative, the viewer doesn't know who committed suicide or what relationship that person had to Paul.

The important questions about who Paul is, whose blood is in the bathtub, and why he is in such distress are answered slowly and incompletely. The viewer of *Last Tango,* then, is presented with more serious interpretational challenges than is the viewer of Howard Hawks' *Red River,* a film that obeys principles of clear and coherent continuity from start to finish. Bertolucci's viewer must sort out the particulars of Paul's distress and his wife's suicide and their marital relationship by working through a plot structure that is not organized to facilitate the answering of these questions.

The Principle of Causality

Causality is the second principle of plot construction. Plot is not a random collection of events. A plot structures events in a time sequence that usually has a clear sense of direction. The story seems to be moving in a certain direction, and, in most cases, the viewer understands that it will come to a very deliberate end, that it will reach a purposeful and satisfying conclusion. Causality is the glue that holds the various events and episodes in the story together. One event in the story causes another, subsequent event. Plots, of course, may differ in the degree to which causality is present as a structuring principle.

Last Tango in Paris
(United Artists, 1972)
Key pieces of story information are withheld from viewers of *Last Tango in Paris* and are revealed only late in the film. As a result, first-time viewers have great difficulty piecing the story together. When Paul visits the scene of a suicide, viewers struggle to grasp its significance for him. The film's narrative design deliberately poses interpretive challenges for viewers. Frame enlargement.

Causality may be either explicit or implicit. Some plots are tightly constructed with events chained in a strong causal sequence. By contrast, other plots are loose, open-ended, or almost shapeless, with causality present in a minimal, and often only an implicit, way.

Explicit Causality   In the classical Hollywood narrative, present in films produced by the Hollywood studios in the 1930s–1950s, plot structure is highly organized and highly directional, that is, it demonstrates **explicit causality.** One event follows another as links in a chain. Each scene and episode in the Hollywood story is carefully integrated into an overall structure so that a chain of events, established early in the film, causes characters to act in goal-directed ways. At the conclusion of the film, the characters either achieve or fail to achieve their goals in a way that brings the narrative to an appropriate conclusion.

John Ford's 1956 production, *The Searchers,* a classic Hollywood film, illustrates this pattern of goal-directed, highly motivated action quite well. At the beginning of *The Searchers,* Ethan Edwards (John Wayne) returns from the Civil War to his brother's cabin in Texas. Ethan has been away for a number of years, engaged in activities that remain mysterious. He arrives at Aaron and Martha's homestead where relations between the brothers are tense and where (it is hinted) Ethan and Martha share an unspoken love. Shortly after Ethan's arrival, Indians attack the homestead, burn the cabin, and wipe out the family, except for Aaron and Martha's two daughters, whom they abduct. Ethan, driven by a powerful hatred of Indians, becomes obsessed with returning his nieces to the white society.

This is the goal-directed activity that generates the rest of the film's narrative and that takes the character on a five-year search. Ethan is accompanied by Martin, an adopted son of Aaron and Martha's. As the plot progresses, Ethan's original goal of rescuing Debbie, the only surviving captive, is replaced by another and darker quest—to destroy her.

Ethan's hatred of the Indians poisons his feelings for Debbie once he realizes that she is living among them as a member of their culture. In its last act, *The Searchers* generates considerable excitement as Ethan closes in on Debbie and chases her down a ravine to the mouth of a cave. He lifts her in his arms and the viewer is afraid that

The Searchers
(Warner Bros., 1956)
Ethan Edwards (John Wayne) looks with horror upon Aaron and Martha's burning cabin in *The Searchers.* Their deaths and the abduction of their daughters prompt his obsessive five-year quest for his surviving niece. Each narrative event in the film is tightly linked to others to form a highly explicit causal chain. Frame enlargement.

he is going to bash her brains out, but in a last-minute turn of events he forgives her, forgives himself, and honors his original quest, returning her to the white society of Texas settlers.

The quest for Debbie, spanning five years in the narrative and most of the film's running time, illustrates how plot in a classical Hollywood narrative is goal directed and explicitly motivated. One event causes another in the chain that forms the narrative. The Indians' attack on the cabin prompts Ethan's quest. Ethan swears to return Debbie to her rightful society. He undertakes a five-year search. During the course of the search, he comes to hate Debbie. What will he do when he finds her? The tension surrounding this latter question generates the climax of the film and its surprising last-minute turn of events in which the character redeems himself in a way that allows him to honor his original goal, the one that had driven the narrative from its beginning.

Causality and the hierarchy of narrative events.   The goal-driven, explicit, **narrative causality** of the classical Hollywood cinema features a clear hierarchy of narrative events. Certain episodes stand out as the most important links in the narrative chain, while others are less decisive and less important. If viewers are asked to summarize this kind of highly motivated film narrative, they can easily identify the most important narrative events. Asked to summarize *The Searchers,* a viewer might say that a band of Indians attacks a Texas homestead, one of the survivors vows revenge and searches for many years for a young girl, kidnapped by the raiders, until finally locating and rescuing her. These events could not be subtracted from the film without radically altering or damaging the story.

The important point here is that not all narratives function in this fashion. Many narratives are more loosely constructed and do not follow such powerful chains of causality. Key episodes do not stand out so clearly. These are narratives that employ implicit causality.

Implicit Causality   Films made outside the classical Hollywood tradition frequently employ alternative narrative structures, for example, a filmmaker might employ **implicit causality.** Here, causality is minimized, the sequence of events is loosely organized, and the viewer's sense of the direction in which the story is moving is weaker.

John Sayles' *City of Hope* (1991) deals with a very broad topic—a decaying urban economy and community in the 1990s. This narrative is very different from *The Searchers.* It is not driven by the personal goals of a protagonist and does not delve into the psychology of that central character. Sayles builds his narrative in an entirely different fashion. Instead of chaining the narrative events to follow the reactions and behavior of a central protagonist, Sayles follows an ensemble, a group, of characters— a corrupt city contractor, his disillusioned son, an idealistic city councilman, a group of cynical policemen, and citizens groups of various racial and ethnic backgrounds who are deeply disturbed by the relentless decay of their city.

The narrative does not concentrate on any one of these protagonists. Instead, it winds through the city to reveal a cross-section of its inhabitants. Summarizing the story of this film is more difficult than with *The Searchers* because narrative events are not tightly tied together and the narrative focus is dispersed among many characters instead of one central protagonist.

The Refusal of Narrative Causality   The range of narrative types in cinema is enormous, extending from explicit causal sequencing (most typical of popular, mass-market films) to more implicit, minimal forms of causation. In addition, radical attempts at narrative deconstruction, at making films that decompose and take apart their own narratives, have been popular among more philosophically inclined directors. In their work, narrative is treated as a problem, as something to be denied or attacked.

French director Alain Resnais, in the classic modernist film *Last Year at Marienbad* (1961), presents a narrative that deliberately refuses to organize itself. *Last Year at Marienbad* deals with a murky, cloudy, unclear set of events taking place at a luxurious hotel. During the film, an unnamed man attempts to persuade an unnamed woman that they have met the year before at a fancy spa. Whether they actually did is never resolved.

Resnais' editing prevents the emergence of clear spatial and time relationships between scenes. For example, a number of shots are joined with matched cuts and continuous dialogue, which imply that no time has elapsed, but the characters' costumes change as do the locales. These are contradictory cues that indicate time is both changing and not changing.

Last Year at Marienbad self-consciously studies the creation of narrative. In the film, a narrative attempts to organize itself but never quite does. The movie opens in a kind of pre-narrative state without characters and without a clear setting. The camera

---

Last Year at Marienbad (1961)
Anti-narrative in *Last Year at Marienbad*. Characters move through richly detailed settings, but the narrative refuses to emerge.

(Museum of Modern Art/Film Stills Archive)

tracks through empty hotel hallways, past doors, friezes, columns, paintings, and tapestries. Voice-over narration, belonging to no clearly identified character, poetically states that this is an environment of soundless rooms where voices sink into rugs so deep that no step can be heard, where halls and galleries are from another age, where hallways cross other hallways that open endlessly onto deserted rooms.

During the course of the camera's movements through this poetically and mysteriously defined environment, a group of individuals appears in frozen, still-life postures, characters existing as sculptures in this strange hotel. Gradually the characters unfreeze, begin to move, and start delivering dialogue, during which the mysterious man attempts to convince the unnamed woman that they have met the year before. The narrative comes to life.

Last Year at Marienbad is a film that deliberately sets out to provoke, puzzle, challenge, and undermine assumptions about what narrative is and how it operates in film. There is no sense of direction to the plot, and no real conclusion is ever reached. Instead, endless repetition—of images, camera movement, dialogue—is the defining structural characteristic. In this respect, Resnais' *Last Year at Marienbad* stands as an extreme departure from the terms of narrative in popular, mass-market movies, and it can be classified as a modernist film in that it does not intend to tell a story so much as to talk about what stories are and how they may be structured in film.

Jean-Luc Godard's *Le Gai Savoir* (1969) is another example of what might be called the "anti-narrative" narrative film. Here, two characters gather in an empty French television studio to inquire into the nature of images and to understand better how television and other visual media communicate. They meet for seven nights, and their comings and goings and their philosophical reflections about the nature of pictures constitute what plot there is. The soundtrack is punctuated by the noise of

Le Gai Savoir (1969)
Godard's *Le Gai Savoir* perversely offers poetry and philosophy in place of a narrative. Many modern, stylistically radical directors believe that all the stories have already been told in cinema, and they reject or deform the medium's storytelling function.
(Museum of Modern Art/Film Stills Archive)

static and by Godard's own voice in a kind of running, anxious commentary about the nature of images and his own film. *Le Gai Savoir* reduces narrative to a minimal presence in order to construct a film that functions more on the lines of an essay than a story. In this respect, like *Last Year at Marienbad*, Godard's *Le Gai Savoir* illustrates the impatience with stories felt by many modern, stylistically radical directors.

Such filmmakers regard narrative as an obstacle to their creative interests. Telling a story gets in the way. It obligates them to create, delineate, and motivate characters and to emphasize the story, treating other, non-narrative elements as background components. Filmmakers whose interests are essayistic, poetic, or didactic often take the medium in a non-narrative direction when they consider narrative to be incompatible with their artistic goals. Viewers of popular movies may find this anti-narrative orientation difficult to understand and, indeed, perverse because the basic pleasure offered by popular cinema is precisely the storytelling function. Such viewers may find the anti-narrative films to be a strange experience or to offer little of the familiar pleasures they are accustomed to finding in movies. But the anti-narrative tradition in cinema is strong, and it has influenced many important filmmakers whose work has enlarged the creative boundaries of cinema.

The Principle of Subplots

Whether a narrative is constructed in a goal-driven, highly motivated fashion in which causality is explicitly present, or whether it involves a weak chaining of events that are connected in a loose fashion, all narratives involve an additional structuring principle. As an accompaniment to causality, subplots are a fundamental narrative element. They are the third principle of plot construction. The distinction between major and minor narrative events is a distinction between those events that drive a narrative forward and cannot be deleted without affecting the logic of the plot, and those events that could, in fact, be removed but which would impoverish the story emotionally or aesthetically.

Subplots are those elements in the narrative in which the viewer's attention is distracted from the main chain of events to focus on a minor character or a secondary episode. Filmmakers often employ subplots, which are woven into the principal sequence of narrative events, to divert the viewer's attention for brief periods. These **digressive subplots** are important in that they add texture and atmosphere to the story. Almost any film narrative will have such digressions. One of the things that distinguishes a classic Hollywood narrative such as *The Searchers* from anti-narrative films such as *Last Year at Marienbad* or *Le Gai Savoir* is that, in the former, *major* narrative events are clearly distinguished from *minor* narrative events, whereas in the latter there is no such distinction. All episodes are treated as equally important to the anti-narrative category, and all may appear to form a kind of extended digression that is the film itself.

Digressive subplots have strategic value as a feature of narrative structure. An audience wants two things from a story. One is that the narrative progress to a satisfying conclusion. This is the need that causality as a structuring principle fulfills. The causal chain of events builds toward an ending that produces satisfaction for the audience by completing and closing that chain of events. Narrative closure is deeply satisfying for viewers.

The audience's second desire, however, is that the narrative, as a source of pleasure in itself, not come to an end. The tension between these desires—that the story continue yet be concluded in a satisfying way—requires the use of digression as a way of extending the narrative and preventing it from ending too soon. Digressive subplots also add depth, texture, and richness to the narrative. Films involving a weak chain of narrative events are films that are full of digressions, whereas the more strongly chained the narrative episodes are, the more infrequent the digressions will be. Few films, though, are without any digression because of its importance as a means of enriching and prolonging the narrative.

Voice and Point of View

All stories involve the presence of **voice** and **point of view.** These terms refer to the manner by which the narrator is understood to speak. Determining narrative voice in film can be very difficult. Films, are made by groups of people, and it is often difficult to say with any certainty which member of the production team—director, cinematographer, editor, sound technician—is responsible for a particular effect on screen. Who is the narrator in film?

Real and Implied Authors

In film, therefore, the distinction that has existed in literary theory between the **real** and the **implied author** acquires a special intensity. The notion of the real versus the implied author was developed by theorist Wayne Booth as a means of avoiding the biographical trap in literary criticism (that is, to avoid the temptation to believe that the "narrative voice" in a work of fiction is that of the author). In discussing the novels of Ernest Hemingway, for example, one cannot reduce their stylistic and literary structure to the facts or the values or the biography of Ernest Hemingway, the man.

Islands in the Stream
(Paramount Pictures, 1977)
George C. Scott as Thomas Hudson in *Islands in the Stream*, a film based on Hemingway's novel. Hemingway's character, Hudson, was a thinly disguised version of himself, and Scott's hair and beard in the film are meant to evoke Hemingway's real-life appearance. The film explicitly points toward its real and implied authors. Frame enlargement.

In other words, for Booth, "Hemingway," the literary persona (and the implied author) seemingly present in the writings, is distinct from Ernest Hemingway, the man, who was born in Illinois in 1899, served as a reporter on the *Kansas City Star,* fought in World War I, settled in Paris after the war, and died in Idaho in 1961. The novels have their own emotional logic and power, and one can speak of "Hemingway," the literary personality that hovers in the shadows of the writings, as being distinct from Hemingway, the man.

A film critic might study the work of such film authors as "Hitchcock," "Ford," "Spielberg," "Godard," "Bertolucci," or "Kurosawa," and treat these as implied rather than real authors, the names as labels given to bodies of film and used to describe the characteristics of those films rather than the characteristics of those individual people. To speak about voice in a Hitchcock film is to describe a narrative world characterized by a certain Catholic conception of sin, guilt, transgression, and punishment. Voice, therefore, is associated with the implied, not the real, author or narrator.

The difficulty with maintaining a hard and complete distinction between the implied and the real author is that many directors do indeed draw upon personal experience in crafting their films so that a correlation does exist between who they are as people and the content of their films. Directors such as Ingmar Bergman, Steven Spielberg, and Alfred Hitchcock have undeniably based aspects of their films on personal experiences. Knowing something about their personal history can help clarify structural features of their films. But biographical correlations can be misleading and easily overemphasized. Because of this, the distinction between real and implied authors is useful to maintain, not in any fixed or absolute sense, but as a way of keeping separate the many ways in which film structure, produced as a collaborative enterprise by teams of filmmakers, and a fictional narrative that creates an imaginary

---

Psycho (Paramount Pictures, 1960)
As a real author, Alfred Hitchcock transformed his personal experiences, interests, and anxieties into brilliant film images and narratives, but the richness of these films transcends any biographical basis they might have. As an implied author, therefore, "Hitchcock" designates a cinematic world of crime, guilt, terror, and madness. Norman Bates (Tony Perkins) inhabits such a world at his motel in *Psycho.* Frame enlargements.

world may fail to correspond with the facts of an individual filmmaker's biography. The real and implied author may overlap in sometimes significant ways but just as often will remain distinct and discrete.

Narrative Point of View

The narrative voice through which a given film speaks will, in turn, help shape narrative point of view. Point of view in the cinema may be either third person or first person. In literature, if point of view is in first person, then the narrator employs the first-person pronoun in a first-person narrative. "I went here." "I did that." Third-person pronouns produce a third-person narrative. "He went here." "She did that." Movies are almost always presented in third-person narration. In most films, the camera assumes a point of view that is detached and separate from the literal viewpoint as seen by each of the characters.

However, there are times when filmmakers want to suggest a character's literal point of view. Such episodes are called **subjective shots** or point-of-view shots or scenes because the camera is literally viewing through the eyes of the character. Generally, the shift from third to first person in film is signaled by showing a character reacting to something off screen, then cutting to a view of what the character sees, the *subjective* view, and then closing the subjective moment with a cut back to the character from a third-person perspective.

Although film generally employs third-person narration, first-person point of view is often implicitly present, far more often than the frequency with which subjective or point-of-view shots are used. Through performance, production design, lighting, color, editing, the use of sound and camera, directors can portray the emotional or psychological perspective of a character in a scene. George Stevens' *Shane* (1953) deals with the arrival of a mysterious gunfighter in a farming community in Wyoming. He stays at the home of farmer Joe Starrett and is revered by Starrett's young son, an impressionable boy whose father is somewhat distant and who yearns for an attractive male authority figure to admire. He finds this figure in Shane, and it is strongly implied that the story of the film is filtered through the point of view of young Joey Starrett.

There are, however, few subjective shots from Joey's perspective. Instead, the systematic visual presentation of Shane as an extremely romantic and idealized figure

Shane (Paramount Pictures, 1953)
Shane's (Alan Ladd) smooth, handsome face, golden buckskins, and refined manner establish an implicitly first-person perspective in *Shane*. It is a boy's view of a romantic and idealized Western hero. Frame enlargement.

clad in golden buckskins establishes an implicit first-person narration, one that correlates with Joey's point of view. Shane's idealized visual and emotional presentation makes him precisely the sort of hero a young boy, starved for adventure, might wish for. This is an implicitly first-person visualization.

Explicit First-Person Narration   Although *extended* point of view in film is rarely first person (except by implication, as in *Shane*), there are a few spectacular exceptions to this rule. *Lady in the Lake,* a detective film made in 1946 from a Raymond Chandler novel, is distinguished by the novelty of having the camera take the detective's first-person point of view throughout. Viewers see the detective when he pauses in front of a mirror or examines his reflection in a store window. At other times his hand or an item of his clothing might intrude into the frame.

More recently, *84 Charlie MoPic* (1989) presented its narrative entirely through a subjective camera as MoPic, a combat cameraman, follows and films a dangerous seven-man reconnaissance mission to the Central Highlands during the Vietnam War. The action is presented as he sees it through the lens of his camera, and the gimmick works well in making the viewer a participant on the mission.

Films rarely employ subjective point of view so extensively, and the reason is clear. When used as much as it is in *Lady in the Lake* or *84 Charlie MoPic,* subjective point of view can become awkward and can interfere with a flexible presentation of narrative information. Filmmakers find it more effective to employ third-person camera positions but to use light, color, sound, performance, and composition to imply the emotional and psychological points of view of characters in a scene. Taken together, these elements of structure help create the cinema's distinctive form of explicit third-person narration with implied first-person components.

THE VIEWER'S CONTRIBUTION TO NARRATIVE

Storytelling and human thought and perception closely correspond with one another. Telling stories is a universal human activity, used when people or cultures need to explain how and why change occurs. Stories organize information and experience into meaningful patterns, and the search for meaning and pattern are basic features of human thought and perception. Stories invite viewers to seek meaning and search for pattern inside the narrative design of the tale. This is why a totally random sequencing of plot events can never constitute a story.

Omission and the Interpretation of Pattern

The omission of plot information, whether at the micro or the macro level, invites the audience to fill in the missing pieces. This is clearly one of the deepest pleasures that stories can offer because, by filling in these missing pieces, readers or viewers help create the overall pattern that is the narrative.

The action of the popular thriller *The French Connection* (1972) deals with a New York cop's obsessive hunt for a powerful French drug smuggler. At the end of the film, the cop corners the smuggler in a warehouse. The cop chases him into a back room, and the camera stays outside the room, leaving both characters off screen. After a pause, a gunshot is heard off screen, and the image fades out. The film is over, and the viewer is left wondering who fired the shot and whether the cop got his man. As the end credits roll, that final gunshot reverberates in the viewer's mind. What did it mean, and why was it presented in such a mysterious way? How does the story *end*? Its structure challenges the viewer to make sense of the film's puzzling conclusion, its final withholding of information, and its lack of narrative closure.

As the ending of *The French Connection* illustrates, storytellers can hold the audience by deliberately omitting bits of information. The viewers infer and fill in the missing pieces as their contribution to the story, binding storyteller and audience in a close creative relationship. In a mystery film, viewers will try to guess the identity of the murderer before the detective or the narrative reveals it. The final shot of the icepick under the bed in *Basic Instinct* (1992) teases the audience with the possibility that the real killer in the narrative is still at large and may strike again.

This activity of filling in by the audience is rooted in a basic operational principle of the human mind—the search for pattern. The acts of seeing, hearing, and remembering impose order and meaning on experience. Perception and interpretation are not mechanical responses to information, but are processes of filling out and filling in by creatively organizing information into meaningful patterns. Narrative operates according to principles that invite this contribution by the audience. The omission of plot information, therefore, contributes not only aesthetically and stylistically to a story, as it clearly does in *The French Connection* and Bertolucci's *Last Tango in Paris,* but also intensifies the vividness of the story experience for the viewer by strengthening the bond between audience and storyteller as they both help create the story.

Causation and the Interpretation of Pattern

Like the omission of detail, narrative causation stimulates interpretive contributions by the viewer. Viewers will seek structure and find pattern even in a weak chain of narrative events. Given only a minimal amount of information, viewers can still assemble a narrative. The scholar Seymour Chatman has made this point in discussing E. M. Forster's famous narrative formula, "The King died and then the Queen died."

Basic Instinct (Carolco, 1992)
The open ending of *Basic Instinct* suggests that the killer is still at large and invites the audience to imagine what happens next. The narrative conclusion is ambiguous and does not tie up all loose ends.

Chatman points out that if the phrase runs, "The king died and then the queen died of grief," this clearly establishes causation. The queen died of grief *because* of the king's death.

However, even the less informative version, "The king died and then the queen died," may imply causation because of the reader/viewer's need for structure. The reader/viewer may attribute causation even to this less-informative version by making inferences to supply the missing links in this mini-narrative. For example, although it is not mentioned, the reader/viewer might infer that the queen's subsequent death is due to grief, thereby perceiving structure and attributing causation even when they are barely present.

The Viewer's Evaluation of Narrative

By choosing to link events in a weakly causal series, filmmakers invite the audience's filling-in activities and can create a very strong bond with the audience as a co-creator of narrative meaning. This consideration points to an important conclusion: meaning is not "in" the film but is formed by the interaction of the film's audiovisual and narrative design with the viewer's own horizon of perceptual and social experience—the viewer's interpretive contribution. The implications of this are enormous. It means that filmmakers cannot control the meaning of their films because the experiences, values,

---

First Blood (Orion Pictures, 1982)
Viewers use a flexible set of standards when evaluating a movie narrative. They assess its artistic quality as well as its correspondence with their own understanding of people, places, or issues that may be contained in the story. Filmmakers cannot control viewer reactions because viewers bring many different perspectives to bear on films. For some viewers, Sylvester Stallone's Rambo is an inspiring hero, to others, a bloodthirsty cartoon figure.
(Museum of Modern Art/Film Stills Archive)

and assumptions that viewers bring to those films, and which establish their basis of interpretation, are incredibly diverse and variable.

Obviously, viewers apply different yardsticks when evaluating the aesthetic qualities of a narrative. Is it coherent? Is it pleasurable? Is it convincing? Does it make sense? These are evaluations of narrative structure—how the story is aesthetically organized and told—and they are applied to the elements of narrative design.

In a story in which events are linked in a tight causal chain, with few digressions, viewers tend to expect an ending that ties up all the loose ends by resolving all outstanding story issues. If viewers are given, instead, an ambiguous ending, as occurs in *The French Connection,* some may feel frustration or anger or betrayal even while others are excited by the ambiguity and are stimulated to fill in the missing information. Viewers routinely evaluate how the story is told and whether, given the type of film it is, the story is told in a satisfying way.

Because so many movies establish screen worlds that are recognizably similar to their own, viewers also tend to evaluate narratives using standards borrowed from personal and social experience. Here, it is not so much narrative design that is being evaluated as the way the narrative portrays people or situations. Arab-Americans protested the Arnold Schwarzenegger thriller *True Lies* (1994) because of its portrayal of Arabic groups as terrorists. Some African-Americans thought that the hyenas in Disney's *The Lion King* (1994) were unpleasantly close to a caricature of African-American people.

These types of assessments of narrative acceptability focus on how a narrative represents social issues, situations, or groups. Viewers make these assessments by measuring the narrative's portrayals against their own understanding of these issues, situations, or groups. Does the narrative square with their own sense of things, or does it seem unreasonably biased or distorted in a way that style cannot justify?

The sets of standards viewers apply when evaluating narratives, then, are quite varied, and they range from judgments about the artistic design of the story to judgments about its success in representing familiar things or people. Filmmakers can influence but they cannot control these evaluations. Although filmmakers may determine the audiovisual structure of their films, viewers are essential co-creators of the meanings that arise from those structures.

SUMMARY

In their most popular form, movies tell stories. However, the film medium can also inform and instruct by observing real events (these movies are called documentaries) or it can represent pure shape, line, color, and form rather than real things (these are experimental, "underground" or avant-garde films). But it is narrative films that have captured the popular audience. The turn toward narrative emerged early in film history and has been present ever since.

Present in all cultures, narrative thinking is an essential human ability. Narratives have three basic sets of elements: a narrator and narrative point of view, a story and plot, and a contract between narrator and audience. Fictional narratives, the kind movies typically employ, grow out of a particular context in which the storyteller and the audience agree to play make-believe in a way that grants the fictional story a special status—its truthfulness is not counted to be as important as its artistic organization and its power to delight and to compel belief.

Films tell their stories by creating plots that may sometimes—through flashbacks or other devices—completely rearrange the proper order of story events. Plots are constructed using principles of selection and omission, causality and digression. Typically, filmmakers will omit information from their stories, either as small bits of detail (microlevel omission) or as larger chunks (macrolevel omission). While selection and omission at the macro level can occasionally cause interpretational problems for the viewer (some filmmakers deliberately intend this), filmmakers generally select and omit detail to draw viewers more deeply into the story by inviting them to "fill in the blanks" and help create its meaning.

Plots are built using causality as the glue to hold events together. Causality can be either explicit or implicit. In more extreme cases of implicit causality, an anti-narrative can result. Digression is a tool filmmakers use to delay the ending of their story. However, in films whose plots are tightly built, with explicit causality, digression is often minimized.

All stories are told by someone. In film, the narrator can be understood, loosely, as the camera, lights, sound, color, set design, costumes, and other elements of structure. Although these can be used to imply a character's point of view, voice in the movies is usually third person, with implicit first-person components, except where a filmmaker will briefly switch to subjective point-of-view shots. Voice is usually an attribute of the implied, rather than the real, author.

SUGGESTED READINGS

Wayne C. Booth, *The Rhetoric of Fiction*, Second Edition (Chicago: University of Chicago Press, 1983).

David Bordwell, *Narration in the Fiction Film* (Madison: University of Wisconsin Press, 1985).

Seymour Chatman, *Story and Discourse: Narrative Structure in Fiction and Film* (Ithaca, NY: Cornell University Press, 1978).

John L. Fell, *Film and the Narrative Tradition* (Norman, OK: University of Oklahoma Press, 1974).

Avrom Fleishman, *Narrated Films: Storytelling Situations in Cinema History* (Baltimore: Johns Hopkins University Press, 1992).

Jane Gaines, ed., *Classical Hollywood Narrative: The Paradigm Wars* (Durham, NC: Duke University Press, 1992).

George M. White, *Narration in Light: Studies in Cinematic Point of View* (Baltimore: Johns Hopkins University Press, 1986).

Chapter 7

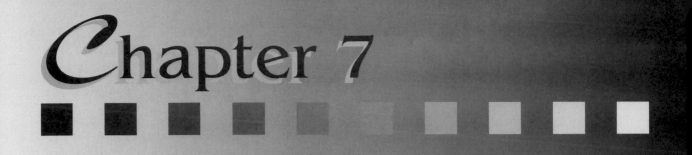

Modes of Screen Reality

Chapter Objectives

After reading this chapter, you should be able to

- explain the basic modes of screen reality
- describe the principles of narrative, character behavior, and audiovisual design that operate in each mode of screen reality
- differentiate ordinary fictional realism, historical realism, documentary realism, and fictional documentary realism
- describe how the cinema functions as a medium that can record properties of the visual world before the camera as well as transform the appearance of that world
- explain how this double capacity for recording and transforming relates to the basic modes of screen reality
- explain the importance of production design for the mode of fantasy and the fantastic and how fantasy settings achieve credibility
- distinguish two modes of cinematic self-reflexivity
- list the elements of genre
- describe the relation of the basic American film genres to modes of screen reality
- explain why multiple modes of screen reality are possible in cinema

Key Terms and Concepts

screen reality
realism
expressionism
fantasy

cinematic self-reflexivity
ordinary fictional realism
historical realism
documentaries

documentary realism
fictional documentary
    realism
genre

This chapter examines how filmmakers use the elements of cinematic structure (lighting, editing, camera position, etc.) to create versions of representational reality on screen. Audiences routinely view a wide variety of films, ranging from comedies and Westerns to serious dramas, science fiction, and gangster films. The worlds represented on screen are uniquely different in each of these genres, and viewers readily accept a variety of screen worlds. Each possible screen world establishes its own validity, and a filmmaker must convince the audience that what they are seeing is plausible and is, taken on its own terms, real.

The concept of **screen reality** pertains to the principles of time, space, character behavior, and audiovisual design that filmmakers systematically organize in a given film to create an ordered world on screen in which characters may act and in which a narrative may unfold. Obviously, different kinds of films create different representational realities on screen and relate in different ways to the actual social worlds inhabited by their flesh-and-blood spectators. A film's screen world is a systematic, artistic transformation of the viewer's personal and social frames of reference. This process of transformation is complex and multileveled. This chapter explains the basic modes or types of screen reality, and why there are several different but equally acceptable modes.

☐ BASIC MODES OF SCREEN REALITY

The cinema can configure physical, social, or psychological reality in a variety of different ways or modes. Cinema has a multimodal capability. It can persuade film viewers to believe in the validity of many uniquely constituted on-screen worlds. There are four fundamental modes of representational reality on screen: **realism, expressionism, fantasy** and the fantastic, and **cinematic self-reflexivity.** (For the purposes of the discussion, each mode will be treated as an ideal type. In practice, however, a given film may draw on elements from several modes.) How do these modes operate and how are films constructed from within them?

Realism

This is one of the most commonly encountered modes of screen reality, and the term *realism* is probably the most overused and overworked item in critical discussions and daily conversations about film. Viewers often say that a film was or was not realistic and base their assessments about whether it was a good or bad movie on how realistic it seemed to be. Although realism is a slippery term with meanings that are often hard to pin down, three broad types or categories of realism clearly exist in film: ordinary fictional realism, historical realism, and documentary realism.

Ordinary Fictional Realism

Many film productions belong to the category of **ordinary fictional realism.** These movies convince viewers that the world on screen does not differ in fundamental ways from the reality they inhabit daily. Time and space behave in these movies much as

Driving Miss Daisy
(Warner Bros., 1989)
Jessica Tandy and Morgan Freeman in a balanced, eye-level medium shot from *Driving Miss Daisy,* part of the film's naturalistic visual style.

they do in viewers' ordinary lives. Characters belong to readily recognizable social worlds and communities, and they neither possess magical powers nor behave in ways that strike the viewer as exotic, strange, or incomprehensible. In other words, films in this category seem to have an ordinary, everyday kind of realism. *Driving Miss Daisy,* the 1989 Academy Award winner as Best Picture, belongs to this mode of representational reality. Three fundamental components of ordinary fictional realism operate in *Driving Miss Daisy.*

Naturalistic Visual Style   The first of these three components is the lack of overly pictorial, expressive interventions in the visual style of ordinary fictional realist films. Explicit, readily recognized stylistic manipulations are generally absent. These might include extreme lighting effects, elaborate camera movements, editing for discontinuity, or elaborate production design.

Like most films in the category of ordinary fictional realism, *Driving Miss Daisy* employs continuity editing to replicate, on screen, basic perceptual cues that viewers use to infer relations of time and space in their daily lives. The film employs the eyeline match, shot-reverse-shot cutting, inserts matching the master shot, the 180-degree rule, and transitional material to prepare for screen direction changes to create strong visual continuity on screen. The action seems to flow over the cuts, and the screen world built from shot to shot links up in a physically coherent way.

The editing style, based on continuity principles, creates a realistic impression of time and space in which the physical constancies in the world on screen do not depart in fundamental ways from those that viewers observe in their own lives. The physical positioning of her son Boolie, and Miss Daisy does not change arbitrarily from shot to shot. With reference to each other and to objects in the rooms they inhabit, their positions remain stable across shot changes and variations in camera angle. In a similar fashion, the lighting, set, and costume design all aim for an unobtrusive naturalism. Visual design and shot construction in *Driving Miss Daisy* achieve an impression of ordinary realism by avoiding cinematic designs that look excessively artificial or elaborately arranged.

Linear Narrative Structure   The second component of ordinary realism is typically found at the narrative level. Films in this mode often employ a linear narrative in which the sequence of events has a teleological logic, that is, events are chained together as a series of causes and effects. The action at the beginning of the film sets in motion events that lead to the final outcome. Daisy's car wreck at the beginning of the film persuades her son that she is no longer capable of driving herself. Acting on this conviction, Boolie hires Hoke to be Miss Daisy's chauffeur, and the remainder of the film studies the close friendship that develops between Daisy and Hoke.

Nonlinear designs.   Narrative designs that are nonlinear tend to pull viewers out of the mode of ordinary realism because nonlinear designs emphasize a film's style and structural design. The kaleidoscopic structure of Woody Allen's *Annie Hall* (1977) presents the story of Alvy Singer's affair with Annie Hall out of chronological sequence, constantly reminding viewers of the film's structural design. This doesn't prevent the audience from enjoying the movie or laughing at the gags or from feeling sadness when Annie and Alvy finally break up. But the audience's relationship to the film is very complex. Viewers are touched by the emotions portrayed on screen while preserving a sense that they are watching an elaborately designed narrative structure whose precision and sophistication distinguish it from the flux and fussiness of daily life.

A fractured and kaleidoscopic time structure, of course, is not the only form of nonlinear narrative construction available to filmmakers. Multiple flashbacks are another common way of breaking up a linear narrative. One of the most famous films to employ multiple flashbacks is Akira Kurosawa's *Rashomon* (1950). The film's story is set in twelfth-century Japan and centers on the details surrounding the rape of a noblewoman and the death of her samurai warrior husband. The events of the crime are recalled differently by four separate narrators—the bandit accused of the rape, the noblewoman herself, the spirit of the dead samurai accessed through a medium, and a woodcutter who was an unseen witness to the tragedy. The film's narrative is composed of these multiple flashbacks, each one narrating a different version of the events under question. In the case of *Rashomon*, the multiple flashbacks signal a didactic intent on the part of the filmmaker and encourage the viewer to extract the following lesson: that truth is relative and that people will perceive those versions of reality that best suit their own self-images.

Plausible Character Behavior   The third component of ordinary fictional realism pertains to the level of plausibility that the viewer ascribes to the behavior of charac-

---

Rashomon (1950)

The complex flashback structure of *Rashomon* creates a nonlinear narrative that emphasizes the artifice of its design. The film's multiple flashbacks undermine a smooth, linear design by forcing the viewer continually to reconsider story information in light of the unfolding flashback material. Through these flashbacks, the memories of the characters intrude upon the narrative in ways that suggest that memory is selective and truth is relative.

(Museum of Modern Art/Film Stills Archive)

ters on screen. At the beginning of *Driving Miss Daisy,* viewers see Daisy absent-mindedly wrecking the family car, followed immediately by her proud denials that she is at fault or that she needs a professional driver. Her refusal to accept her declining abilities and her son's gentle concern for her welfare are readily understandable human motives, and they strike the viewer as entirely plausible motivations for the action in the film that follows.

Not all films in the ordinary fictional realism mode are as successful in displaying plausible character behavior as in *Driving Miss Daisy.* The classic Western *Red River* (1948) has created controversies about its climax in which the expected gunfight between John Wayne and Montgomery Clift does not occur. In the last minutes of the film, the John Wayne character, bent on revenge and swearing to kill his adopted son (portrayed by Montgomery Clift) changes his mind and forgives the young man. A sudden, abrupt, and unexpected comic reconciliation ensues. *Red River* is recognized as a classic of the Western genre, but since 1948, when the film was released, critics and viewers have been arguing about whether the change in John Wayne's character is plausible or realistic, given the stress the narrative has placed on the character's ruthless, selfish, and violent personality.

In films with star performers, the star's screen personality can complicate a viewer's assessment of the plausibility of a screen character's portrayal. Viewers have complex expectations about star personas and these often mandate the kinds of roles stars should play. Clint Eastwood's violent *Dirty Harry* films have been consistent box-office successes, while his more off-beat and unusual roles as a country-western singer in *Honkytonk Man* (1982) or as a Hollywood film director in *White Hunter, Black Heart* (1990) have been relative commercial failures. The relation of

---

Red River (United Artists, 1948)
The abrupt conclusion of *Red River,* in which John Wayne and Montgomery Clift trade punches and then become friends again, strikes many viewers as an implausible turn of events. The formulaic nature of genre films, such as Westerns, conditions viewers to expect certain kinds of narrative events. Because of this, genre filmmakers are often more tightly bound in their work by what an audience expects and what a genre requires than are filmmakers whose work places them outside genre boundaries.

a star's persona to the type of characters portrayed by the star is extremely important in affecting how viewers will respond to those portrayals. If a star steps too far outside the parameters of his or her accepted image, the star may be courting audience rejection.

Because the ordinary fictional realist mode can seem so familiar and accessible, critics and viewers sometimes mistakenly regard it as an easy accomplishment or as synonymous with no style at all. However, the elements of linear narrative, unobtrusive visual design, and plausible character behavior do not denote the absence of cinematic style. They should not be misunderstood to be a kind of zero-degree level of style, nor should one assume that a filmmaker can achieve these elements of ordinary fictional realism easily. Like all the other modes, this one is highly constructed, involving the deliberate design and manipulation of elements of cinematic style. The appearance of ordinary realism is one that is *constructed* and *created*.

Historical Realism

Ordinary fictional realism generally represents a time or place not too far removed from the social world of the film's audiences. Many films made in the mode referred to as **historical realism,** however, try to recreate a more distant past. Such films include Martin Scorsese's *The Age of Innocence* (1993), set in late-nineteenth-century, aristocratic New York society; James Ivory's *The Remains of the Day* (1993), set among the British aristocracy in the decade prior to the start of World War II; and Steven Spielberg's Oscar-winning *Schindler's List* (1993), which aims at a visual and cultural recreation of Poland and Germany during the Nazi era.

The historical realist mode attempts to convince the viewer of the reality of the world on screen through the accumulation of authentic period detail. Therefore, production design is extremely important in this mode. Nominees for Academy Awards in the categories of art direction and costume design are often dominated by historical realist films. In 1994, for example, the nominees included the three historical realist films just mentioned: *The Age of Innocence, The Remains of the Day,* and *Schindler's List*.

The Age of Innocence (Columbia Pictures, 1994)
Production design is a key element of style that helps establish the period setting of films in the mode of historical realism. Sets and costumes in *The Age of Innocence* embody with fine detail the aristocratic world of late-nineteenth-century New York society.
Schindler's List (Universal Studios, 1993)
Liam Neeson as Schindler. The film's black and white cinematography combined with its meticulous production design to emphasize its historical realism.

To achieve this detail, filmmakers working in this mode conduct extensive historical research. Janusz Kaminski, the cinematographer for *Schindler's List,* based the visual design of his images on the photography of Roman Vishniac, who photographed European Jewish communities in the 1920s and 1930s and who published these photographs in his book, *A Vanished World.* Seeking to re-create the visual appearance of these communities for the film, Kaminski imitated Vishniac's photographs. Kaminski notes that he tried to work as if he were photographing the film using the technology of 50 years ago, with no fancy lights, dollies, or tripods.

Documentary Realism

Concepts of realism in the cinema are closely tied to traditions in which the camera is used as an instrument of reportage and documentation. Films that fall into this tradition are frequently termed **documentaries,** although such films may employ a wide range of cinematic styles and structures. Although the topic of documentary filmmaking is an extremely broad one and generally falls outside the confines of this textbook, a word on the subject is in order in relation to concepts of realism.

Even though the camera is used as a recording instrument to capture events, situations, and realities that may be transpiring independently of the filmmaker, the camera is also an instrument of style. A filmmaker's choices of lenses, film stocks, and positions and angles subtly transform the raw material of the event unfolding before it so that what is taking place becomes a cinematic event that has its own stylistic organization and design. The cinema has dual capabilities: the camera can *record* the same kinds of visual information about space and the positioning of objects that viewers use in their perception of everyday life. However, filmmakers can *transform* this information by using it to create fantastic, unreal, impossible, or heavily stylized images. Moreover, the narrative style and logic of many films is shaped by generic story conventions that viewers understand and use as a basis for evaluating the acceptability of a film's tale. The cinema transforms as well as records, and if one is to understand how films work one must understand both of these activities.

It is naïve, then, to believe that documentary filmmaking is the equivalent of raw reportage. The inevitable choices a filmmaker makes about lenses, camera positions, lighting, sound, and editing transform the raw material in front of the camera into an organized cinematic design.

Assumption of a Referent   All documentary films exist in a state of tension, caught between the camera's recording and transforming functions. The documentary filmmaker wants to report an event that has occurred but must transform that event into cinema. How, then, does the concept of realism operate within the documentary tradition? Are documentary films essentially like fiction films in that they speak a language of structure and style that is unique to the cinema?

To some extent, documentaries are like fiction films. In each, a filmmaker confronts the same array of choices—where to put the camera, where to cut the shot, how to join several images together, whether and how to impose a narrative logic upon the events depicted. Despite these similarities, however, two unique characteristics distinguish **documentary realism.** First, audiences and most documentary filmmakers assume the existence of a noncinematic referent, some person, event, or situation that exists prior to, and independently of, the film that is being made. This assumption does not hold for fiction films in which the characters are clearly made up for the purposes of the story.

Absence of Fictional Elements   The second basis on which documentary realism rests is the perceived absence in the film structure of key fictional elements. These elements might include the presence of actors performing a role or the presence of a narrative structure that alters the time chronology of the event. Audiences and most documentary filmmakers assume that fictionalizing tendencies begin with the presence of actors and an invented narrative structure. Critics charged that *Roger and Me* (1989), the documentary about the collapse of the auto industry in Flint, Michigan, violated ethics of documentary filmmaking because it rearranged and reordered the chronology of events leading to the demise of the General Motors auto plant. The film collapsed and telescoped events that occurred over a long period of time so that they appeared to occur virtually overnight. Assumptions of a noncinematic referent and the absence of key fictional elements are central to the mode of documentary realism, but, in practice, there is considerable flexibility and room for individual films to negotiate their own unique approaches with reference to these issues, particularly with reference to the cinema's capacity for stylistic commentary.

Documentary poesis.   Many recent documentaries make no claim of reportorial objectivity and come close, instead, to a form that might best be described as an extended poetic essay. Errol Morris' *The Thin Blue Line* (1988) reexamines the 1976 murder of Dallas policeman Robert Wood through interviews with Randall Adams and David Harris. Harris was originally arrested for the killing, but he swore that hitchhiker Randall Adams was the killer. Adams was arrested, convicted, and sentenced to death, and Harris was released. Harris subsequently confessed to the crime. Adams, who had maintained his innocence from the beginning, was exonerated as a result of this film.

The Thin Blue Line (Miramax, 1988)
The Thin Blue Line mixes standard documentary elements, such as interview footage with real people, with highly stylized crime scene reenactments. The poetic results show how imaginative and creative documentary style may be. Interview footage with Randall Adams, filmed in a straightforward manner, contrasts with the visually expressive crime reenactments. Note the tight framing of the gun, and the dark, low-key lighting. Frame enlargements.

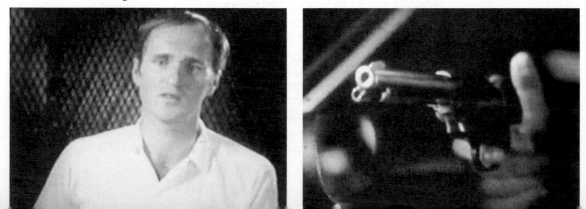

The Thin Blue Line powerfully illustrates the flexibility of documentary realism. It deals with an actual, noncinematic event through interviews with the principal people involved. Intermixed with the interview footage, however, are re-creations of the shooting, employing actors, an original, moody musical score by celebrity composer Philip Glass, and a deliberate, stylized editing design that runs through the entire film.

Director Errol Morris wanted to avoid the style of such popular journalistic documentaries as *60 Minutes*. The editing on *60 Minutes* directly compares and contrasts the positions taken by the subjects of the show's interviews by intercutting different speakers, one after the other. Witness A claims that condition X is true and then a direct cut shows witness B claiming that condition Y is, in fact, true.

In *The Thin Blue Line,* Morris forbade editor Paul Barnes from employing this type of editing. Barnes could not cut directly from shots of Adams to shots of Harris or vice versa. On the soundtrack viewers hear one man speaking after the other but never see them together in adjacent shots. Adams and Harris are interviewed separately, and each talks about what brought him to Dallas on the eve of the fatal shooting. Moving back and forth between the recollections of each man, the film establishes two parallel lines of action in the double series of events that brought each man to the same city. The editing imposes a deliberate visual design that separates the interview footage of each man from the interview footage of his antagonist. Instead of cutting directly between the footage of Adams and Harris, Barnes separates them by interspersing shots of the Dallas skyline.

The editing is an artificial creation by the filmmakers. It imposes a visual design upon the narrated events as well as an ethical structure. The ethic, in this case, emerges from Morris' intention to avoid what he perceives as the exploitative journalistic practice of setting one person up to be immediately contradicted by another witness. The filmmakers impose an artificially constructed cinematic design upon their material. Is this a violation of documentary realism? No, because such realism co-exists with the cinema's enormous capability for stylistic manipulation and transformation. In this case, the editorial design does not change the fact that the film refers, without falsification, to a noncinematic referent and includes interview footage with the actual participants.

What about the crime scene reenactments that are clearly fictional elements? Director Morris and editor Paul Barnes wanted to avoid the usual style of fake dramatizations employing well-lit full-figure shots that show an actor impersonating a real person. Instead, they chose to play the reenactments in dark light with very tight (close-up) camera framings that prevent viewers from seeing many details. This design imposes an artificial visual style upon the reenacted event that signals to viewers that it is not real, that it is, in fact, a reenactment, and that, by employing such an artificial design, the filmmakers know the difference between the two. The reenactments place fictionalizing elements within the film. The shooting is *reenacted* by actors. In principle, this is a violation of documentary realism, but the film employs a self-conscious visual style to alert the viewer that these reenactments belong to a manipulated and stylized level of reality and that the filmmakers realize this and want the viewer to know it, also.

Fictional documentary realism.   *The Thin Blue Line* demonstrates that documentary filmmakers can shuttle between realistic and nonrealistic styles in the interest of creating cinematic and poetic effects with great success. While the stylized reen-actments in the film have an arty, unreal quality to them, the sequences with Harris and Adams utilize two fundamental codes of documentary film practice: interview footage with the principals involved in an event and voice-over narration.

A filmmaker may deliberately use the codes of documentary filmmaking but apply them to a wholly fictitious event. Such films can best be described as **fictional documentary realism.** Rob Reiner's *This Is Spinal Tap* (1984) is a well-known example of a fake documentary. In the film, director Reiner plays fictitious director Marty DiBergi who is making a documentary film about the British rock group Spinal Tap. No such group exists, of course, except in the pretend world of this film parody that accurately skewers many of the conventions of rock documentaries.

The film opens with Marty DiBergi (Reiner) seated by a camera and lighting equipment telling viewers about his first meeting with Spinal Tap in 1966 and explaining the genesis of "the documentary, the, if you will, rockumentary you are about to see." DiBergi talks directly to the camera with cinema equipment prominently displayed behind him. Since documentaries are thought by viewers to be more real than fiction films, filmmakers may confirm this by displaying the cinema equipment used to create the images on screen. Such on-screen display of camera equipment is unthinkable in the mode of ordinary fictional realism, but, within documentary realism, it serves to authenticate the special nonfiction status of the film by communicating to the audience that the filmmaker is not trying to "fool" viewers into mistaking the film's images for reality itself.

Other codes of rock documentaries the film employs include people-on-the-street interviews with fans talking about what "Tap" means to them. These interviews are intercut with faked concert footage and faked behind-the-scenes glimpses of backstage preparation for concerts. Other faked documentary codes include a series of interviews with the band members (all of whom, of course, are actors) and even faked black-and-white kinescope footage (supposedly from 1965) dramatizing an early television appearance by Tap (like the Beatles on Ed Sullivan).

This Is Spinal Tap is an intelligent and funny satire of rock documentary filmmaking. It uses basic documentary codes, but the difference is that the film lacks a

This Is Spinal Tap
(Embassy Pictures, 1984)
This Is Spinal Tap applies documentary techniques to completely fictitious events and characters. The film looks like a documentary but is really an elaborate hoax. Representational reality may be unreliable or ironic. In the case of *This Is Spinal Tap,* the filmmaker expects the audience to recognize this irony.

real referent. It looks like a documentary, sounds like a documentary, but is, instead, an exercise in fictional documentary realism. *This Is Spinal Tap* illustrates how a given mode of screen reality is rule based. By imitating many of the rules or codes of documentary filmmaking, the filmmakers skillfully simulate the appearance of a documentary. It is up to the viewer to appreciate the irony, to understand that the film has no authentic noncinematic referent, and that it does indeed contain abundant fictionalizing elements.

Expressionism

Expressionism is an extremely stylized mode of screen reality. Expressionism in its pure form as characterized by German cinema in the 1920s is distinct from expressionism as it survives in contemporary cinema.

German Expressionism in the 1920s

The expressionist mode in its purest form is found in 1920s German cinema. Expressionism began in German painting and theater in 1908 and, by the 1920s, had spread to the cinema where it characterized a series of classic films including *The Cabinet of Dr. Caligari* (1919); an early version of Dracula, *Nosferatu* (1922); and the science fiction classic *Metropolis* (1926).

In these and other classics of early German cinema, the expressionist style was extravagantly anti-realist and used explicit stylistic manipulations to give a deliberately artificial design to the image. This was achieved largely through a series of distortions in the mise-en-scene. Lighting designs employed a prevalence of shadows and violent visual contrast. Low-key designs were common. Decor and set design were extremely stylized. Normal rectilinear architectural forms were replaced with bizarre, distorted forms employing diagonal lines.

Expressionist filmmakers integrated the actors' physical appearance and movements with these architectural forms. In the accompanying illustration from F. W.

Nosferatu (1922)
Expressionistic integration of character and decor in *Nosferatu*. Note how the vampire's elongated body fits within the arched doorway. Expressionist distortions included architectural design as well as the human figure. The expressionist style thus linked people and settings to form a uniquely stylized screen reality. Frame enlargement.

Murnau's *Nosferatu,* the vampire's thin, elongated body is linked at a visual level with the arched door frame in which he lingers before pouncing upon his victim. Expressionist acting frequently employed a distorted physical appearance, and, as the image from *Nosferatu* illustrates, these strange body types could function as architectural forms of their own, integrated seamlessly with the shapes and textures of the set design.

Expressionist filmmakers frequently employed odd camera angles to enhance the de-centering of the screen world. The camera's positioning, the lighting design, and the decor all work together to achieve maximum distortion in expressionist mise-en-scene. These distortions were often correlated with a particular kind of subject matter. Characters might be grotesques as in the vampires of *Nosferatu* or the mad doctor in *Metropolis.* They often inhabited fantasy realms of myth as in Fritz Lang's *Seigfried,* or futuristic worlds as in Lang's *Metropolis.* Correlated with these extra-human or subhuman characters were their extreme and sometimes deranged emotional states. The terror of the victim of the sleepwalking killer in *The Cabinet of Dr. Caligari* and the killer's own anxiety-laden flight across the rooftops are expressively conveyed in the wild decor pictured in the accompanying illustration.

German expressionism entered the United States via a wave of emigré German filmmakers working in Hollywood and was popularized in the series of horror films produced in the 1930s at Universal Studios. In James Whale's 1931 production, *Frankenstein,* the emphasis on grotesque characters and diagonal visual forms creates a sense of unease in a world that appears off kilter and de-centered. In the opening scene, Dr. Frankenstein and his evil assistant Fritz hide in a graveyard, waiting until the gravediggers have finished burying a body. They plan to dig it up and steal the corpse for use in their gruesome medical experiments. Visual design, with its emphasis upon extreme anti-realism and distortion, is used effectively in the service of the film's horror content.

Metropolis (1926)
Grotesque characters inhabited the screen world of German expressionism, prompting one prominent critic to label it a "haunted screen." Rotwang, the mad inventor of *Metropolis* (1926), creates a humanoid robot. Frame enlargement.

The Cabinet of Dr. Caligari (1919)
Expressionist set design created a bizarre, strange, off-kilter world in the classic *The Cabinet of Dr. Caligari,* the first expressionist film. Note the disturbing diagonal lines suggesting disorder and instability throughout the set in place of normal rectilinear architecture. Frame enlargement.

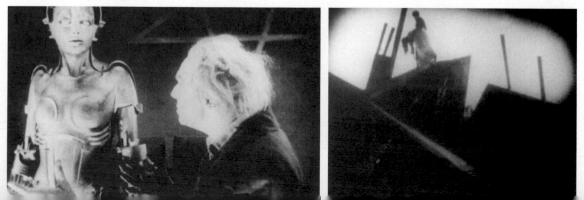

Frankenstein (Universal Studios, 1931)
Expressionist set design in the Universal horror genre. Dr. Frankenstein (Colin Clive) digs
up a fresh corpse in *Frankenstein*. Classic expressionist motifs include the morbid setting and
its sloping diagonal design. Frame enlargement.
The Black Cat (Universal Studios, 1934)
Boris Karloff, Universal's reigning king of horror, plays a devil worshipper in *The Black Cat*.
He stands before a recognizably expressionistic altar. The expressionist manner of visualizing
characters and settings quickly transcended its German roots to become an essential mode of
screen reality, indispensable to world cinema. Frame enlargement.

Expressionism as a Style in Contemporary Film

Although the pure expressionism that characterized German cinema of the 1920s is
rarely found in contemporary filmmaking, modern directors often employ highly
explicit pictorial distortions.

Expressionism and Hitchcock.   Alfred Hitchcock was probably the best-known filmmaker who kept the expressionist heritage alive. Consider the following illustrations
from his films. In *Psycho* (1960), a striking, low-angle shot of Norman Bates, the psychopathic killer, dehumanizes his face. By emphasizing the working of his gullet as he
chews on some candy, it transforms him visually into a bird-like creature. This is
appropriate because Norman is a taxidermist by hobby and keeps his office stuffed
with birds of prey, which he has mounted on the walls. Hitchcock said that these birds
are perfect symbols of Norman himself. They are birds of the night—predators—and
he sees his own guilt reflected in their eyes.

In *Notorious* (1946), a woman who is coerced into spying for the U.S. government is shown, in an early scene, waking up with a hangover. She looks up and sees
a government agent hovering in the doorway of her bedroom. Hitchcock employs a
subjective expressionistic shot to represent her point of view and to make the agent
seem threatening and sinister. The agent initially appears as a silhouette. As he
advances, she turns her head to look up at him, tracking his movements, and his figure pirouettes upside down across her field of vision.

In *Vertigo* (1958), to suggest the approaching despair and madness of the detective hero (James Stewart), Hitchcock included a completely artificial sequence. The

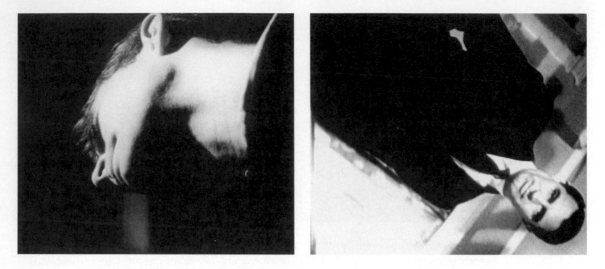

Psycho (Paramount Pictures, 1960)
This strange, low-angle shot of Norman Bates (Anthony Perkins) in *Psycho* turns him into a bird. This adds a symbolic dimension to the narrative since Norman is a taxidermist specializing in stuffing predatory birds. The bizarre image suggests that Norman, too, is a predator, a creature of the night, like his stuffed birds. Hitchcock appreciated the special power of expressionistically distorted images to transform normal visual reality. Frame enlargement.

Notorious (RKO, 1946)
In *Notorious*, Cary Grant, as an American government agent, appears in this bizarre, upside-down perspective. The angular distortion represents the anxious point of view of a character reclining on a bed. In this respect, the visually-unstable point of view is very close to the original aims of German expressionism, which were to visually represent subjective states of mind. Frame enlargement.

---

detective's nightmare hallucination is represented, in part, through animation. As shown in the accompanying still, the bouquet of flowers, held by a ghostly character in the film, suddenly splits apart and the petals advance menacingly toward the viewer. Sometimes modern audiences become confused about the level on which they are meant to interpret this scene, unsure whether to view it as the artificial visual design it so clearly is. Hitchcock departs from realism so thoroughly here that it confuses some modern film viewers, who are uncertain whether they are seeing an example of inferior visual effects or a genuinely radical visual design.

As these examples from Hitchcock's cinema illustrate, the director learned from the expressionists about the power of a distorted visual image, and he employed such visual designs systematically throughout his career when he needed to suggest intensified states of emotional disturbance.

Expressionist credit design.   A more recent production, Martin Scorsese's *Cape Fear* (1992), employs a number of striking expressionistic motifs in the opening title design. The film deals with a vengeful psychopath, newly released from prison, who wreaks a terrible plan of destruction on the family of the lawyer he blames for his conviction. The film's title is derived from the river in which the climax is set. The title

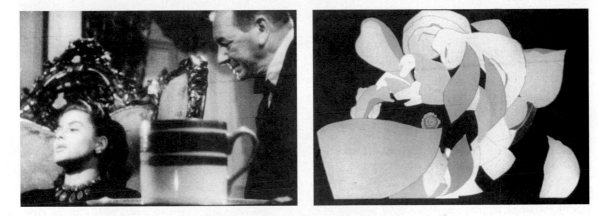

Notorious (RKO, 1946)

With a subtle expressionistic touch, Hitchcock designs this shot from *Notorious* so that the cup of poison (*foreground*) looms gigantically beside the woman who is being poisoned (Ingrid Bergman, *background*). To get the shot, Hitchcock instructed his prop crew to construct an enormous cup and then placed the camera in this low-angle position to emphasize its size. Frame enlargement.

Vertigo (Paramount Pictures, 1958)

One of Hitchcock's most radical expressionist touches is this sudden switch to animated footage in *Vertigo*. Flower petals swirl toward the camera in a threatening manner. Viewers often react nervously, unsure how to interpret the obviously artificial effect. Frame enlargement.

---

also evokes poetically and symbolically the climate of terror and anxiety that is established in the story.

During the opening credit sequence, a number of distorted expressionistic forms are reflected in the waters of the Cape Fear River. A predatory bird swoops down near the surface of the water, its shadow extended and disturbed by the river's rippling surface. Superimposed over the water is a terror-stricken eye, glancing about with extreme agitation. Later in the sequence, a screaming mouth appears, the teeth fearsomely exposed. Next looms a classic expressionist figure, the black shadow of an executioner, skewed on a diagonal. Finally, a drop of blood drips from the top to the bottom of the screen, bringing with it a wave of red color.

Cape Fear (Universal Studios, 1992)

The diagonal shadow of a murderer haunts the river's surface in the expressionistic title design of *Cape Fear*. Frame enlargement.

MARTIN SCORSESE

Martin Scorsese has charted a uniquely modern path through American cinema, glancing self-consciously off established genres such as the musical and gangster films and bringing to them a European-styled openness of narrative, ambiguity of character, moral perspective, and an extraordinary cinematic self-consciousness. With respect to the latter, Scorsese has an encyclopedic knowledge of old films and voraciously views other directors' works. He fully understands the traditions from which his own films derive. Because of this love for the medium and its past, Scorsese has been especially active in efforts to preserve and restore old films, such as *Lawrence of Arabia* (1962), and to pressure Eastman Kodak into developing film stocks with more stable dyes to protect against color fading. He shot *Raging Bull* (1980) in black and white because of the then-unresolved problem of color fading.

Educated at New York University, where he subsequently taught from 1968–1970, he directed his second feature, *Boxcar Bertha* (1972), under legendary B-movie producer Roger Corman. Scorsese then dramatically displayed great cinematic maturity and his own intensely personal style in *Mean Streets* (1973), a vivid portrait of four male friends in New York's Little Italy that combined a diffuse narrative, an aggressively moving camera, and improvisatory, unpredictable performance styles. The latter derive largely from Scorsese's remarkable collaboration with actor Robert De Niro. Together, they form one of the most striking actor-director relationships in cinema history. De Niro's mercurial, quicksilver, threatening persona is an essential part of Scorsese's accomplishments in his

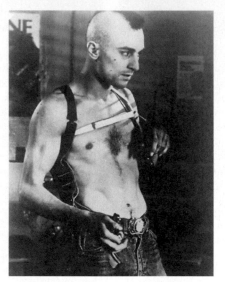

Taxi Driver (Columbia Pictures, 1976)
In *Taxi Driver,* Scorsese and actor Robert DeNiro collaborated to produce their most powerful and chilling creation—the psychopathic cab driver Travis Bickle and the hellish urban world he inhabits. Scorsese's expressionistic style visualizes Bickle's dementia with astonishing and distrubing vividness, and De Niro supplies some of his most brilliant improvisations.

revision of Hollywood's musicals (*New York, New York,* 1977), gangster films (*Goodfellas,* 1990), horror films (*Cape Fear,* 1992), and boxing films (*Raging Bull*). In addition, De Niro contributed unforgetable portraits of a psychopath in *Taxi Driver* (1976) and of a nebbishy fan in *The King of Comedy* (1983).

Because of his unconventional visual and narrative style, Scorsese labored for many years without due recognition from the Hollywood film industry. The late 1970s and early to mid-1980s were an especially difficult period for him when he was uncertain that he could continue to support himself as a director. However, he enjoyed great critical acceptance with *Goodfellas* in 1990 and immediately followed that with two shrewd career moves. *Cape Fear,* executive produced by Steven Spielberg, demonstrated his ability to manufacture a mainstream (if highly unpleasant) horror film, and *The Age of Innocence* (1993) dramatically expanded his screen domain beyond the familiar urban milieu of crooks, psychopaths, and losers (to which he returned in *Casino,* 1995). The lavish, sensitive portrait of nineteenth-century New York aristocratic society in *The Age of Innocence* demonstrated that Scorsese was not only a major filmmaker (many already knew that) but that he possessed a surprising artistic range.

After many years of laboring in the wilderness, Scorsese has at last earned respect and acceptance from the Hollywood film industry. Like John Ford, the old-time Hollywood director he greatly admires, Scorsese is today an acknowledged master of his medium and an integral part of the mainstream industry. No longer knocking at its door, he is now inside the club.

A dissolve links the end of the credit sequence to a close-up of the eyes of the lawyer's young daughter. She will become a special target of the psychopath's plan of vengeance. Here, Scorsese revives an expressionist technique used to striking effect in Murnau's vampire classic *Nosferatu*—the use of negative images. To suggest the phantom world, Murnau photographed Dracula's coach and horses as negative images. Scorsese pulls viewers out of the expressionist title sequence and inserts them into the world of the narrative proper by using negative imagery, suggesting, at a visual level, what the narrative will establish—a world in which human behavior and values are dangerously inverted.

Contemporary expressionism constitutes a powerful mode of screen reality permitting a filmmaker to introduce selected visual distortions into a scene or film in ways that are correlated with the representation of emotional, social, or psychological disturbances or abnormalities.

Fantasy and the Fantastic

Fantasy and the fantastic are modes of screen reality that are closely related to expressionism. There is some overlap but there are also important distinctions. Expressionism can co-exist with a realism frame as in the films of Alfred Hitchcock. By contrast, in films employing a fantasy or fantastic mode, settings and subjects, characters and narrative time are displaced from the viewer's own realm into alternative, often future, realms where normal laws of time and space may not apply. Characters might have superpowers, like Superman, or advanced technology that lends them superpowers, like Robocop. Adventurers can pilot starships to new galaxies as in *Star Wars* (1977), and artificial beings, created by mad inventors, can become suburban hairdressers, like Edward Scissorhands.

Star Wars (Twentieth Century Fox, 1977)
The limits of a filmmaker's imagination are among the few constraints operating on films in the fantasy mode. Strange creatures and fantastic characters with outlandish costumes populate these films. In *Star Wars,* an imperial stormtrooper sits astride this bizarre creature.

The Importance of Production Design in Fantasy

Production design is crucially important to the mode of fantasy and the fantastic. Films employing this mode achieve the bulk of their effects through the use of production design. Consider the work of Tim Burton, one of the most popular filmmakers currently working within this mode. His films include *Batman* (1989), *Edward Scissorhands* (1990), *Batman Returns* (1990), and *Beetlejuice* (1988), and, as producer, *The Nightmare Before Christmas* (1993). The opening moments in *Edward Scissorhands* and *Batman* clarify how Burton and his collaborators employ production design to establish the nature of the fantasy and fantastic worlds in those films.

The Fantasy Mode in *Batman*   The opening credits of *Batman* feature a tracking camera exploring what seems to be a dark, shadowy, and cold landscape. The viewer sees it in pieces and in small details. The precise nature of the place remains unknown until the end of the credit sequence, when a long shot reveals that what viewers think is a physical place is, instead, the Batman emblem. Because viewers see the camera tilt down from the sky, they assume that a locale is being described. The tilt down from the sky cues the viewer to expect ground-level information—topographical detail such as mountains or plains or man-made structures such as houses or skyscrapers.

Thus, viewers can reasonably hypothesize that the serpentine corridors through which the camera tracks is the Batcave. At the end of the sequence, the full shot

---

Batman (Warner Bros., 1989)

Production design is critically important in establishing the fantasy mode of *Batman*. The gigantic and grim Gotham City is a fanciful transformation of modern cities and provides the visually striking setting for the story. Using indoor sets, mattes, and miniature models, the production design suggests a monumental urban landscape that is dark, cold, gray, largely devoid of color, light, open space, or human values. Suffocatingly dense and heavy, Gotham City chokes its inhabitants with architecture that suggests an absence of freedom or hope.

reveals that the camera has been moving through a completely unreal location, one that is not even a locale at all, one which is, instead, the symbolic emblem of the fantasy character Batman. The cinematography of Roger Pratt and the production design of Anton Furst are masterfully contrived to mislead the eye and brain of the film's audience. The switch from an *implied* locale to Batman's symbolic emblem establishes the initial transformation of setting from everyday life into the realm of costumed superheroes that defines the film's fantasy world.

The Fantasy Mode in *Edward Scissorhands*   *Edward Scissorhands* was photographed by Stefan Czapsky with production design by Bo Welch. As in *Batman,* the opening moments of *Edward Scissorhands* emphasize production design information in order to establish essential qualities of the film's fantasy mode. The first image is the Twentieth Century Fox logo, but the familiar logo is transformed thematically. In place of the usual colors, viewers see white snow and icy blue. These evoke the film's fantasy world of which Edward Scissorhands' ice sculptures are dominant emblems.

The camera then pans and tracks to a monster-movie style door, modeled on the set design of the horror films produced by Universal Pictures in the 1930s. The door opens onto darkness, and the camera tracks inside, promising gothic images and horrors to come. This promise is gently fulfilled as the story deals with an artificial man, Edward Scissorhands, created by an inventor and given a real heart and brain but left unfinished when the inventor dies. Edward is afflicted with giant scissors at the end of his arms in place of hands. After the camera tracks into the dark doorway, a montage follows, composed of shots of weird machines linked by fades. These machines are associated with the inventor and with Edward's artificial world, and they are accompanied by the credits and by gargoyle-like sculptures.

At the end of the credits, the first image of the narrative proper returns viewers to the snowfall imagery, and the action fades-in on a gothic-looking castle atop a mountain. The castle, though, is obviously a miniature model and is meant to look so. The film's visual design presents the castle as an explicit miniature in order to emphasize and display qualities of visual artifice. These enable the film to establish a counter-reality, a reality of fantasy and the fantastic. The camera tracks away from the castle to the inside of a child's room where an elderly woman tells a bedtime story that is the film's story of Edward Scissorhands, how he was invented and how he fell in love with an ordinary, real woman. This narrative device—the bedtime

Edward Scissorhands
(Twentieth Century Fox, 1990)
All things are possible in the fantasy mode, even a gothic castle perched in the middle of suburbia.

GEORGE LUCAS

Although he has directed very few films, Lucas' influence on contemporary film is enormous. A graduate of the University of Southern California Film School, Lucas took one of his student projects, expanded and enlarged it into his first feature as director. *THX-1138* (1971) is a grim, science-fiction vision of a totalitarian future. Its sober and somber tone is galaxies removed from the spirited hi-jinx of his subsequent *Star Wars* series.

Lucas followed *THX-1138* with the hugely popular *American Graffiti* (1973), portraying the bittersweet antics of high school graduates at summer's end on the threshold of the sixties. Its complex sound design resulted from Lucas' collaboration with sound designer Walter Murch, who also worked with Lucas on *THX-1138*. Lucas is extraordinarily sensitive to the intricacies of sound, and he teamed with another top sound designer, Ben Burtt, on the *Star Wars* trilogy.

Released in 1977, *Star Wars* was one of two films in the mid-1970s that changed Hollywood. The other was Steven Spielberg's *Jaws* (1975). These films made more money than anyone dreamed a film could make and inaugurated the blockbuster era. Lucas planned *Star Wars* as a kind of old-time Hollywood cliffhanger and took extraordinary care to achieve what were then state-of-the-art special effects. He formed Industrial Light and Magic at San Rafael, California, in 1976 to do the film's effects work. ILM is now an established

leader in the effects industry, breaking new ground in digital effects for Spielberg's *Jurassic Park* (1994). Through ILM, Lucas has exerted a profound influence over the effects design of contemporary films. Through the mix of adventure and effects-driven fantasy he perfected in *Star Wars*, Lucas has helped shape the very definition of a Hollywood blockbuster.

Following *Star Wars*, Lucas stepped out of the director's chair and turned his attention to executive producing. In this capacity, he oversaw completion, and co-wrote, the other two films in the trilogy (*The Empire Strikes Back*, 1980; *Return of the Jedi*, 1983) and each of the three Indiana Jones films directed by his pal Steven Spielberg (*Raiders of the Lost Ark*, 1981; *Indiana Jones and the Temple of Doom*, 1984; *Indiana Jones and the Last Crusade*, 1989).

Together with Spielberg, and separately through his own films and ILM, Lucas has changed the face of American film. His work embraces the simplicities of formulaic melodrama and avoids the thematic complexity and nuances found in the work of other leading American directors such as Sidney Lumet, Robert Altman, and Woody Allen. This had led some critics to charge that his films perpetuate an adolescent hunger for spectacle and constant visual thrills. But there is no denying the enormous popular acceptance of his work or its tremendous trend-setting importance for mainstream filmmaking.

Star Wars (Twentieth Century Fox, 1977)
With *Star Wars*, Lucas embraced the cliffhanger style of old movie serials and aimed to fashion a modern mythic parable. The film's extraordinary success helped change Hollywood filmmaking forever. Over the next two decades, Lucas' work and production facilities would help spearhead the special-effects revolution in contemporary film.

story—places the film securely in the realm of folklore, myth, and fantasy, and it grounds the film's childlike qualities of wonder and mystery.

Tim Burton's alternate world of gothic invention has been so firmly established as the governing style in the opening minutes of the film that Burton can get away with a subsequent, outrageous establishing shot showing the castle perched atop its mountain and located at the end of an ordinary street in a suburban neighborhood. The accompanying still conveys the flagrantly outrageous and fairy-tale contrast between the castle and the surrounding neighborhood. The viewer accepts this image, understanding that all is permissible in a realm of fantasy and the fantastic. In its opening moments, the film has employed sophisticated production design to thoroughly evoke and establish such a world.

Achieving Credibility in the Fantasy Mode   The production design of *Batman* and *Edward Scissorhands* stresses the highly artificial and fantastic worlds inhabited by the Caped Crusader and Edward. Many of the sets in these films look deliberately unreal. Other fantasy films, however, insist upon the credibility and validity of the fantastic settings, rather than their artificiality. One method that *Star Wars* employs to convince the viewer that the fantasy world is valid is the use of real-world perceptual information to lend a perceived authenticity to the invented props and settings. In *Star Wars'* first scene, a series of spaceships approaches the camera, and then, in a reverse angle cut, they fly away into a great void. The rumble and roar of the ship's engines, heard on the soundtrack, lends a perceived physical weight and authenticity to these fantastic images. This is due, in part, to the depth and volume of the sound but also because the sound design makes use of the Doppler effect.

The Doppler effect is the term given for the way sound changes pitch as its source approaches and then moves away from the observer. As the observer and source come closer together, the pitch of the sound will increase (become higher) and, when they are more apart, it will decrease (become lower). Drawing closer to the sound source, the observer hears a frequency that is higher than the actual emitted frequency. Drawing apart, the observer will hear one that is lower. The sound design of the scene incorporates this physical phenomenon so that the sound of the ship's engines changes systematically (the pitch rises) in shots where the ships approach the camera, and, when they fly off into the distance, the pitch lowers.

Notice the complexity of the film's stylistic transformation of a perceptual correspondence. Although the perceptual information presented here is physically accurate for Earth-bound experience, in the context in which it occurs in the film it is completely impossible and imaginary. In space there is no sound because there is no medium, such as the air or atmosphere on Earth, which can transport sound waves. Consequently, the spaceships should be making no perceivable noise at all. This, of course, would be dramatically flat and uninteresting. Accordingly, the viewer readily accepts the fantasy proposition that spaceships traveling through a void make noise.

Fantasy and the fantastic can be an utterly convincing mode of screen reality in which production design is emphasized to establish important dimensions of the imaginary world on screen. As the example from *Star Wars* illustrates, filmmakers use real-life perceptual experience in fabricated situations to lend credence and a sense of validity to the fantastic settings and action.

Cinematic Self-Reflexivity

Each of the preceding modes of screen reality, however unusual or fantastic their settings and design, aims to persuade the viewer that the world depicted on screen is real and is, for the purposes of the narrative, a valid world whose premises are not questioned within the context of the film. The science-fiction world that George Lucas created in the *Star Wars* films is, taken on its own terms, a self-enclosed and internally valid world.

By contrast, the mode of cinematic self-reflexivity makes no pretense that the world represented on screen is anything other than a filmic construction. Films made within the tradition of cinematic self-reflexivity remind viewers that what they are watching is, after all, a movie. Self-reflexive films tell the viewer that the reality on screen is only a movie reality. These acknowledgments take a variety of forms. Typically, they fall into two categories: either comic or having didactic intent.

Comic Self-Reflexivity

The tradition of self-reflexivity most commonly found in popular, mass-market movies employs a comic design. Throughout *Annie Hall,* director and star Woody Allen continually interrupts the narrative with a series of humorous asides and confessions made to the camera. By speaking directly to the camera, of course, he is also speaking directly to the audience. During one scene in which Alvy Singer (Woody Allen) and Annie Hall (Diane Keaton) quarrel over whether she said going to psychoanalysis will change her life or change her wife, Alvy breaks off the argument, turns to the camera, and reminds viewers that they know what was said because they have been there all along, listening to the quarrel. Likewise, in a subtle way, the tradition established by director Alfred Hitchcock of making guest appearances inside his own films reminds viewers of his controlling presence as director and, therefore, of the film's status *as* a film.

Multiple Levels of Comic Self-Reflexivity in *Wayne's World*

Witty, comic self-consciousness occurs in the *Wayne's World* movies, spun-off from TV's popular *Saturday Night Live* characters, Wayne and Garth, who are hosts of their

Annie Hall
(United Artists, 1977)
Woody Allen, as Alvy Singer, turns toward the camera and speaks to the film's viewers in this scene from *Annie Hall*. Allen breaks the illusion of make-believe in this moment of comic self-reflexivity. In popular films, such self-reflexivity is quite common in comedy but very rare in drama. Frame enlargement.

own local-access cable television talk show. In *Wayne's World* (1992), Wayne and Garth give viewers a tour of the local doughnut shop, one of their favorite hangouts. A moving camera follows them, and they periodically turn and talk to it. The scene features a double level of comic self-reflexivity. Level one includes the dialogue and performances by Wayne and Garth. Level two includes the movements of the camera, which proves to be somewhat unpredictable and uncooperative.

As Wayne and Garth enter the doughnut shop, the camera follows them. Wayne turns toward the camera and begins a series of confessional remarks. "This is Stan's Doughnut Shop. Excellent munchables. This is the manager, Glen. He is here 24 hours a day. I recommend the sugar pucks. They're excellent. Come on." As Wayne speaks, he walks up to the counter and points toward Glen. Then, saying "Come on," he motions the viewer and the camera toward him and exits frame right, expecting the camera to follow.

Instead, the camera stays with Glen, who begins walking to the left. Glen, it turns out, is a lunatic. He, too, speaks in the familiar confessional mode, telling the camera, "I'd never done a crazy thing in my life before that night." He angrily asks why, when you kill a man in combat, it's considered heroism, but if you kill a man in the heat of passion, it's called murder. His lunatic remarks are interrupted by Wayne, off screen, calling impatiently, "Hello, what do you think you're doing?" Wayne then enters the shot and says, "Only me and Garth get to talk to the camera. Come on." Now the camera behaves, following Wayne to the right.

Garth then enters the frame and nervously confesses to the camera and to the viewer that he has nothing to say. He then fakes the camera out, exclaiming "What's that?" and points off frame. The camera pans in the direction of his gesture but finds nothing. As the camera pans back to the left, the viewer sees Garth hurrying away.

As noted, two levels of self-reflexivity operate in this scene. One involves Wayne and Garth's comic remarks, the intimate confessional mode that they strike up with the camera and, by extension, with the viewers. The second level of self-consciousness is the more interesting one. It involves the camera's unpredictable and uncooperative behavior. Instead of following Wayne as commanded, it strikes up a relationship with the deranged night manager, Glen, and waits patiently as Glen delivers a rambling monologue that implies that he's killed a man. Eventually, Wayne reasserts his control

Wayne's World
(Paramount Pictures, 1992) Wayne (Mike Myers) regains control of the camera from the lunatic doughnut shop manager in *Wayne's World*. This self-reflexive moment plays to a hip, ironic attitude in the film's viewers. Wayne smiles knowingly to the camera, telling viewers that, of course, it's all just a movie. Frame enlargement.

over the camera only to have Garth fake out the camera's attention as a means of escaping from its gaze.

Throughout this scene, the film makes fun of the mode of ordinary fictional realism that treats the camera as an unacknowledged and unseen witness to the action. Under ordinary fictional realism, the viewer is never reminded of the camera's presence, and it is this mode that Wayne and Garth so cleverly skewer. The comic possibilities of the self-reflexive mode are based on the viewer's understanding of the norms that are being violated. The humor in these films derives partly from the viewer's familiarity and long acquaintance with the mode of ordinary fictional realism that Wayne, Garth, and Woody Allen play so expertly against.

Didactic Self-Reflexivity

The second category of self-reflexive film style is used for didactic purposes and falls within the aesthetic tradition identified with the theater of playwright Bertolt Brecht. As a Marxist, Brecht sought to have a direct impact upon his social world and historical period through his art. Brecht was an active playwright and poet from the 1920s until his death in 1956, and his plays include such classics as *The Threepenny Opera, Galileo,* and *The Caucasian Chalk Circle.*

Impatient with the conventions of the theater of his day, Brecht created his own theatrical forms that he termed "epic" and that involved various attempts to break down the barriers that separated spectators from the play they were watching. Brecht considered the illusion of naturalism or realism, as created in theater or film, to be an obstacle that prevented play-goers or film viewers from reflecting upon the connections between their own lives and the events depicted on stage or screen.

He wanted his plays to become a stimulus to social action and reform, to have direct real-world consequences, and so he deliberately broke with realist and naturalist traditions by incorporating explicitly didactic techniques into his theater. Actors on stage might speak directly to the audience, or the social contradictions dramatized by the action of a play might be announced directly via titles projected upon a screen above the stage.

The Brechtian Legacy in Film   Brecht's work in the theater continues to exert an enormously powerful influence upon filmmakers. French director Jean-Luc Godard is probably the most famous Brechtian filmmaker currently working. Godard's films offer a virtual catalogue of Brechtian cinematic techniques, that is, film techniques that break the illusion of reality, the impression that the spectator is watching a real, authentic world on screen rather than a movie. These techniques enable Godard to speak directly to his audience as author, rather than indirectly through the characters and action of the film. *Weekend* (1967), Godard's savage satire of modern consumer society, employs three kinds of didactic, Brechtian, self-reflexive techniques. These are the use of printed titles, nontraditional camera techniques, and the incorporation of imaginary characters and moments of performance self-disclosure.

Titles.   Title cards break up the narrative action of *Weekend,* which follows the comic and violent misadventures of a middle-class couple journeying across France on holiday. The printed titles offer ironic and poetic commentaries upon the narrative. During the opening credits of the film, two title cards announce that this is "a film adrift in the cosmos" and "a film found on a dump." A long musical sequence in the middle of the film, during which a pianist performs a Mozart sonata as the camera tracks three times around the perimeter of a farmyard, is introduced by several flash-cut inserts of the title "Musical Action."

Throughout the film, title cards serve to (1) introduce and set off a given scene from the surrounding context of the narrative, (2) tell viewers what it is they are about to see, (3) remind viewers of the filmmaker's intrusion upon the narrative, and (4) emphasize the way the filmmaker has chosen to shape and organize the structure of the film. Each of these functions is consistent with the Brechtian goal of breaking the illusion of reality exerted by the screen world by reminding the viewer about the film's methods of constructing its images and narrative.

The title card "Totem and Taboo" prefaces the film's most horrific sequence, dealing with the cannibalism and mutilation of English tourists at the hands of a guerrilla army based in the countryside. This title derives from a famous book by Sigmund Freud dealing with primitive social organization and behavioral taboos in human ancestry. Here, the self-reflexive qualities are multiple. In addition to the four functions described above, the title card tells the viewer that the scenes that follow will contain shocking and taboo imagery, as indeed they do, and, for viewers who know the reference, this acknowledgment positions the scenes in relation to Freud's famous work.

Nontraditional camera techniques.   Nontraditional camera techniques are a second method of creating self-reflexive style in *Weekend*. Two sequences stand out for the use of radical camera work. The tracking shot along the row of stalled cars and the circular tracking movements around the farmyard during the musical interlude extend the length of these shots and scenes to a point many viewers find unbearable, especially since no new narrative information is being disclosed. The tracking shots go on for so long that the viewer is invited to contemplate the movements of the camera in such a way that those movements become the very subject of the shots. These shots emphasize the presence of the moving camera to such a remarkable degree that the style becomes self-reflexive in that the viewer grows acutely aware of its visual design.

Once again, it is important to note that here, as elsewhere, the moment of self-reflexivity plays off a viewer's awareness of the norm that is being violated. In this

Weekend
(New Yorker Films, 1967)
Storybook characters dressed in fairy-tale costumes help shatter a realistic tone in Godard's *Weekend*. Dressed in these outlandish costumes, Emily Brontë and Le Gros Poucet step into the film from some alternate poetic reality. They quarrel with Corrine and Roland, who promptly burn them for violating the standard of realism. Frame enlargement.

case, the norm is that camera work and camera movement remain generally unobtrusive in most commercially produced films.

Imaginary characters and performance self-disclosure.   *Weekend* is filled with imaginary storybook characters. These establish a third area of self-reflexive technique. During one episode in the middle of the film, the vacationing couple, Corinne and Roland, encounter poet Emily Brontë dressed in a storybook costume. Brontë is accompanied by a wholly imaginary character, Le Gros Poucet.

Corinne and Roland ask for directions to their destination, Oinville, but Brontë and her companion reply with metaphysical riddles. When Roland asks for the directions, Brontë inquires whether he is interested in poetical or physical information. When Roland tells her that they only want to know how to get to Oinville, Brontë tells him that physics doesn't really exist, only individual sciences, prompting Roland to mutter, "What a rotten film. All we meet are crazy people." His remark is a moment of performance self-disclosure in which the actor steps out of character to evaluate the quality of the film in which he appears. Of course, Godard does not believe he's making a rotten film and so the evaluation is ironic. During another example of performance self-disclosure, Corinne grabs the poet Brontë and says angrily, "This isn't a novel. It's a film. A film is life."

For the Brechtian tradition, this is the attitude to be combatted and motivates the use of self-reflexive techniques. By breaking the spell of reality cast by film or play, these techniques point to the enormous difference between life and the constructed spectacles on stage or screen.

The scene culminates in a moment of horror. Roland drives away Brontë's companion and then sets her on fire. As the poet burns and cries, Corinne says that this is bad, they shouldn't really be burning her, prompting Roland to remark, "Can't you see they're only imaginary characters?" Godard, the director, then reveals the emotional paradox upon which cinema rests. Corinne replies, "Why is she crying, then?"

Although the film presents Brontë as an imaginary storybook character dressed in a fairy-tale costume, her fiery destruction by Roland strikes the viewer as a moment of true horror, an unspeakable obscenity. Despite her obviously fictional status, a sadness attaches to the destruction of the Emily Brontë figure, and this paradox—the film's ability to compel emotional belief from the viewer even while acknowledging the fictional artifice of its characters—is made explicit in Corinne's remark about the storybook character's tears.

The legacy of Godard.   The self-conscious and radical cinematic techniques of Godard have exerted an enormous influence on other filmmakers, as has the Brechtian tradition that inspired Godard himself. Spike Lee is a contemporary director who freely mixes modes of screen reality in his films, incorporating ordinary fictional realism, fantasy sequences, and modes of self-reflexivity. The black and white narrative of *She's Gotta Have It* (1986), for example, is punctuated by one striking color sequence, a musical fantasy, which departs greatly in tone and style from the surrounding narrative.

In *Do the Right Thing* (1989), Lee displays a precise understanding of how Brechtian techniques can be used to contain and control the emotions generated by the story on screen. During the famous racial slur sequence, a gallery of characters hurl insults at targeted racial groups. A young Italian man (John Turturro) vents a stream of intensely obscene insults about African Americans, Mookie (Spike Lee) gives vent to an equally obscene stream of insults about Italian Americans, a Hispanic gang member insults Koreans, a cop insults Hispanics, and a Korean merchant condemns Jews. Each character is filmed in an identical fashion, the camera tracking in quickly from long shot to medium close-up in a way that adds visual emphasis to the stream of verbal invective.

The sequence is emotionally powerful and dangerous because it gives full-throated voice to various racisms. Spike Lee realized that he needed to break and contain the emotions that were unleashed on screen and that were likely to be aroused in the film's audiences. Accordingly, he breaks the hypnotizing power of the racist rhetoric with an explicitly didactic, Brechtian conclusion. A black radio deejay breaks into the montage, telling the characters to cool down, shut up, and break that nonsense off. The racial antagonisms among the various groups—whites, blacks, Jews, Koreans—are heartily condemned by the deejay, and a note of calm and sanity is restored at the scene's end.

Filmmakers such as Lee or Godard who employ self-reflexive techniques in a didactic manner tend do so because they want to maintain some measure of control over the social impact of their films and the messages inside those films. The Brechtian tradition is a major aesthetic influence on filmmakers who want to speak directly to their audience and to assert maximum control over the impact of their social messages.

Impact on Viewers of Self-Reflexive Techniques

The comic and didactic modes of cinematic self-reflexivity tend to pull viewers out of the reality represented on screen by reminding viewers that this reality is a cinematic construction. It is important to note, though, that the implied reality of the screen world is extremely powerful. It can sustain the digressions and intrusions of self-reflexive techniques. Such techniques typically dispel, *momentarily,* the emotional pull

Do the Right Thing
(Universal Studios, 1989)
Mookie (Spike Lee) in the famous racial slur sequence from *Do the Right Thing.* Director Lee uses a self-reflexive technique to maintain artistic control over the sequence's inflammatory stream of racist insults. By alternating between different modes of screen reality, Lee evokes the special, poisonous intensity of racial hatred and then contextualizes it with a clear and direct condemnation. Frame enlargement.

the viewer experiences from the on-screen world, but it is difficult to disrupt this emotional pull for long. It tends to quickly reassert itself.

In *Weekend,* for example, despite all of the title cards, the radical camera movements, and the moments of performance self-disclosure, the basic spectacle of Corinne and Roland's comic and increasingly violent car journey across France is exceptionally compelling. Although one appreciates the social responsibility that Lee demonstrates as director when he brings on the calm deejay to conclude the racism scene in *Do the Right Thing,* one nevertheless remembers the scene for its extraordinarily hypnotic stream of racial insults.

The represented world on screen can be manipulated by filmmakers using self-reflexive techniques, but the represented world tends to retain, for the spectator, its own emotional integrity and validity. Viewers know that Wayne and Garth are just movie characters. Wayne and Garth admit this themselves, but viewers still want to spend time with them. The cinema can compel emotional belief in its representational reality even when filmmakers admit to viewers that it's all fake.

◻ GENRES AND SCREEN REALITY

Much commercial filmmaking falls into clear genre categories. How do genres relate to the basic modes of screen reality? **Genres** are clearly defined types of films that follow a set of visual and narrative patterns that are unique within the genre. The most popular and historically significant American film genres include the Western, the gangster film, the musical, film noir, the horror film, and the science fiction film.

Genres constitute unique variants of screen reality, and they can fall within any of the basic modes. For example, horror films tend to fall within the mode of fantasy and the fantastic, whereas many contemporary musicals, such as *Fame* (1980) or *A Chorus Line* (1985), represent a conjoining of ordinary fictional realism and a fantasy

The Sand Pebbles
(Twentieth Century Fox, 1966)
The settings, costumes, and stories of many films fall into easily recognized patterns. Steve McQueen's helmet and rifle in this shot from *The Sand Pebbles* clearly announce that this is a war film. Frame enlargement.

mode. In contemporary musicals, the dramatic sections are typically consistent with ordinary fictional realism, while the musical sections explicitly break with realistic time and space in favor of a stylized emphasis upon color, spectacle, music, and movement.

Elements of Genre

A film genre is a set of interrelated stories and their associated settings and visual images. The stories become generic by virtue of heavy repetition, and they can be repeated over and over again because they express underlying social values and value conflicts that remain significant in the culture. Generic rules, or codes, specify the kinds of events and situations that can occur within the stories. These rules or codes are repeated throughout the body of the genre so that a viewer who is familiar with horror films, or Westerns, can easily anticipate the types of stories and situations likely to occur in a given film. Moreover, many codes are unique to a given genre. What viewers accept in a musical film might appear ridiculous in a gangster film.

Repetition of story situations throughout a genre produces two effects: it enables viewers familiar with the genre to anticipate likely narrative developments and outcomes, and it enables filmmakers to achieve highly concentrated meanings within the genre. Consider these simple terms common to Westerns: "gunfighter," "Indian," "cowboy" "posse." Each word conjures up a host of associated images and potential story situations for viewers who are familiar with the genre.

A viewer critical of genres, who objects that all Westerns or all horror films are the same, is missing the point. Film scholar Robert Warshow has pointed out that "one does not want too much novelty" from a genre film. Fans of a genre derive pleasure from the small variations that are worked out within the pre-established order of story and setting. Repetition of familiar material is very important, and too much novelty or originality can place a film outside a genre's framework.

Genres and the Construction of Screen Reality

How do genres construct screen reality? How do American film genres relate to the basic modes of screen reality? Available space does not permit a profile of every American film genre. However, for the sake of brevity, several of the most important genres will be profiled here from the standpoint of their relationship to modes of screen reality.

The Western

The Western is one of the oldest screen genres. Indeed, the Western as a cultural category pre-exists the cinema. It emerged near the end of the nineteenth-century and was established in a variety of pre-cinematic forms: the dime novel, the Puritan captivity narratives, the Leatherstocking tales (1823–1841) of James Fenimore Cooper, theatrical plays and shows (e.g., Buffalo Bill's Wild West Show), and painting (ethnographic studies of Indian cultures as well as Frederic Remington's action scenes). The Western, then, already existed when the cinema was invented at the turn of the century. The cinema supplied movement and exciting visual images to flesh out existing cultural stories about westward expansion and the conflict between settlers and Native

The Western is one of the oldest screen genres and achieved enormous popularity by the 1910s. William S. Hart was one of the most well-known and most popular Western stars from this period. Frame enlargement.

The Searchers (Warner Bros., 1956)
With the rocky buttes of Monument Valley at his back, John Wayne rides in from the desert at the beginning of *The Searchers*. Wayne's character is a wilderness figure, and the highly stylized opening, typical of many Westerns, stresses that he will remain forever so. Frame enlargement.

Americans. The Western achieved a striking early popularity in the cinema. By 1910, approximately 20 percent of all American pictures were Westerns.

Like each of the other genres to be discussed here, the Western is far too complex for easy or quick summary. Nevertheless, among the social values that are in opposition at the heart of the genre, the conflict between cultural ideas about civilization and the wilderness is paramount. The following illustration from *The Searchers* (1956) illustrates the highly conventionalized opening typical of many Westerns in which the protagonist, or central character, a man of violence, approaches a community or settlement. A narrative situation, the approach of the violent individual to the community, is linked to a particular setting and image, the desert and wilderness. The long shots integrate the character with the surrounding wilderness, and, by showing how large and expansive the wilderness is, they stress the fragility and vulnerability of the settlement or community.

This pattern of imagery demonstrates the rule-governed nature of genres. A central conflict at the heart of Westerns is the struggle between violence and law, and this is epitomized in the narrative and in the visual contrast between the wilderness and the community or settlement. As a figure of violence, the gunman comes from the wilderness (violence) to the community (law), and, frequently at the end of the films, he leaves in the opposite direction to return to the mountains or plains.

One more example from Westerns will demonstrate the link between a genre's images, settings, and underlying social values. In many Westerns, the violent skills of the protagonist are tested in a public arena. This arena is typically a saloon. The accompanying illustrations show a clear pattern connecting story situation, image, and setting. In each case, armed and violent confrontations occur in close proximity to the bar within the saloon. The genre has coded this location in terms of a particular kind of dramatic action that may occur there. In Westerns, schoolrooms are impermissible locations for violent confrontations. Gunfights or brawls almost never occur there.

Modes of Screen Reality in the Western   Westerns typically integrate elements from several modes of screen reality. Detailed period costumes and props establish an aura of historical realism that co-exists with a narrative emphasis on exaggerated action and adventure and heroes and villains with supremely powerful wilderness skills. This latter emphasis tends to deflect the historical realism of the genre into a highly charged fantasy mode.

Gangster Films

The gangster film is nearly as old as the cinema, having clear precursors in the early silent era. The genre emerged as a powerful force in American film, however, at the time of the Great Depression. In the years 1930–1932, three films—*Little Caesar, The Public Enemy,* and *Scarface*—defined the essential narrative patterns, settings, images, and types of social conflicts that would characterize the genre during the next decades.

In the classical gangster structure, the narrative focuses on the rise and fall of a career criminal, from his early, humble, frequently immigrant, origins to the zenith of his success, and then to his decline from power and violent death. This narrative pattern characterizes *Little Caesar, The Public Enemy,* and *Scarface,* as well as many later

The Gunfighter
(Twentieth Century Fox, 1950);
Shane (Paramount Pictures, 1953);
El Dorado (Paramount Pictures, 1967)
Violent showdowns at the saloon's bar.
Gregory Peck (background) faces down an impudent young gunman in *The Gunfighter.*
Shane (Alan Ladd) protects his honor in a brutal fistfight in *Shane.* Robert Mitchum cleans out the saloon in *El Dorado.* Frame enlargements.

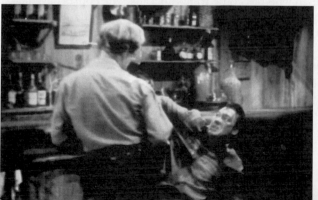

Little Caesar
(Warner Bros., 1931)
One of the biggest in a long line of movie gangsters, the snarling Rico Bandello (Edward G. Robinson) in *Little Caesar.* Rico is so smug and self-centered that when death finally comes, he can scarcely believe it. Riddled by a police machine gun, he asks in disbelief, "Mother of Mercy, is this the end of Rico?"

gangster films, including the *Godfather* films, Brian De Palma's 1983 remake of *Scarface,* and Mario Van Peebles' *New Jack City* (1991).

Movie Gangsters and the Critique of Society   In this classical structure, the gangster hero incarnates a perverse version of the American myth of success. He is an inverted and dark embodiment of the Horatio Alger myth. His determination and persistence yield great economic success, and, of course, eventual violent death. The roots of the gangster film in American culture include the Horatio Alger myth of success, as well as the example of the nineteenth-century robber barons, who, like the film gangster, amassed great fortunes through frequently ruthless methods. The genre's cultural roots also include the impact of the Great Depression and its demonstration of economic injustice, and the influence of Prohibition in terms of eroding respect for law and order and generating popular sympathy for the rum-running gangster.

Each of these cultural factors helped make the movie gangster what he was and ensured that the genre contained a sustained critique of society. If society, after all, had created gangsters such as Little Caesar or Scarface, then how healthy could society be? Francis Ford Coppola's *The Godfather* (1972) opens ironically over a dark screen, as a voice intones, "I believe in America." As the lights come up, Don Corleone confers with an Italian man who has come to him because the courts have failed to provide justice. His daughter has been raped and assaulted, and the legal system failed to convict her assailants. He seeks from Don Corleone a more primitive kind of justice.

With his ability to exercise violent retribution and his rejection and repudiation of established society, with his attainment of great economic success and power, the gangster character has always appealed to an implicit dissatisfaction on the part of movie audiences with their own social and economic status. This appeal is nowhere more apparent than in the conventions that surround the death of the movie gangster. As dictated by the rules of the genre, the gangster's death must be spectacular,

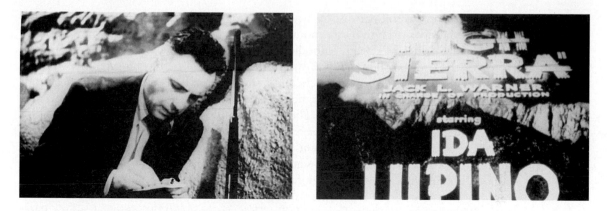

High Sierra (Warner Bros., 1941)
Cornered in the Sierra Nevada mountains, Roy Earle (Humphrey Bogart) dies a noble death, and the film's credit design, with titles rolling toward the heavens, suggests that in death Earle has at last found freedom and transcendence. Frame enlargement.

and the circumstances surrounding the death often contain a powerful social critique. In *High Sierra* (1941), Roy Earl is a romantic and sympathetic gangster, with great compassion and empathy for poor and downtrodden individuals. When he is gunned down at the end of the film, his death is presented as a cowardly act by the legal authorities.

Roy Earl is not simply killed, he is shot off a mountain top and falls from a great height, a hero of legendary stature finally brought down by callous authority. Shot in the back, he is felled by a police sniper. His death is witnessed by Marie, the woman he loved, and in the closing moments of the film she murmurs, "Freedom," equating Earl's death with a final escape from unjust social authority. The end credits are

White Heat
(Warner Bros., 1948)
Cody Jarrett (James Cagney) seconds before his explosive death in *White Heat*. Jarrett's white-hot end is a cautionary note for the nuclear age. Jarrett's spectacular death is a moment of such visual brilliance that it has become part of cinema's folklore, comparable to King Kong's last stand atop the Empire State Building. Both monsters, Kong and Jarrett, find an unforgettably poetic death. Frame enlargement.

presented on a scroll that moves toward the top of the frame in a visual design that echoes the distant High Sierra mountains and symbolizes the idea of transcendence and escape that Earl's death embodies in the narrative.

At the conclusion of *White Heat* (1948), the psychopathic gangster Cody Jarrett immolates himself atop a huge chemical storage tank. In one of the most famous moments in all American cinema, he screams, "Made it, Ma, top of the world!" just before he and the tank explode. The erupting mushroom cloud, which is the film's final image, situates Jarrett's crazed violence within the post-war atomic age and its nuclear anxieties. Jarrett is a violent psychopath, yet the energies of violence embodied in modern society and represented by the atomic weapon and the mushroom cloud are infinitely greater. The ending of the film suggests a nuclear apocalypse. Jarrett has made it to the top of the world, and now the world ends.

The famous montage that concludes *The Godfather* (1972), in which editor Peter Zinner cuts back and forth between the baptism ceremony for Michael Corleone's infant son and the execution of Corleone's enemies, suggests Michael's own violent and corrupt nature and also the violence and corruption at the heart of established society. Michael has attained a position of eminence, wealth, and political power, and he commands sufficient social prestige to ensure a proper baptism for his son in one of the city's largest and most prominent churches, even as he wipes out his enemies.

Each of these films presents the gangster's death in a spectacular manner that contains an implicit social critique. The conventions of the genre mandate that the gangster have a great deal of charisma. The gangster's appeal invites the viewer to ask about the kind of society that produces such seductive forms of corruption and violence.

Modes of Screen Reality in the Gangster Film   Many gangster films, such as *The Godfather,* rich as it is in period detail, obviously draw upon the mode of historical realism in establishing settings and locales for the story. The gangster, however, usually has appetites for power, wealth, and violence sufficiently vast as to surpass the psychology and behavior of characters typically found in the mode of ordinary fictional realism. Like the cowboy, the movie gangster is a highly charged cultural symbol. He embodies at once the dangers of chaos, lawlessness, and popular resentment of legal authority. The movie gangster represents a highly complex social fantasy about the prize and price of success. The gangster genre, therefore, weaves elements of fantasy and historical realism.

The Musical

Whereas the Western and the gangster film deal with the problem of violence and its relationship to law and social order, the musical is a considerably more lighthearted genre. As noted, contemporary musicals, such as *Fame* and *A Chorus Line,* attempt to strike a somewhat realistic style, whereas earlier musicals, from the 1930s through the 1950s, offered extremely stylized and anti-realistic designs. The basic narrative convention during the genre's height of popularity from the 1930s–1950s centered on the courtship rituals of a romantic couple who sang and danced to express their desire for each other.

Modes of Screen Reality in the Musical   Whereas normal continuity principles prevail throughout the narrative proper of the classical musical and are used to sim-

With their joyous optimism and happy romance, the musical couple is in love with love and each other. Dance expresses this celebration. Ginger Rogers and Fred Astaire are the most famous couple in musical film history. They courted each other on the dance floor in ten films.

ulate normal laws of time and space, the musical sequences radically disrupt realist style and normal relations of time and space. At least for the duration of the musical scenes, the films occupy the mode of fantasy and the fantastic.

Permissible visual design in musical scenes can radically stylize the screen world and includes the wild geometric forms of Busby Berkeley, popular in the 1930s, and the overtly pictorial lighting and color design of the ballet sequences from Vincente

A Star Is Born
(Warner Bros., 1954)
In their extreme visual stylization, song and dance in the musicals break with the conventions of ordinary fictional realism. The pleasures offered by color, sound, and movement are the only things that matter in this mode. Judy Garland performing "Swanee" in *A Star Is Born*. Frame enlargement.

Minnelli's *The Bandwagon* (1953) and *An American in Paris* (1951). In the latter film, the compositions and color schemes evoke the style of French Impressionist painters.

Contemporary audiences frequently have trouble accepting the conventions of classical musical films. The transition points from everyday reality to the musical scenes with their extravagant song, dance, color, lighting, and camerawork often seem jarring for contemporary audiences. Modern viewers may react with disbelief and nervousness at those points at which a character in a classical musical suddenly breaks into song and dance.

Once again, though, it is important to understand the connection between these visual and narrative conventions and the underlying social values they express. The classical musicals—*Singing in the Rain* (1952), *Meet Me in St. Louis* (1944), *The Bandwagon* (1953), and *An American in Paris* (1951)—belong to a less cynical age and, as films, express a cultural optimism and innocence that contemporary viewers find quite foreign. The musical is a joyous celebration of life, romance, and desire, whereas modern audiences may be more accustomed to cynical representations of life on movie screens.

The Horror Film

For obvious reasons, the musical appeared with the arrival of sound in the American cinema in the late 1920s. Like Westerns and gangster films, though, horror has roots in the early silent period and existed as a literary and theatrical genre long before the invention of cinema. Critic Robin Wood defines the basic narrative situation in horror films as one whereby "normality" is threatened by the monster. In monster films from *Frankenstein* (1931) and *Dracula* (1931) to *Halloween* (1978) and *The Fly* (1988), normality is often defined in terms of the romantic, heterosexual couple, although this is not an invariable pattern. John Carpenter's remake of *The Thing* (1982), for example, is set amid an all-male community of scientific researchers based in Antarctica.

Aside from the obvious physical danger it typically poses to ordinary, normal characters in the films, the monster also threatens categories of social normality through its configuration. Whether a vampire, a mummy, a werewolf, or a vengeful psychopath, the monster represents a confusion, or a violation, of social categories that specify boundaries between normal and abnormal, human and animal, living and dead. The monster typically occupies an uncertain middle ground between these cultural categories, neither living nor dead, neither fully human nor fully animal, abnormal but bearing disturbing traces of the human.

The accompanying illustrations of some of the screen's most famous monsters—Lon Chaney's wolfman, Jason, Bela Lugosi's Dracula, Boris Karloff as Frankenstein's monster, Freddie Kreuger—demonstrate that the monstrousness of the monster lies precisely in its display of both human and inhuman characteristics. As such, the horror film questions the viewer's most deeply cherished notions about what it means to be a human being. By centering on imaginary creatures who dwell in the margins of human life and consciousness, the horror film terrifies viewers by undermining their secure sense of where human identity lies in relation to the world of the dead, of animals, or of things.

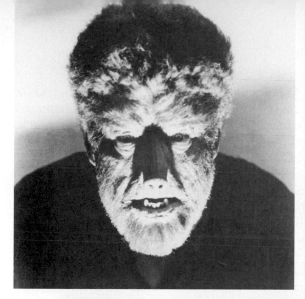

The greatest and most
enduring monsters are
those that remain
recognizably human
while being undeniably
monstrous. This
recognition that
human identity and
monstrosity are one is
the genre's deepest
secret and most
profound source
of terror.

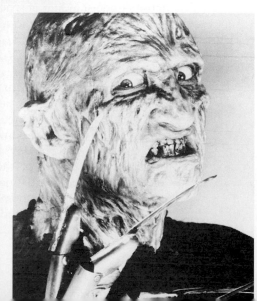

Evolution of the Horror Film   The evolution of the horror film demonstrates how genre conventions change. Old conventions become exhausted, and filmmakers search for new ones in their never-ending challenge to retain the interest of the audience. Horror films of the 1930s and 1940s tended to end on a very comforting note. The monster was destroyed, and the romantic couple reached safety unharmed.

By the 1970s and 1980s, however, in such films as *Halloween* and the never-ending *Nightmare on Elm Street* and *Friday the 13th* series, the monster became indestructible and undefeatable. Freddy, Jason, and Michael Myers of the *Halloween* films, remain alive at the end of each episode, and viewers know they will come back again to haunt and terrify. Contemporary horror films, therefore, are far more disturbing and unsettling than horror was in previous decades, when narrative conventions insisted that normality be restored and secure at film's end. Perhaps because the modern viewer's sense of what is normal is more precarious and more easily undermined, the destruction of order and security may strike contemporary audiences as a more authentic vision of life. The monsters today are everywhere, and they cannot be defeated.

Modes of Screen Reality in the Horror Film   Offering visions of imaginary monsters, horror often occupies a fantasy and fantastic mode. Some horror films, though, such as Alfred Hitchcock's *Psycho,* draw heavily on realist expressionist elements and offer a vision of human depravity that is disturbing precisely because it is not located in a fantasy realm.

SUMMARY

Because the camera has a double capacity, functioning as a medium that can both record properties of the visual world set before it and manipulate and transform the appearance of that world, filmmakers can create differing styles or modes of screen reality. The mode of ordinary fictional realism employs an audiovisual and narrative design that strives to replicate on screen, with a fair degree of resemblance, the spectator's understanding of space, time, causality, and the dynamics of human behavior.

The expressionist mode makes available to filmmakers a range of extremely explicit stylistic distortions and manipulations that are used to express heightened, extreme, or abnormal states of feeling, thought, or behavior. The mode of fantasy and the fantastic establishes a realm of time and space far removed from ordinary reality in which character behavior can retain recognizably human dimensions or possess magical and extraordinary powers and abilities.

Finally, the mode of cinematic self-reflexivity is available to filmmakers who want to reveal and display the constructed and artificial basis of the cinema. Typically, filmmakers employ this mode for either a comic effect or for communicating an urgent social message directly to their audience. In the latter case, filmmakers will use this mode if they feel that the necessity of having to speak indirectly through characters and a story will prevent them from getting their message across or may leave the message itself muddied and muddled.

While the cinema has four distinct stylistic modes available to it, the divisions and boundaries between these modes are not hard and fast. In fact, many films incorporate one or more distinct modes. Musicals such as *Singin' in the Rain* or *An American in Paris,* for example, typically draw on ordinary fictional realism as well as fantasy and the fantastic. These stylistic modes are extremely flexible, and filmmakers can move in and out of several different modes.

Screen reality is constructed partly by the manipulations of film design discussed in this chapter, and it can vary widely across films and become concentrated in one or more forms in particular genres. In genres, the modes of screen reality are highly charged with cultural meaning. Screen reality, however, is also constructed by viewers. Representational reality seems real only when a viewer decides that it does. Representational conventions change over time, as does viewer response to them. Contemporary audiences react with disbelief when gunshot victims in 1940s movies clutch their stomachs, double over, and slowly sink out of frame. Screen reality exists in relation to viewers who judge its perceived levels of credibility and validity. By manipulating film structure, filmmakers hope to influence viewers' judgments, but their ability to control viewer response is limited. Like so much else about film, the creation of screen reality is a collaborative production.

SUGGESTED READINGS

Edward Buscombe, ed., *The BFI Companion to the Western* (New York: Da Capo Press, 1991).

James Donald, *Fantasy and the Cinema* (London: British Film Institute, 1989).

Jane Feuer, *The Hollywood Musical,* second edition (Bloomington: Indiana University Press, 1993).

Bill Nichols, *Representing Reality: Issues and Concepts in Documentary* (Bloomington: Indiana University Press, 1992).

William Paul, *Laughing Screaming: Modern Hollywood Horror and Comedy* (New York: Columbia University Press, 1994).

Andrew Tudor, *Monsters and Mad Scientists: A Cultural History of the Horror Movie* (London: Blackwell, 1989).

Chapter 8

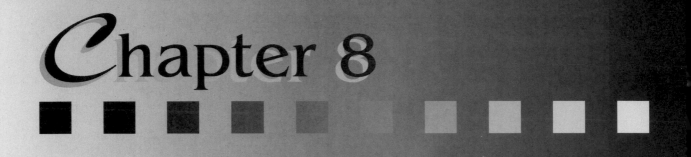

Hollywood International

Chapter Objectives

After reading this chapter, you should be able to

- describe the box-office performance of American films in world markets
- explain how the American film industry facilitates the marketing of its product
- describe three key forms of Hollywood's stylistic influence on world cinema
- explain how contemporary filmmaking operates within an integrated market
- define blockbuster production

- define product tie-ins and product placement
- describe the international marketing of *Jurassic Park*
- compare and contrast the original European version of *The Vanishing* with its American remake and explain how Hollywood absorbs and transforms foreign film style

Key Terms and Concepts

gross
integration
ancillary markets

blockbuster
diversification
product tie-ins

product placement
homage

Movies are as much a business as they are an art. Considered either artistically or economically, the cinema is a global phenomenon. Movies are seen by millions of people throughout the world, and filmmakers have an enormous opportunity to communicate cross-culturally to viewers in different countries and diverse social communities. In turn, a film's profit potential is not restricted by national borders. Box office champions top profit lists because of their outstanding performances in a global market. American cinema dominates the world's movie screens, exerting a powerful influence. In response to this influence, foreign filmmakers alternatively accept and reject the model of filmmaking promoted by the Hollywood system.

This chapter and Chapter 9 place the cinema in an international frame, artistically and economically. This chapter examines the global economic dominance of Hollywood film in terms of the box-office performance of American films throughout the world, how the American industry facilitates the international marketing of its product, and Hollywood's stylistic influence on world cinema. The next chapter examines important stylistic alternatives to Hollywood in the international cinema. Filmmakers wanting to develop an indigenous national style often reject the style of American cinema. These discussions will show that the greatest international box-office popularity has been achieved by a fairly narrow range of film styles and subjects. Although seen by the greatest numbers of people, these should not be misidentified as representing all that the cinema has to offer.

☐ THE GLOBAL DOMINANCE OF HOLLYWOOD

To understand Hollywood's position in the world's cinema market, one must first grasp the size of that market and the relative performance of American films therein. In 1993, *Variety,* the film industry's business journal, conducted its first global box-office survey, and the findings were striking. The total world **gross** (the *gross* is the total box-office receipts earned by a film) was $8 billion. Of the top-earning 100 films, 88 were U.S. productions, and only six were non-English language pictures. In other words, American film production accounted for 88 percent of the highest grossing films throughout world markets. The number-one film in the world that year was Steven Spielberg's *Jurassic Park,* grossing $338 million in the U.S. market and $530 million overseas. For Universal, the studio producing the film, the world market was more important than the domestic U.S. market in terms of box-office revenue.

Other leading films that year dramatically illustrate the importance of the overseas market. *Home Alone 2,* Twentieth Century Fox's follow-up to its phenomenally successful *Home Alone* (1990), grossed $139 million in the U.S. market and earned $106 million overseas. The performance of Warner Bros.' Steven Seagal-action thriller *Under Siege* (1992) was more striking. It earned $38 million in the U.S. market, but $66 million overseas. More impressive still was the international popularity of Francis Ford Coppola's *Bram Stoker's Dracula* (1992). It grossed $48 million in the United States. Without the overseas market, this paltry U.S. return would stamp the film as a clear failure. Overseas, however, it earned $107 million.

Not all films, of course, do better overseas than domestically. For some, the pattern is reversed. *Sleepless in Seattle* (1993), which grossed $126 million in the United States, returned only $62 million overseas, and the popular Tom Cruise vehicle, *The Firm* (1993), grossed $158 million in the U.S. market, but only $95 million overseas. Overseas performance often depends on the relative popularity of a film's star.

Jurassic Park
(Universal Studios, 1993)
The spectacular dinosaurs in *Jurassic Park* helped ensure that film's extraordinary box-office success. These computer-generated monsters moved with unprecedented vividness and wrung huge profits from thrilled audiences. Breakthrough achievements in computer-generated imagery gave the film its special appeal. Frame enlargement.

Tom Cruise has more limited appeal overseas than does Sylvester Stallone. Stallone's *Cliffhanger* (1994) grossed $84 million in the United States and $139 million overseas.

The Integrated Market

The *Variety* survey shows the size of the global market and the preeminent position of American films in that market. The organization of the U.S. cinema industry facilitates this dominance. Hollywood is an integrated entertainment producer catering to integrated domestic and international markets.

Integration describes the ability of a corporate film producer through its products to generate revenue across a wide variety of media and markets. Warner Bros.' Batman has proved its profit potential as a comic book character, a television series, a motion picture, a soundtrack album, a book about the making of the film, a Saturday morning cartoon series, and a wide range of toys, games, clothing, and other associated products carrying the Batman logo. Revenue earned by the Batman character from these products, both domestically and overseas, returns to Time-Warner, the parent corporation that owns the rights to the character and controls many of the media in which that character is marketed.

Ancillary Markets

The integrated market arose from two conditions: the declining importance of theatrical box-office revenues and the growth of **ancillary markets,** alternative media environments in which consumers watch motion pictures. These ancillary markets include the foreign theatrical market, broadcast and pay cable television (both domestically and worldwide), and home video royalties realized through rental and sale of videotapes.

The year 1986 was a historic one for the film industry. For the first time ever, revenue from home video rental and sales surpassed box-office revenues. In every year since then, the video market has outpaced the U.S. theatrical market. When the other

Batman is really the name for a stream of products: movie, comic book character, soundtrack album, toys, clothing, and games. A successful film performs well across these integrated markets. It must have multiple market appeal and be capable of generating sales of many different lines of associated products. Frame enlargement.

ancillary markets—foreign theatrical, cable and broadcast television, domestically and worldwide—are added to the video market, the declining importance of theatrical box-office revenue is striking. In 1986, for example, box-office ticket sales represented less than 30 percent of total film revenues.

For better or worse, the markets for motion picture entertainment are now integrated, and corporate survival depends on diversified control of these markets. This environment creates a distinct rationale for blockbuster production. A **blockbuster** is any hugely profitable film. The most successful blockbusters easily gross hundreds of millions of dollars in the world markets. Many blockbusters feature a fantasy narrative and state-of-the-art special effects. The blockbuster film, whether *Batman, Terminator 2, Star Wars, E.T.,* or *Jurassic Park,* has enormous audience appeal that spreads across a variety of media categories. These films do a huge business in both theatrical and ancillary markets. Their huge audience makes blockbuster films ideal for generating revenue from an integrated market. But to create blockbusters a film company must be properly organized. Today, **diversification** is the hallmark of a corporation such as Time-Warner, which also owns Warner Bros. studios. That is, Time-Warner's diverse business activities are spread across a range of products, media, and associated markets. Diversification positions a film studio to compete in an integrated entertainment market, to perform in overseas markets, and to market blockbuster films more easily.

Warner Communications Incorporated (WCI) in the 1980s   Throughout the 1980s, Warner Bros. belonged to Warner Communications Inc. (WCI). Motion picture entertainment was simply one part of the large range of leisure-time business operations carried out by WCI.

WCI's leisure-time businesses operated in six large umbrella areas: recorded music and music publishing included Warner Bros. Records, Atlantic Records, Electra, Asylum, Nonesuch Records, and Warner Bros. Music Publishing; filmed entertainment included the Warner Bros. film studio, Warner Bros. Television, Panavision equipment, Warner Home Video, and the Licensing Corporation of America; publishing and related distribution included Warner books, *Mad Magazine,* and D.C. Comics; cable communications included Warner Amex Cable Communications, a joint venture between Warners and American Express, and the Movie Channel; consumer electronics and toys included Atari, Malibu Grand Prix, and Knickerbocker Toys; finally, other miscellaneous operations included ownership of the New York Cosmos Soccer Club, Warner Cosmetics, and the Franklin Mint.

What are the advantages of such diversification? A diversified company can offset any loss accruing to one area of business operations from profits associated with others. The major advantage, however, is that WCI is able to keep in house all revenues accruing from the performance of its products across a wide range of media markets. For example, in the 1980s Batman was a WCI-controlled product. The Batman character originated in D.C. Comics, which WCI owned and published. The *Batman* film was produced by Warner Bros., falling under WCI's filmed entertainment area. A book about the making of the *Batman* movie was published by Warner Books, also a WCI holding. The soundtrack album appeared on Warner Bros. Records, and revenue from the release of the film to the home video market was generated through Warner Home Video.

WCI's Licensing Corporation of America enables the company to maintain control over its Batman character and revenue from that character, and even from products and markets not directly controlled by WCI. Merchants who want to produce and market a line of Batman games, toys, or costumes must pay a fee for the use of the character to the Licensing Corporation of America. In this way, regardless of how the Batman character appears—as a movie, record album, book, video viewed in the home, comic strip, or toy model or board game—WCI is assured a steady stream of revenue. Corporate diversification ensures outstanding product performance by maintaining control over an integrated market.

Time-Warner in the 1990s   In January 1990, Time, Inc. purchased WCI, creating an enormous combination of interlocking media companies. Time, of course, is the nation's leading magazine publisher with such titles as *Time, People, Sports Illustrated,* and *Fortune,* and it is also active in book publishing through its subsidiary Little, Brown. In addition to the Time, Inc. publishing titles and WCI's areas of media activity, the new Time-Warner company also includes Six Flags Entertainment, which encompasses seven theme parks that count about 20 million admissions annually, and HBO with its 18 million pay cable subscribers.

Time-Warner also has partial investments in a wide range of other domestic companies. These include Turner Broadcasting System, Courtroom T.V. Network, Comedy Central, E! Entertainment Channel, Black Entertainment Television, QVC Incorporated, and Hasbro Toys. Overseas, Time-Warner has investments in cable television, radio, and motion picture operations in Germany, the United Kingdom, Hungary, Scandinavia, Latin America, Australia, New Zealand, Japan, Denmark, and Portugal. These investments enable the corporation to perform in overseas markets.

Film and Product Merchandising in the Integrated Market

Film-based product merchandising is extremely important in this integrated global market and is a direct function of these patterns of corporate diversification. Blockbuster films—*Jurassic Park, Terminator 2, Star Wars*—generate huge profits and often feature mechanical or fantasy characters that lend themselves to manufacture and merchandising across diverse product lines. Film-based merchandising takes two forms: the product tie-in and product placement.

Product Tie-ins   In the mid-1970s, Steven Spielberg's *Jaws* and George Lucas' *Star Wars* announced the arrival of the blockbuster film by dramatically increasing the potential box-office income of motion pictures. The phenomenal impact of *Jaws* in the summer of 1975 was intensified by the enormous range of product tie-ins. **Product tie-ins** are products that bear the logo or likeness of characters in the movie or that re-package other aspects of the film, such as its music or narrative, in the case of records and books. Product tie-ins are "tied-in" with the release of the film, that is, they are marketed simultaneously with the film's release. For *Jaws* these product tie-ins included T-shirts, plastic tumblers, the soundtrack album, a paperback book about the making of the movie, beach towels, bike bags, blankets, costume jewelry, shark costumes, hosiery, hobby kits, inflatable sharks, iron-on transfers, games, posters, sharks' teeth necklaces, sleepwear, children's sweaters, swimsuits, ties, and water pistols.

Terminator 2 (Tri-Star Pictures, 1991)
Terminator 2 cost a lot of money to make, but it grossed huge sums in worldwide markets. Blockbuster films are aggressively promoted and very profitable. Like *Terminator 2*, they become movie events. Although the huge budgets of many blockbusters may seem to make them very risky ventures, their track record is most impressive. Given the ancillary markets worldwide, a heavily advertised and promoted blockbuster rarely loses money. Frame enlargement.

Today, the marketing of diverse product lines tied in to the visibility of a high-profile film is a standard feature of film distribution. The product tie-in, characteristic of contemporary film merchandising, shows how closely tied contemporary filmmaking is to diverse areas of consumer leisure-time activity and, indeed, to popular culture, itself.

Product Placement A second category of contemporary film merchandising demonstrates how deeply modern film is tied to the consumer economy. **Product placement** is a form of product advertising that appears within the motion picture. Today, if Mel Gibson or Sylvester Stallone drink a can of beer in a movie, it is not going to be a generic fictitious label such as Ajax beer. It will be a popular, commercially available beer such as Budweiser or Michelob. Product manufacturers pay a placement fee to studios for their brand labels to appear on screen. The size of the fee depends on how prominently the product is displayed. This income is now an important revenue source for studios, which accounts for the growing frequency of product placement.

In 1990, The Center for the Study of Commercialism, based in Washington, D.C., conducted a study to determine the pervasiveness of product placement. They found that the year's top-grossing film, Paramount Pictures' *Ghost*, contained 23 references to 16 different brand-name products. The second highest-grossing film that year, Disney's *Pretty Woman*, contained 20 references to 18 brand names. *Total Recall*, which was the sixth highest-grossing film that year, was the champion in terms of

Jaws
(Universal Studios, 1975)
While *Jaws* terrified summer audiences, it was accompanied by a marketing blitzkrieg pushing shark products. Blockbuster films are huge engines driving the leisure-time economy. They stimulate massive cycles of consumer purchasing. Their economic impact is far more significant than the artistic merits they possess.

product placement. It contained 55 references to 28 brand-named products including Heinz catsup, *U.S.A. Today*, Ocean Spray juices, the Hilton Hotel, Pepsi, Fuji Film, Hostess snacks, Panasonic T.V., Nike shoes, Coca-Cola, Kodak film, Sony television, Beck's Beer, Campbell's soup, Northwest Airlines, Killian Red Beer, Miller Light Beer, Miller Genuine Draft Beer, Gordon's Liquor, Jack-in-the-Box restaurants, ESPN, and Evian Water.

Given the emphasis on product placement in today's Hollywood, obvious issues of creative control arise. Do paid advertisements within the context of a film narrative subtly alter the shape and focus of that narrative? At least with respect to certain films, the answer is an unqualified yes. In the case of *Total Recall*, the influence of product placement seriously compromised the theme of the film. *Total Recall* is a science fiction thriller in which the villains are ruthless futuristic corporations in league with

Ghost (Paramount Pictures, 1990); **Pretty Woman** (Touchstone Pictures, 1990)
Ghost, with Demi Moore and Patrick Swayze, and *Pretty Woman*, starring Julia Roberts, carried high levels of product placements. Such films illustrate the growing tendency for motion pictures to function as an advertising medium.

gangsters running a brutal mining operation on Mars. The film's criticism of corporate control was certainly compromised by its massive reliance on corporate product placements. Product placement rendered the film's anticorporate satire less than consistent. At a minimum, product placements will bias the social perspective of a film toward an unquestioning or unexamined acceptance of the contemporary consumer economy with its engineered, leisure-time markets and products.

International Marketing of Jurassic Park

The importance of the global market and of product licensing and merchandising in that market is dramatically illustrated by the performance of *Jurassic Park,* the number-one film in world markets in 1993. The overseas release of *Jurassic Park* quickly followed its domestic premiere. The film opened in the United States on June 11, 1993, and overseas, first in Brazil, on June 25. In July, the picture opened throughout the rest of Latin and South America as well as in the United Kingdom, Japan, South Korea, Taiwan, the Philippines, Hong Kong, and Thailand. Markets in the Philippines, Hong Kong, and Thailand are especially prone to piracy, that is, the manufacture of unauthorized video copies of a popular film prior to its theatrical release. The distributor released the film quickly to those markets to decrease the allure of pirated copies. In August, September, and October, *Jurassic Park* opened in an additional 33 countries.

The film did extraordinarily well throughout the world in its opening week. In the United Kingdom, for example, Spielberg's dinosaur epic grossed $14 million in its first week, in Japan, $15 million. It grossed $13 million in Germany and $14 million in France.

Products associated with *Jurassic Park* included ice cream, frozen pizza, cakes, juices, cookies, key rings, chairs, sneakers, and, of course, toy dinosaurs. Video and computer games were a huge chunk of the product merchandising associated with the film. Ocean Software paid $2 million prior to the film's release as an advance royalty in exchange for worldwide rights to all *Jurassic Park* video games. It was a good deal. In France the film opened on October 20, and, by the end of December, Ocean Software had already sold 250,000 video games there. So stunning was the early performance of *Jurassic Park*-themed computer games, food, clothing, books, and toys that the Vice-President of International Merchandising for MCA/Universal, the studio conglomerate that produced the film, predicted that international sales of *Jurassic Park*-licensed products would outperform domestic U.S. sales.

Total Recall
(Tri-Star Pictures, 1990)
Total Recall, starring Arnold Schwarzenegger, featured more product placements than any other film of 1990. The film's satirical content suffered from the constant on-screen product advertising.
(Museum of Modern Art/Film Stills Archive)

E.T.
(Universal Studios, 1982)
Despite its longtime position as box-office champ before being dethroned by *Jurassic Park*, *E.T.* never realized its full potential as a catalyst for product marketing. In comparison with the early 1980s, the film industry today heavily depends on product placement and marketing for additional revenue streams. Throughout the 1980s, the film industry carefully reorganized itself to capitalize as much as possible on the profit potential of diverse leisure-time markets. Frame enlargement.

Long-term planning before the film's release helped ensure the successful marketing of the film and its associated products. The previous international box-office champion was another Spielberg film, 1981's *E.T.: The Extra-Terrestrial*. Marketing executives at the studio believed they fumbled the ball with *E.T.* more than a decade ago. Because the main character in *E.T.* is an ugly little alien, executives underestimated the market potential for product tie-ins, and they actually had difficulty finding manufacturers who were interested in bringing out *E.T.*-themed lines of merchandise.

Marketing executives were determined not to repeat this mistake with *Jurassic Park*. They would not underestimate the market for Speilberg's new mechanical creatures. Accordingly, two years before the film's premiere, the studio integrated teams of licensing, promotional, and manufacturing personnel to prepare for the film's global launch. A major component of the marketing strategy was *limited* disclosure of information about the film, never too much at any one time. Marketing programs were drawn up in countries throughout the world using only one graphic illustration from the film, an image showing the head of a dinosaur tipping over a Park vehicle. Speilberg did not want to give away too much about the film in early trailers and publicity. This ensured that the audience would stay interested and be kept in suspense about the mysterious new film prior to its release.

As the film's premiere drew closer, minimal, teasing information gave way to full media blitzes. For example, the film premiered September 3 in Sweden, Finland, and Norway and two weeks later in Denmark. Television was the major media form promoting the picture in these Scandinavian countries. Massive advertising campaigns saturated television viewers with promos for the film. In Norway, 97 commercials were presented in the nine days before the film's premiere. Heavy television advertising also wetted viewers' appetites in Sweden, Denmark, and Finland. As a result, from the less-than-24-million people inhabiting these countries, the film scored $15 million in box-office revenue.

Spielberg's Assessment Surveying the extraordinary performance of his film in global markets, Spielberg likens its appeal to the magic of a compelling story told

STEVEN SPIELBERG

Judged by box-office receipts, Steven Spielberg is the most popular filmmaker in the world. *Jurassic Park* (1993) broke world box-office records, and the top-grossing film it displaced was *E.T.* (1982), another Spielberg creation. His other hits—*Jaws* (1975), *Raiders of the Lost Ark* (1981), and *Indiana Jones and the Last Crusade* (1989)—are among the largest-grossing films of all time. But unlike Spielberg's public, critics remain divided over the merits of his work. Aside from the recent and atypically adult *Schindler's List* (1993), Spielberg's films have been determinedly child-oriented. Centered on special-effects "toys"—the mechanical shark, the spacecraft and aliens of *Close Encounters of the Third Kind* (1977) and *E.T.*—the brilliant style of the films evokes a narrow range of uncomplicated feelings, mainly awe and wonder, issuing from unexpected encounters with fantasy creatures. Until *Schindler's List*, critics were baffled that such a talented filmmaker seemed so uninterested in expanding his range and tackling subjects with some human complexity.

As a filmmaker, Spielberg was a genuine boy wonder. Unlike his contemporaries, he did not attend film school but went straight into the industry. Born in Cincinnati in 1947, he was just 21 when hired as a tele-

Jaws, (Universal Studios, 1975); **E.T.** (Universal Studios, 1982)
Speilberg's films are the top money makers of all time. *Jaws* was an efficient thrill machine that terrified summer audiences. and *E.T.,* (frame enlargement) cast a potent spell of childlike wonder and mystery. Built around mechanical characters, both films are driven by special effects.

around a campfire. In earlier times, communities would sit around the campfire and listen attentively as a storyteller cast a spell with tales of magic and fantasy. Today, Speilberg points out, the gathering around the campfire is the entire world. From Europe to Asia to Central and South America, people gather in multiplex theaters. "That's what has thrilled me most about the *Jurassic Park* phenomenon. It's not vision director by Universal Studios where he was in charge of episodes of *Night Gallery, Marcus Welby,* and *Columbo.* His first feature film, *Duel* (1971), made for television, was a gripping metaphoric story of a travelling salesman menaced on the road by a mysterious, anonymous truck driver.

At the age of 26, Spielberg began filming a similar story about a confrontation between ordinary people and the unknown, but this time with an aquatic setting. *Jaws* (1975), the work of a hungry young filmmaker eager to prove himself, caused a sensation the summer of its release. People were afraid to go in the water, just as they had been afraid to take showers when Hitchcock had finished with them in *Psycho* (1960), a decade-and-a-half earlier. A ferocious thrill machine, *Jaws* evoked a primitive terror in its audience that Spielberg never again attempted to duplicate.

He quickly turned to spirited evocations of childlike wonder and adolescent adventure: *Close Encounters of the Third Kind* (1977), *Raiders of the Lost Ark* (1981), *E.T.* (1982), *Indiana Jones and the Temple of Doom* (1984). Their spectacular success obliterated his only early career misfire, *1941* (1979), an overblown and unfunny attempt at a World War II slapstick comedy.

With *The Color Purple* (1985), Spielberg offered a controversial interpretation of Alice Walker's novel about a black woman's experiences in the South, but additional efforts to step away from his usual material were more misfires. *Empire of the Sun* (1987), a World War II film, and *Always* (1989), a remake of a classic 1943 Hollywood film, were critical and commercial disappointments. Although Spielberg returned to childhood fantasy with *Hook* (1991), a version of Peter Pan, it was so overproduced and visually cluttered that he seemed to be losing his magic touch.

However, the spectacular one-two punch of *Jurassic Park* and *Schindler's List* in 1993 reaffirmed his stature commercially and now also artistically. Although *Jurassic Park* was a sloppily plotted and mechanical film, its computer-generated dinosaurs came to life with unprecedented vividness. *Jurassic Park* cleaned up at the box office, while *Schindler's List* rejuvenated Spielberg's artistic career as the film no one thought he could make. This grim, black-and-white film portrays the horrors of the Nazi extermination camps in Poland with a depth of emotional feeling and an adult sensibility that Spielberg had never before demonstrated in his work. With *Schindler's List,* he seemed to be remaking himself as a new, more ambitious filmmaker. He has extended his cultural and historical ambitions and his moral sense of personal obligation by helping launch a vast project documenting and recording the oral histories of Holocaust survivors, which will be digitized and will become part of the world's historical record. Spielberg feels a special urgency in carrying out this project since many of these survivors are now quite elderly. Through this oral history project, Spielberg is acting as artist, historian, and citizen of the world, rather than as a blockbuster filmmaker.

Spielberg's career exemplifies the tensions and trade-offs of blockbuster filmmaking. His work has been enormously profitable, yet has generally stayed within narrow boundaries and, excepting *Schindler's List,* has avoided challenging or complex portrayals of adult life. He has the clout to finance and direct any film he desires any way he desires. It will be interesting to see whether he chooses to stay safely within the fantasy-blockbuster format or to further explore the newfound cinematic maturity displayed in *Schindler's List.*

domination by American cinema, it's just the magic of storytelling and it unites the world, and that is truly gratifying."

Speilberg certainly deserves to feel satisfied. After all, he remains box-office champion. *E.T.* held the number one spot for more than a decade, and *Jurassic Park* will certainly do so in the foreseeable future. However, more than the magic of good storytelling is at work in the global performance of *Jurassic Park*. Without corporate diversification and control of an integrated market, the *Jurassic Park* phenomenon could not exist. The economic framework in which these films operate cannot be dismissed.

Impact of the Blockbuster Film

Jurassic Park is a blockbuster film. Besides being highly profitable, these films often have two additional characteristics. Their stories frequently depend on fantasy or special effects (this is the magic that Spielberg referred to) and their characters are often superhuman or mechanical and nonhuman (the shark in *Jaws*, the robots in *Star Wars*, the alien in *E.T.*, the robot in *Terminator 2*, and the dinosaurs in *Jurassic Park*). These kinds of characters lend themselves quite well to reproduction across diverse product lines. (Not all blockbusters have each of these elements. *Forrest Gump* (1994), *Home Alone* (1990), and *Beverly Hills Cop* (1984), for example, are not dependent on mechanical or nonhuman characters. *Gump*, though, is a special-effects showcase, while *Home Alone* and *Beverly Hills Cop* boast cartoonlike plots with ultrapowerful heroes (played by Macaulay Culkin and Eddie Murphy) at their center.) Blockbuster films frequently have popular appeal and market potential across a wide range of media sources and merchandise lines. As such, the shark frenzy generated by *Jaws* in 1975 and the dinosaur craze created by *Jurassic Park* in the mid-1990s represented economic phenomena far greater than the films themselves. The shark and dinosaur markets extended well beyond the revenues created by motion picture ticket sales.

Here lies an important principle represented by blockbuster production. The blockbuster motion picture is merely the hub of a giant wheel of interconnected services and

---

Beverly Hills Cop (Paramount Pictures, 1984); **Forrest Gump** (Paramount Pictures, 1994)

Blockbuster films include a range of star vehicles and characters. Eddie Murphy's cop, Alex Foley, appeared in three *Beverly Hills Cop* films, and Tom Hanks' *Forrest Gump*, was a charming simpleton. Typically, though, blockbuster films contain some combination of special effects and cartoonlike, sometimes mechanical, characters and stories.

products. The film provides the stimulus for a huge array of merchandising and marketing underway in the nation's and the world's restaurants, toy stores, and other retail outlets. Blockbuster filmmaking is really about more than just the film. Successful blockbuster production stimulates the creation of a huge network of associated products and productions. This is why the integrated market is so important. Since the appeal of blockbuster film characters crosses media classes and product lines and because an enormous amount of money is at stake, parent corporations who own the film studios that produce those characters must maintain control of this integrated market.

This is done by tightly controlling the multiple ways consumers encounter the film and/or its characters. Whether consumers view it as a theatrical motion picture, as a video on home television, or by way of pay cable, whether they listen to the film's music on a soundtrack album, or read a paperback book about the making of the movie, buy dolls, games, or clothing tied in to the film's characters, the revenue streams generated by these media markets stay within the corporation. By licensing the use of the blockbuster characters to other manufacturers, the potentially huge revenue stream generated by product tie-ins throughout the world helps enlarge corporate earnings.

In its truest sense, blockbuster filmmaking is about production and manufacture of commodities on a national and global scale. Film is only a means toward this pattern of global production. Understood in economic terms, the blockbuster film's importance is measured only by its ability to stimulate a huge wave of consumption of film-themed, leisure-time products and services. With their blockbuster productions and aggressive promotional campaigns, American film studios have made the world their marketplace. The danger is that global film production becomes increasingly homogenized, increasingly the same from country to country, given over to special-effects-driven fantasy narratives or violent action spectacles featuring superhuman heroes. Because of this, as Chapter 9 shows, many filmmakers in other countries, fully aware of the global influence of Hollywood filmmaking, have extended film style in explicitly alternative directions. These alternatives co-exist with myriad ways in which Hollywood functions as a role model for foreign filmmakers. The American cinema absorbs, modifies, and influences the work of foreign directors, some of whom eventually come to work in Hollywood.

☐ INTERNATIONAL INFLUENCE OF HOLLYWOOD STYLE

The American cinema influences foreign directors in three key ways. Hollywood (1) stimulates filmmakers to absorb selected aspects of American cinema into their own work, (2) employs emigré directors, and (3) remakes foreign films and then distributes these overseas.

Influence on International Filmmaking Style

Hollywood films are popular throughout the world. Directors in other countries incorporate examples and quotations from American films in their own work to demonstrate their affection for Hollywood film. French directors Francois Truffaut and Jean-Luc Godard include extensive homages to Hollywood in their films. (An **homage** is a reference in a film to another film or filmmaker.) Truffaut paid his respects to his beloved Hollywood director, Alfred Hitchcock, in *The Bride Wore Black* (1968), and Godard's first film, *Breathless* (1959), is styled as a playful variation on American gangster pictures and Hollywood star Humphrey Bogart. Virtually the entire career of fellow French director Claude Chabrol is a variation on Hitchcock-style films of crime and psychological suspense.

The Case of Kurosawa   Although he is a master of cinema in his own right, Japanese director Akira Kurosawa is extraordinarily receptive to the example of Hollywood. In *The Bad Sleep Well* (1960), a thriller about corrupt corporations, Kurosawa borrows from Warner Bros. crime films of the 1930s in using montages of newspaper headlines to announce major plot developments. *Yojimbo* (1961), a samurai film about a warrior who manipulates two criminal gangs into annihilating each other, uses for its main set a dusty, wide street in a T-design that recalls the main street of many a Hollywood Western. The climactic showdown in *Yojimbo* occurs on the street just as it has in countless Hollywood Westerns. *Yojimbo* also includes a reference to the well-known Western *High Noon* (1952).

At the conclusion of *Sanjuro* (1962), two samurai confront each other, staring silently like gunfighters before a gunfight. They draw their swords like guns from holsters, and the faster draw wins. Quicker to get his sword out of its scabbard, the hero kills his opponent. Kurosawa has clearly modeled this showdown on Western gunfights. By the time Kurosawa made *Kagemusha* (1980), another samurai drama, he worked from the influence of Hollywood Westerns and simultaneously played off that influence. Many of the film's horizon shots of samurai on the march were modeled on the Monument Valley compositions of John Ford in a series of famous Hollywood westerns (these included *Fort Apache,* 1948; *She Wore a Yellow Ribbon,* 1949; and *The Searchers,* 1956).

Kurosawa borrowed from Ford, but he also played off and against Hollywood tradition. The climax of *Kagemusha* features a charge by samurai mounted on horseback against an opposing clan armed with rifles. The scene visualizes an important Japanese battle that has historic significance because it was the first demonstration of

Yojimbo (1961)
Kurosawa's popular samurai film *Yojimbo* makes reference to the design of classical Hollywood Westerns. It concludes with a "high noon" style showdown on the town's dusty main street.
(Museum of Modern Art/Film Stills Archive)

the effects of organized firepower upon an army carrying only swords and lances. As the riders charge, they are cut down by their enemy's firepower.

Kurosawa had the riflemen appear to shoot the horses out from under the riders, deliberately reversing a well-known Hollywood convention in which one invariably fired to hit the rider and not the horse. This convention can be seen in John Ford's classic 1939 Western, *Stagecoach*. During the climax, a band of Apache Indians, armed with rifles, chases the stagecoach and its inhabitants across the plains. The chase is thrilling and long, mainly because the Indians never shoot the horses pulling the coach. Instead, they try to hit the riders on and in the coach. Ever since the film was made, critics have pointed to the artificial quality of this chase in which the Indians never do the logical thing by shooting the horses. Making *Kagemusha,* Kurosawa deliberately departed from this time-worn convention. Kurosawa is an internationally famous director, but his relationship with the American cinema is by no means unique. He is one of many directors who define themselves by and against Hollywood filmmaking.

Absorption of Foreign Filmmakers

Because of its prestige, the American cinema continually attracts and absorbs talented foreign filmmakers who, in turn, influence and change American film style. Beginning in the late 1920s a major wave of emigré filmmakers arrived in Hollywood from Germany. These included cinematographer Karl Freund, directors Fritz Lang, F. W. Murnau, and Ernst Lubitsch, script writer Carl Mayer, and actors Emil Jannings and Conrad Veidt. Lang had directed such classic German films as *Metropolis* (1926) and *M* (1931), and beginning in 1934 he established a long career in Hollywood, frequently specializing in dark, crime films before he returned to Germany near the end of his career to direct his final films in the early 1960s.

Many of the American cinema's enduring classics were created by filmmakers who began their careers in other countries. The jaunty adventure classic *The Adventures of Robin Hood* (1938), the popular romantic drama *Casablanca* (1942), and the super-patriotic portrait of composer George M. Cohan, *Yankee Doodle Dandy* (1944), were all directed by Michael Curtiz, who was born in Hungary and worked in Germany during the early part of his film career. Hollywood's superstar director Alfred Hitchcock arrived in the United States in 1939 after a long and distinguished career as director in the British cinema. While apprenticing in the British system as an assistant director, Hitchcock worked and studied in Germany for two years, absorbing the style of expressionism then prevalent in German cinema. Hitchcock's subsequent American movies are strongly marked by the elements of German expressionism that he found so impressive while studying in Germany in 1924 and 1925.

Recent Emigré Filmmakers

In recent years, emigré directors have created some of the American cinema's most distinguished and popular films. Peter Weir established his career in Australia with such memorable films as *Picnic at Hanging Rock* (1975), *The Last Wave* (1978), and *Gallipoli* (1981), the latter film starring Australian actor Mel Gibson who, of course, subsequently became a major Hollywood star. Weir then went on to direct the well-regarded American films *Witness* (1985) and *Dead Poets' Society* (1989) with such established American celebrities as Harrison Ford and Robin Williams. Weir's colleague in the Australian cinema, George Miller, established his international reputation with the hits *Mad Max* (1979) and *The Road Warrior* (1981), both starring Mel Gibson. In the American cinema, Miller directed one segment of *Twilight Zone—The Movie* (1983), *The Witches of Eastwick* (1987), and *Lorenzo's Oil* (1992).

The Hollywood career of Dutch director Paul Verhoeven is even more spectacular. He established his reputation with the well-regarded Dutch films *Soldier of Orange* (1977) and *The Fourth Man* (1979), before embarking on a series of popular American hits. These include *Robocop* (1987), *Total Recall* (1990), and *Basic Instinct* (1992). *Robocop* is that rare example of a thinking person's action film. Verhoeven studied the contemporary action thrillers of Sylvester Stallone and Arnold Schwarzenegger and determined to beat them at their own game by providing ultra-kinetic, supercharged thrills and extreme violence. This he did while infusing the action spectacle with a sharp, on-target and biting satire of an American media culture dominated by entertainment-oriented television shows (popularly known as infotainment) and a caustic portrait of early 1980s economic and social policies. Seeing the excesses and irrationalities of contemporary American culture as only the outsider can, Verhoeven skewers that culture with a remarkable satire.

Robocop shows the dual influences at work when Hollywood absorbs foreign talent. The film's sharp social satire is facilitated by Verhoeven's status as a cultural outsider. On the other hand, its spectacular violence and supercharged action narrative are standard formulas of contemporary American film. Despite Verhoeven's success, his career illustrates one of the ironies resulting from absorption into the Hollywood industry. Foreign filmmakers absorbed into the Hollywood system rarely work with the kind of artistic freedom or produce the stylistically unusual works that drew Hol-

Robocop
(Orion Pictures, 1987)
The critical and popular success of *Robocop*, a savage social satire of 1980s America, launched the Hollywood career of Dutch director Paul Verhoeven. Like many foreign filmmakers before him, Verhoeven found the huge resources and popular impact of Hollywood filmmaking to be powerful lures. Unlike some of his less successful predecessors, though, Verhoeven enjoyed great popular success with his American productions.

lywood to them and them to Hollywood in the first place. Verhoeven, for example, has yet to produce for U.S. screens anything like the haunted, surreal dreamworld he captured in his Dutch film *The Fourth Man* (1979).

Remakes of Foreign Films

In addition to absorbing emigré talent from the cinemas of other nations, American filmmaking exercises international influence by remaking foreign hits and then distributing the remakes overseas. The Richard Gere-Jodie Foster vehicle, *Sommersby* (1993), was a remake of a popular French film, *The Return of Martin Guerre*. Overseas, *Sommersby* grossed $90 million, compared with $50 million in the United States. Such recent American comedies as *Three Men and a Baby* and *The Man with One Red Shoe* were also remakes of popular French hits. While Hollywood remakes of foreign hits have been especially common in recent years, it is not a new trend. The classic Western *The Magnificent Seven* (1960) Americanized Akira Kurosawa's magnificently filmed Japanese epic, *Seven Samurai* (1954).

The challenge Hollywood faces in remaking foreign hits is to translate story material from one cultural context to another. In some cases, the translations are fairly successful, as with *Three Men and a Baby*, mainly because the original was a piece of comic fluff not bound closely to a particular cultural context. By contrast, the Americanized Western *The Magnificent Seven* simplifies and eliminates much of the historical and philosophical complexity of the Japanese original, because no parallel cultural relationship exists in the American West with that of the Japanese samurai warrior and the peasant farmer in medieval Japan. Unable to translate the class conflicts and historical framework of Kurosawa's feudal drama to the American West, the screenwriters working on the remake simply eliminated large segments of the original film. As a result, although the American remake is somewhat entertaining, it has never achieved the international stature of Kurosawa's film.

What changes when Hollywood remakes a foreign film? The recent case of *The Vanishing* shows Hollywood's impact in reorganizing the original film and tailoring it to fit the American market.

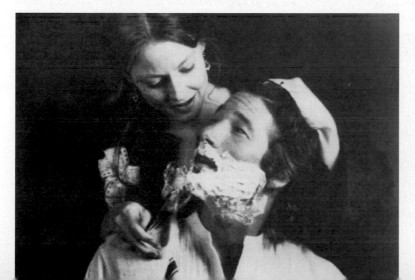

Sommersby
(Warner Bros., 1993)
American films draw on world cinema for inspiration. Hollywood today is quite fond of remaking foreign pictures. *Sommersby*, with Jodie Foster and Richard Gere, was a Hollywood remake of the French film, *The Return of Martin Guerro*. It went on to perform well in overseas markets.

The Vanishing: Two Versions

The Hollywoodizing of foreign film is clearly demonstrated in the two versions of *The Vanishing,* both directed by George Sluizer. Originally, *The Vanishing* was a French/Dutch co-production released in 1988. The film did very well in international distribution and won several top awards at film festivals. Noting the film's success, Hollywood thought it could be a viable commercial property as a remake. Director George Sluizer came to the United States to direct the project. The American version of *The Vanishing,* starring Jeff Bridges, Kiefer Sutherland, and Nancy Travis was released in 1993.

The American film industry exerted an extremely powerful influence on director Sluizer. The distinguishing features of his original picture were revised to fit contemporary American horror film conventions. These revisions reduced the uniquely disturbing psychological power of the original and turned it into a standard, formulaic horror film produced for American screens.

Narrative in Two Versions of *The Vanishing*

The story in each version of *The Vanishing* is superficially similar, turning on the mysterious disappearance of a young woman and the determined efforts by her lover to find her. In the original version, while vacationing in France, Rex Hofman and Saskia Wachter stop for gas at a local station. Saskia goes inside to buy drinks while Rex waits by the car. When she fails to return, Rex goes into the station looking for her, but she has vanished without a trace. During the next three years, Rex relentlessly papers the city with posters carrying Saskia's photograph, soliciting information about her whereabouts. He also appears on local television shows pleading his case. A parallel narrative in the film follows Raymond Lemorne, a university chemistry professor, family man and sociopath who is compelled to prove that his behavior exceeds ordinary moral categories. He devises an elaborate scheme whereby, posing as a weak man with an arm in a cast, he can lure a naive woman into his car, sedate her with chloroform, and abduct her. The film implies that Saskia has fallen victim to Lemorne's plan.

Intrigued by the spectacle of Rex and his determined efforts to discover Saskia's fate, Lemorne contacts Rex and promises that if Rex accompanies him to the site of Saskia's disappearance, he will tell Rex everything. With diabolical calculation, Lemorne plays on Rex's desperate need to know Saskia's fate. He persuades Rex to

The Vanishing (1988)
In the original version of *The Vanishing,* Raymond Lemorne is a vicious, inhuman sociopath who looks perfectly normal. The film's special creepiness comes from its suggestion that, beneath this outward normality, lies the most unspeakable evil. By contrast, in the American version, the killer looks quite sleazy and unpleasant. This establishes a less-disturbing philosophical outlook in the remake. Frame enlargement.

drink coffee laced with a sleeping pill, telling Rex that, if he does so, he will experience exactly what Saskia experienced. Knowing that to drink the coffee means he will die, as did Saskia, Rex nevertheless complies. In the final scene, Rex awakens, entombed in a coffin, buried alive. In the final moments of the film, Rex scratches vainly at the wooden lid and cries out Saskia's name.

In the American remake, the story is similar at first, but eventually veers off in a contrived and unsatisfying direction. Jeff (Kiefer Sutherland) and Diane (Sandra Bullock) are vacationing in the Northwestern United States. Diane disappears, Jeff spends three years trying to find out what happened to her, and, eventually, Barney (Jeff Bridges), Diane's abductor, contacts him. Jeff drinks from Barney's cup of coffee, and he wakes up buried alive beneath the earth. Earlier in the film Jeff found a new girlfriend, Rita (Nancy Travis). At the climax of the story, she tracks Barney to his secluded cabin and rescues Jeff. Rita and Jeff kill Barney. In the final scene of the film, they dine in a restaurant and laugh about the whole affair.

The disturbing narrative in the original French/Dutch production of *The Vanishing* was recast to fit contemporary American narrative formulas. Three major changes were imposed upon Tim Krabbe's original novel and screenplay. These result in emphases on (1) romance, (2) a reassuring, "happy" ending, and (3) standard horror film conventions which will be discussed later in the chapter.

Emphasis on romance and the loving couple.   The entire middle section of the remake focuses on the relationship between Rita and Jeff and adds considerable narrative complications in place of the elegant simplicity of the original film's narrative. In a convoluted subplot, Jeff tries to write a book dealing with Diane's disappearance and prevents Rita from seeing the contents of this book. Jeff has promised Rita that he would forget about Diane, and Rita exerts considerable pressure to coerce Jeff's loyalty towards her. As Jeff writes his secret book, he slips away one weekend a month, dons a fake uniform, and tells Rita he is in the Army Reserves, in order to continue his hunt for Diane's abductor. Eventually, Rita catches on to Jeff's deception, and this leads to many additional scenes in which the couple argue over Jeff's obsession with Diane and Rita's need for an exclusive commitment to their relationship.

In the original version, Rex did find a girlfriend, Lieneke, in the middle section of the film. However, this relationship remained a minor and subsidiary part of the

The Vanishing (Hollywood remake, 1993)
The American remake of *The Vanishing* emphasizes a romantic subplot between Jeff (Kiefer Sutherland) and Rita (Nancy Travis). The romance is formulaic and uninspired. Its comforting presence replaces the disturbing spiritual perspective of the original. Frame enlargement.

narrative, the major focus of which was the psychological cat-and-mouse game between Raymond and Rex. Eventually, Lieneke leaves Rex, realizing that a relationship with him is impossible because of his obsessions, and they reach this decision without any of the melodramatic emotional fireworks expended by the couple in the American remake. Indeed, the acting by the cast in the original production is cooler and more aloof than the theatrical and histrionic styles employed by the American actors.

A major alteration, then, in the remake of *The Vanishing* emphasizes elements of traditional romance because these are lacking in the original production, at least after the disappearance of Saskia at the beginning of the film. The story is reconfigured to bring a new love interest into Jeff's life and to have that occupy the long middle section of the film. Romantic love is an enduring characteristic of Hollywood productions, and belief in the power of romance to reconfigure one's life and re-create one's destiny is an essential part of the mythology of the couple constructed by Hollywood films. Accordingly, the narrative of *The Vanishing* is overhauled and retrofitted with these elements. In the end, love, in the form of Rita, saves the day.

Emphasis upon a happy, comforting ending.   The most striking difference between the two versions is the last minute rescue of Jeff in the American remake, whereas, in the original, it is Rex who perishes. The ending of the American version is comforting and reassuring while the original possesses considerable psychological terror. In the original, the camera remains in the coffin, with Rex gasping for breath as the image fades out and the end titles appear, leaving the viewer in a state of acute anxiety and considerable psychological tension.

The last-minute rescue in the American remake alters not only the outward structure of the narrative, it changes the philosophical and metaphysical design as well. In the original version, the narrative is a grim meditation on the inevitability of death. Nothing of this survives in the remake. Both versions are based on a novel called *The Golden Egg* by Tim Krabbe, and the golden egg imagery plays a huge role in the narrative design of the first version but no role at all in the remake.

Both films include an opening scene in which the lovers are driving through a dark tunnel and run out of gas. In the original version, this introduces the imagery of the golden egg. As Rex and Saskia drive through the darkened tunnel, she describes a recurring nightmare in which she is inside a golden egg, unable to get out, flying

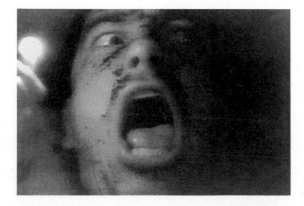

The original version concludes in the most terrifying way possible. Buried alive, unable to escape, Rex suffocates in a frenzy of panic. It is a ferociously grim ending that nothing in the remake matches. Frame enlargement.

through space for eternity. She adds that lately she dreams about a second golden egg flying in space. At this early point in the narrative, the viewer may not realize that this is a death dream. However, the enclosure of Saskia and Rex by the darkened tunnel clearly prefigures their final, if separate, entombment. During the tunnel sequence, a soprano vocal on the soundtrack adds an element of mystery and mysticism and marks the scene as seemingly significant.

When Rex and Saskia run out of gas in the tunnel, they quarrel because he ignored her earlier warnings about being low on gas. She tells him she is scared, and a truck approaches them from behind. She turns, sees its looming lights, and cries out, "the golden egg!" Saskia stays to look for a flashlight to guide their way out of the tunnel, while Rex angrily leaves her behind, determined to walk to a station to refill their spare gas can. She cries after Rex, imploring him not to leave her alone. The camera stays inside the car with Saskia, and the viewer sees her thrashing about, looking for the flashlight in the car's confined space. This, too, prefigures her protracted struggles in the final, confined space of her life, the coffin provided by Lemorne. Rex returns with the gas, and Saskia extracts a promise from him never to abandon her again.

In the original version, this promise is binding. By drinking Lemorne's drugged coffee and submitting to Saskia's fate at the end, Rex honors this promise and rejoins Saskia in oblivion. Even before this, however, Rex begins to share Saskia's dream. One afternoon with Lieneke, Rex has a seizure lying on the grass. He seems possessed, thrashes in place and cries out "the golden egg" and Saskia's name. This, too, prefigures death, since Rex will struggle and cry out like this in the coffin. Rex subsequently tells the television interviewer that he regularly has Saskia's dream and believes that they will meet each other again inside a golden egg. The golden egg and the dream shared by Rex and Saskia, and the imagery of the enclosing dark tunnel at the opening of the film establish the entire narrative as an advance toward a delayed but prefigured death.

Because Jeff is saved at the conclusion of the remake, the production team evidently thought that the dream of the golden egg had to be removed from the narrative. It was a costly choice because it meant that the narrative in the remake would work only on a literal and mundane level, whereas the original enriched its states of anxiety and terror with a cosmic, mystical dimension. In the remake, Jeff and Diane do drive through a tunnel and run out of gas, but there is no dialogue about a shared dream. There is no prefiguring of a final entombment. The tunnel sequence in the

Jeff and Diane run out of gas in a dark tunnel in the American remake, but the scene remains mundane and without metaphysical mystery. Frame enlargement.

remake is a mundane scene that works only on a literal level and fails to evoke the original version's sense of mystery and metaphysical predestination.

By contrast with the original's evocation of predestined death and cosmic horror, the final scene in the remake concludes the narrative on a trivializing note. Jeff and Rita enjoy a dinner in a restaurant with Jeff's publisher. A waiter arrives offering them coffee, and Jeff and Rita look at each other, laugh, and reply that they don't drink coffee any more. On this comic note, the end credits roll. Their laughter is meant to comfort the audience and end the film on a reassuring note, but it winds up trivializing the narrative that has preceded it.

Use of contemporary horror conventions.   Among the most unfortunate changes made in adapting *The Vanishing* to an American market is the use of contemporary horror conventions. As do many horror films today, *The Vanishing* contains extensive stalking sequences in which the killer relentlessly hunts his prey. Whereas the original film began with Rex and Diane stuck in the tunnel, the remake opens with a series of long scenes showing Barney perfecting his plans and methods for abducting a woman. The sustained focus of the film initially is on Barney, and Jeff and Diane do not appear until much later. When they finally arrive at the gas station, extensive cross-cutting shows Diane going inside for drinks and Barney stalking her. Viewers know the killer is already at the station waiting to do mischief, and they wait uneasily for Diane to fall into his clutches.

This narrative design diminishes the sense of terrifying mystery evoked by the original film, where the killer is only gradually revealed. At the very beginning of the remake, viewers meet the killer, learn how he plans to abduct his prey, and then wait for Diane to walk into the trap. As a result, the remake generates suspense instead of metaphysical mystery and gives viewers a clear and anticipated *abduction,* rather than a *vanishing.* Viewers know what will happen to Diane before it happens. It is a simple, if diabolical, abduction. In the original version, viewers don't learn until the end what happened to Saskia. She simply vanishes from the face of the earth. Instead of mystery, the remake offers a literal, ordinary crime.

Other stalking sequences show Barney hunting Rita at Jeff's apartment and the extended hunt and chase between Rita and Barney at the cabin during the film's climax. During this sequence, the film conforms to the most unfortunate of contemporary horror conventions, namely, a gratuitous emphasis on explicit violence. The elegant psychological narrative of the original contained little overt violence. The re-

Unlike the original version, the American remake reveals the killer (Jeff Bridges) right at the beginning, and he looks very creepy. Frame enlargement.

The elegant psychological suspense of the original, in which no overt violence occurs, degenerates into the usual horror film bloodbath in the remake as Rita goes after the killer with a variety of weapons. Frame enlargement.

make degenerates into a routine bloodbath. Struggling with Barney, Rita clubs him, stabs him, and burns him with a cigarette lighter, while Barney, in turn, tries to cut Rita's head off with a handsaw. Eventually, Rita frees Jeff, and Jeff clubs Barney to death with a shovel. Gross-out physical effects replace the psychological emphasis of the original.

Conforming to the American Market   This case study of two versions of *The Vanishing* demonstrates the way that Hollywood lures foreign filmmakers with the promise of access to its glamour and resources. The chance to make an American picture in Hollywood with popular American stars is extraordinarily tempting because the scale of the technical resources and cultural power available within the Hollywood system is so high. Furthermore, the global reach of its product ensures that the successful emigré director, such as Paul Verhoeven, can have a much larger potential audience.

In return, however, the industry imposes its own demands on the careers and artistic vision of the emigré filmmaker. Both versions of *The Vanishing* are directed by George Sluizer, but this is less important than one might at first think. Comparison of the two films shows that it is not the director, but the American production system, with its assumptions about what audiences want to see, how horror film narratives should be designed, and how much violence is necessary to ensure marketability, that exerts the determining influence over construction of the remake.

These dynamics are enduring ones. Many emigré filmmakers arriving in Hollywood find that, in crucial respects, they are accorded less freedom than in their home industry and that the unique or unusual features of their work, which attracted Hollywood to them in the first place, are not always welcomed in their American productions. Sluizer's original version of *The Vanishing* is sophisticated and inventive. Its merits, though, did not survive its cross-cultural transformation into an American remake. Since it would become a standard American horror film, Hollywood really needn't have hired Sluizer to direct the project, but few foreign directors will turn down an offer from Hollywood. These dynamics illuminate the reciprocal influences prevailing between Hollywood and the international cinema. Hollywood absorbs influences from overseas, and, at the same time, transforms and domesticates those influences according to the perceived demands of the American market.

SUMMARY

American filmmaking exerts a global influence throughout world markets. This influence has a clear economic basis. American film studios are owned by diversified parent corporations whose holdings equip them to compete in an integrated, world entertainment market. Blockbuster filmmaking, driven by special effects and mechanical or superhuman characters, is an ideal vehicle for dominating domestic and world cinema markets. The blockbuster film is enormously popular, generates huge overseas interest, and lends itself to extensive lines of product merchandising. With its multinational corporations and blockbuster productions, the American cinema is able to perform aggressively in global markets.

Hollywood exerts strong international influence not just economically, but stylistically as well. The style and content of American films have a major impact on world cinemas in three ways: (1) foreign filmmakers borrow images, characters, and story situations from the American cinema, (2) filmmakers who have established their careers in other countries come to Hollywood to make American films, and (3) Hollywood remakes foreign films according to the norms and standards of American film and popular culture.

Despite its impact on world markets, the influence of the American blockbuster cinema is limited. Although blockbuster films may threaten to homogenize the tastes of world cinema audiences, American and international film culture remain extraordinarily diverse and contain many film styles and approaches to filmmaking that differ from the norms of blockbuster filmmaking.

SUGGESTED READINGS

Tino Balio, ed. *The American Film Industry,* rev. ed. (Madison: University of Wisconsin Press, 1985).

Roger Ebert and Gene Siskel, *The Future of Movies: Interviews with Martin Scorsese, Steven Spielberg and George Lucas* (Kansas City, MO: Andres and McMeel, 1991).

Fred Goldberg, *Motion Picture Marketing and Distribution* (Stoneham, MA: Focal Press, 1991).

Peter Lev, *The Euro-American Film* (Austin, TX: University of Texas Press, 1993).

Philip M. Taylor, *Steven Spielberg: The Man, His Movies and Their Meaning* (New York: Continuum, 1992).

Justin Wyatt, *High Concept: Movies and Marketing in Hollywood* (Austin, TX: University of Texas Press, 1).

Chapter 9

The Cinema in an International Frame

Chapter Objectives

After reading this chapter, you should be able to

- explain how visual and narrative designs in the international cinema differ from the norms of American filmmaking

- describe two key features of the international film art movement of the 1950s

- identify and describe the basic film styles of five key international auteurs

- explain the aims of Italian neorealism and describe its cinematic techniques

- assess the legacy of Italian neorealism and its influence on subsequent filmmakers

- describe the theoretical and historical origins of the French New Wave and discuss the stylistic approaches of key New Wave directors

- explain the origins of New German Cinema and compare the film styles of its key directors

- describe the artistic and generational dynamics at work in the emergence of new wave film styles

- recognize and appreciate the diversity of artistic styles in the international cinema

Key Terms and Concepts

auteurism
surrealism
new wave

neorealism
temporal ambiguity
open narrative

melodrama
antinarrative

The cinema is a global medium. As such, it displays an extraordinary diversity of styles. A close familiarity with the norms of American filmmaking is but a first step toward a comprehensive understanding of the cinema's broad range of artistic styles and accomplishments. Previous chapters emphasized mostly American films and filmmakers. The international context must now be stressed. It presents an astonishing range of cinema styles and approaches and demonstrates the medium's great flexibility in its methods of storytelling and image design. In an international context, Hollywood becomes one reference point amid many others.

A survey of milestones in the international cinema turns up unique visual and narrative designs and many filmmakers whose work is a distinct departure from the norms of American filmmaking. This chapter examines some of these alternatives within two major categories: international auteurism and the phenomenon of national film movements.

☐ THE INTERNATIONAL AUTEUR CINEMA

Auteurism, the belief that certain directors can function as independent artists whose films display a unified personal style and design, characterized French film criticism throughout the 1950s and inspired the French New Wave directors in the 1960s. In turn, auteurism influenced American film criticism and film production beginning in the 1960s. In some ways, auteurism was not a new insight. Throughout cinema history, many important directors certainly exerted the key artistic influence on the style and themes of their films. These included Frank Capra and John Ford in Hollywood; Alfred Hitchcock in the British and Hollywood industries; Carl Dreyer, a Danish director who worked in a variety of European countries; and Sergei Eisenstein, Fritz Lang, and F. W. Murnau, from the classic silent era in Russian and German cinema.

What was distinctive, though, about the international auteur period beginning in the 1950s was (1) a new insistence upon the old idea that film was an art and the director was its key visionary, and (2) the emergence into worldwide distribution of an international cinema dominated by key superstar directors. International film culture in the 1950s and 1960s emphasized the recognition of outstanding international auteurs.

The auteur filmmaker, of course, was not a European phenomenon. Hollywood had its own auteurs. In an earlier period, these included John Ford, Alfred Hitchcock, and Orson Welles, while contemporary figures include Martin Scorsese, Francis Ford Coppola, Tim Burton, and Steven Spielberg. The 1950s international film art movement, though, tended to promote the international auteur. Since this chapter examines cinema in an international context, these auteurs are discussed here. (Hollywood auteurs are discussed and profiled throughout the other chapters.) Among the most important of the international auteurs were Michelangelo Antonioni, Ingmar Bergman, Luis Bunuel, Federico Fellini, and Akira Kurosawa.

Michelangelo Antonioni

Italian director Michelangelo Antonioni's earliest films were documentary shorts made within the tradition of *neorealism* that dominated Italian cinema of the period. These included *People of the Po* (1943) and *Dustmen* (1948). Consistent with neorealism, these were bleak, unsentimental portraits of working class life.

In his feature films, however, beginning with *Story of a Love Affair* (1950), Antonioni began an examination of lovelessness and alienation among the middle and upper classes. From *Story of a Love Affair* to *Il Grido* (1957), Antonioni develops the distinctive visual and psychological features of his soon-to-be-famous cinematic style. These include (1) the use of long takes and sequence shots, (2) silent, dead stretches within scenes during which the narrative is suspended while the film concentrates on moments of emotional stillness and psychological alienation between the characters, and (3) an increasingly precise compositional design that describes, through the positioning of characters and objects, the spatial coordinates of alienation.

Antonioni gained international prominence with *L'avventura* in 1960, which was honored with a special jury award at the Cannes Film Festival for the beauty of its images and for its invention of a new cinema language. Beginning with *L'avventura,* the distinct components of Antonioni's style—the use of long takes, moments of silence and narrative suspension, and the refinement of visual strategies for embodying states of psychological alienation—achieve a strikingly sophisticated and elaborate design.

Visual Design in *L'avventura*

L'avventura presents a deliberately mysterious and unresolved narrative. Set among the wealthy Italian leisure class, the film examines a boating party consisting of Anna, her boyfriend Sandro, her friend Claudia, and other guests. The group interrupts its swimming to go ashore on a rocky Mediterranean island. On the island, Anna tells her boyfriend that she no longer feels anything for him and wants to go away. Shortly thereafter, she vanishes. Her comrades find no trace of her on the island. She has simply disappeared.

The island itself is rocky and barren, and Antonioni explores this landscape with a distinctive visual brilliance. After Anna's disappearance, Antonioni spends an extraordinary amount of time, with very little dialogue, examining the visual and spatial relations of isolated characters placed against rocks, sea, and sky. The narrative is nearly suspended during these long scenes, as the imagery emphasizes the isolation of small characters dwarfed against an immense, forbidding, and empty landscape. The scenes are virtually silent, with long hiatuses between dialogue. These are the empty, dead moments so common in Antonioni's films during which the fragile emotional connections among characters break down. Antonioni's compositions during the island search display the most famous feature of his cinematic design—his extraordinary ability to create visual environments in which architectural design or features of landscape displace, obliterate, or swallow up the human figure.

The story in *L'avventura* remains an enigma. Anna is never found, nor does the viewer ever learn why and how she vanished. Her friends Claudia and Sandro become lovers but they are estranged at the film's end. No answers are forthcoming, and all of the characters seem to have reached an emotional dead end. By leaving the narrative profoundly unresolved and celebrating ambiguity, Antonioni implicitly pointed to the huge distance between his cinematic style and the tidy and reassuring conventions of storytelling in the American cinema, where all the narrative questions are neatly resolved before the final fade-out.

Elaboration of Style in *L'eclisse*

Antonioni continued to explore his concerns about lovelessness and psychological alienation in the modern world in a pair of films that, with *L'avventura,* are regarded

L'avventura (1960)
A barren island landscape and images of human isolation and anguish in Antonioni's *L'avventura*. Antonioni's special cinematic skill lay in placing his characters in physical settings in which visual design externalizes the characters' psychological problems. Frame enlargement.

as his trilogy. These are *La Notte* (1960) and *L'eclisse* (1962). His visual and narrative strategies reached a point of extreme concentration and emphasis by the time he made *L'eclisse*. The film begins with the disintegration of a love affair between Vittoria (played by Monica Vitti, who starred in all three films of the trilogy) and Ricardo. In the first scene, Vittoria announces to Ricardo that their affair is over and she is leaving. Later, she has a brief relationship with her mother's stockbroker but that, too, dissolves by the end of the film, and the viewer, once more, is left with a powerful vision of human disconnection.

The opening scene of *L'eclisse* demonstrates the extraordinary complexity and power of Antonioni's compositions. The first shot of the film is a close up of a lamp and books with a white object resting on top of the books. Significantly, this composition lacks any apparent human presence. After a few seconds, though, the camera pans right to reveal Ricardo sitting at his desk. The white object on top of the books turns out to be his elbow. His body is bisected by a pyramid sculpture and bordered by a second lamp on the right of the frame.

This compositional design is typical of Antonioni. In his cinema, human beings are overwhelmed by and entangled with the things that surround them—for example, tables, chairs, and buildings. The looming physical presence of their material environment overwhelms their attempts at love and communication. Antonioni's compositions are precise, visual statements of this sad psychological condition.

Withholding the Establishing Shot   Shot two shows Vittoria, with her back to the camera, standing in front of some curtains. She turns to face the camera and reaches for something out of frame. Antonioni's visual design here is quite distant from the continuity principles of the American system. Antonioni uses no establishing shot to clarify the spatial connections between the fields of view presented in shot one and shot two. The viewer assumes, for the sake of the narrative, that the two characters inhabit the same room, but the visual information in the film does not specify their actual physical relation to one another.

L'eclisse (1962)
Changing compositions in the opening shot of *L'eclisse*. After lingering on the image of the table lamp and books, the camera pans right to reveal Ricardo. Note how the composition splinters his body. Frame enlargements.

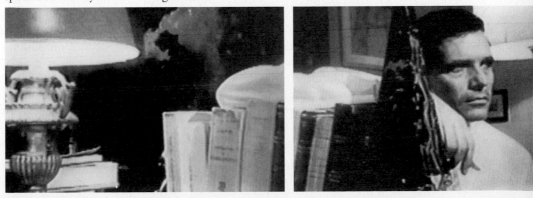

The second and third shots of *L'eclisse* present more fragmentary views of the scene. Unlike Hollywood's continuity editing, Antonioni's visual designs prevent the viewer from integrating shot information in a perceptually satisfying way. Frame enlargements.

Shot three presents another composition that the viewer cannot integrate into the established spaces. A picture frame encloses an ashtray and a series of porcelain figurines. A hand, which the viewer assumes is Vittoria's, reaches through the picture frame and rearranges these objects.

Antonioni frustrates the viewer's desire for psychological integration and closure. This is a significant point. By withholding the establishing shot, by building the sequence out of fragmented details, Antonioni frustrates the viewer's desire to integrate those details into a larger pattern or visual environment, and this ensures that the viewer begins to feel disconnected and cut-off, just like the characters.

Without any dialogue, Antonioni spends two-and-a-half minutes visually describing the emotional distance between Vittoria and Ricardo and the way that this psychological distance is externalized into their relationship with the environment. The images are eloquent, from the opening shot of Ricardo's body fragmented by the everyday objects of his room to later imagery of Vittoria staring lifelessly into space, with her presence and body dehumanized to become one more object of visual decor in the room. By withholding establishing shot information and by extending the long, dead silences between Vittoria and Ricardo, Antonioni creates a series of fractured, splintered spaces that do not cohere.

Antonioni ends the film with an even more dazzling example of visual form. Vittoria's affair with the stockbroker has become sterile and unfulfilling. She leaves his apartment and walks off into the city. A five-and-a-half minute montage follows, concluding the film. In this montage of 44 shots, Antonioni explores the city's empty, nonhuman spaces, a visually alienating, disturbing, and anxiety-provoking environment. The narrative is suspended, the main characters have been removed from the stage, but the film goes on during the final montage to explore in a poetic and nonnarrative way a cluster of visual impressions and accumulating anxieties.

Antonioni's Later Career

On the basis of his growing international reputation, Antonioni made several films in English, the first of which, *Blow Up* (1966), was a popular and critical hit. Its successor, *Zabriskie Point* (1969), performed dismally at the box office. Stunned by this failure, he returned to documentaries and made a nearly four-hour film about the Chinese revolution, *Chung Kuo cina* (1972).

He did not return to feature fiction films until making *The Passenger* in 1975. With this film, Antonioni re-engaged his familiar themes of alienated identities and disrupted lives. A television news reporter (Jack Nicholson) in the Middle East assumes the identity of a dead man found in a Moroccan hotel and is drawn unwittingly into violent political intrigue. At the end of the film, Antonioni executes a dazzling, seven-minute tracking and zoom shot. The camera pulls away from the reporter in his hotel room to move through the street and courtyard, then returns to the hotel window to reveal a narrative ellipsis—the reporter is dead. The narrative implies that he has been murdered by the agent responsible for the death of the original political operative found in the Moroccan hotel. The conclusion of *The Passenger* shows Antonioni working with undiminished visual brilliance and continuing to experiment boldly with narrative, as when he moves the camera away from the major action during the film's climax as the reporter is killed.

Unfortunately, however, Antonioni suffered a stroke in 1985, ending his filmmaking career. He has not worked since, but with films such as *L'avventura, L'eclisse,* and *The Passenger,* Antonioni established himself as an international director of the first rank. His distinguished work presents a series of unique cinematic narratives and landscapes in which the human figure is radically de-centered, in which characters lead emotionally dislocated lives, in which narrative is disrupted and attenuated, and in which a psychology of alienation prevails. Each of these features marks an immense distance from the norms and style of the American cinema.

Ingmar Bergman

Ingmar Bergman established his career in the small state-subsidized Swedish film industry. Since the state guaranteed to cover production and distribution costs of approved projects that fail to turn a profit at the box office, Bergman worked in a relatively pressure-free artistic environment, without the constant box-office worries of Hollywood directors. As a consequence of this relative freedom from box-office pressures, Bergman's films are extremely severe, often unrelentingly grim, and focus on human spiritual problems and crises of religious faith. Light, humorous moments are rare in Bergman's films (except for his few comedies). Bergman felt compelled to use film to explore some of humankind's deepest spiritual and emotional problems, and this led him to make films whose stark tone and extremely austere visual design would seem to be box-office poison, at least when measured by Hollywood's standards of what an audience wants. Bergman, though, found astonishing popular success and became an international cinema giant.

After training in the theater, Bergman, the son of a Lutheran minister, began his directing career with *Crisis* (1946) but did not achieve his first significant international recognition for a decade. *Smiles of a Summer Night* (1956), a light-hearted sex comedy, announced Bergman's arrival as an internationally recognized director. Following that production, Bergman launched into a series of unrelentingly sober and challenging examinations of human spiritual crises and religious dilemmas. *The Seventh Seal* (1956) is an extraordinary evocation of the plague years of the Middle Ages and tells an allegorical

The Seventh Seal (1956)
By playing chess with Death, the Knight (Max von Sydow) hopes to uncover the mysteries of life. The stark lighting and elegant composition are hallmarks of Bergman's work in this period. *The Seventh Seal.* Frame enlargement.

tale of a wandering knight engaged in a desperate chess game with Death. Death has come to claim the knight, but the warrior uses the game as a delaying tactic. Death agrees to spare him as long as the game goes on, and the knight uses this temporary respite to try to find, in the closing moments of his life, an answer to the question of why suffering must exist in a world presided over by a presumably benevolent God.

The cinematography is by Gunnar Fischer, and the cast includes Max von Sydow, Gunnar Björnstrand, Bibi Andersson, and Gunnel Lindblom, all of whom became regular members of Bergman's stock company. Bergman shot his films quickly and worked with a small cast of technicians and performers. Subsequent additions to this stock company included the actors Liv Ullmann and Erland Josephson and cinematographer Sven Nykvist, replacing Fischer on the later productions.

Bergman followed *The Seventh Seal* with *Wild Strawberries* (1957), one of his most famous films, about a science professor, traveling to receive an honorary doctorate, who is overwhelmed by memories and dreams of his youth, his parents, and his children. Late in life and with great anxiety, he confronts the ultimate question about whether his life has had meaning.

Wild Strawberries (1957)
An elderly professor, en route to receiving an honorary degree, re-evaluates his life in *Wild Strawberries,* one of the best of Bergman's introspective, psychologically probing films. Victor Sjöström, who had been a major Swedish director during the silent era, plays the professor. Frame enlargement.

The Trilogy

In the early 1960s, Bergman commenced a stark trilogy of films focusing on the religious and philosophical problems of God's silence in world torn by cruelty and violence. These films were *Through a Glass Darkly* (1961), *Winter Light* (1963), and *The Silence* (1963). In each of these works, the narrative covers a short period of time, the cast is very small, and the range of emotions evoked is fairly restricted. *Through a Glass Darkly* deals with the schizophrenic breakdown of a young woman and the detached, cruel response of her father who studies her disintegration in order to write about it in a novel. *Winter Light* deals with a village pastor's personal crisis when he is called on to give communion but lacks faith himself. *The Silence* deals with the fate of two sisters in a strange, mythical city where the inhabitants speak an unknown language. The two sisters become progressively more estranged from one another and from the world about them.

Cinematic Design in *Persona*

In 1966, Bergman made one of the most distinguished films of his long and illustrious career, *Persona,* a drama about the exchange of identities between a theater actress and the nurse attending her. For inexplicable reasons, the actress ceases speaking. The nurse entrusted to her care is obsessed with uncovering the mystery behind the actress' silence. This silence creates a void that eventually engulfs the personality and mind of the nurse. The two women merge identities, a moment Bergman captures in a mystical and mysterious image in which each woman's face is superimposed on top of the other, creating a composite, third, yet nonexistent, persona.

Persona is Bergman's most cinematically self-conscious and assured film. Many of his other films contain exquisite cinematography by Gunnar Fischer and Sven Nykvist but have a literary quality due to a primary reliance on dialogue and acting performances. In *Persona,* by contrast, Bergman draws attention to the apparatus of the cinema and points to the illusions that the cinema creates—illusions of time, space, narrative, and characterization—in developing the film's story about the exchange of identity and the breakdown of language.

Bergman establishes this self-conscious referencing of cinema at the film's beginning. The narrative commences when a doctor assigns the nurse to care for Mrs.

Persona (1966)
The human personality as enigmatic, seductive, and destructive. Bibi Andersson and Liv Ullmann merge identities in *Persona.*
(Museum of Modern Art/Film Stills Archive)

Vogler, the actress who has stopped speaking. This scene, though, occurs seven minutes into the film. The preceding six minutes are a poetic montage, which includes the opening credits and is constructed out of brief, kaleidoscopic visual impressions.

The first image of the film is the firing of the carbon arc inside a motion picture projector. The analogy, of course, is with the beginning of cinema and the beginning of *Persona*, the film Bergman is making. As *Persona* begins, the shots evoke the beginning of the projection experience. The viewer sees images of film running through the gate of a projector and countdown leader flashing on a screen. A brief cartoon image follows and then an image of a hand signing in the language of the deaf.

A kaleidoscope of disjointed images follows, including shots of a tarantula crawling on a glass screen, a sheep with its throat being cut and its organs removed, a crucified hand with a nail pounded into it, a landscape with trees, an iron-spiked fence, a mouth, an old woman's face, a boy lying on a platform covered by a sheet, a dangling hand, an old woman's hands at rest, feet, a face with eyes closed jump-cut with the eyes opening. On the soundtrack, dissonant music alternates with a phone ringing and dripping water. The boy under the sheet changes positions and then he sits up and turns toward the camera. He runs his hand across the lens of the camera. A reverse angle cut shows the boy in front of what appears to be a motion picture screen. On this screen, the faces of the nurse and Mrs. Vogler dissolve one into the other. Their superimposition suggests the merging of consciousness that will be the theme of the film.

At this point, *Persona*'s credit sequence begins with white letters on a black screen. Brief shots flash as subliminal images between the credits—a Vietnamese monk on fire, the boy's face, the women's faces, lips pressed against glass, various landscapes, and, fading in from a white screen, a door through which the nurse emerges to receive her assignment from the doctor. At this point the narrative proper begins.

This complex, kaleidoscopic montage preceding the narrative in *Persona* virtually defies analysis. Its poetic, non-narrative qualities are far removed from the standards of American popular cinema. The images are evocative, disturbing, anxiety-provoking, taboo (the imagery of the sheep with its throat cut), and constitute a poetic and rad-

In the poetic and mysterious prologue of *Persona,* an unidentified boy touches a screen containing the luminous image of the nurse (Bibi Andersson). Bergman's images are often symbolic and nonliteral, and they challenge viewers to interpret their mystery. Frame enlargement.

ical digression from the narrative of the film. That narrative, however, never establishes the kind of driving causal force that propels events in a Hollywood film. Bergman's narrative is a small, slender thread from which he creates mysterious images and an elliptical drama of psychological breakdown.

Bergman's Later Career

Bergman followed *Persona* with a series of internationally acclaimed films. *Hour of the Wolf* (1968), *Shame* (1968), and *The Passion of Anna* (1969) present elliptical, mysterious, and metaphorical narratives about the process of artistic creation, the closeness of artistic perception and madness, and the relation of the artist to a world in which violence and war are normal conditions. *Cries and Whispers* (1972), one of Bergman's most famous films, focuses with unbearable psychological intensity on the relationship among four women brought together in a turn-of-the-century manor by one's impending death from cancer.

Since *Cries and Whispers,* Bergman continued to work prolifically, realizing an adaptation of Mozart's opera, *The Magic Flute* (1975), a difficult and intense study of the breakdown of a marriage, *Scenes from a Marriage* (1974), a nightmarish vision of a female psychiatrist's decent into madness, *Face to Face* (1976), and, as his farewell to filmmaking, *Fanny and Alexander* (1982), with sumptuous costumes and art direction in a story about a young boy and his family in turn-of-the-century Sweden. The film's magical atmosphere, wider-than-usual emotional range, and vivid production design made it very popular. It earned four Academy Awards for Best Foreign Film and for its costumes, art direction, and cinematography. Bergman announced that this was to be his final film. Although he made one additional 16mm project for Swedish television, he has apparently retired from the world of cinema.

Like Antonioni, Bergman is a giant of the international screen—one who created a unique, distinctive, and unmistakably personal world on film. Bergman's characters suffer intense psychological and spiritual anguish, and he is relentless in using the camera to probe the nuances of emotional torment, spiritual despair, and the mysteries of artistic creation. His psychological poetry, minimal narratives, grim subject matter and sparse, stark visual style are in sharp contrast with the style of popular commercial films.

Luis Bunuel

While Antonioni and Bergman achieved fame in their native countries of Italy and Sweden, Luis Bunuel was an itinerant filmmaker, working alternately in Mexico, Spain, France, and the United States. He was a true freelancer, not at home for very long in any national cinema industry. But irrespective of the country in which he worked, Bunuel honored the surrealist impulse to explore, and even celebrate, the forces of social anarchy and the subconscious, irrational mind.

Presaged by the Dadaist movement (1916–1920) in modern art, which was committed to anarchy and the breakdown of order in art and society, surrealism appeared as a fully articulated movement in 1924 when André Breton in Paris issued his Surrealist Manifesto. **Surrealism** intended to overthrow social and artistic conventions.

Influenced by Freudian psychoanalysis, surrealism attempted to access the subconscious and irrational mind by creating art whose content and style was frankly fantastic and dreamlike. Surrealist images typically emphasize an illogical and unexpected combination of things or places as when a character in Bunuel's *Un Chien Andalou* opens an apartment door in the city and steps outside onto a beach by the sea or when, in David Lynch's *Blue Velvet* (1986), a character finds a human ear in the woods. Long after the surrealist wave had crested in modern art, Bunuel continued to explore the collision of dream and reality, social decorum and irrational impulse.

Calculated Assaults on Social Propriety

In 1928 Bunuel teamed with the surrealist artist Salvador Dali to make *Un Chien Andalou*, one of the most scandalous films of its time. A determined assault on the conventions of good taste and bourgeois morality, Bunuel and Dali's film is a catalog of sexual and religious taboos and anticontinuity approaches to narrative construction. From an editing standpoint, correct continuity matches fail to occur. The implied angles of a character's line of sight are incoherent, and characters improperly appear inside their own point-of-view shots. From a social and moral standpoint, the Bunuel/Dali film attacks the very act of seeing and the institution of cinema, itself. In the film's opening moments, Bunuel performs one of the most shocking and famous acts in the history of cinema. He stands behind a young woman, takes out a straight razor, and brings it close to her eye. The film cuts to a long shot of thin clouds slicing across a full moon and then to an extreme close-up of the razor slicing into an eye, which disgorges a viscous fluid.

The shot, of course, depends on a trick effect. Rather than the actress' eye, Bunuel slices the eye of a dead animal photographed in extreme close-up. Nevertheless, the act is shocking and never fails to provoke a gasp even from jaded, contemporary audiences. For once, the camera does not cut away from the promised, outrageous event. This assault on the eye, both literally and figuratively, is an emblematic gesture indicating Bunuel and Dali's aims in *Un Chien Andalou*. The film's elliptical, disjointed, dreamlike, and completely irrational narrative constantly frustrates the audience's desire to draw an integrative interpretation of the dissociated events in the film and also scandalizes the audience with a catalog of outrageous images that violate social decorum and propriety.

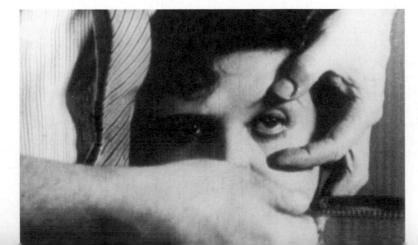

Un Chien Andalou (1928)
The most shocking and audacious act in the history of cinema. To make his artistic intentions perfectly clear, at the beginning of *Un Chien Andalou,* director Bunuel slices into an eye. Frame enlargement.

A Cinema of Assault and Subversive Play

The assault on the eye is emblematic of Bunuel's entire career in which he challenges the viewer's social values and perceptions of reality. Bunuel is a humorist who celebrates the power of the irrational and the unexpected in life. His goal is to subvert the spectator's belief in an ordered and reassuring universe. Bunuel's films delight in strange juxtapositions of unusual objects, as when, in *Un Chien Andalou,* the protagonist suddenly appears strapped to a piano on top of which is a bleeding animal carcass, and, with great effort, tries to pull it across the room.

Because dreams and unconventional erotic practices are, in their nature, opposed to the everyday world of ordinary logic and social morality, Bunuel regarded them as having a liberating potential. This assumption was consistent with his surrealist belief that subversive art could liberate and shake-up time-worn social perceptions and attitudes, and this was his reason for including such material in his films. As a surrealist, Bunuel believed that, by exploding the logic and conventional practices of everyday life, he could open a space for freer and less inhibited human behavior and perception.

Because his films were anticlerical and portrayed sexual perversions, Bunuel and his cinema were long an enemy of the Catholic church, especially in Spain where the authorities tried to destroy all copies of *Viridiana* (1961), a parable about the attempts of a devout and saintly young woman to lead a Christian life but which end in disaster for herself and for everyone in her life. In the mid-1950s Bunuel worked in France and then returned again to Mexico in 1958 to direct *Nazarin,* a film about a saintly priest whose efforts to conduct a spiritual life and follow the example of Christ, ironically, lead to his being hunted by the police as a criminal and thrown into jail. Bunuel's point was that, in present-day society, efforts to lead a genuinely Christian life are doomed to failure. *Viridiana,* shot in Spain, was a continuation of this idea and aroused the wrath of the Spanish authorities even though it won the top prize at the Cannes Film Festival.

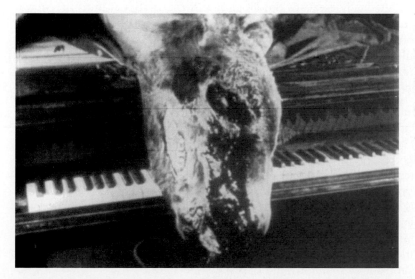

Bunuel's subversive assault on order, rationality, art, and religion compelled his use of surreal, antirational imagery. A bleeding animal carcass is draped over a piano in *Un Chien Andalou.* Frame enlargement.

The Exterminating Angel   In 1962, Bunuel returned again to Mexico to film *The Exterminating Angel,* one of his most famous and surreal films. The narrative focuses on twenty dinner guests who gather for a sumptuous banquet hosted by a wealthy socialite. After dinner, the guests find they cannot leave. They take off their jackets and bed down for the night on furniture and the floor. In the morning, they are still trapped in the room and remain so for several weeks. Paradoxically, no one from the outside can break in.

During their confinement, the veneer of polite bourgeois manners gradually crumbles. Desperate for water, the guests break through the ornate walls of the mansion with a pick axe, rupture a water line, and gather in a frenzy for the available water. Searching for food, they find a flock of sheep running through the house and butcher and eat them. One guest, in delirium, sees a disembodied hand scuttle across the floor. With unexpected aggression, it grabs her neck and attempts to strangle her. All pretense to civilized manners gone, the guests smash the furniture in the room and build a bonfire on the living room floor. Two guests are found dead (suicide victims), and the remaining guests try to kill a scapegoat victim to break the mysterious spell that holds them in the mansion.

Eventually, the guests find that they are in the same positions as on the original night. They re-trace their steps, trying to re-create their words and gestures from the original evening in an effort to undo the spell. This formula works, and they can now leave the room. They go outside where the authorities cheer them as refugees from a prison camp. To give thanks, they enter a church, but Bunuel's universe remains irrational. Following the ceremony, along with the other members of the congregation, they remain trapped inside the church. A huge flock of sheep breaks into the building, while violence in the streets erupts outside.

Bunuel's film style lacks the visual complexity of Antonioni or Bergman. The secret to his surrealist style lies in his method of narrative construction. He presents the most illogical and outlandish events as if they were completely normal. *The Exterminating Angel* opens on a world that initially obeys normal laws of time and space, but the narrative gradually escalates the illogical and the irrational until the viewer completely accepts the absurd premise of the film. As a surrealist, Bunuel aims to depict the chaotic emotional and social impulses that he believes lie beneath the artificial order established by social conventions and propriety. To get at these chaotic impulses and desires, he proceeds deliberately, gradually, and with a completely logical presentation of the illogical.

Narrative Structure in *The Discreet Charm of the Bourgeoisie*   The logical presentaton of the illogical distinguishes one of his best and most famous films, *The Discreet Charm of the Bourgeoisie,* produced in France in 1973. A group of wealthy and cultured friends repeatedly tries to have a civilized dinner party, alternately at restaurants and at their respective homes. A series of strange events frustrates each of their attempts. Patronizing a restaurant, the dinner party discovers that the manager has just died and is laid out in the very next room. They lose their appetites. The party attempts `to dine at a friend's house, but a group of soldiers, taking a break from maneuvers, comes to the house expecting to be fed. Accepting a dinner invitation from another friend, the group arrives at the home, only to find themselves mysteriously on stage in front of an auditorium of restless spectators.

The Discreet Charm of the Bourgeoisie (1973) A violent, unrealistic, irrational universe constantly disrupts the efforts of the bourgeoisie to complete their dinner party in *The Discreet Charm of the Bourgeoisie*. Nevertheless, they persist, and the film leaves them on the road, still looking for their dinner. Frame enlargement.

Bunuel presents these strange and bizarre events as if they were completely normal and logical. Moreover, Bunuel interrupts the narrative with scenes showing various characters waking from sleep and announcing that everything just seen in the film was a dream. This continually reframes the narrative as a series of dream episodes with the result that the order and structure required for a coherent narrative breaks down. Dreams are embedded within dreams so many times that the viewer is no longer sure who dreamt what or what level of reality governs events in the film. This peculiar structure enables Bunuel to mount an attack on the logic and structure of conventional realist narratives and places the film far outside the style of the Hollywood model, in which relations of time and space in a film's narrative are clearly established. Under the Hollywood model, dream episodes have explicit boundaries that clearly delineate them from the remaining body of the narrative.

In Bunuel's final film, *That Obscure Object of Desire* (1977), he assaults the logic of conventional narrative and cinematic representation by casting two different actresses with similar features in the same role—a young Spanish woman who tempts and teases a French widower. Accordingly, the character of the young woman continually changes her appearance, depending on who plays her and no one else in the film ever apparently notices. With this tactic and with typical surrealist wit, Bunuel calls into question not just the integrity and unity of the personality, but also conventions of cinematic representation that have always required that a character be portrayed by a single performer unless that character is seen in the narrative at different stages in his or her life.

Bunuel's Legacy

Bunuel's surrealistic film style assaults virtually all of the continuities of time and space, of narrative logic, and of character representation that commonly prevail in the Hollywood film industry and in the commercial film industries of other countries. His work is an obvious source of inspiration for contemporary specialists of the irrational such as David Lynch (*Eraserhead* (1978), *Blue Velvet* (1986)) and for genres that celebrate antilogical and irrational narratives, such as rock music videos. But unlike these more popular representatives of mass culture, Bunuel was a true anarchist in spirit, whose art retains its biting, socially subversive edge untainted by commercialism.

Federico Fellini

Like the early work of his colleague Michelangelo Antonioni, Fellini's first films superficially fall within the style of Italian neorealism. *The White Sheik* (1952), *I Vitelloni* (1953), and *La Strada* (1954) are realistic in outward style but are so strongly allegorical as to infuse their narratives with a powerful poetic and symbolic resonance. With *La Dolce Vita* (1960), Fellini turned his images away from the tradition of realism that had dominated Italian cinema since the mid-1940s and toward the hyperreal, surreal, and fantastical images for which he was to become famous. *La Dolce Vita* focuses on the professional and personal life of a journalist in Rome and opens with a strange series of long shots showing a statue of Christ transported by helicopter across the city, and it ends with a fantastic sequence in which a huge, weird fish is captured by the city's inhabitants.

In *8½* (1963), Fellini delved into the world of filmmaking with the self-reference that would become a hallmark of his cinema. In the film, a film director, Guido, who may represent Fellini himself, is creatively blocked, unable to complete his latest project, and retreats into an adolescent world of dreams and fantasies. The film ends with fantasy imagery in which Guido, dreaming now of himself as a boy, directs performers in a three-ring circus.

Fantasy and Spectacle

Juliet of the Spirits (1965) continued this emphasis on the inner world of fantasy and dream, achieved through an extreme distortion of the exterior world of people and objects. Juliet (played by Giulietta Masina, Fellini's wife and frequent collaborator) escapes into a private world of hallucination to avoid the unpleasantness of her marriage to an unfaithful husband. The striking feature about Fellini's work, here as in other films, is that Juliet's dreams and reveries are not radically different in visual style and emotional tone from her daily life. Fellini's extraordinary ability to impart a sense of weirdness and circus-like spectacle to everyday reality gives Juliet's daily life a marked element of strangeness to which her dreams offer only a limited stylistic contrast. Compare these images from the film. In the first shot pictured here, Juliet reclines at the shore and watches a group of her neighbors arrive to frolic on the beach. Fellini makes these neighbors appear dreamlike in their odd attire and strange behavior. This, though, is Juliet's reality. In the second shot, Juliet is having a dream

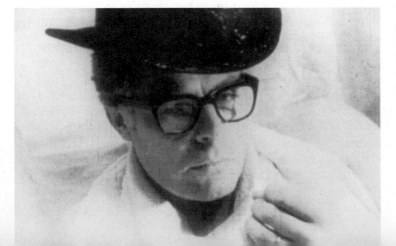

8½ (1963)
Marcello Mastroianni plays the frustrated film director in Fellini's self-referential *8½*. Frame enlargement.

Juliet of the Spirits (1965)
Fellini's cinema transforms reality into spectacle and pageant. These images from *Juliet of the Spirits* representing fantasy and reality look identical. The odd promenade of beachgoers from Juliet's waking reality looks just as strange as her weird dream of a boat at sea with the top of a submerged man's head visible in the foreground. Frame enlargements.

about meeting a mysterious boatman on the shore. The visual style of the dream and its elements of oddness and unreality are not substantially different from the previous image drawn from Juliet's daily reality.

An Alternative to Hollywood Norms

Fellini's cinema, then, displays an extraordinary ability to transform the surfaces of everyday life, imparting to them a strange, odd, circuslike appearance and atmosphere. Not surprisingly, Fellini increasingly turned toward extreme spectacles and circus pageantry. *Satyricon* (1969) was a lavish but harsh view of ancient Roman decadence, and *The Clowns* (1970) took the circus as its subject matter. In 1974, Fellini examined his own youth in the autobiographical, extremely stylized *Amarcord*. Remembering episodes from his boyhood, Fellini visualized them as a series of encounters with bizarrely configured people and places.

In subsequent films, such as *Casanova* (1976), *City of Women* (1981), *And the Ship Sails On* (1984), and *Ginger and Fred* (1986), Fellini continued to pioneer a unique path away from conventional realism and toward a world of exaggerated spectacle, circus atmosphere, and the subjective imagery of private dreams and hallucinations. Unlike Bunuel's work, though, which is extremely critical of conventional society, Fellini's extravagant imagery is uniquely personal and lacks the sardonic, anarchic, antisocial impulses of Bunuel. Bunuel's dream imagery is subversive. Fellini's is personal and joyously poetic. The almost complete subordination of narrative to style in Fellini's films places his work far from the norms of Hollywood cinema. Fellini's style is radically antirealistic, his world on screen an extremely personal pageantry of spectacular and theatricalized characters.

Akira Kurosawa

Unlike the other auteur filmmakers, Kurosawa's cinema does not radically break from the models of narrative and style associated with the American cinema. Kurosawa does

Drunken Angel (1948)
In *Drunken Angel* and other films of the postwar years, Kurosawa portrayed the efforts of a defeated nation to recover from the devastation of war. His treatment of gangsters and doctors, crime and sickness symbolized a recommended course of national recovery.
(Museum of Modern Art/Film Stills Archive)

not display the austere, narrow emotional range of a Bergman, the anarchic, antisocial impulses of a Bunuel, or the delight in a fantastical circus atmosphere of a Fellini. But, in more subtle ways, Kurosawa's style poses a genuine alternative to the norms of the American cinema. Although he began making films during the Second World War in Japan, Kurosawa made his mark in the immediate postwar years with a series of urban dramas focusing on the physical, emotional, and spiritual conditions of life in a defeated and ruined nation. These films included *Drunken Angel* (1948), *Stray Dog* (1950), and *Ikiru* (1952).

Kurosawa also attained fame with a series of vibrant, visually spectacular period films, many of which were set during the violent turmoil of Japan's sixteenth century. Kurosawa's period films include *Rashomon* (1950), an international classic about a rape and murder that is recalled in strikingly different terms by each of the four witnesses called to testify; *Seven Samurai* (1954), in which seven warriors defend a village of farmers against marauding bandits (a film that exerted a tremendous influence on the American cinema and was remade in 1960 as an American western, *The Magnificent Seven);* and *Throne of Blood* (1957), a widely admired version of *MacBeth* set during the civil wars in the sixteenth century. Kurosawa also adapted Shakespeare's *King Lear* as *Ran* (1985), also set in the sixteenth-century period that has had such significance for him as an artist. Kurosawa's samurai film, *Yojimbo* (1961), inspired the line of "spaghetti westerns" directed by Sergio Leone beginning with *A Fistful of Dollars* (1964).

Kurosawa's Cinematic Style

Kurosawa's stylistic elements include extremely rapid montage editing as well as the long take. The battle scenes in *Seven Samurai* feature a then-unprecedented use of rapid-fire editing to capture the ferocity of the battle, but in *Kagemusha* (1980), Kurosawa opens the film with a static, seven-minute shot that holds on three characters who remain largely motionless for the duration of the shot. Kurosawa's editing is a marked departure from Hollywood norms of continuity cutting because he rarely repeats camera set-ups throughout a scene. Under the Hollywood system, filmmakers created continuity by repeating camera set-ups at various points throughout a

Throne of Blood (1957)
Kurosawa is best known for his period films dealing with the samurai wars of the sixteenth century. Transposing Shakespeare to this setting, he made the acclaimed *Throne of Blood*.
(Museum of Modern Art/Film Stills Archive)

scene. This provides continuing reorientation for the viewer and helps maintain a strong continuity of character position and screen direction. By avoiding this, Kurosawa's editing demands constant perceptual reorientation from the viewer since the camera's angles of view are everchanging.

In a scene from *Seven Samurai*, several farmers from the village come to town to hire samurai for protection against bandits. They spend the night at a run-down inn, sharing the room with some local ruffians who are contemptuous of the farmers and with a boastful, arrogant, but humiliated samurai. Instead of repeating camera positions, Kurosawa uses set-ups that offer a novel and sometimes bewildering perspectives on the action. The scene contains nineteen different camera set-ups and only five repetitions of a previous set-up. Some of these repetitions, though, are deceiving because they begin with a familiar framing but then use camera movement to shift to

Kagemusha (1980)
A static camera and a seven-minute shot provide the daring opening of *Kagemusha*, Kurosawa's epic about the end of the samurai era in Japan. Despite his fondness for scenes of physical action and the moving camera, Kurosawa also loves still, static compositions. He integrates movement and action with moments of quiet and contemplation as few other filmmakers have.
(Museum of Modern Art/Film Stills Archive)

Seven Samurai (1954)
Ferocious action is a Kurosawa hallmark. Rapid-fire editing, telephoto lenses, and moving cameras plunge viewers into the battle scenes of *Seven Samurai*.
(Museum of Modern Art/Film Stills Archive)

a new position. Kurosawa's cutting, unlike Hollywood editing, demands ongoing perceptual reorientation by the viewer.

Kurosawa's use of multiple cameras when filming and his reliance on the telephoto lens are other essential features of his style and point to important differences from the Hollywood cinema. In Hollywood's practice, scenes are restaged and reshot each time a new camera perspective is needed. By contrast, Kurosawa permits the action of a scene to run through in its entirety and captures it using up to six cameras running simultaneously. He believes he gets better performances from the actors this way, and it is a distinctly different mode of production from the American system that restages action for coverage by a single camera.

Kurosawa's use of telephoto lenses ensures that his images have a different visual appearance from those in the American cinema. The extreme long lens that Kurosawa favors imposes a radical foreshortening of the representation of depth. Foreground and background areas of composition are compressed in ways that impose a distortion on normal perspective. This minimizes the viewer's perception of spatial depth in Kurosawa's shots. In sum, while Kurosawa's films fall into familiar genres—police thrillers, medical dramas, battle epics—his unconventional methods of filming and editing and his use of telephoto lenses clearly differentiate his work from the style of American cinema.

Each of these auteurs—Antonioni, Bergman, Bunuel, Fellini, and Kurosawa—achieved international prominence during the 1950s and 1960s and created a body of film different in subject matter and cinematic design from the norms of American filmmaking. As such, their work demonstrates the extraordinary range of stylistic options that are available to filmmakers and the enormous flexibility of the elements of cinema. This flexibility showcases the transformative power of the cinema, its ability to go beyond a reproduction of the surface appearance of things. These directors created uniquely stylized approaches to image and narrative construction. Their highly imaginative work demonstrates that the cinema is infinitely powerful in its ability to reconfigure, on screen, the visual and physical realities of daily life and to reshape, through narrative, the viewer's sense of time and causality.

☐ CINEMA AND SOCIETY: THE NEW WAVE PHENOMENON

A second striking feature of the international cinema and of film history, in general, is the tendency for a new national film style to coalesce around a group of young film-makers and critics who issue written proclamations about the need for cinematic alternatives and their intention of creating them. Thus, a **new wave** or a new direction and design within an existing national cinema is born. New wave directors are typically impatient with existing cinema styles and are intent on creating alternatives. This section examines three of the most famous examples of the new wave phenomenon: Italian neorealism in the 1940s, the French New Wave of the late 1950s and 1960s, and the New German Cinema of the 1970s.

Italian Neorealism

Neorealism exerted tremendous influence over Italian filmmakers throughout the 1940s and 1950s. Directors Antonioni and Fellini both had to work free of this influence before developing their own unique cinematic styles. Neorealist filmmakers aimed to truthfully portray Italian social reality by avoiding the gloss and glitter of expensive studio productions, emphasizing instead location filmmaking, a mixture of non- and semiprofessional performers, and simple, straightforward visual technique. Although it emerged in the 1940s and had peaked and declined by the end of the 1950s, neorealist style continues to be highly influential. Ermanno Olmi's *The Tree of Wooden Clogs* (1978), for example, is true to its neorealist origins in its simple, quiet, unsentimental focus on peasant life.

Goals of Neorealism

Neorealism developed as a reaction against the Fascist film style that typified Italian cinema under Mussolini. Mussolini invigorated Italian cinema through construction of the vast national studio, Cinecitta. But films produced during the Fascist years came to be known derisively as "white telephone" films because they focused on upper-class characters in sumptuous surroundings leading lives of leisure and decadence, allegedly spending most of their time talking on white telephones.

In 1942, critic and screenwriter Cesare Zavattini called for a new kind of film, equating entertainment films under the Fascists with perpetuation of a false consciousness and a false view of reality. Zavattini urged filmmakers to use the cinema as a medium for documenting and recording authentic social reality, rather than for creating glossy, if entertaining, fantasies. Zavattini urged filmmakers to show the everyday rather the exceptional, to show things as they are rather than as they seem, to show the relation of the people to their society rather than to their dreams, and to show the common people, workers and peasants, rather than idealized heroes and wealthy, upper-class socialites.

In 1943, critic Umberto Barbaro coined the term *neorealism* to describe this approach to cinema. Luchino Visconti's *Ossessione* (1943), a dramatization of an American crime novel, signaled a decisive break with the white-telephone tradition. Visconti gave this tale of desire and murder a vivid national setting by capturing the bleakness and poverty of the contemporary Italian countryside. In 1945, Roberto Rossellini's *Open City* received international acclaim and marked the full-blooded emergence of the neorealist style. Portraying the efforts of an Italian resistance leader, a Communist guerrilla fighter, and an Italian priest to fight the Nazi authorities occupying Rome, *Open City* vividly illustrates the methods and techniques of neorealist filmmaking.

Neorealist Techniques   Neorealist filmmakers such as Rossellini preferred to shoot on location rather than using artificial sets and to employ non- or semiprofessional actors. They also wanted to avoid intricate plots and fancy narratives. They believed that elaborate plotting and intricate storytelling impose a false structure on reality. *Open City* honors these techniques. The film was shot on location in Rome shortly after the Nazi occupation and tells a fairly simple story. Critics and viewers worldwide were stunned by the film's realistic evocation of a city ruined by warfare, crushed under the Nazis' authoritarian and cruel grip.

Like those of other neorealists, Rossellini's cinema techniques marked an explicit departure from the visual style of American cinema and of Italian white-telephone films. With their big stars and glossy production values, Hollywood cinema and the Italian white-telephone films offered disconnected views of social reality for a country with an active peasantry struggling to emerge from the wreckage of war. Accordingly, the neorealists rejected the glossy production techniques of studio filmmaking.

The neorealists employed a casual, open style of composition instead of deliberate and complex framings. Characters might move fluidly in and out of the frame instead of being artfully arranged within the shot. Camera set-ups tended to be functional and basic, without elaborate camera movement. The neorealists avoided expensive cinema equipment such as booms and dollies and the extravagant camera movement these make possible. These signal the vast resources of a film studio, and, hence, a kind of glossy manipulation and reworking of the raw social reality that a film documents.

Lighting set-ups tended to be very sparse and unadorned. The neorealists avoided the elaborate high-contrast and low-key lighting popular in American cinema at this time because these designs required and expressed the availability of expensive studio resources. Editing was relatively unimportant in neorealist films. Neorealist filmmakers avoided montage as a way of achieving effects because it, too, was considered to be overly artificial and manipulative of the viewer's response.

Using these simple approaches, neorealist directors concentrated on what was in the frame rather than on the properties of the image itself. In other words, unlike directors such as Alfred Hitchcock or Michelangelo Antonioni, neorealist directors did not want to create images so complex and self-conscious that they called attention to themselves as artificial creations. Instead, they wanted to portray authentic subjects rooted in the conditions of postwar Italian society. Cinema techniques were to be unobtrusive and simply used as a means of capturing, rather than falsely transforming, these social realities. Neorealists emphasized the observational, rather than the transformative, capabilities of cinema.

Neorealism in *Open City*   These cinematic approaches are neorealist ideas. In practice, a given filmmaker is likely to deviate from them. Rossellini's *Open City* illustrates the application of these principles as well as significant departures from them. Rossellini's use of non- and semiprofessional actors, authentic settings, a story rooted in Italian social reality, and sparse, unadorned camera techniques are consistent with neorealist ideals. To gain a sense of the gap between artistic idea and the realities of actual filmmaking practice, though, it will be helpful to examine where the film also falls short of these ideas.

In *Open City* there are four significant stylistic departures from neorealist ideas. First is the film's humor, which is clearly contrived as a way of manipulating viewer response and modulating the emotional tone of the film. The priest, although he is heroic and maintains a valiant resistance against the Nazis even unto death, is both the butt and source of comic episodes. Early in the film, playing soccer with a group of boys at his parish, he is bopped on the head by the ball. Later in the film, in its funniest scene, he smacks a garrulous old man on the head with a frying pan to shut him up so that Nazi soldiers, passing nearby, will not hear him.

The film needs the humor in these and other episodes because otherwise, it is an unrelentingly grim depiction of the costs of resistance and the valor of heroic sacrifice. By the end of the movie, most of the main characters are dead—murdered by the Nazis. The humor offsets the grimness of the picture and provides a temporary but much-needed respite and relief, but it is, clearly, the result of aesthetic calculation by the filmmaker.

A second clear stylistic departure from the neorealist idea of minimal manipulation is Rossellini's use of explicit religious symbolism. During the climax of the movie, Don Pietro, the priest, and Manfredi, the Communist leader, are captured by the Nazis. In an attempt to break the priest and extract vital information from him, they torture Manfredi. During this brutal scene, the film draws a series of visual analogies with the suffering of Christ, even positioning Manfredi in a crucifixion pose. Elsewhere in the film, the Nazis murder the fiance of an Italian resistance fighter. When Don Pietro cradles her body, Rossellini films this as an extended *Pieta* composition.

Third, the film employs a series of expressive, visually manipulative compositions. At the end of the film, as Don Pietro is about to be executed by a firing squad, the camera photographs the priest in the foreground while his Nazi executioners line up behind him in the distance. It is an extremely powerful, tense, and unsettling composition

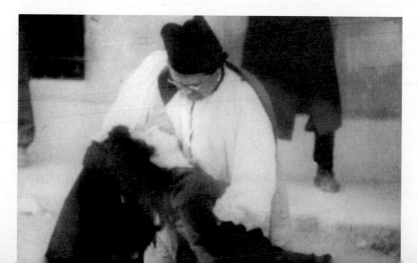

Open City (1945)
Don Pietro cradles the body of Pina (Anna Magnani) in an explicit *Pieta* composition that relates Pina's sacrifice to Christian iconography. The camera lingers on this image for a long time. Frame enlargement.

This powerfully expressive composition on the brink of Don Pietro's death places the viewer directly in the line of fire and emphasizes the priest's anguish and faith. It is an extraordinary image and is quite calculated in its design and effects. Frame enlargement.

because it places the viewer in close proximity to the anxiety and suffering of the priest and directly in the line of fire. Such an expressive composition is, in a pure sense, untrue to the neorealist idea of minimal use of cinematic technique to engineer emotional responses from viewers. Nevertheless, it is a highly effective composition at this point in the film. The emotional response it arouses is appropriate to the subject matter, and its degree of compositional artificiality is minimal, especially when compared with the baroque compositions employed by Alfred Hitchcock or Orson Welles in the American cinema.

Last, the editing in *Open City* sometimes departs from the idea of minimal aesthetic manipulation by the filmmaker. Perhaps the most striking use of technique to make an editorial point lies in the sound editing employed during the torture sequence late in the film. While Manfredi is being beaten and burned by his interrogators, the Nazi officer in charge grows bored with the spectacle. He leaves the torture room to enter an adjoining room where another group of officers lounges about a piano, partying. The lounge is a haven of culture and comfort. It contains the piano, fine furniture, drink, and expensive food. As the Nazi officer opens the door to cross from the torture chamber to the lounge, a sound mix dissolves the screams of the prisoner into the sound of the piano so that the two overlap.

Rossellini's point, here, is that Nazi culture has its basis in death. The musical performance in one room accompanies torture in another, and sound editing relates the two acoustically by having the sounds of one overlap the sounds of the other. The acoustical relation is intended to point to a political relation. From a strict standpoint this technique is artificial, an imposition by Rossellini upon the materials of social reality he seeks to observe and document. In practice, however, a filmmaker must balance artistic ideas against the actual effects that can be obtained or are needed, and as a practicing filmmaker Rossellini made the right choice here. The effect is subtle and cinematically sophisticated, and it does not otherwise intrude upon what remains an essentially unadorned style in the film.

Expressive sound editing overlaps piano music from the Nazi officers' lounge with the screams of their victims in the adjoining torture chamber. The sound dissolve enables Rossellini to make a political point about the relation between Nazi culture and death. Frame enlargement.

The Legacy of Neorealism

Italian neorealism declined in the late 1950s, in part because Italian political culture became hostile to the populist worker and peasant-based visions of the neorealists, but also probably because of the unrelenting seriousness and occasional grimness of the pictures themselves. Nevertheless, neorealism remains of lasting historical and stylistic importance because it demonstrated, after years of studio filmmaking focused on wealthy characters and narrative fantasies, how powerful the cinema can be as an instrument documenting authentic social realities. Furthermore, it demonstrated how artistically effective the results could be when a filmmaker rejects the norms of studio style associated with make-believe narratives, and, through simplification of technique, attempts honestly to return to a straightforward representation of social conditions. The legacy of neorealism is powerful and fundamental—it defines an essential approach to social realism in the cinema and exerts an enormous influence on subsequent filmmakers interested in using the camera to explore social realities.

The French New Wave

Similar generational dynamics are at work in the emergence of the French New Wave in the 1950s. As in Italian neorealism, a novel film style emerged along two fronts—in both theory and practice.

Theoretical Foundation of the New Wave

A radical shift in thinking about French cinema was pioneered in Alexandre Astruc's essay "Le Camera-Stylo," published in 1948. Astruc called for filmmakers to use the cinema as writers and painters have employed their mediums, to achieve a highly personal style. Astruc asserted that after years of an essentially commercial existence the cinema was now emerging in its own right as an art, like painting and the novel, whose practitioners could and should use it in a highly personal way. Astruc employed the term *the camera-pen* to designate the work of a filmmaker who uses the language of cinema to visualize his or her thoughts in an artistic way.

An important center for much new thinking and writing about French cinema was the community of critics working for the film journal *Cahiers du Cinema*. These critics included Francois Truffaut, Jean-Luc Godard, and Claude Chabrol, all of whom became, in a few years, important New Wave directors in their own right. In 1954, Truffaut published the essay "A Certain Tendency of the French Cinema," which attacked the studio-bound, literary, theatrical style of filmmaking, heavily dependent on plot and dialogue, which then prevailed. Truffaut claimed that a rededication to the importance of the image and a personal use of cinema was the corrective medicine needed to rejuvenate the artistry of French cinema.

In this essay, Truffaut also proclaimed a new policy for authors writing in the journal *Cahiers du Cinema*. The journal's criticism would henceforth emphasize the unity of themes and visual structure in the films of auteur directors, those directors who functioned as authors influencing and guiding the design and organization of their films. The auteur director was the film's author, responsible for its artistic vision, its visual and narrative structure.

The French critics claimed that, even in the Hollywood system where the producer typically had the ultimate administrative authority over a film's production, important auteurs prevailed. These auteur directors included Alfred Hitchcock, John Ford, and Howard Hawks. Although they tended to work in established genres such as the detective film and the Western, their movies seemed to have strong recurring themes and signature visual elements.

Technical Features of New Wave Style

It was to be expected, then, that when the *Cahiers* critics put down their pens and took up cameras, their films would explore the medium in highly personal and idiosyncratic ways. Indeed, the styles of French New Wave films, the first of which premiered in 1959, were extremely unusual, inventive, and experimental. French New Wave films employed innovative technology and a style that broke the rules of traditional French and Hollywood studio filmmaking. Among these new technologies were light-weight cameras that permitted the stylistic feature of location shooting. New Wave directors also employed fast film stock that enabled them to shoot on location under a variety of light conditions. With more flexible light requirements, they could shoot in a greater variety of physical environments.

Third, New Wave films employed Nagra tape recorders that were distinguished by their light weight and sophisticated sound recording capabilities. The Nagra recorders enabled directors to employ direct sound, to capture environmental sources of sound on location as opposed to creating a soundtrack in a recording studio during postproduction. Each of these technical features was extremely important in enabling New Wave films to break with traditional French and Hollywood studio style in which both sound and image were highly processed and refined by shooting on indoor sound stages.

Initial New Wave Productions

These stylistic and technical features distinguished the first group of New Wave films to arrive in theaters in 1959. Jean-Luc Godard's *Breathless* was an homage to American gangster movies, and particularly Humphrey Bogart, in a tale of a small-time gangster on the run from the police. It featured the revolutionary technique of jump-cutting in which Godard edited sequences with an unprecedented roughness, ragged-ness, and abruptness of transition from shot to shot. In the jump cut, portions of the action are left out, disrupting continuity so that the flow of action seems to break and jump from one moment to the next. In the film's early sequence where the thief shoots a policeman, Godard uses several jump cuts to fragment continuity.

Alain Resnais' *Hiroshima, Mon Amour,* the second of the three New Wave films to premiere that year, typified an even looser, more free-wheeling approach to cine-matic time and space. This film marked a distinctive New Wave contribution to cin-ematic style, replacing traditional studio continuity methods in which transitions from place to place and from one time frame to another were clearly marked.

Temporal Ambiguities in *Hiroshima, Mon Amour* Exploring the love affair between a French actress and a Japanese architect in postwar Hiroshima, Resnais' film takes the viewer in and out of several different time periods and states of conscious-ness, with transitions that are abrupt and not always clearly marked. The films **tem-poral ambiguity** lies in the way it mixes time frames, blending past and present so they are not easily separable, thereby making the time frame of the narrative uncer-tain and indefinite. For example, in one of the film's most famous temporal juxtapo-sitions, the French actress looks at her Japanese lover lying in bed. She glances at his hand, triggering a memory flashback, visualized on screen by a flash intercut of the hand of her dying German lover in wartime France. As the film progresses, tracking shots that explore the architecture of postwar Hiroshima are intercut with similar

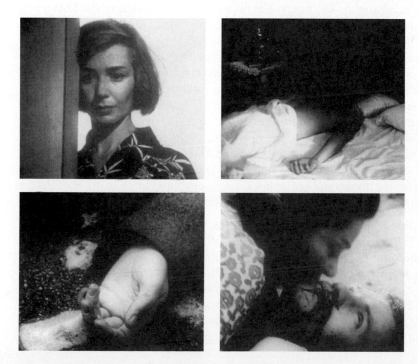

Hiroshima, Mon Amour (1959)
In *Hiroshima, Mon Amour,* time is fragmented and reorganized by memory and desire. Looking at the hand of her sleeping Japanese lover, the French actress recalls the twitching hand of her dying German lover years earlier in World War II. Resnais' film fulfills Astruc's call to use cinema to reveal the workings of human consciousness. Frame enlargements.

The poetic, metaphoric prologue visualizes the paradox of love in a nuclear age of mass destruction. Nuclear ash covers the entwined arms of embracing lovers. Frame enlargement.

tracking shots that explore the architecture of wartime France in ways that suggest the simultaneity of past and present, the existence of the past inside the present, within the minds of the characters.

The opening of *Hiroshima, Mon Amour* exemplifies its radical design. The film begins with a series of shots showing two bodies embracing and covered by what seems to be radioactive fallout. On the soundtrack, a man and a woman's voices engage in a poetic dialogue. She asserts the necessity of remembering the horrors of war and he counters by insisting that, in time, even memories of the most horrifying tragedies must fade and vanish.

Throughout this long, poetic dialogue, no fictional characters appear. The bodies embracing, covered with fallout, remain anonymous. The viewer cannot see their faces, nor correlate them with the voices on the soundtrack. Instead of introducing characters within a narrative, the camera explores, in a series of hypnotic tracking shots, the streets and buildings of Hiroshima, the banks of the river Ota into which victims of the bombing fled following the firestorm, and the faces and gnarled figures of bomb survivors. By withholding the narrative and characters from the opening sequences of the film, director Resnais and screenwriter Marguerite Duras establish an overt, explicitly symbolic and metaphoric tone, enabling the film to articulate a philosophical interest in the effects of time on human memory.

Narrative Openness in *The 400 Blows*   Francois Truffaut's *The 400 Blows* was the third film of 1959 to announce the emergence of New Wave. Truffaut's film is an unsentimental account of an adolescent delinquent named Antoine Doinel (played by Jean-Pierre Leaud), whose adventures Truffaut followed in four additional films over the next twenty years. *The 400 Blows* was shot on location in Paris and features fluid editing, extremely quick transitions from shot to shot and scene to scene, and a lyrical energy and delight in location filming that distinguished the film from the set-bound studio productions Truffaut had criticized in his 1954 essay.

The 400 Blows (1959)
Jean-Pierre Leaud as Antoine Doinel in Truffaut's *The 400 Blows,* the first of several films tracing the life of Doinel.

(Museum of Modern Art/Film Stills Archive)

Instead of offering the clean narrative closure typical of French and Hollywood studio films, Truffaut's film concludes with a deliberately ambiguous ending. Eluding the authorities one last time, Antoine Doinel runs free down to the beach and looks uneasily about. The film ends with a freeze frame of his anxious face, deliberately refusing a concluding statement about the character's fate and inviting the viewer to contemplate the ambiguities and open-endedness of life. The narrative remains **open.** Its chain of events are not brought to a definite conclusion but are suggestive of ongoing events extending beyond the end point of the film.

Each of these New Wave directors enjoyed long and prolific careers. Truffaut directed a wide range of films, including other New Wave classics such as *Shoot the Piano Player* (1960) and *Jules and Jim* (1961) before embarking on a pair of Hitchcock-style thrillers, *The Bride Wore Black* (1968) and *Mississippi Mermaid* (1969). Truffaut continued his Antoine Doinel series with a contribution to the anthology film *Love at Twenty* (1962) and with *Stolen Kisses* (1968), *Bed and Board* (1970), and *Love on the Run* (1979). His *The Wild Child* (1969) and *The Story of Adele H.* (1975) are exquisitely mounted period films, and *Day for Night* (1973), one of his most popular pictures, is a loving valentine to the movie industry, a film about the making of a film by a movie director played by Francois Truffaut.

Godard's Later Career

Jean-Luc Godard became the most important and cinematically influential director of the New Wave. Godard's films, following *Breathless,* were ever-more-radical attempts to break down the normative conventions and styles of the commercial cinema. *Weekend* (1967), examined in previous chapters, was Godard's violent rejection of consumer society and his own acknowledged end to narrative filmmaking. *Le Gai Savoir* (1968) was an ambiguous visual essay on the effects of language, film, comic strips, and television on human consciousness and society. The film has no story. Instead, it focuses on two characters who meet in a television studio at night to reflect upon images and language.

At the end of the 1960s, Godard joined a collective filmmaking group called Dziga Vertov and produced such pictures as *British Sounds* (1969), *Wind from the East* (1969), and *Tout va bien* (1972) in which he explored the connections between images, cinema, and ideology in a politically forceful manner. As Godard's style became more radical, however, and his interest in a politically rigorous interrogation of the nature of cinema became more pronounced, his films, not surprisingly, became more inward and withdrawn and their ideal audience smaller.

In the mid-1970s, Godard experimented with film/videotape combinations in such works as *Numero Deux* (1975) before returning to theatrical filmmaking with *Sauve Qui Peut LaVie* (1980) and other features including the controversial *Hail Mary* (1984), a contemporary re-telling of the Immaculate Conception that offended many Catholics, and a typically eccentric adaptation of *King Lear* (1986).

Resnais' Later Career

In subsequent films, Alan Resnais continued to explore the effects of memory and time on human consciousness. *Last Year at Marienbad* (1961), scripted by Alain Robbe-Grillet, assaulted narrative with a story deliberately constructed like a labyrinth, mystifying the viewer as to time structure and narrative tense. In the film, a man tries to

Sauve Qui Peut LaVie (1980)
A signature Godard composition: a character posed before a declamatory background in *Sauve Qui Peut LaVie.* Godard uses such images as self-reflexive moments. Image and text contrast and contend with one another. The effect is often ironic and playful. Cain and Abel, cinema and video. The implied relationship is counterintuitive. If anything, video, and the alternate, nontheatrical delivery systems of which it is part, will kill cinema (theatrical film).
(Museum of Modern Art/Film Stills Archive)

persuade a woman that they have met the year before at a posh resort in Marienbad. She denies this, and for the remainder of the film, they meet and re-meet and have the same conversation in different settings and implied time frames. Clear, temporal referents and narrative causality break down in *Last Year at Marienbad*.

In *The War Is Over* (1966) Resnais applied his interest in time and the effects of memory to a political framework, examining the past and present life of a middle-aged Spanish revolutionary whose ideas are called into question by a younger group of Parisian Leftists. Resnais' *Providence* (1977) put the viewer inside the mind of a dying British novelist and studied the way memory and desire can reconfigure the realities of time and place.

Other New Wave Filmmakers

Other important French New Wave directors include Claude Chabrol, whose long career is virtually a variation on the works of Hitchcock. Chabrol's films include *Les Biches* (1968), *The Butcher* (1979), *Just Before Nightfall* (1971), and *Masks* (1987). Also associated with the New Wave are Louis Malle (*Murmur of the Heart,* 1971), Eric Rohmer, whose series of "moral tales" include *My Night at Maud's* (1967), Jacques Rivette, whose films explore the outer, temporal boundaries of cinematic narratives, for example, *Out One Specter* (1972) is a four-and-a-half hour condensation of a thirteen-hour original; and Agnes Varda, whose *Cleo From Five to Seven* (1962), *One Sings the Other Doesn't* (1977), and *Vagabond* (1985), explore, from a feminist perspective, the psychological and emotional landscape of women's lives in contemporary society.

Significance of the New Wave

The French New Wave illustrates a fundamental dynamic of film style, namely, a process of generational revolt, wherein a collective of young directors attempted to throw off the inherited styles and forms of the dominant cinema that confront them as they enter the industry. The results of their experiments rejuvenated the traditional industry that, in time, absorbed their work. This dynamic characterized Italian neorealism and appeared again in connection with the New German Cinema.

Last Year at Marienbad
(1961)
Resnais aimed for a total ambiguity of time and setting and for the destruction of narrative in *Last Year at Marienbad*. The mysterious hotel is the real star of the film. The seductive tracking shots down the hotel corridors may have influenced Stanley Kubrick's camerawork in *The Shining* (1980). Frame enlargement.

Bonnie and Clyde (Warner Bros., 1967); **Easy Rider** (Columbia Pictures, 1969)
Influenced by the French New Wave cinema, *Bonnie and Clyde* and *Easy Rider* broke
prevailing film styles in the American cinema. Frame enlargements.

The remarkable success of New Wave visual and narrative experiments can be
measured, in part, by their profound influence on the American cinema. In 1967,
Arthur Penn's *Bonnie and Clyde* was a major commercial hit. Penn's free-wheeling
approach to direction and storytelling, his novel mixture of comedy and tragedy, slapstick and graphic violence, and the rapid montage editing and abrupt transitions supplied by editor Dede Allen were inspired by the rule-breaking of the French New
Wave, which blended genres, moods, and styles in an often-irreverent fashion and
which demonstrated that a more flexible and fluid film style could be enormously
popular. Following *Bonnie and Clyde, Easy Rider* (1969) also showed New Wave
influence, as did the freer, less studio-bound filmmaking that soon characterized the
post-1960s American cinema.

New German Cinema

During the 1960s a group of young filmmakers impatient with the inherited forms
of the older, established German cinema pioneered a New German Cinema. As with
Italian neorealism and the French New Wave Cinema, this was accompanied by the
issuing of manifestoes and proclamations describing the intent and aims of the new
orientation and by an ongoing contrast between the new film style and the norms of
the American cinema.

In 1962 at the Oberhausen Film Festival, twenty-six young directors signed a
manifesto declaring a break with existing film traditions and the need to redefine German cinema. Among the signers of the Oberhausen manifesto were Volker Schlondorff (*Young Torless* (1966), *The Tin Drum* (1979) and, for American television,
Death of a Salesman, 1985), who became a major figure in the New German Cinema,
and Alexander Kluge, whose *Yesterday Girl* (1966) established a certain continuity
with the French New Wave, using such techniques as jump cuts, hand-held camera-

work, and inter-titles, in telling a New Wave-style story of a young woman who drifts into a life of petty crime.

Other important directors associated with the emergence of the New German Cinema in the 1960s were Jean-Marie Straub and Danièle Huillet, whose work was among the most radical experiments at attenuating the emotional effects of narrative, and, indeed, of cinema itself. *Not Reconciled* (1965) and *The Diary of Anna Magdalena Bach* (1968) feature intentionally flat, unemotional acting, the use of direct sound, an unclear temporal structure, and, in the latter film, long concert performances, with no audience shown, interspersed with brief narrative scenes.

Subsequently, Volker Schlondorff, with his wife Margarethe von Trotta, directed *The Lost Honor of Katherina Blum* (1975), which, accompanied by von Trotta's own *The Second Awakening of Christa Klages* (1977), examined women allied with political extremists in Germany's 1970s climate of terrorism and increasing state authoritarianism. The work of Agnes Varda in the French New Wave and von Trotta within the New German Cinema highlight the important contribution of women filmmakers in the contemporary international cinema. Varda's and von Trotta's feminist perspectives help shape an alternative social and ideological voice within their films, sensitive to the emotional, social, and political problems and place of women in contemporary society.

By the early 1970s, filmmaking in Germany was state supported in an important way. Government television helped fund theatrical films, which were then shown on public television after their theatrical distribution. This arrangement provided a major stimulus for production and auteurship since the government frequently sought to promote the work of filmmakers who had established a distinctive authorial voice for themselves.

Fassbinder and the Politics of Melodrama

Among such filmmakers were Rainer Werner Fassbinder, one of the most prolific of modern directors. Fassbinder embarked on a long series of politically charged melodramas inspired by the work of Hollywood director Douglas Sirk in the 1950s. Fassbinder's *The Bitter Tears of Petra von Kant* (1972), *Fear Eats the Soul* (1973), and *Fox and His Friends* (1974) examined how power dynamics in personal relationships

Fox and His Friends (1974) Fassbinder (*left*) performing in his *Fox and His Friends*. During his relatively brief career, Fassbinder worked at a fiery pace to complete an amazing 41 films in 17 years.

(*Museum of Modern Art/Film Stills Archive*)

embody types of oppression found at large in society between established and stigmatized groups.

Fassbinder considered melodrama to be an effective vehicle for examining the political aspects of personal relationships because, in melodrama, everything—emotions, gestures, behavior—are oversized and are therefore capable of becoming subjects of the film through their exaggeration and stylization. **Melodrama** is based on exaggerated emotional displays, on clear moral distinctions between hero and villain, and on a narrative style in which the twists and turns of the plot determine character behavior. Melodrama tends to be the predominant dramatic style of popular cinema. Fassbinder treats melodrama with great self-consciousness and uses it to describe how society, with its power hierarchies, deforms even the private sphere of one's personal life. Fassbinder's work is influenced by, yet is self-conscious about and critically distant from, Hollywood melodrama.

Herzog and Mystical Cinema

In contrast to Fassbinder's relentless interrogation of the ways that people will internalize the social power structure and live it out in their personal lives, Werner Herzog tended to avoid depictions of social and political issues in his films. Instead, his work celebrated mystical and antirational states of mind and modes of existence. In films such as *Even Dwarfs Started Small* (1970), *Aguirre, the Wrath of God* (1972), *The Great Ecstasy of Sculptor Steiner* (1974), *Every Man for Himself and God Against All* (1975), and *Heart of Glass* (1976), the characters are grotesques, supermen, mystics, or oddities.

Herzog's images aim not for social clarity, but rather for the evocation of mystery and the unknowable. The opening of *Heart of Glass,* for example, includes a long mystical prologue of clouds, mountains, and waterfalls accompanied by a poetic recitation on the dissolution and rebirth of the earth. The narrative that follows deals with a community that loses the secret for creating ruby-colored glass, a secret on which its social identity depends, and begins to disintegrate. The story is diffuse, scattered, and is built from scenes in which the actors are all hypnotized. These hypnotic

Aguierre, the Wrath of God (1972)
Klaus Kinski's Spanish explorer in *Aguirre, the Wrath of God* is one of many memorable madmen and lunatics who populate Herzog's films.
(Museum of Modern Art/Film Stills Archive)

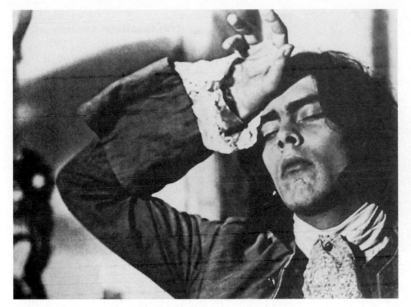

Heart of Glass (1976)
Herzog hypnotized his actors in
Heart of Glass to create some of
the oddest performances in
cinema. It was all part of his
cinematic pursuit of the poetic
and mystical attributes of
human life.
*(Museum of Modern Art/Film
Stills Archive)*

trances make the performances seem weird and other-worldly, a style that is well-suited to the film's mythological parable about dissolution and rebirth.

Antinarrative in Wender's Films

Fassbinder and Herzog represent opposite poles of social criticism and mystical anti-rationalism within the New German Cinema. Between their extremes is the work of director Wim Wenders, whose movies focus on wandering, drifting, alienated characters, creating a kind of collective antinarrative. Convinced that narratives construct misleading versions of reality by imposing an artificial structure on the essentially disorganized nature of daily life, Wenders attenuates the narratives in his films with sustained attention on objects, dead silences, and states of dissociated consciousness.

The Goalie's Anxiety at the Penalty Kick (1971) focuses on the psychological disintegration of a soccer goalie, suspended from his job, who subsequently murders a woman and then drifts around in a state of extreme psychological disengagement. The dissociation of the character is structurally described by a narrative that is loose, disconnected, and without apparent direction. **Antinarrative** films tend, paradoxically, toward the elimination of narrative by employing lots of digression, avoiding a clear hierarchy of narrative events, and by suppressing the causal connections among events. By breaking down narrative links between events, Wenders creates his antinarrative. *Alice in the Cities* (1973), *The Wrong Move* (1974), and *Kings of the Road* (1976) constitute Wenders' "road trilogy" of antinarratives about drifting characters.

Wenders' other work includes a tribute to legendary American director Nicholas Ray, *Lighting Over Water* (1980), an attempt to make an American studio film under producer Francis Ford Coppola, *Hammett* (1982), and *The State of Things* (1982), a bitter and sardonic reflection on his disappointing experience with Coppola. Wenders scored a major critical and box-office success with *Wings of Desire* (1987), about a

The Goalie's Anxiety at the Penalty Kick (1971) Wenders relentlessly focused on the alienation and mental breakdown of an unemployed goalie in *The Goalie's Anxiety at the Penalty Kick*. For Wenders, telling a story was less important here than exploring a drifting, aimless, despairing state of mind. The film was one of Wenders' many antinarrative experiments.
(Museum of Modern Art/Film Stills Archive)

melancholy angel (Bruno Ganz), drifting and watching over the city of Berlin, who becomes fascinated by human beings. Longing to feel what they feel, he enters their world and falls in love with a young trapeze artist.

Importance of the International Cinema

The careers of Fassbinder and Wenders illustrate the same dynamic that was at work in Italian neorealism and the French New Wave. Their cinema forms a continuing and conscious relationship to the norms of Hollywood filmmaking and the icons of the American cinema. Although their films establish explicit alternatives to the methods and techniques of studio filmmaking and conventional movie narratives, as alternatives their work plays against these more established norms. The global presence of Hollywood film elicits a series of explicitly formulated cinematic alternatives that chart new stylistic approaches.

This short survey of some key international filmmakers and movements can only begin to suggest the abundance of alternative styles and forms of narrative filmmaking. Third World political filmmaking, for example, in Cuba, Latin America, Africa, and China offers a vibrant embrace of revolution, a world view very different from that of Hollywood film. East European cinema, working through metaphor and social allegory, offers a sustained critique of Soviet authoritarianism. The cinema thrives in India, the Middle East, Asia, and the Pacific rim. Films here are uniquely influenced by social norms and cultural frameworks that are quite different from those that inform Hollywood production.

The availability of international films at local video stores and on cable television enables viewers to become citizens of the world and allows the cinema to function as an infinitely rich medium offering uncountable sources of pleasure. This chapter sketched only a few of these alternative sources. Many, many more remain to be explored, offering viewers an exciting and unpredictable social, cultural, and visual journey. Film can become a window on the world, enlarging one's social horizon and establishing a context in which the Hollywood cinema becomes simply one reference point among many.

SUMMARY

Cinema exists within an international framework, the product of multiple cultures and nationalities. In this international framework, Hollywood filmmaking has been a global and dominant influence. The corporate structure of the American industry and its multinational reach accentuates the impact of contemporary Hollywood blockbusters. Although this results in some erosion of variety and diversity in the international cinema, as audiences clamor to see more films like the popular Hollywood blockbusters, one should not overstate or overemphasize this development.

Of greater importance is the flourishing diversity of artistic styles throughout film history. While Hollywood exports a certain kind of film to cinemas throughout the world, many filmmakers in other countries explore alternatives to the norms and style of Hollywood film. Cinema has an enormous creative potential for redefining methods of storytelling and image design. Periodically these coalesce around a national movement to revise film style or create new waves of film production.

As a part of this process, Hollywood both inspires and absorbs foreign influences. In Germany, Fassbinder pays homage to the works of his beloved Hollywood director, Douglas Sirk, even while politicizing those Sirk-inspired melodramas. Jean-Luc Godard works free of the Hollywood influence apparent in his early works such as *Breathless* to reach a point of extreme stylistic reduction and near-total rejection of narrative in films such as *Le Gai Savoir*.

Hollywood draws foreign directors to its studios. Peter Weir, George Miller, and Paul Verhoeven all make highly successful and profitable films within the Hollywood industry, and their work, like the work of other generations of emigré filmmakers in Hollywood, has subtly changed the style of American filmmaking.

The cinema is a medium of enormous creative potential, and the huge range of film styles prevailing in the international cinema testifies to this potential. A sophisticated understanding of cinema requires an understanding of the importance of Hollywood filmmaking as well as knowledge of the work of filmmakers who are not a part of the Hollywood model. This work should include the alternative narrative and image styles of Antonioni, Wenders, Resnais, and Godard, the psychological and spiritual focus of Bergman, the pageantry and spectacle of Fellini, the thrilling genre work of Kurosawa, the playful subversiveness of Bunuel, and the dedicated social visions of neorealist filmmakers.

The broader the range of film styles, international auteurs, and national cinema movements that the viewer becomes familiar with, the greater are the pleasures that the cinema has to offer. Virtually every reader of this textbook is an accomplished master at watching Hollywood films. To now broaden that mastery through an exploration of alternative cinema styles and movements is to deepen the pleasure and excitement that the movies can offer.

SUGGESTED READINGS

Peter Bondanella, *The Cinema of Federico Fellini* (Princeton, NJ: Princeton University Press, 1992).

Luis Bunuel, *My Last Sigh,* trans. Abigail Israel (New York: Knopf, 1983).

Timothy Corrigan, *New German Film* rev. ed., (Bloomington: Indiana University Press, 1994).

Robert Phillip Kolker, *The Altering Eye: Contemporary International Cinema* (New York: Oxford University Press, 1983).

Paisley Livingston, *Ingmar Bergman and the Rituals of Art* (Ithaca, NY: Cornell University Press, 1982).

James Monaco, *The New Wave: Truffaut, Godard, Chabrol, Rohmer, Rivette* (New York: Oxford University Press, 1976).

Stephen Prince, *The Warrior's Camera: The Cinema of Akira Kurosawa* (Princeton, NJ: Princeton University Press, 1991).

Sam Rohdie, *Antonioni* (London: BFI, 1990).

Chapter 10

Film Criticism and Interpretation

Chapter Objectives

After reading this chapter, you should be able to

- explain what criticism is and what purposes it serves
- describe how communication signs are multidimensional
- explain the task of the critic and how criticism functions as rhetoric
- define and distinguish three basic modes of film criticism
- describe three stages in the creation of criticism
- explain the deductive method of criticism
- distinguish explicit or first-order meanings from latent or second-order meanings
- recognize critical interpretation as a strategic reorganization of a film's structure and meaning
- list and define three types of attributional errors
- learn how to develop a framework of interpretation
- learn how to create and practice film criticism

Key Terms and Concepts

criticism
sign
polyvalence
rhetoric
newspaper review
general-interest journal-
    based criticism

scholarly criticism
identification
description
deduction
interpretation
latent meaning

interpretive
    reorganization
framework of
    interpretation
attributional errors

Previous chapters explored the methods filmmakers use to create images and tell stories in both the American and the international cinema. Once the film is finished, critics and viewers take over, interpreting what they see and debating its meaning and merits. What is film criticism, and what is film theory? How are the two related? Why, in fact, do they exist? What purposes do they serve, and what pleasures do they offer? This chapter explores the nature of film criticism, and Chapter 11 examines film theory.

☐ WHY CRITICISM EXISTS

Whether carried out by casual viewers or professional critics who are paid for their services, criticism and interpretation are inevitable. **Criticism** is the attempt to discover and interpret the meanings and intentions of the film or filmmaker that extend well beyond a film's surface features. Like all forms of expressed communication, these meanings are complex and multidimensional. Through their criticism, critics often develop new interpretations or perspectives on the work in question.

Human communication occurs through the exchange of **signs.** Signs stand for and represent the meanings and ideas to be communicated. Signs are the currency of communication, exchanged among communicators in order to transmit meaning. Different modes of communication have their own unique types of signs. In spoken language, these are the acoustical properties of word-sounds and their associated concepts or referents. In the cinema, signs include the pictures of the world that a given film presents to viewers and that are structured by the elements of camera placement, editing, sound, and mise-en-scene. Signs express meaning. As they circulate through society and among individuals, human communication takes place.

Polyvalence of the Sign

Signs have many potential meanings, that is, they possess a principle called **polyvalence.** It is the job of criticism and interpretation to describe these meanings and to organize them in a hierarchy of emphasis or importance. An example will clarify the principle of polyvalence. *Rambo: First Blood Part II* (1985) was the second of three films in which Sylvester Stallone played Vietnam warrior John Rambo. In the film, Rambo returns to Vietnam many years after the war to search for Americans missing in action who may still be held in captivity. Prevailing against overwhelming odds, Rambo manages to rescue several Americans and bring them home.

At the end of the film, exhausted by his heroic exploits and angry at the duplicity of American governmental bureaucrats, Rambo delivers a speech in which he identifies

Rambo: First Blood Part II (Tri-Star Pictures, 1985)
Rambo: First Blood Part II. Does Sylvester Stallone's warrior, John Rambo, express old-fashioned American patriotism, or is the character a calculated attempt to cash in on Cold War politics? Film criticism provides the answers to this kind of question.

(Museum of Modern Art/Film Stills Archive)

himself as a spokesperson for all Vietnam veterans and announces that what they really want is simply for their country to love and honor them. "I want what they want and what every other guy who came over here and spilled his guts and gave everything he had wants—for our country to love us as much as we love it."

Rambo was a big hit at the box office, and its extraordinary popularity would seem to indicate that the moviegoing audience responded positively to Rambo's hero-ics and to his plea at the end of the film that America accept its Vietnam veterans and acknowledge their honor. Many veterans, however, objected to the film and to Rambo's speech. Some were offended that Stallone tried to identify himself with them and wrap himself in their cause. They pointed out that Stallone never served in Vietnam, and they felt their cause was poorly represented by a blood-thirsty and car-toonish character such as Rambo.

These differing responses to the film illustrate the principle of polyvalence, the multidimensionality of its signs and their meanings. A popular audience seeking action and spectacle enthusiastically embraced *Rambo,* but many Vietnam veterans found it to be a grossly distorted portrayal of the war. With regard to Rambo's speech at the end, is it a noble plea to honor Vietnam veterans or a cynical exercise in polit-ical opportunism calculated in terms of its likely box office effect? It is the job of crit-icism and interpretation to answer such questions. Because film images and narratives are extraordinarily complex, that is, polyvalent, debates about their meaning are inevitable. Herein lies the need for criticism and interpretation.

☐ THE TASK OF THE CRITIC

Film criticism does not mean criticizing a movie in the sense of pointing out its flaws or failed ambitions. Criticism is not a negative act. The critic tries to come to terms with the multidimensional meanings of a given film. The critic (1) teases out implicit or subtle meanings, (2) clarifies seemingly contradictory messages or values in a given film, and (3) creates a novel way of interpreting or understanding a film. This last function is the central act of criticism: the creation of a novel interpretation that extends or deepens a viewer's appreciation of a film.

Criticism as a Rhetorical Act

Film criticism is a rhetorical act because the critic works and persuades by virtue of the power and sophistication of his or her rhetoric or command of the language. **Rhetoric** is the use of language to persuade and influence others. There are two sources of pleasure in good criticism. The first is a re-experiencing of the film through the critic's descriptions and interpretations, and the second is an engagement with the critic's own use of language. So important is this latter source of enjoyment that many people read critics even when they usually disagree with them or when they have not even seen or read the work being examined. Even when disagreeing with a particular critic, a reader still might enjoy the way that a critic writes or talks about movies.

Since criticism is fundamentally a rhetorical act, the critic needs to know how to write well, how to construct an argument, and how to select evidence and employ it carefully to persuade readers of the rightness of his or her interpretation. Although it is primarily an exercise in rhetoric, criticism also has an empirical dimension because the critic must reference ideas against the evidence of the film. Interpretations must always be grounded in a careful description and selection of evidence from the film under discussion. Misidentification or explicit attributional errors weaken the critic's argument and will lessen a reader's support for the interpretation that is being constructed.

☐ MODES OF CRITICISM

Film criticism differs greatly depending on the forum in which it occurs and the audience to whom it is directed. Film criticism falls into three basic modes: newspaper reviewing, general-interest journal-based criticism, and scholarly criticism. The objectives and implied audience differ for each mode.

Newspaper and Television Reviewing

Film reviews in the daily newspaper or as part of a television news or review program are probably the most familiar modes of film criticism. **Newspaper and television reviews** are reviews prepared for a general audience; they perform an explicit consumer function. The reviewer answers the moviegoer's most basic and most immediate question—should I see this movie? Newspaper and television movie reviews are usually very short, and the reviewer must address this question right away. The reviewer typically does this by giving a highly personalized and subjective response to the movie. Newspaper and television critics use terms that describe the intensity of their subjective reactions. If they like a film, they call it dazzling, stunning, hilarious, or sensational. If they don't like it, the film is a "turkey" or "it bombed."

What the Newspaper/TV Critic Does

By concentrating so intensively on the issue of whether they liked or disliked a film, the newspaper or television reviewers display for their audience a series of emotional responses to the movie under discussion. These responses enable audience members to decide whether they should see the film. If the reviewer is trusted, and he or she hated the movie, the consumer will probably stay away from it. Sometimes, though, an inverse relationship prevails—many moviegoers decide they'll probably like a movie if a disliked reviewer hated it.

In addition to providing a highly detailed description of their subjective responses to films, newspaper and television reviewers also provide a plot summary (without disclosing the ending—this is a cardinal rule in this mode of criticism) and a discussion of the stars who appear in the film. These, too, serve an explicit consumer function. People want to know what a movie is about before deciding whether to see it, and, typically, they seek out films that feature their favorite performers.

Finally, the newspaper or television reviewer may also include a brief statement of the film's general theme. Reviewers of the recent Kevin Costner epic *Dances With Wolves* (1990), for example, stressed how the film's noble and heroic portrayal of the Sioux constituted a reversal of traditional Westerns that presented Indians as savages and villains. This judgment, however, overlooked or disregarded many Westerns that preceded *Dances With Wolves* that did present a heroic and sympathetic portrait of American Indians. The thematic content of *Dances With Wolves* was hardly new or revolutionary, although newspaper and television critics responded as if it were.

Emphasizing personal, subjective responses often means that newspaper and television reviewers are not able to provide historical perspective on the films they discuss, nor are they able to clarify how those films relate to earlier works, as in the case of *Dances With Wolves*. The newspaper or television reviewer is also unlikely to provide much analysis or description of a film's audiovisual structure, of how a filmmaker employs the elements of editing, sound, or mise-en-scene.

Newspaper and television reviewers, then, typically concentrate on four things: a description of their subjective responses to the film, a plot summary, a discussion of star performance, and a brief statement of the film's theme. Coverage of these areas enables reviewers to serve the explicit consumer function of helping the reader or listener decide whether they should see the film.

General-Interest Journal-Based Criticism

General-interest journal-based criticism is that criticism that falls somewhere between newspaper and television reviewing and the highly technical, scholarly criticism. It is written for such literate but general-interest publications as *The New Yorker, The New Republic, The Village Voice*, and *The New York Review of Books*, in which the reviewer has more space in which to explain his or her reviews and does not need to provide the same urgent, consumer function as the newspaper or television reviewer. As a result, the general-interest journal critic can offer a more detailed and sophisticated discussion of a film's structure and messages.

Pauline Kael

One of the best known general-interest journal critics is Pauline Kael, the former reviewer for *The New Yorker* magazine from 1967–1991. During her tenure, Kael was a powerful and influential critic. She was an early champion of the career and works of directors Sam Peckinpah and Robert Altman. An exceptionally good writer, Kael aggressively trumpeted the merits of films she loved and was a merciless opponent of those she deemed mediocre or inferior.

Kael and *Last Tango*   Perhaps Kael's most famous review was her glowing rave for Bernardo Bertolucci's *Last Tango in Paris* (1972). Bertolucci's film about the affair between a young woman and an aging widower in Paris was extremely controversial in its day because of its sexually frank content. Kael met the controversies head on in a spirited defense of the film in which she proclaimed that Bertolucci and Marlon Brando, its director and star, had altered the face of an art form.

Kael's method.   Kael went far beyond the immediate consumer function of the newspaper or television reviewer. She began the review by establishing what she considered to be the revolutionary character of this film, the degree to which it changed the face of its medium. She compared it to the premiere of Stravinsky's *The Rite of Spring*

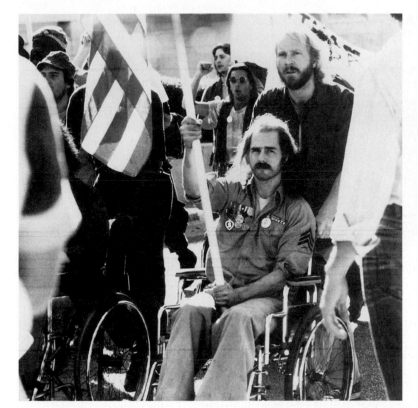

Born on the Fourth of July
(Universal Pictures, 1989)
For readers, one of Kael's
greatest assets was the intensity
of her opinions. She passionately
embraced the films she liked
and mercilessly condemned
those whose artistry she found
lacking. She championed the
work of Robert Altman, Sam
Peckinpah, and Martin Scorsese,
and could be harsh toward films
she didn't like, such as *Born on
the Fourth of July*.
*(Museum of Modern Art/Film
Stills Archive)*

(*Le Sacre du Printemps*), a musical composition that she maintains was comparably shocking and unconventional for its first audiences.

Bernardo Bertolucci's *Last Tango in Paris* was presented for the first time on the closing night of the New York Film Festival, October 14, 1972; that date should become a landmark in movie history comparable to May 29, 1913—the night *Le Sacre du Printemps* was first performed—in music history. There was no riot, and no one threw anything at the screen, but I think it's fair to say that the audience was in a state of shock, because *Last Tango in Paris* has the same kind of hypnotic excitement as the *Sacre,* the same primitive force, and the same thrusting, jabbing eroticism. The movie breakthrough has finally come. Exploitation films have been supplying mechanized sex—sex as physical stimulant but without any passion or emotional violence. The sex in *Last Tango in Paris* expresses the characters' drives. Marlon Brando, as Paul, is working out his aggression on Jeanne (Maria Schneider), and the physical menace of sexuality that is emotionally charged is such a departure from everything we've come to expect at the movies that there was something almost like fear in the atmosphere of the party in the lobby that followed the screening. Carried along by the sustained excitement of the movie, the audience had given Bertolucci an ovation, but afterward, as individuals, they were quiet. This must be the most powerfully erotic movie ever made, and it may turn out to be the most liberating movie ever made, and so it's probably only natural that an audience, anticipating a voluptuous feast from the man who made *The Conformist,* and confronted with this unexpected sexuality and the

Last Tango in Paris
(United Artists, 1972)
Pauline Kael's famous review of *Last Tango in Paris* used a carefully chosen rhetorical style to praise the film and placed it within a detailed film historical and cultural context. Newspaper/television reviewers cannot offer such comprehensive discussion. Frame enlargement.

new realism it requires of the actors, should go into shock. Bertolucci and Brando have altered the face of an art form. Who was prepared for that?*

Kael's comparison of *Last Tango* with *The Rite of Spring* was a strategic rhetorical move. Stravinsky's composition, though initially attacked as ugly and offensive, is today regarded as a classic. By using it as a gauge for measuring initial reactions to *Last Tango,* Kael helped legitimize the film by favorably comparing it to an already-established artistic masterpiece. In doing so, she left no doubts about the high esteem in which she held the film and about her belief in it as art.

Kael's opening discussion of Stravinsky illustrates one of the most important services the general-interest journal critic performs (and that the brief format of newspaper or TV reviewing does not permit)—placing the film under discussion into a broad cultural and historical context. After briefly summarizing the film's plot, Kael explored in considerable detail the history of Brando's screen persona, how the film drew upon it and exploited it, and the way Bertolucci's direction was influenced by traditions of French and Italian cinema. Her references here include films that many of her readers may not have seen. These include Jean Renoir's *La Chienne* and *La Bete Humaine,* Jean Vigo's *L'Atalante,* Luchino Visconti's *Ossessione,* and Roberto Rossellini's *Open City.*

> The colors in this movie are late-afternoon orange-beige-browns and pink—the pink of flesh drained of blood, corpse pink. They are so delicately modulated (Vittorio Storaro was the cinematographer, as he was on *The Conformist*) that romance and rot are one; the lyric extravagance of the music (by Gato Barbieri) heightens this effect. Outside the flat, the gray buildings and the noise are certainly modern Paris, and yet the city seems muted. Bertolucci uses a feedback of his own—the feedback of old movies to enrich the imagery and associations. In substance, this is his most American film, yet the shadow of Michel Simon seems to hover over Brando, and the ambience is a tribute to the early crime-of-passion films of Jean Renoir, especially *La Chienne* and *La Bête Humaine.* Léaud, as Tom, the young

*"Last Tango in Paris," © 1972 by Pauline Kael, from *For Keeps* by Pauline Kael. Used by permission of Dutton Signet, a division of Penguin Books USA Inc.

director, is used as an affectionate takeoff on Godard, and the movie that Tom is shooting about Jeanne, his runaway bride, echoes Jean Vigo's *L'Atalante.* Bertolucci's soft focus recalls the thirties films, with their lyrically kind eye for every variety of passion; Marcel Carné comes to mind, as well as the masters who influenced Bertolucci's technique—von Sternberg (the controlled lighting) and Max Ophuls (the tracking camera). The film is utterly beautiful to look at. The virtuosity of Bertolucci's gliding camera style is such that he can show you the hype of the tango-contest scene (with its own echo of *The Conformist*) by stylizing it (the automaton-dancers do wildly fake head turns) and still make it work. He uses the other actors for their associations, too—Girotti, of course, the star of so many Italian films, including *Senso* and *Ossessione,* Visconti's version of *The Postman Always Rings Twice,* and, as Paul's mother-in-law, Maria Michi, the young girl who betrays her lover in *Open City.* As a maid in the hotel (part of a weak, diversionary subplot that is soon dispensed with), Catherine Allegret, with her heart-shaped mouth in a full, childishly beautiful face, is an aching, sweet reminder of her mother, Simone Signoret, in her *Casque d'Or* days. Bertolucci draws upon the movie background of this movie because movies are as active in him as direct experience—perhaps more active, since they may color everything else. Movies are a past we share, and, whether we recognize them or not, the copious associations are at work in the film and we feel them. As Jeanne, Maria Schneider, who has never had a major role before, is like a bouquet of Renoir's screen heroines and his father's models. She carries the whole history of movie passion in her long legs and baby face.

These comparisons with other films enable Kael to contextualize *Last Tango* within the traditions of cinema that have nourished Bertolucci and whose marks are apparent in *Tango*. The comparisons also enable Kael to display her own credentials as a sophisticated film critic whose horizons of cinema experience extend well beyond the present film under discussion. Notice how different this aspect of her reviewing is from the norms of newspaper and television reviewing that mandate that the critic focus almost exclusively on the immediate film under discussion. Finally, Kael's lively writing style, and willingness to champion the cause of films she believes in, conveys her deep love for the medium of cinema and her joy in sharing that passion with readers.

The Virtues of Journal-Based Criticism

In her long career, Pauline Kael exemplified the merits and virtues of the general-interest journal-based critic. She was witty, intelligent, informed about the history and culture of the cinema and passionately in love with the medium. As a writer, she had the space necessary to explore her ideas in detail. Readers of her criticism were the beneficiaries, and her writing on film went well beyond the reviewer's immediate task of separating the good from the bad. Her essays capture broad aspects of film history and culture, and they dissect the spirit of the times in which the films were made. As important critical documents, they have been collected in several volumes representing the decades of her work.

Scholarly Criticism

Unlike newspaper and television reviewing or even general-interest journal-based criticism, scholarly criticism contains almost no focus on the consumer function of telling

Dead Again (Paramount Pictures, 1991) Scholarly criticism of contemporary films, such as *Dead Again,* starring Emma Thompson and Kenneth Branagh, does not address consumer-oriented questions— Is this a good film? Should one see it?—but rather explores in detail particular artistic, cultural, or theoretical issues. Frame enlargement.

the reader whether they should see the film or skip it. Instead, **scholarly criticism** is criticism that explores the significance of a given film in relation to issues of theory, history, or technology. It appears in such journals as *Film Quarterly, Cinema Journal, Screen,* and *Wide Angle* and is written for an audience of scholars rather than general readers. Scholarly critics, therefore, use a more demanding and specialized vocabulary, accessible to scholars if not to general readers. Authors of essays explore theoretical and historical questions rather than issues of merit, that is, whether a given film is good or bad. Scholarly criticism often draws on one or more models of film theory.

Scholarly criticism is illustrated by this analysis of Kenneth Branagh's *Dead Again* (1991) that appeared in *Cinema Journal,* an academic publication read largely by university-trained film scholars and graduate students. The film's story is about the murder in the 1940s of Margaret Strauss, allegedly by her composer husband, Roman, and the consequences of that death many decades later. The authors of the essay analyze the film as an example of postmodernism, that is, as a film whose style and content are largely defined by reference to earlier traditions of film and literature.

> In the wake of numerous critical pronouncements concerning the nature and viability of postmodernism as a descriptive, critical, and political category, it seems appropriate to interrogate a current instance of popular filmmaking in order to test the viability of this discourse. In this essay, we look at *Dead Again* (1991), a film that might be deemed "postmodern" through its deployment of numerous thematic, intertextual, stylistic, and self-reflexive strategies.*

The authors then go on to analyze in detail the numerous ways in which *Dead Again* quotes from the cinematic past.

> With its thematic focus on the past, *Dead Again* is a film that seems to encourage the audience to play with it, to identify its numerous allusions to other films, genres, and film stars. To analyze the narrative for its meaning would seem to violate the playfulness that the film seems to invite. The film defies classification according

*"Dead Again or Alive Again," by Marcia Landy and Lucy Fisher in *Cinema Journal* vol. 33:4, pp. 3–10. Used by permission of the authors and the University of Texas Press.

to a single generic mode. In the allusions to other works, we are given a mélange of different forms: crime detection, thriller, melodrama, and the occult. For Caryn James, this mixture is a hallmark of post-modern cinema. As she notes, such films "rejuvenate old genres . . . by being them and by mocking them at the same time." In *Dead Again,* the allusions to other works include most prominently Hitchcock's *Rebecca* (1940). The Gothic imagery associated with Manderley is reiterated in the image of the Strauss mansion. Furthermore, Roman and Margaret Strauss's portrayal, as well as that of Inga, the housekeeper, plays off the dominant characters in the Hitchcock film. In its adherence to the crime thriller genre, *Dead Again* resurrects incidents, character types, and conventions associated with crime detection and with aggression toward female victims in such films as *Dial M for Murder* (1954), *Frenzy* (1972), and *Psycho* (1960). There are also numerous allusions to images and characters from such thrillers as *Journey into Fear* (1942) and *The Stranger* (1946), especially to the elusive, deceptive, or malevolent identity of the male protagonist. British and Hollywood melodramas of the 1930s and 1940s are also referenced, including films such as *Gaslight* (Dickinson [1939] and Cukor [1944]), which involve questions of a woman's sanity. Like *Dead Again, Humoresque* (1946) and *The Seventh Veil* (1945) are melodramas that foreground musicians. The latter, starring Ann Todd and James Mason, closely parallels Branagh's film with its plot involving a pianist and her moody, domineering, and mysterious guardian. Through these allusions, *Dead Again* thus fuses the genres of crime detection, thriller, and melodrama. Furthermore, it effects another hybridization by conflating the woman's film with the male melodrama. . . .

The allusions to other films and the conflation of genres are deployed in a number of ways: as clues for the audience, as narrative markers, as selective moments in history (and particularly in the legacy of representation), as an homage to the commercial cinema. The rather complicated collage of citations and genres upsets conventional expectations concerning plot and character. For example, the audience is bombarded with clues which might lead to an understanding of the diegetic past. Thus the beginning of the film with its montage of newspaper clippings involving the death of Margaret Strauss, the stages of Roman Strauss's sentencing, and the introduction of the newspaperman, Baker, would appear to present the film's enigma: was Roman Strauss guilty of murdering his wife? However, the opening scene of Strauss on death row invokes a sequence from Welles' script to *Heart of Darkness,* where the viewer witnesses events through the eyes of a condemned man. Furthermore, it also suggests Monsieur Verdoux's walk to death at the end of Chaplin's 1947 film, another story of a woman-killer. Knowledge of other filmic texts seems required to understand this one.

In the spirit of *Citizen Kane* (1941), the enigma turns out to be the nature of storytelling itself, involving the mystery of who is the keeper of knowledge. Whose story is this? Who is telling the tale and to what ends? Whose point of view are we invited to explore? The film inserts characters that resurrect the hermeneutics of *Citizen Kane,* especially in Strauss's whispered words to Baker (a descendant of Jed Leland), which invoke the puzzle of "Rosebud." In *Dead Again*'s hydra-headed interest in investigating and uncovering the past, it asks us to discern who is the narrator: the newspaperman, the hypnotist, or the doubled figure of Roman Strauss and Mike Church? The narrator is certainly not the tripled figure of Margaret and Grace/ Amanda, played by Branagh's wife to quadruple the equation. These problems concerning narration would seem to underscore the film's indeterminacy and instability, a characteristic that we might consider as centrally identified with the postmodern.

This scholarly analysis is extremely different from what a reviewer writing for a newspaper or general-interest journal would produce. First of all, it is not a review oriented to a potential consumer but a detailed analysis of how the film is postmodern by virtue of its extraordinarily rich sets of references to other works of film and literature. The authors provide minimal plot summary, only enough to make their analysis clear, and they are less interested in reaching a clear verdict about the quality of the film (the reviewer's eternal question of whether a film is "good" or "bad") than with explaining how it works as a visual narrative that constructs a network of relationships with prior films and directors.

Accordingly, the authors discuss in detail how director Branagh and the film play off the work of Orson Welles, Charles Chaplin, and Alfred Hitchcock and such specific films as *Citizen Kane, Rebecca, Gaslight,* and *Monsieur Verdoux.* The authors explore these relationships with references to critical concepts of postmodernism, voyeurism, psychoanalysis, and gender and genre issues. Instead of the consumer-oriented function of newspaper reviewing, or the part-consumer-part-analytic focus of general-interest journal-based criticism, the emphasis here is entirely analytic and is geared to a smaller audience of specialist readers familiar with the critical concepts and film references employed in the essay. Note how the tone of the writing differs from Pauline Kael's work, which compared *Last Tango* to other films and filmmakers. The scholarly tone is less emotional than Kael's approach and is more analytic and informational.

The clearest measure of this specialized readership lies in the language employed in the essay. It is densely compacted with information, loaded with names, terms, and concepts, and the authors do not always elaborate on their meaning or background because they assume their readers are already knowledgeable in these areas. For these reasons, the essay's language might seem forbidding or excessively difficult for non-specialist readers.

Scholarly criticism seeks to analyze how the narrative or audiovisual design of a film works with reference to existing traditions of cinema or other arts and with ref-

---

Citizen Kane (RKO, 1941); **Dead Again** (Paramount Pictures, 1991)
Scholarly criticism may attempt to clarify the cinematic traditions and influences that operate on a film. Orson Welles' *Citizen Kane,* influenced the visual and narrative design of *Dead Again.* The wealthy composer in *Dead Again* has a striking emblem (the treble clef) on the gate to his estate, just as Charles Foster Kane has (the letter K) in the earlier film. The emblems are emphasized at very similar points in each film's narrative. Frame enlargements.

erence to basic critical concepts or models of film theory. Unlike newspaper or general-interest journal-based criticism, scholarly criticism performs virtually no consumer function. Instead, it appeals to specialized film scholars interested in expanding their knowledgeability of given films and filmmakers.

☐ CREATING CRITICISM

Components of Film Criticism

Whether one is writing for a newspaper, general-interest magazine, or scholarly journal, there are three stages in the creation of criticism. These are the stages of identification, description, and interpretation.

Identification and Description

Identification and **description** identify and describe passages or elements of the film relevant to the critical interpretation being developed. They generally occur together. The purpose of identification and description is to simplify and reduce the wealth of material in the film that the critic confronts. In this respect, they are strategic tools, enabling the critic to omit nonrelevant details. A verbal description of a visual sequence can be endless because of the huge quantity of visual, narrative, and behavioral cues present in even a few seconds of film. Critics, therefore, need to reduce and simplify the material with which they are working.

Employing a Deductive Method   The method by which the critic works is **deduction,** that is, using the general goals of the criticism to guide the search for supporting evidence. The selection of information proceeds deductively, with selection criteria established by the general goals of the analysis. These goals are the themes or ideas that the criticism seeks to establish. Without such general goals, identification can only pick up disconnected bits of information. Suppose, by way of example, that a critic was developing an interpretation of Alfred Hitchcock's *Psycho*. Such a critic might want to deal with the theme of voyeurism as Hitchcock develops it throughout the film. Norman Bates, the psychopathic killer, has a secret peephole in his motel office that he uses to spy on attractive women guests as they undress for bed.

During one of the most intense scenes in the film, Hitchcock films Norman peeping through the hole in his wall, watching one of the guests whom he is about to murder undressing before she takes a shower. Hitchcock first shows Norman's eye, brightly lit, as it peers through the hole and then switches to a subjective shot, representing Norman's point of view, as the camera itself peers through the hole, thus aligning character viewpoint and spectator viewpoint in one voyeuristic moment. By identifying and describing this subjective shot, a critic can link it to the more general theme of voyeurism, which, in this example, is guiding the selection of details for analysis.

Working deductively, the critic uses the general goals or premises of the criticism to guide a search for relevant material in the film. Refining these general goals permits more efficient identification of relevant material. The critic, for example, might seek to explore the theme of voyeurism in *Psycho* based on an understanding of

Hitchcock's use of cinema. Hitchcock believed that the cinema offers moviegoers essentially voyeuristic pleasures. In the darkened theater auditorium moviegoers permit themselves to see things they would ordinarily shun in daily life—sex, violence, aberrant or criminal behavior. Hitchcock believed that viewers experience the pleasure of the Peeping Tom, witnessing forbidden sights without being held accountable for what is seen.

Knowing these terms by which Hitchcock understood the cinema and its pleasures, the critic of *Psycho* could seek out aspects of the film's visual design that reflect Hitchcock's regard for the film viewer as a voyeur. The critic would emphasize the moment in which Hitchcock makes the viewer share Norman's voyeuristic view through the peephole and would also select, as a relevant detail, the film's opening scene in which the camera, after panning the skyline of Phoenix, Arizona, cranes down toward a hotel window and then peeks in to glimpse a pair of lovers reclining on a bed.

In this camera movement, the critic could argue, Hitchcock literally visualizes voyeuristic behavior. The critic could suggest that the camera prowls to the window and then peers beneath the curtain to see the semiclothed lovers. The critic would be justified in labeling such a shot a voyeuristic moment because the movements of the camera seem to call to mind the actions of a Peeping Tom.

Notice the deductive method of proceeding. Armed with an understanding of Hitchcock's equation of cinema and voyeurism, the critic selects details that illustrate

Psycho (Paramount Pictures, 1960)
In *Psycho,* Hitchcock turns the viewer into a peeping Tom. Note how the switch to Norman's subjective view of Marion Crane (Janet Leigh) through the peephole forces the viewer to share Norman's psychopathic point of view. Frame enlargements.

 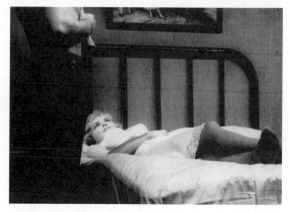

Psycho (Paramount Pictures, 1960)
Hitchcock's camera explicitly simulates the movement of a prowling voyeur, drawing closer
to a darkened window, then peering inside to see two partially clad lovers in a bedroom.
Frame enlargements.

this. Hitchcock's emphasis on voyeurism established an interpretive framework that, in turn, provided selection criteria, enabling the critic to select relevant aspects of visual design. The themes or ideas that the criticism seeks to establish—here, the idea that *Psycho* exhibits a voyeuristic design—enable the critic to select relevant details and to omit nonrelevant details.

Precision in Labeling   The critic must precisely label those elements of film structure that are being identified. The camera's movement toward the window and then underneath the blinds need to be identified and described as a moving camera shot and labeled as either a tracking or a crane shot. The camera movement is crucial for Hitchcock's effect. The moving camera implies not just the prowling activity of the Peeping Tom but also the voyeur's progressive focusing of attention, the drawing closer to a private and secret moment and its sudden revelation in the image of the lovers. Identifying and describing these features of camera movement are key to linking this scene with the general theme of voyeurism that guides the criticism. Strong and precise description of the camera's movements integrates this scene with the critical premise and strengthens the force of the critic's argument and its effect on the reader.

In a similar fashion, the critic should recognize and precisely describe the use of a subjective shot in the scene in which Norman looks through his peephole at his victim, Marion Crane. This shot represents Norman's point of view and also the viewpoint of the film's spectator. Good criticism would explore the implications of these aligned viewpoints. What does it mean for Hitchcock to invite the film's viewer to share the perspective of the central character, a psychopathic killer? What kind of relationship is Hitchcock suggesting exists between Norman and the film's viewers who share his space and his view of Marion?

Creating Rhetorical Force   By precisely identifying carefully selected details, and matching these details to the critical premise, the critic's descriptions become a part of the interpretation being developed. The interpretation grows out of the descriptions and seems to follow inevitably from them, provided the criticism is performed with sophistication and intelligence. When this is not the case, the reader will feel that the critic is stretching things or trying to justify an interpretation that does not fit the evidence.

Interpretation

The third component of criticism, **interpretation,** is the assignment of meaning to a scene or film that it does not immediately denote. A critic's interpretive framework guides the search for details and the description of those details in order to create a strong link with the interpretive premise. Film images and narratives are polyvalent. They express more than one thing or idea at a time. A film's first-order meanings are those that are immediately expressed or denoted by the characters, dialogue, story, and visual design. In general, criticism is the act of reorganizing these elements of a film to emphasize its latent or second-order meanings, those that are not immediately expressed at the surface level of character and story.

Latent Meaning and Interpretative Reorganization   Don Siegel's classic 1956 science fiction film, *Invasion of the Body Snatchers,* is about residents of a small town who become inhuman duplicates, their bodies and minds snatched by aliens who hatch from mysterious pods. The film portrays the efforts of a small band of heroes to struggle against the aliens' efforts to impose total conformity and mind control.

Since the film premiered, critics have been fascinated by its ambiguous, latent meanings. **Latent meaning** is indirect, implied by a film's narrative and audiovisual design. It is not direct, immediately obvious, or explicit. Many critics suggest that *Invasion of the Body Snatchers* is politically symbolic of the McCarthy period during which it was made, a time when anti-Communist witch hunts were conducted throughout the country, creating extraordinary pressures to conform to a pro-American, anti-Communist political agenda. The elements of terror and mind control, given a science fiction setting in the film, are analogous to real political and social forces in the United States during the decade of the 1950s, and many critics develop interpretations of the film that stress this analogy.

The film, however, is extraordinarily ambiguous and polyvalent. Although few critics are content to argue that it is simply and only a science fiction fantasy with no bearing on the then-contemporary American political climate, others point out that the film's ambiguities cut in several directions. While the movie can be construed as an anti-McCarthy political satire, it can also be taken in the opposite direction, as a conservative pro-McCarthy warning to the country. After all, in the movie itself, the alien menace is real, undetected by the casual observer, and working insidiously to corrupt and destroy the community from within. These are precisely the terms by which Senator McCarthy warned Americans about Communism. Since the hysteria in the film is entirely justified given its science fiction setting, some critics argue that the film is actually a part of the witch hunt atmosphere of the 1950s rather than an attack upon it.

Invasion of the Body Snatchers is an extremely rich and ambiguous film, and the distinctions between its first-order meanings—the science fiction setting, characters, and story—and the latent second-order meanings—meanings that bear upon the McCarthy period in the United States—illustrate how the act of interpretation involves a reconfiguration of a film's narrative and images in order to draw out implicit dimensions of meaning. This is the act of **interpretive reorganization.** Critical interpretation reorganizes Siegel's film as a politically symbolic treatment of contemporary American culture.

Establishing Frameworks of Interpretation   To uncover latent dimensions of meaning, the critic employs **frameworks of interpretation,** the intellectual, social, or cultural frames of reference that a critic applies to a film in order to derive an interpretation of that film. Frameworks of interpretation guide the selection of relevant details for analysis. The critic interpreting *Invasion of the Body Snatchers* as a political allegory needs to know something about the McCarthy period of the 1950s and the anxieties and political ambiguities it unleashed and fed on. This might require additional and special research, but no critic can proceed without a framework of interpretation. Otherwise, the deductive process of criticism is impossible. To develop frameworks of interpretation, the film critic needs to do much more than simply watch movies. The critic must be sufficiently well read, educated, and cultured to possess numerous frameworks of reference or interpretation that can be applied to films and that can nurture works of criticism. The broader a critic's social and cultural frames of reference, the richer the criticism that is produced.

Attributional Errors

As a critic applies frameworks of interpretation to a film, selecting and describing details, and then assigning meaning to those details in order to develop an interpretation, the critic needs to be cautious about committing common attributional errors.

Invasion of the Body Snatchers (Allied Artists, 1956)
Dr. Miles Bennell (Kevin McCarthy) frantically warns unsuspecting motorists of the alien menace in *Invasion of the Body Snatchers*. The film's social ambiguities work in different directions. Is it an attack on McCarthy-era paranoia or an expression of that paranoia? It is up to the critic to decide.

Attributional errors occur when a critic erroneously attributes an effect in film to a given creator. Common attributional errors stem from three sources. Two involve errors of intended meaning and the third involves errors of assigned authorship.

Errors of Intended Meaning   Two common types of attributional errors are those of intended meaning. Critics, by nature, assign meanings to films. However, not every effect or apparent design within a film is meaningful, understood in terms of the intentions of its creators. Sometimes filmmakers do things simply because they like the effect, not because they are trying to express a particular idea or feeling. In fact, unlike critics, filmmakers are often reluctant to speak or think self-consciously about the design implications of their work.

Easy Rider (1969) broke a lot of the rules of conventional studio filmmaking. Viewers instantly notice the flash cross-cutting between scenes and remember this long after seeing the film. Viewers might legitimately wonder why the filmmakers employed this technique, and a critic might develop an interpretation in which flash cross-cutting becomes emblematic in some way of the film's view of society in the late 1960s or its themes of freedom and violence. Such an interpretation could be very interesting and might enrich one's understanding of the film, but the critic would commit an attributional error if he or she argued that the filmmakers employed flash cross-cutting with a particular intended meaning in mind.

The film's editor, Donn Cambern, admitted that the flash cross-cutting developed simply because it was an unusual way of handling scene transitions. Cambern described the origin of the flash cross-cutting by saying, "That came about in looking for a way to simply make a transition from one scene to the other. We literally had to experiment to find how long those cuts needed to be in order to convey the idea . . . . At first we said, 'Ah! We got something great here,' so we started pumping it every place. Speaking of redundancy, it got to be absolutely indulgent. I don't remember how many times it's used, but it's not that much. But people remember

Easy Rider
(Columbia Pictures, 1969)
Easy Rider broke many conventional rules of filmmaking, but not all of the film's visual techniques were meant to convey particular meanings. While critics search for meaning and tend to attribute it to most, if not all, features of a film's design, film-makers themselves often work intuitively and may have very practical, rather than symbolic or expressive, reasons for shooting or editing a scene in a particular manner. Frame enlargement.

the technique." As Cambern's remarks indicate, not every aspect of visual design has a particular meaning. Sometimes the effects themselves are their own end and provide the filmmaker with sufficient incentive for executing the scene that way.

In addition, films and their audiovisual design are polyvalent in ways their creators never intended. Audiences see meanings that the filmmakers may not have intended or even expressly did not intend. Steven Spielberg wanted the execution scenes in *Schindler's List* (1993) to horrify audiences. He never wanted the violence in such scenes to elicit laughter, but it did from at least one audience of high school students who apparently found the violence less than horrifying. Spielberg was fascinated by this and remarked that some modern viewers have become desensitized toward screen violence.

Sam Peckinpah's *Straw Dogs* (1971) is one of the most controversial violent films of the early 1970s. A meek college professor (Dustin Hoffman) slaughters a gang of thugs who break into his house. Critics widely condemned the film for what they perceived as Peckinpah's glorification of violence, which leads the viewer to applaud the bloody deeds of the professor, but director Peckinpah stated that he viewed the professor as the villain of the film and a thoroughly reprehensible character. Critics attributed a meaning to the director that was at odds with the filmmaker's own stated intentions.

These examples illustrate the two most common types of errors regarding intended meaning. A critic commits an attributional error of intended meaning when asserting that (1) some effect or scene has a specific intended meaning never expressly planned by a filmmaker or (2) some effect or scene has a specific meaning intended by a filmmaker that is expressly different from the meaning the filmmaker did intend. The first type of error attributes intended meaning to an effect that is without any such meaning, and the second type misconstrues the intended meaning that is there.

Straw Dogs
(ABC Pictures, 1971)
Professor David Sumner (Dustin Hoffman) resorts to violence in the climax of the ultrabloody *Straw Dogs*, which offended many critics who thought the film glorified violence. Director Sam Peckinpah intended a more ironic view of violence as both compelling and horrifying and of Sumner as a pitifully deluded character. Critics' reactions may fail to correspond with a filmmaker's intentions. Frame enlargement.

WRITING FILM CRITICISM

Learning to write good film criticism can be fairly easy. As a developing film critic, you can follow these basic steps (all of which assume that you have already found a film to critique): establish an interpretive framework, apply the framework, and draw interpretive conclusions.

Developing an Interpretive Framework

Start out by establishing a framework of interpretation to apply to the film. The framework of interpretation specifies what to look for in the film being critiqued. Without such a framework, criticism is impossible and deteriorates into an effort to patch together disconnected pieces of information. To develop a framework of interpretation, research subjects or issues addressed by the film as a basis for evaluating how the film treats them. View other films produced by the same director or by a director or team of production personnel on a relevant topic or genre to become familiar with a body of work to which the film being critiqued can be related.

Study some of the film theories discussed in Chapter 11 and attempt to apply them to the film. One should also read what other critics have said about the film because this will stimulate thinking and help generate ideas. It will also show how other writers have constructed their critical arguments. Remember, though, that the goal of criticism is to produce a novel or original interpretation, not to recycle someone else's ideas.

Star Wars
(Twentieth Century Fox, 1977)
Good film criticism enhances one's understanding of a given film's design and expressive meanings. Indeed, the critic helps establish those meanings. With *Star Wars,* the critic could discuss the film's stylistic debt to early movie serials or the symbolic implications of the stark clash between good and evil at the heart of the narrative

Cinematic meaning, of course, does not derive solely from a filmmaker's intentions. This is an important point. Because filmmaking is a collaborative art, viewers often cannot know what the intentions of a single artist working on a production may have been. Viewers are free to interpret and derive meaning from films in their own fashion. Critics, though, often assert that specific elements of style have particular meanings intended by filmmakers. It is these assertions that may be vulnerable to the

To develop a framework of interpretation, go beyond the film itself to establish a social, philosophical, aesthetic, or historical context into which the film may be placed. Two measures of good criticism relevant here include the richness and comprehensiveness of the interpretive frame and how well the interpretive frame coincides with the film.

Application of the Framework

Once the objectives are clear, you then need to view the film at least two or three more times. Search for material to identify as a potential fit with the interpretive frame. Having found it, carefully isolate it from the rest of the film through a strategic description. This description will simplify and reduce the amount of film material it is necessary to work with. Strategic identification and description make it possible to efficiently reorganize the film in ways that fit the interpretations being developed.

Because of this, each repeated viewing can become more efficient and quicker since you will become more efficient at finding and extracting the needed information. A VCR is an excellent study tool because it permits you to freeze the action or repeat it as many times as necessary to check for details. Search the film for key scenes, character interactions, aspects of narrative structure, and elements of audiovisual design that can be integrated with the framework of interpretation. The other chapters in this text highlight features of audiovisual design and narrative that you might wish to isolate for critical analysis. If it doesn't fit, don't force it. The people reading the criticism will know whether the interpretations are false or unworkable for the film.

Remember to simplify the sequences discussed by eliminating unnecessary information. This is what is meant by strategic description. Don't describe everything in the scene, only what is important for the argument developed. Precisely label all aspects of visual design, quote dialogue accurately, and spell character names correctly. A critic who fails to do this loses credibility.

Building an Argument

There is no single formula or method for constructing a critical argument. However, all the rules normally associated with good writing also apply to film criticism. Build an argument, in a coherent and legitimate way, that your novel interpretation of the film reveals important patterns and layers of meaning that are not immediately apparent or explicitly conveyed with a casual viewing.

Be careful, therefore, to build the argument by clearly guiding the reader through all the steps and stages of critical thought, from outlining the initial critical premises to the citation of supporting evidence and the statement of conclusions. Good writing is clear, connected, and forceful. Because criticism is a rhetorical act, the quality of the writing is as important as the quality of the ideas in swaying the reader to your positions. Finally, remember that good criticism is provocative. If the ideas are challenging, if the connections established across the images, and narrative episodes are novel and insightful, you will enrich the readers' understanding of the film and may even send them back for another, wiser viewing.

two fallacies discussed here. Note, however, that uncovering these errors typically requires documentation of a film's production history. This is true, as well, for the next error of attribution.

Errors of assigned authorship. The third type of attributional error is an error of assigned authorship. Because filmmaking is a collaborative process, it is often difficult to assign responsibility for a particular effect or aspect of visual design to an individual craftsperson. The color design of *Do the Right Thing* (1989) is the contribution of production designer Wynn Thomas working in collaboration with director Spike Lee and cinematographer Ernest Dickerson. The kaleidoscopic structure of *Annie Hall* (1977) owes as much to editor Ralph Rosenblum as it does to writer/director Woody Allen.

These cases are documented through interviews with the principal artists involved. With most films, the precise areas of collaborative influence remain undocumented. Accordingly, a critic almost never knows with certainty who was responsible for what in a given film. Critics commonly attribute effects to the director. This is a kind of critical shorthand, a necessary, but somewhat misleading procedure. The director is merely one key player among many and should in no case be regarded as the sole author for all of a film's finished effects or design.

The Stages in Creating Criticism

Three stages are essential for creating good criticism. First, when viewing a film, the critic sees within that film the potential application of a given framework of interpretation. The work of criticism is the application of this frame to the film. Before starting to build the interpretation, the critic may research more fully the framework of interpretation that he or she wants to apply. For example, if the critic is interpreting *Invasion of the Body Snatchers,* he or she might research the McCarthy period of the 1950s or the existence of documentation on the political attitudes and, specifically, attitudes toward McCarthyism of director Don Siegel, screenwriter Daniel Mainwaring, and other members of the cast or crew.

Second, armed with a fully elaborated framework of interpretation, the critic applies this framework to the film by selecting and describing relevant details, aspects of cinematic structure, and elements of the narrative that can be regarded as meaningful according to the framework employed. Quantity of evidence carries considerable weight here. The more evidence *from the film* the critic can isolate, the more aspects of its visual or narrative design that are integrated into the argument being constructed, the more persuasive the critical interpretation will be.

Third, by assigning meaning to these details, by placing them within the interpretational frame, the critic reorganizes the film's structure. The newly reconfigured film will seem inevitably to embody the meanings the critic has assigned to it. With the best criticism, these meanings become an enduring part of the film itself and help shape the context in which it is seen by new viewers.

SUMMARY

Film criticism is the use of language to impose a new organization upon a film, its images and narratives, and/or an audience's experience of that film. By translating pictorial material into words, criticism is a rhetorical act and depends, for its persuasive effect, on the critic's skills at language and intellectual sophistication. As a rhetorical act, film criticism also includes an empirical dimension. By selectively citing details of audiovisual and narrative design, the critic reorganizes a film's structure to emphasize or draw out implicit meanings not apparent on a casual viewing. The critic employs a deductive method, applying an interpretational framework to the film and using it to guide the selection of details for analysis. These details are then integrated into the intrepretive framework, helping the critic build a novel interpretation of the film.

Criticism assumes a number of distinct forms. Newspaper reviewing is heavily consumer oriented, designed to answer the reader's question about whether a given movie is worth seeing. As such, newspaper criticism tends toward plot summary, descriptions of the film's characters, and the performances of stars in those roles.

The general-interest journal-based critic usually has more space to practice the craft. As such, this critic goes into greater detail about the artistic traditions to which a given film belongs and in describing the particular visual and narrative style employed by a filmmaker. The consumer function, here, is less urgent. Scholarly criticism is written for a community of scholars rather than for the general reader. As such, it employs a specialized language and draws on one or more distinct theoretical models.

Whatever the form of criticism employed and whatever the theoretical model, criticism involves several distinct stages. The critic selects and identifies relative features of the film under discussion and describes them in sufficient detail to communicate to the reader their important features and then relates these elements of cinema to the critical interpretation being developed.

Narratives and visual signs in the cinema are polyvalent, that is they contain multiple meanings. They are multidimensional and complex. As an example of this, any five people are likely to provide different accounts of what a particular film means. This is the condition that makes criticism necessary and enjoyable. Often, viewers feel that their experience of a film does not come to an end with the final credits. They want to kick the movie around in their heads a bit more or talk about it with friends to get a better understanding of what they are thinking or feeling. To do this, they may also read critical interpretations of the film, and, if the criticism is good, it enriches their understanding and experience and may even drive them back to the film for another viewing.

Because criticism, though, is rhetorical and because the multidimensional range of meanings implicit in any film is vast, a critic's interpretation is likely to vary according to (1) the forum—newspaper, general-interest journal, scholarly journal—in which it is performed, and (2) the particular theoretical model employed. The daily newspaper reviewer's assessment of a movie is likely to be rushed and extremely clear cut: it's either a good movie or a bad one, one that viewers should see or avoid at all costs. The assessment of a general-interest journal-based critic is likely to be more measured, multilayered, and ambivalent. Similarly, what a psychoanalytic scholarly critic sees in a film and finds significant may differ considerably from what a cognitive scholarly critic or ideological critic deems worthy of analysis.

The fact that a single movie can give rise to such a range of criticism and interpretation should not leave viewers feeling frustrated about the enterprise of criticism or doubtful of its usefulness. Instead, viewers should take this as proof of the creative and conceptual richness of the cinema and of the many ways it addresses an audience. The critic reimposes meaning and psychological closure upon the inherently ambiguous and provocative experience of watching a movie. This richness is cause for celebration and is one more reason for loving and embracing the medium of cinema.

SUGGESTED READINGS

David Bordwell, *Making Meaning: Inference and Rhetoric in the Interpretation of Cinema* (Cambridge, MA: Harvard University Press, 1989).

Pauline Kael, *Movie Love: Complete Reviews 1988–91* (New York: Plume, 1991).

Mark Crispin Miller, ed., *Seeing Through Movies* (New York: Pantheon, 1990).

Jonathan Rosenbaum, *Placing Movies: The Practice of Film Criticism* (Berkeley: University of California Press, 1995).

Andrew Sarris, *Confessions of a Cultist: On the Cinema, 1955–59* (New York: Simon and Schuster, 1970).

Steve Vineberg, *No Surprises, Please: Movies in the Reagan Decade* (New York: Schirmer Books, 1993).

Chapter 11

Models of Film Theory

Chapter Objectives

After reading this chapter, you should be able to

- explain the nature of film theory and the types of questions it investigates

- describe the characteristics, strengths, and limitations of realist models

- describe the characteristics, strengths, and limitations of auteurist models

- describe the characteristics, strengths, and limitations of psychoanalytic models

- describe the characteristics, strengths, and limitations of ideological models

- describe the characteristics, strengths, and limitations of feminist models

- describe the characteristics, strengths, and limitations of cognitive models

- select the most appropriate theoretical model for the particular type of questions that need answers

- understand that multiple theoretical perspectives are required because the cinema is multidimensional

Key Terms and Concepts

realist film theory
deep-focus cinema-
    tography
long take
perceptual realism

auteurist film theory
psychoanalytic film theory
voyeurism
ideological film theory
ideology

feminist film theory
cognitive film theory
fetishizing techniques
perceptual processing
interpretive processing

More so than newspaper and television reviewers and general-interest journal critics, scholarly critics use film theories to build critical interpretations. What, then, is film theory? Earlier chapters examined audiovisual design in the cinema and the viewer's contribution to the screen experience. A logical concluding point in the exploration of cinema is to examine the nature of film theory because theory tries to answer the question, what is cinema? Film theories are systematic attempts to think about the nature of cinema, what it is as a medium, how it works, how it embodies meaning for viewers, and what kind of meanings it embodies. Each film theory approaches these questions from different angles. Most theories represent an application of some previously existing philosophical, social, or aesthetic framework to the film medium rather than a true medium-specific theory of meaning or effect.

This chapter examines six models of film theory that have shaped the thinking of film scholars in important ways. These are the realist, auteurist, psychoanalytic, ideological, feminist, and cognitive models of film theory. Each model is especially good at dealing with some aspects of film style and the viewer's experience while being limited in its ability to deal with other aspects. Depending on the model employed, critics emphasize certain features of films at the expense of others. Very different portraits of the film medium emerge within critical writing depending on the theoretical model employed.

☐ REALIST MODELS OF THE FILM EXPERIENCE

This textbook has emphasized that the cinema has a double capacity. It both records and transforms the people, objects, and situations before the camera lens. Filmmakers use cinema as a recording medium to document existing social realities or to explore the complexities of human behavior and psychology. Filmmakers also use it as a transformational medium by employing the complex tools of their craft to create highly striking, original, and inventive images and narratives. The elements of mise-en-scene, sound and image editing, and camera placement and movement enable filmmakers to achieve extraordinary manipulations of visual and acoustical design in their films. This tension within the cinema between its recording and documentation functions and the power it gives filmmakers to stylize and transform reality creates problems for film theory when it attempts to locate a basis for realism and for realistic film styles.

Elements of Realist Theory: Bazin

Realism in the cinema is generally based on a film style that aims to capture, with minimal distortion, the essential features of real-world situations and events, or, in the case of fictionalized events, give them the appearance of real-world status. Typically, **realist film theory** suggests that there is a threshold beyond which stylistic manipulation in cinema is deemed unfair, misleading, or distorting of reality. Italian neo-realists, for example, aimed to define such a threshold by holding the filmmaker's manipulations of style to a minimum.

Of course, questions about where social or psychological reality properly lies are extremely difficult problems. French theorist Andre Bazin offered an ingenious solution. His essays on the cinema, composed during the 1940s and 1950s, exerted an enormous influence on the thinking of those film critics writing for the journal *Cahiers du Cinema,* who would later themselves become film directors (see the section on the French New Wave in Chapter 9). Bazin based his theory of cinematic realism on an ethical assumption and recommended specific elements of film form as a basis for realist style.

Ethical Components of Bazin's Realism

Realistic film styles for Bazin were those that tended to respect the viewer's experience of reality. Bazin emphasized that each individual's perspective on the world was, to some extent, uniquely his or her own and differed from the perspective of others. For Bazin, reality possessed an ambiguous quality. Different people viewing the same scene or situation extracted different interpretations. Bazin believed that filmmakers should develop a style that respected these ambiguities and that did not unfairly coerce or manipulate viewers into sharing one single, mass emotional response to the scene or film. Bazin argued that filmmakers should employ techniques that actually enhance the ambiguities of reality and afford spectators ample room for developing their own interpretations and responses to a scene.

Technical Basis for Bazin's Realism

Bazin argued that certain formal techniques were more or less suited to representing the ambiguities of reality on screen and for affording spectators freedom in developing their responses. Filmmakers should avoid montage or highly manipulative editing.

Psycho (Paramount Pictures, 1960)
Mass emotion films, such as *Psycho,* fail Bazin's test of a realist film by provoking all spectators to share a uniform emotional response (fright, in the case of *Psycho*). Frame enlargement.

Bazin criticized filmmakers who used manipulative montage editing to exert control over the audience and to elicit mass emotional reactions to films. Montage-oriented directors who would fail Bazin's ethical basis for a realist aesthetic include such masters as Alfred Hitchcock and Steven Spielberg.

The shower sequence from *Psycho* (1960), showing a violent murder in extremely brief shots edited at a frenzied pace, achieved Hitchcock's goal of making the audience share a single, uniform response—a scream. Hitchcock said about *Psycho* that he wasn't interested in the actors or their performances or even the story, but only in using the elements of pure cinema, primarily editing, to make the audience experience a mass emotion. A similar strategy operates in Steven Spielberg's *Jaws* (1975), where editing, specifically cross-cutting, creates considerable suspense and terror about the shark's attacks. Like *Psycho, Jaws* is a mass-emotion film in which filmmakers use technique with brilliance and sophistication to ensure that all members of the viewing audience experience the same intense reactions.

This uniformity of response is precisely what Bazin wanted to avoid. Montage editing has an inherent tendency to manipulate the viewer's response. Bazin argued that filmmakers wanting to reproduce the ambiguities of reality should employ **deep-focus cinematography** (where great distance separates sharply focused foreground and background objects) and the **long take** (shots of long duration) in a style that minimizes the importance of editing.

Shots employing deep focus create highly articulated foreground and background areas. Viewers have multiple areas of interest to study in a deep-focus shot, rather than a single central area of interest. For Bazin, such shots are theoretically more ambiguous than shots composed using a narrow plane of focus, thus affording viewers multiple ways of organizing and perceiving the frame. By avoiding montage, long takes enhance this visual ambiguity by extending in time the deep-focus compositions. For Bazin, deep focus "brings the spectator into a relation with the image closer to that which he enjoys with reality. Therefore, it is correct to say that independently of the contents of the image, its structure is more realistic." By contrast, for Bazin "montage by its very nature rules out ambiguity of expression."

Bazinian Filmmakers

Bazin praised the work of directors who employed these techniques. Bazin greatly esteemed French director Jean Renoir for his use of deep-focus cinematography and for his tendency to employ camera movement rather than montage. Bazin admired American director Orson Welles. In *Citizen Kane* (1941), Welles filmed entire scenes in only one or two lengthy shots. In the scene in which Kane's parents make arrangements with a banker to raise him and to act as young Charlie Kane's guardian, Welles composed most of the scene in two shots. The action begins with a long shot showing young Charlie playing in the snow and then the camera pulls inside the window of young Charlie's home to reveal his parents and the banker. The camera tracks in front of his mother as she crosses from the window to a table to sign the papers. Then, as she rises again and crosses back to the window, the camera follows her. In the second shot of the scene, the camera is outdoors and tracks across the porch of the cabin to young Charlie in the snow, where the adults join him and announce his fate.

The two extended takes that largely compose this scene, running nearly four minutes, represent a clear stylistic alternative to the standard rules of continuity editing that would have mandated using first a master shot and then inserts matching action to the master. As Bazin pointed out with respect to Welles' films, "dramatic effects for which we had formerly relied on montage were created out of the movements of the actors within a fixed framework."

The supreme example of a filmmaker who employs deep focus, rather than montage, to create rich compositions with multiple areas of interest is the French director Jacques Tati. In films such as *Playtime* (1967), editing plays virtually no creative role at all. This comic film about the encounters of a bumbling Frenchman with a bewildering modern world of steel skyscrapers and plastic commodities is played out entirely in lengthy shots composed in deep focus where an amazing number of things are happening simultaneously within the frame.

Strengths of Bazinian Realism

Bazin's theory of realism has an extraordinary strength. It stresses the ethical contract that exists between a filmmaker and an audience, and it challenges filmmakers and

Citizen Kane
(RKO, 1941)
Deep focus in *Citizen Kane*. Young Charles Kane plays outside while his parents sign away control of his future to a banker. Note the crisp focus in foreground, mid-ground, and background. Frame enlargement.

viewers to think about the cinema's potential for unfairly manipulating its audiences. Bazin cited ample evidence throughout film history to support his argument that the ethically motivated filmmaker, seeking to respect the viewer's experience of reality, should avoid a style that is overtly manipulative and based in montage.

If Bazin was right that individuals' subjective experiences of reality are varied and that a basis for realist style lies in employing cinematic tools that respect this variety, then it follows that filmmakers who use their cinematic power to manipulate audiences into holding socially objectionable reactions are engaging in an unfair or unethical exploitation of their viewers. Although Bazin wrote about film beginning in the 1940s until his death in 1958, his work has important implications for contemporary film in this respect. Among the most controversial of contemporary horror films are the so-called slasher films, such as *Friday the 13th, The Toolbox Murders,* or *Driller Killer,* which feature elaborate scenes in which a psychopathic killer stalks and murders attractive young women and men. These films typically use subjective shots to show the victims as they are being stalked and slaughtered from the killer's point of view.

Following Bazin, one could object on ethical grounds that this kind of stylistic manipulation is unnecessarily sadistic. It elicits only the most violent of desires from audiences and treats viewers with a measure of brutality, cruelly enforcing a limited range of socially questionable physical and emotional responses. These films trigger a mass emotional response from the audience. For a Bazinian realist, such films fail to respect the integrity of each viewer and the uniqueness of each one's approach to reality. Bazin's theory of realism has much to say about the ethical contract that exists between filmmakers and viewers and about the extraordinary potential for coercing emotions that filmmakers have at their command.

Weaknesses of Bazinian Realism

The major weakness of Bazin's realist aesthetic is that it exists as a potential and as an idea that is never fully realized in any given film. Some of the filmmakers Bazin cites as practitioners of deep focus or the long take also employ montage. *Citizen Kane* includes a number of celebrated sequence shots composed in deep focus, but it also employs some striking montages.

Very few films do without the expressive power of editing. In *Rope* (1948), Alfred Hitchcock came close to dispensing with editing. Most of the shots in *Rope* run a full ten minutes. Hitchcock cut only when the camera ran out of film, and even then he went to great pains to disguise the cut by having it occur at moments when a character suddenly crosses in front of the camera, blocking its view. Hitchcock, however, discontinued this experiment after *Rope,* recognizing that without editing he had very little ability to create dramatic and psychological rhythm and tempo. Few films representing a pure application of Bazinian principles exist.

A second weakness of Bazinian theory lies in its tendency to minimize the degree to which even deep-focus–long-take cinematography can manipulate the viewer's perceptions. In Jacques Tati's *Playtime,* when Tati needs viewers to look at a particular area of the frame, he uses a sudden loud noise, a rapid movement, or a bright color to draw attention to that area. Even within the deep-focus–long-take approach, filmmakers can still guide and influence viewer perceptions.

Other Realist Models

Bazinian theory, of course, is not the only basis for a theory of film realism. An alternative approach emphasizes the ways that cinema style and technique have a basis in **perceptual realism,** that is, the ability of picture and sound in cinema to correspond with the ways viewers perceive space and sound in the real, three-dimensional world. Film technique builds on and manipulates the viewer's ordinary perceptual habits and ways of processing the visual and auditory world. Through lighting, sound design, and camera placement, filmmakers build sources of three-dimensional information into their images and can selectively emphasize these sources. Wide-angle lenses emphasize depth cues. Continuity editing ensures that the screen world corresponds in important ways to a viewer's experience of time and space in daily life. Viewers look to films for reference and correspondence with facets of their own experience, but give filmmakers extraordinary latitude in achieving this. Accordingly, the cinema incorporates dimensions of social and perceptual realism into its visual and narrative designs, but these co-exist with and are counterbalanced by the medium's transformative abilities. Cinema reconfigures, stylizes, and creatively distorts the correspondences between the screen world and a viewer's nonfilmic social and perceptual experience. An adequate understanding of cinematic realism, based on these correspondences, must also acknowledge their limitations and the transformative properties of cinema that exist in tension with them. In sum, realism is a concept that must be carefully qualified when applied to the cinema.

☐ AUTEURIST MODELS

Auteurist film theory studies film authors. Auteurist theory, accordingly, studies film as a medium of personal expression in which great directors leave a recognizable stylistic signature on their work. Auteur critics usually consider this author to be the director. The term *auteur* derives from the French word meaning *author,* and this model of criticism is now the most commonly employed and deeply ingrained method of thinking about film.

In the 1930s and 1940s, during the high period of the Hollywood studio system, directors were often hired functionaries who filmed the script as economically and quickly as possible and who answered to the film's producer. Today, by contrast, many directors achieve superstar status and even directors who have made only one or two films are allowed to place their name above the film title and claim possessive credit.

Auteurist criticism originally developed among the French New Wave critics and then was imported to the United States in the 1960s. Today, director studies are among the most common forms of film criticism. They trace the style of key directors regarded as important artists and as the major creative influence shaping the materials and design of their films. Such directors include Akira Kurosawa in Japan, Ingmar Bergman in Sweden, Federico Fellini in Italy, and, in the United States, Alfred Hitchcock, John Ford, Francis Ford Coppola, Martin Scorsese, and many others.

Elements of Auteurism

An auteurist critic looks for consistency of theme and design throughout a director's films. In practice, the critic looks at three correlated elements: cinematic techniques, stories, and themes. Across the repertoire of a director's films, the auteur critic looks for recurring stories, themes, and audiovisual designs.

The Case of Hitchcock

In the case of Alfred Hitchcock, a director frequently studied from an auteur perspective, these consistent and recurring elements include stories about characters falsely accused of crimes (the so-called "wrong man" scenario, found in such films as *The Thirty-Nine Steps, The Wrong Man, Strangers on a Train,* and *North by Northwest*) and visual elements such as cross-tracking shots, the subjective camera, high-angle shots, mirror imagery, and long stretches of film without dialogue but with an intensively visual design that Hitchcock called "pure cinema."

Hitchcock's Film Style as Biography   In addition, the critic developing an auteur study of Hitchcock might seek correlations between Hitchcock's upbringing and private life and the subjects and techniques of his films. An auteur critic might draw a connection between Hitchcock's intense relationship with his mother and the frequently recurring mother figures in the films, or between Hitchcock's Catholic upbringing and attendance at a Jesuit school and the narratives of guilt, sin, transgression, and crime so common in his films. Hitchcock's fascination with crime, his attendance of murder trials at England's Old Bailey Court, his visits to the Black Museum of Scotland Yard, his attraction to the suspense writer Edgar Allen Poe, and his fascination with celebrity killers such as England's famed John Christie, who buried the bodies of his victims under the floorboards of his house, would *seem* to have an obvious bearing on the films.

The auteur critic could also draw on anecdotes told by Hitchcock as a standard part of interviews, such as the imprisonment story about the time his father allegedly took him to a police station where Hitchcock was locked in a cell, then subsequently released with a warning by the police that "this is what we do to nasty boys." By telling such anecdotes, Hitchcock encouraged the search for connections between his personal life and his films. He said, "I was terrified of the police, of the Jesuit fathers, of physical punishment, of a lot of things. This is the root of my work."

To the extent that the auteur critic can find consistent themes, stories, and audiovisual designs running through the body of a director's films, and can even tie these

North by Northwest (MGM, 1959)
"Wrong man" imagery in Hitchcock's classic *North by Northwest*. An innocent advertising executive (Cary Grant), mistakenly identified as a murderer and a government agent, is pursued by enemy agents intent on killing him.

Psycho
(Paramount Pictures, 1960)
Hitchcock's lifelong fascination
with crime certainly influenced
his screen work. He studied the
career of England's famous
murderers and helped create
some of the screen's most
famous villains. Norman Bates
(Tony Perkins) in *Psycho* remains
one of cinema's most chilling
monsters. Frame enlargement.

elements to the filmmaker's private life, the critic can argue that such a director is a
true auteur whose films embody a personal and artistic vision.

Strengths of the Auteur Model

Auteur criticism has helped elevate the cinema to the level of art in the eyes of critics, filmmakers, and the general public. By stressing the uniformity and integrity of a
director's artistic vision, the auteur critic argues in favor of a unified body of work.
By doing so, the critic implies that film is more than just a business and a product
manufactured for profit. By stressing film as an art, auteur criticism undeniably bol-
sters the power of directors relative to producers and other members of the production crew and has helped legitimize the film medium.

Moreover, in many cases, the director is the catalyst of a production, the key crew
member who synthesizes, directs, and helps guide the contributions of other personnel. Production designers and cinematographers emphasize the need to subordinate
their artistic visions and interests to the desires of the director in an effort to help the
director get the results he or she wants. With many directors, therefore, it is legitimate to argue in favor of some degree of auteurism.

Weaknesses of the Auteur Model

The weaknesses of auteur criticism lie in its tendency to commit the attributional
errors discussed in Chapter 10. If one looks at enough films of any director, undeni-
able visual and narrative patterns will probably begin to emerge, but not all of these
patterns are meaningful and not all of them should be attributed to the director.

Not every effect or apparent design within a film has a clear meaning intended
by production personnel or the director. Filmmakers sometimes execute an effect

simply because they like the way it looks or even, more mundanely, because they had to shoot or edit a scene the way it appears on screen due to uncooperative weather, loss of footage, or simply running out of money. Many factors that influence the look of a finished film are things over which filmmakers have little or no control.

Even more damaging to the auteur critic's search for a sole author is the fact that film production is collaborative. It is often impossible to assign responsibility for an effect to a particular individual such as the director. Alfred Hitchcock collaborated with the screenwriters on most of his films. Hitchcock's contribution was to kick around a few ideas and make sure the stories incorporated opportunities for his interest in visual effects. Constructing a narrative from scratch and building it into an elegant finished structure was not one of Hitchcock's strengths. He needed the services of accomplished screenwriters.

Some of his finest films, *Notorious* (1946) for example, about American agents infiltrating a nest of Nazi spies in Brazil, were shaped by decisive creative intervention from the producer. In the case of *Notorious,* producer David O. Selznick insisted again and again that the scripts Hitchcock and his writers were turning in were not good enough and needed merciless revision. As was his custom, Selznick even offered specific suggestions for changing the characters and story situations. Only when Selznick was satisfied with the revisions was Hitchcock allowed to begin filming.

There is no effective way for auteurist criticism to deal with the problems posed by collaboration. The auteur critic detects consistent patterns across the body of a director's films and hopes that those things attributed to the director are, indeed, justified. In most cases, the auteur critic attributes things to the director on faith, without documentation, in the form of interviews or written records about who on the crew did what. Many auteur critics respond to this problem by claiming that, by "Hitchcock," they mean not the private individual, but rather the body of films with their unified themes and visual designs. Accordingly, "Hitchcock" becomes a construction required by criticism, referring to the films or texts and not to the man. This stratagem is a way of dealing with the objection that a critic can never really know who is responsible for what in a film, and it corrects some, but not all, of the reasons for making the objection.

Vertigo
(Paramount Pictures, 1958)
James Stewart, as detective Scotty Ferguson, hangs precariously, high above San Francisco, in *Vertigo*. In film after film, Hitchcock took his characters and viewers to the edge of the abyss and forced them to look at the darkness and chaos below. In doing so, he created a distinctive cinematic universe, but he did not work alone. He depended on the vital input of his collaborators. Hitchcock may be an auteur, but the cinema remains a collaborative medium. Frame enlargement.

A final weakness of auteur criticism should be noted. In some cases, the critic's attempt to discover a unified body of work produces bias and distortion. Minor films are elevated to the status of masterworks, and, in the most extreme form, a critic may regard even a minor film by an auteur director as a greater work than an undeniably major film, such as *Casablanca* (1942), by a nonauteur director (in this case, Michael Curtiz).

☐ PSYCHOANALYTIC MODELS

Drawing primarily from the writings of Freud and French psychoanalyst Jacques Lacan, **psychoanalytic film theory** emphasizes film's reinforcement of unconscious sources of pleasure or anxiety. For psychoanalytic theory, the film medium activates deep-rooted psychological, sometimes infantile and nonrational, desires and anxieties.

Elements of Psychoanalytic Models

Voyeuristic Pleasures

Psychoanalytic critics examine the way that cinema organizes and manipulates a viewer's pleasures and attractions to the screen spectacle. The cinema activates what psychoanalytic critics refer to as the "scopic drive," a primary pleasure obtained from looking at things. In the cinema, the scopic drive acts in viewers as a kind of **voyeurism,** that is, a pleasure derived from looking at characters and situations on screen.

Voyeuristic or scopic pleasures can be aroused in two ways by the cinema. First, cinema techniques, such as close-ups, draw the viewer's attention to aspects of the screen spectacle that arouse the viewer's nonrational pleasure. Psychoanalytic critics have examined the way that male directors will use long, loving, lingering close-ups to examine the glamorous, sexy appearance and costuming of female stars, such as Marlene Dietrich or Marilyn Monroe, who embody male erotic desires.

Fetishizing the Body   Psychoanalytic critics describe Dietrich's elaborate costuming and ritualistic visual presentation in a series of films she made for director Josef von Sternberg (*Morocco* (1930), *Shanghai Express* (1932), *Blonde Venus* (1932), *The Scarlet Express* (1934), *The Devil Is a Woman* (1935)) as a kind of visual fetish. With lingering visual attention, the camera studies the precise outline, design, and appearance of Dietrich as an erotic object.

Fetishizing techniques can also apply to the presentation of male stars. Long, loving close-ups dwell on the glistening, extraordinarily defined muscles of Sylvester Stallone or Arnold Schwarzenegger in their films. For psychoanalytic critics, this visual attention emphasizes the bodies of Stallone and Schwarzenegger as idealized sexual objects conforming to an exaggerated cultural ideal of male potency and power.

Through the use of such cinematic techniques as the close-up, film organizes the visual attention of its audience around such erotically charged objects as the body of a Marilyn Monroe or a Sylvester Stallone. Psychoanalytic critics believe that, in doing so, films activate the spectator's pleasures in looking, voyeuristic in nature, and the spectator's scopic desire to possess an object through a controlling gaze.

Elaborately costumed and posed in the films of Joseph von Sternberg, Marlene Dietrich becomes a point of concentrated visual focus, commanding the camera's attention and receiving its lingering gaze.

(Paramount Pictures)

Taboo Images   A second way the cinema can appeal to the voyeuristic pleasures of its viewers is by displaying taboo or forbidden, subjects and images. Films offer spectacles of sex and violence that excite viewers in ways they would deny in polite society. Viewers of *The Silence of the Lambs* (1991) eagerly spend time in the thrilling company of serial killer Hannibal Lecter, whereas in real life they would shun such a person. Unlike real-life violence, bloodshed and killing on screen give many viewers intense aesthetic pleasure. For psychoanalytic critics, the cinema's ability to excite viewers with spectacles of sex and violence illustrates its powerful appeal to an audience's primitive, nonrational, unconscious desires. Polite society restricts outward expressions of sexual or aggressive behavior, but the cinema displays these in extremely arousing ways.

Strengths of the Psychoanalytic Model

Psychoanalytic criticism emphasizes the complex ways that film arouses an audience's emotions and desires. These desires are not always conscious or fully understood by viewers, yet film seems able to reach deep inside viewers' minds to influence the ways

Rambo III
(Carolco, 1988)
Sylvester Stallone's engorged, glistening muscles in *Rambo III* add a sexual excitement to the film's violence, especially since they receive such extraordinary visual attention throughout the film. Male, as well as female, stars may function as erotic objects.

The Silence of the Lambs
(Orion Pictures, 1991)
Hannibal Lecter (Anthony Hopkins) in *The Silence of the Lambs* exerts a powerful fascination for viewers who are repulsed by his monstrousness yet attracted by his wit and intelligence. The special power such a character has over viewers may require a psychoanalytical explanation since it seems to exceed a viewer's rational judgment that such a person is evil and to be avoided. Frame enlargement.

viewers understand the world, themselves, and their own feelings. Sometimes the emotional response of an audience is so extraordinarily intense and concentrated, the audience aroused to such an unbearable pitch, that a psychoanalytic explanation seems warranted.

As an example, consider the opening of Luis Bunuel's and Salvador Dali's *Un Chien Andalou* (1922), which features one of the most horrific images in screen history. The scene leaves audiences shocked and gasping for breath, much as if they had been hit in the solar plexus. In the scene, discussed in Chapter 9, a man (played by Bunuel) stands behind a seated woman. He pulls out a straight razor and opens her right eye. The film then cuts to a long shot of clouds slicing across a moon, as the audience breathes a sigh of relief, thinking that, as usual, the camera has turned away from something that promises to be too horrifying.

In the next moment, though, the filmmakers show what viewers most dread. The razor slices into an eye which pops and disgorges a blob of gelatinous fluid. This is an old movie, and violent images have a way of becoming less intense and horrifying over time. This, though, is not one of those cases. The image has a special, sustained power to disturb and nauseate viewers. Contemporary audiences recoil with the same intensity and disgust viewers felt in 1922.

A psychoanalytic explanation can help here. As Freud suggested, among all the parts of the body that might potentially be wounded, people seem most sensitive about their eyes. Freud connected this anxiety to fears of castration. Whatever one might think of such a connection, Freud seemed correct in noting the special intensity of the terror over the threat of wounds to the eyes. When an object or situation is so highly charged with emotional energy, psychoanalysis looks toward the unconscious for an explanation. The anxieties seem, in some way, to be fundamental and primitive components of human identity, and, for psychoanalytic theory, the unconscious is the most primitive part of the mind. Psychoanalytic theory, then, enables critics to ask why certain film images seem so highly charged with emotion and how, in such moments, does the cinema provoke and intensify the reactions of its audience.

Weaknesses of the Psychoanalytic Model

There are several weaknesses to psychoanalytically-based criticism. The first is that psychoanalytic theory is based on ambiguous clinical data. The case studies, the analyses of patients' behavior and dreams that form the basis of the theory, are accessible as data only through the interpretations an analyst has placed on them. A scholar wanting to check the validity of psychoanalytic claims cannot do so by going back to the original patient, the original dream, or behavior. These can never be retrieved except through the analyst's published interpretations. The scientific status of psychoanalytic theory, therefore, is weak because the information on which the theory is based is either inaccessible or unavailable for re-examination. This means that psychoanalytic film theory must pretend to have a clinical basis that it, in fact, never does.

Second, it has a tendency to overextend itself, to be used as a means of explaining all dimensions of an audience's emotional response to movies. Psychoanalytic critics tend to see the cinema as a medium that plays on mainly irrational desires and irrational perceptions. On the contrary, though, many dimensions of viewer response to movies are entirely rational and do not require special explanation with reference to the unconscious mind. Among these are the demands for reference and correspondence with experience that viewers expect from a photographically-based medium such as cinema.

Psychoanalytic theories emphasizing irrational states of mind and desire are best applied to certain categories of films rather than to all films. Horror films, for example, are especially deserving of psychoanalytic attention because of the way they activate primitive fears and anxieties and center on monsters and supernatural beings who, arguably, represent irrational terrors. Selectively applied to films that elicit exceptionally charged and nonrational responses from viewers, psychoanalytic theory can clarify the special qualities of these responses. Psychoanalytic theory is less useful as a means of explaining how all films operate.

IDEOLOGICAL MODELS

Critics use **ideological film theory** to examine the relationship between movies and society and, specifically, how film represents social and political realities. An **ideology** is a set of beliefs about society and the nature of the world that involves assumptions and judgments about the nature of right and wrong, good and evil, justice and injustice, law and social order, and human nature and behavior.

Ideologies are systems and patterns of thought characteristic of a particular society or social subgroup. All societies or social subgroups contain ideologies, which people in those societies or groups internalize by virtue of growing up in that culture or gaining membership in that group or subculture.

Societies contain multiple ideologies, and these are not always coherent or harmonious. Because of this, all societies are subject to ideological tensions and conflicts. Among conflicting ideologies in American culture are the commitments to individual freedoms, on the one hand, and, on the other, the power of state and local governments to enforce law and maintain public order.

The ongoing controversies over gun control illustrate these conflicting ideologies. Proponents of gun control emphasize the need for government to ensure public safety by getting guns off the street. Opponents emphasize the individual right to own and bear arms. Such conflicts are difficult to resolve and tend to arouse a great deal of emotion on each side, as the ongoing battles about gun control illustrate. Ideological conflict is a typical social phenomenon arising from the simple fact that not all of the belief systems that circulate through a society are compatible or consistent with one another.

Elements of Ideological Criticism

Ideological film critics study the ways film portrays society and gives voice to one or more social ideologies. The ideological critic often starts by describing certain social trends or habits of thought and then demonstrates how these are represented in given bodies of film. Ideological critics, for example, emphasize the way that many Hollywood Westerns, showing the settling of the wilderness by white European settlers and Indians as villains and as obstacles to be removed, support traditional cultural beliefs about manifest destiny, about the inalienable right of European settlers to claim the wilderness and divest Native Americans of their land.

Levels of Ideology

Social ideologies exist in films on either first- or second-order levels. *Rambo: First Blood Part II* (1985), about a super American warrior who returns to Vietnam many years after the war and defeats the Vietnamese in battle, offers American culture a kind of substitute and vicarious symbolic victory in a war the nation lost. By virtue of its explicit treatment of social, political, and historical topics, it is an overtly ideological film. Its story deals with anxieties about the role of the United States as a world superpower and with lingering questions about its defeat in Southeast Asia. As such, the images and narrative of *Rambo* are ideological in an immediate, explicit, first-order way.

Films that are ideological on a second-order level present social messages and portraits of society that are implicit, indirect, and subtle. Examples of second-order ideological films are *Back to the Future* (1985) and *Field of Dreams* (1989), both of which are intimately connected to the mood of the era in which they were produced, especially the nostalgic myth of a return to the past represented by 1980s political culture.

In *Back to the Future,* the hero, Marty McFly (Michael J. Fox) travels back in time, and Ray Kinsella (Kevin Costner) from *Field of Dreams* mysteriously re-creates the past in an Iowa cornfield of dreams. Both characters meet their parents from the past and, by doing so, reclaim their boyhood but with an adult understanding. An ideological critic would show how these narratives correlate with the political culture of the 1980s, particularly its nostalgic embrace of an ideal past and the folklore of small towns and close-knit communities that underlay the appeal and vision of the Reagan presidency.

Unlike *Rambo,* where political ideologies are right up front and out in the open, *Back to the Future* and *Field of Dreams* do not strike one immediately as political films. An ideological critic, however, could argue that these films are nevertheless closely entwined with the political culture of their period. As such, despite their immediate appeal as entertainment vehicles, they are ideological in a second-order, implicit, and indirect way.

Ideological Point of View

Just as films may be either directly or indirectly ideological, they may also take up a variety of positions with respect to the ideologies they portray and the views of society developed in their narratives. Although a wide range of such positions exist, three main categories are the most important. An ideological critic distinguishes among films that support established social values, films that criticize established social values, and films that offer an incoherent, ambiguous, or unresolved representation of social values.

Position One: Ideological Support   The first ideological position—support for established social values—is illustrated by such films as *Top Gun* (1986) and *Rocky IV* (1985), both of which are explicitly connected to the political culture of the 1980s. *Top Gun* portrays the grit and resolve the hero needs to become a U.S. Navy pilot and climaxes with an aerial dogfight between the hero and a group of Soviet warplanes. The military is a basic social institution, and *Top Gun*'s glowing portrait of military heroism places the film in a position of clear support for the institution and its values.

Rocky IV climaxes with a politically symbolic boxing match between Rocky and an evil, robotlike Soviet opponent. The match occurs in the USSR, and the film presents it as an obvious test of wills between the two countries, with Rocky and his opponent symbolizing their respective political cultures. The political culture of the 1980s emphasized the need to revive America's military power after years of presumed neglect and abandonment, and the film visualizes this theme through Rocky's transformation from a lazy, wealthy, retired exfighter, unconcerned about the Soviets at the beginning of the movie, to a highly motivated warrior committed to defeating them and rehabilitating the honor of his country at film's end. As such, the movie clearly supports major themes of the era's dominant political culture.

Correlating portraits and groups.   To identify a film as one that supports established social values, a critic must carefully specify the social groups to whom those values

Top Gun
(Paramount Pictures, 1986)
The ideological content of *Top Gun* reinforces Cold War perceptions of the need for a strong U.S. military to counter Soviet threats. The film's ideological content is straightforward and unidimensional.

(Museum of Modern Art/Film Stills Archive)

Philadelphia (Tri-Star Pictures, 1994)
The ideological content of *Philadelphia*, was argued over by commentators and critics who focused on the film's portrayal of a homosexual man (played by Tom Hanks) with AIDS. Some critics charged that the film minimized the character's gay identity and sexuality in the interest of appealing to heterosexual audiences that have traditionally avoided gay-themed films. Frame enlargement.

correspond. With respect to *Top Gun* and *Rocky IV*, this can easily be done by citing the official, publicly proclaimed positions of the Reagan presidency.

Obviously, though, because societies contain multiple communities and multiple ideologies, films can support established social values that have currency within one community or subgroup but are disdained or rejected by other subgroups. *Longtime Companion* (1990) examines the spread of AIDS in the 1980s by focusing on a small, closely-knit community of gay men in New York City. When released, the film was controversial because its affectionate, supportive portrayal of gay life clashed with the social values of groups convinced that gay sexuality is wrong and/or that blamed the gay community for the spread of AIDS.

A critic's description of the ideological position of a film, then, irrespective of its particular point of view, must specify two things—the constellation of social values within the film and the film's attitude toward them, and, second, the social groups to whom those values belong.

Position Two: Ideological Critique   Films offering a genuinely critical view of established social values are less common in the American industry than those that offer clear support for such values. Nevertheless, in the late 1960s, films such as *Easy Rider* (1969) and *The Wild Bunch* (1969) presented heroes who were outlaws or rebels dissatisfied with and struggling against what was then termed "the establishment." Audience sympathy in *Easy Rider* and *The Wild Bunch* lay with the outlaw rebel and not with mainstream society, and the heroes' rebellion exposed the pettiness and intolerance of mainstream society. More recently, *Robocop* (1987) offered a savage critique of the social Darwinism that underlay 1980s' economic policies, especially those cutting the social safety net from under the poor while revising the tax laws to benefit the wealthy.

Outside relatively rare social satires such as *Robocop*, social critiques from a left-wing perspective are uncommon within the American industry. By contrast, European filmmakers are much sharper in their political critiques. Italian director Gillo Pontecorvo, in *The Battle of Algiers* (1965) and *Burn!* (1969), critiqued the imperialism of France and England at the time of their empires in these films about heroic guerrilla struggles for revolution and independence. This kind of left-wing, socially critical filmmaking is virtually nonexistent in the American industry.

OLIVER STONE

With much thunder and rage, Oliver Stone brings leftist politics back into mainstream American cinema, although to call his political vision left-wing is to give it more coherence than it actually possesses. After serving in the infantry in Vietnam and subsequently studying filmmaking at New York University, Stone scripted several violent, pulp films (*Midnight Express*, 1978; *Conan the Barbarian*, 1982; *Scarface*, 1983; *Year of the Dragon*, 1985) and directed a routine horror film, *The Hand* (1981).

In his second film as director, the remarkable *Salvador* (1986), he began to define his niche as a powerful, sometimes strident, critic of American society and foreign policy. Completed during the Reagan era of the early and mid-1980s as a criticism of the Reagan administration's support for a brutal military regime in El Salvador, Stone's film is an act of political courage and commitment. Like most of his work, however, it is not fully coherent. It skillfully dissects the duplicity of U.S. policy in El Salvador and the violence of the regime the United States supported, but backs away from acknowledging the peasant revolutionaries as a viable alternative. As a result, Stone cannot find any solution to the horrors he portrays, and his political engagement turns into despair.

Stone's next film, *Platoon* (1986), put him in the big leagues as a filmmaker. As an antidote to the comic book fantasies embodied by Sylvester Stallone's Rambo character, Stone's film was hailed by veterans and critics as the most realistic portrait of the war yet made. *Platoon* does have a surface realism, but it also employs explicit religious symbolism and generic nar-

Platoon (Orion Pictures, 1986)
Platoon was one of the most influential films of its decade. Avoiding Rambo-style heroics, it shows the war as a horrifically destructive event. The film mixes realism with religious symbolism, as in the Christian imagery employed in this shot showing an American soldier's death. Stone returned to the war in several subsequent films, but *Platoon* remains his best work on that subject. Frame enlargement.

The reasons are not hard to understand. Many millions of dollars are at stake in a film production today, and Hollywood is not eager to risk losing big chunks of its market with hard-edged social criticism. It is easier and potentially more profitable to reinforce existing ideologies than to challenge them in fundamental ways.

Position Three: Ideological Incoherence   While genuine ideological criticism is rarely found in the American industry, Hollywood films more commonly assume a position of ideological incoherence. This is an easily understandable result from the

rative formulas. Its political view of the war is murky, but it portrays with great intensity the suffering and loss of American soldiers.

Stone next applied his *Platoon* narrative formula—a young man torn between good and bad father figures—to American capitalism in *Wall Street* (1987), and then made one of his least-popular but best films, *Talk Radio* (1988), which powerfully portrays the free-floating popular rage and anxiety that he believes threatens American society and democracy.

A pompous, grandiose style and an increasingly strident tone mar his subsequent films. *Born on the Fourth of July* (1989) contains an extraordinary Tom Cruise performance as Vietnam vet Ron Kovic, but Stone's audiovisual style is unrelentingly bombastic. The viewer is pummelled by its grandiloquence and by a one-dimensional view of how young Kovic was brainwashed by macho, jingoistic American culture, personified by John F. Kennedy in the period the film portrays.

Stone apparently revised his view of Kennedy for *JFK* (1991), which portrays a dovish president eager to withdraw from Vietnam and assassinated by Washington powers intent on prosecuting the war. While the film is structurally brilliant in its complex montage editing and clear summary of a mountain of assassination data, Stone characteristically weakens his case and renders it less compelling by resting his argument on the entirely speculative and unproved thesis that Kennedy was going to withdraw from Vietnam. As a result, the film occupies a muddy middle ground,

neither a clear fiction, nor a responsible historical document.

Attacked by many media commentators for the conspiracy theories of *JFK,* Stone lashed back with *Natural Born Killers* (1994), an ugly account of two mass murderers whose crime spree is glamorized by the news media and who are portrayed as celebrities by reporters eager to promote the latest scrap of tabloid sensationalism. The film is a mishmash of disjointed, MTV-style technique—flash cuts, off-kilter camera angles, jerky hand-held camerawork, random pans, and other visual manipulations that exist for their own sakes. The film glorifies and embodies what it pretends to attack—the violence and ugliness in modern American society and its promotion via film and television. Stone's film reinforces the very phenomenon it pretends to satirize.

Stone's films are vociferous, cinematically powerful attacks upon what he sees as the power structure in American society. In carrying out this project, he is virtually unique among contemporary American directors who generally prefer box-office returns to social messages. But Stone faces a quandary. American society offers no clear left-wing alternatives to the system he opposes. As a result, he has no effective ideological position from which to speak and criticize and few alternatives to offer. It will be interesting to see, in his future films, how and whether Stone can work through this problem.

conditions of mass market production. Major studio films are designed for consumption by large, heterogeneous audiences composed of diverse groups, communities, and subcultures. To appeal to these diverse groupings, Hollywood often puts, ideologically, a little of this and a little of that into a film. The resulting ideological mix creates a sufficiently ambiguous product calculated to attract as many members of the target audiences as possible while offending as few as possible. Ideological incoherence enables Hollywood films to appeal to viewers' differing ideological orientations.

The Wild Bunch
(Warner Bros., 1969)
The savage violence of *The Wild Bunch* contained a powerful indictment of society. The film viewed society as being hopelessly corrupt, and its outlaw heroes were only slightly less bad than everyone else.
(Museum of Modern Art/Film Stills Archive)

Ideological incoherence and market appeal.   The futuristic social satire, *Total Recall* (1990), portrayed ruthless corporations exploiting workers on a Martian mining colony and using the media back on Earth to camouflage and disguise political reality. Excessive product placements in the film undermined its social satire. *Total Recall* was 1990's product placement champion, the film that featured the most product placements of any produced that year. The anticorporate social satire of *Total Recall* did not coincide with the constant corporate advertising for real products carried on in the film through the product placements. The extensive product placements helped tame the film's anticorporate satire and provided a greater degree of social familiarity and ideological comfort to viewers watching the film's disturbing futuristic world.

In *Rambo III* (1988), which was set in Afghanistan following the Soviet invasion, Rambo's boss, Colonel Trautman (Richard Crenna), is captured by a brutal Soviet officer. Trautman offers him a history lesson, saying, "You know there won't be a victory. Every day your war machines lose ground to a group of poorly armed, poorly equipped freedom fighters. The fact is that you underestimated your competition. If you'd studied your history, you'd know these people have never given up to anyone. They'd rather die than be slaves to an invading army. You can't defeat a people like that. We tried. We already had our Vietnam. Now you're gonna have yours."

This speech is a clear example of an incoherent ideological mix. It offers, surprisingly enough, a leftist analysis of the U.S. role in Vietnam, with the United States as the invading force crushing an indigenous people's desire for freedom. It then places this analysis in the service of Cold War perceptions of the Soviet menace in Afghanistan and employs the political terminology of the Reagan administration (the Afghan rebels as "freedom fighters," a term Reagan used to refer to the soldiers in Nicaragua, funded by the United States, who were opposed to the Nicaraguan revolution).

The resulting mixture of a left-wing analysis of the Vietnam War and right-wing, Cold War, anti-Soviet perceptions produces a conceptual mismash in which the discourse becomes unintelligible and breaks down, even as its content is intended by the filmmakers to attract a diverse audience composed of both liberal and conservative members. Ideological incoherence serves a strategic economic function in the current film industry, enabling films to offer broad-based appeals to diverse and frequently conflicting social groups.

Narrative and Ideology

A final component of ideological film criticism should be noted. This is the close relationship that exists between narrative and ideology. Ideological film critics regard narrative as an especially good vehicle for ideology. A film's narrative traces and explains a series of changes in a situation or a state of affairs, and, by doing so, can embody an ideological *argument*.

Fatal Attraction (1987), for example, tells a story about a happily married stockbroker whose casual adultery produces a nightmare for his family when the woman he is seeing turns out to be a violent psychopath. In telling a story that moves from the allure of casual sex and the excitement of adultery to terror and anxiety and concludes with the death of the villainess and the reunification of the family, *Fatal Attraction* constructs an argument about the importance of family and fidelity and about the violation of trust and love that results from adultery in this framework.

Note, though, that this is an ideological argument, and that all of these categories—family, love, fidelity, adultery—are ones that the film carefully constructs in the course of developing its argument. As such, one can quarrel with some of the definitions. Was it really necessary, for example, to turn the stockbroker's lover into such a monster? In the real world, adultery does not inevitably have such horrific and monstrous consequences. It is essential for the film's ideological argument, though, that these consequences ensue.

Fatal Attraction
(Paramount Pictures, 1987)
Fatal Attraction builds its ideological argument about marriage and family through its narrative about a violent threat to the family of Dan and Beth Gallagher (Michael Douglas and Anne Archer). The film's ideology is conveyed by its narrative.

Strengths of the Ideological Model

Ideological criticism has the great strength of clarifying the multidimensional aspect of film content, especially the way that a given movie may reflect and embody diverse currents of social opinion and belief. Because many films are ideological in an implicit and second-order way, such criticism usefully uncovers otherwise-unnoticed aspects of social meaning. Good ideological criticism prevents viewers from becoming too complacent, too naïve about the way film can display and distort important social and political realities. Ideological criticism keeps viewers vigilant against the egregious screen distortions of important social issues.

Weaknesses of the Ideological Model

The major weakness of ideological criticism occurs when a critic too quickly collapses different levels of meaning, moving too fast from the specificity of the film, the particulars of the characters and their situations, to the extraction of a more abstract and generalized ideological message.

Moving too quickly from the particular and concrete details of a film's characters and story situations to a more abstract social message that a film is said to contain is a common error of ideological analysis. It may be that the ideological argument of *Fatal Attraction* is that sex is bad if it takes place outside of marriage, but the enormously complex concrete details of the film, and the intricacies of its narrative, should not be reduced to such an abstract and blanket statement. Sophisticated ideological analysis maintains a clear separation between these levels.

☐ FEMINIST MODELS

Critics use **feminist film theory** to discover and describe a distinctively female perspective on film, as well as those ways in which the cinema might be found uniquely pleasurable by female viewers. In practice, feminist models of criticism blend elements of psychoanalytic and ideological analysis. The psychoanalytic component is found in attempts to understand the ways cinema arouses the pleasure and desire of its audiences and how this might differ on a gender basis. The ideological component is found in the efforts of feminist criticism to relate the portrayal of women in films to particular social attitudes, assumptions, and practices that may be found in the more general society of which those films are a part.

Elements of Feminist Criticism

Images of Women in Film
Feminist film criticism tends to assume two forms. The first is an analysis and description of how a male-dominated film industry has selectively shaped images of women in films that have been created largely by men. Many feminist critics have discussed the way that visual spectacle and the use of the close-up function in film to present women as essentially visual and erotic objects for the contemplation of an ideal male

Feminist criticism and theory often look at the images of women in mainstream films. Stars such as Marilyn Monroe projected a powerful, and limiting, idea of what a woman should be.

audience. For feminist critics, the extraordinary visual attention given to the bodies of stars such as Marilyn Monroe or Marlene Dietrich turns these performers into erotic objects for a male audience.

Feminist analyses of the portrayal of women focus on narrative strategies as well as specifically visual ones. A feminist analysis of *Fatal Attraction* might concentrate on the fate of the film's nominal villain, Alex (portrayed by Glenn Close). A feminist critic could emphasize the way the film ideologically constructs the character of Alex as a monster, whose outrageous behavior toward the hero's family requires that she undergo an extraordinary amount of suffering and physical punishment to atone for her crimes.

Because the film presents Alex as such a monster, the feminist critic could suggest, quite reasonably, that *Fatal Attraction* regards female sexuality uncontained by the institutions of marriage and family with a great deal of fear, suspicion, and loathing. Alex is an independent, single, aggressive, and sexual woman. In the film, she is ideologically suspect because of these very qualities. By creating and then destroying this monster, the film offers a traditional message about the ideal role of women as wives and mothers rather than as single professionals.

Feminist Filmmaking

The second focus of feminist criticism is closely related to the first. It is the discovery of alternative feminist forms of filmmaking and images of characters. What difference does it make to a film's imagery and narrative if the writer and/or director are female, rather than, as is usually the case, male?

The feminist critic has a fairly wide range of filmmakers and models of filmmaking from which to choose. The critic could examine the work of a director such as Kathryn Bigelow, who specializes in the action genres traditionally associated with male directors. Her films include *Blue Steel* (1990), an urban police thriller, and *Point*

Break (1991), about a string of perfect bank robberies and the FBI agent sent to investigate. Since films such as *Blue Steel* and *Point Break* are genre pictures, the feminist critic would be interested to uncover the minor variations that a director such as Bigelow might create within these standard and traditional formats.

With regard to independent films, a feminist critic could emphasize the important influence of a female director on productions that are not slotted into particular genres or targeted to be large crowd pleasers employing traditional formulas. Two such films are *The Piano* (1993) and *Orlando* (1993).

The Piano.   *The Piano,* written and directed by Jane Campion, stars Holly Hunter (Best Actress Oscar-winner for the role) as a mute, Victorian, unwed mother who travels to New Zealand to fulfill an arranged marriage to an English farmer living there. Ada arrives in New Zealand accompanied by her child and her piano. The film explores her torturous reception as both a woman and an artist. She confronts a culture that is alien to her and that places her into the most restrictive of sex roles, expecting her to be a dutiful wife to a well-meaning but insensitive and brutal husband (played by Sam Neill).

The most telling measure of his insensitivity is his refusal to transport her piano from the beach to their plantation home. Unable to speak or unwilling to do so for reasons that in the film remain mysterious, Ada's only form of communication with the world is her music. Denied this by her husband, who abandons the piano and who later mutilates one of her hands, Ada becomes progressively more alienated from her surroundings, sexually, emotionally, aesthetically. A feminist critic could emphasize the improbability of a male screenwriter or director demonstrating this degree of sensitivity to a woman's psychological and physical plight and such a complex metaphorical understanding of the close relationship between the social position of women and control over the rights to speech, art, and communication.

Orlando.   Sally Potter's *Orlando* (1993) examines the consequences of gender roles and how they affect the way people live their lives. Potter's film is adapted from a Vir-

The Piano
(Miramax, 1993)
In *The Piano*, Holly Hunter portrays Ada, an unmarried mother coping with life in a rustic, remote New Zealand community. Written and directed by a woman, the film emphasizes Ada's viewpoint and treats the narrative's male characters as supporting, rather than lead, players. Frame enlargement.

ginia Woolf story about a young man during the Elizabethan era who lives for over four centuries without aging but who mysteriously changes into a woman. Orlando thus experiences the world from the perspective of each gender. Living as both a man and a woman, Orlando comes to appreciate the uniqueness of each gender's role and how socially conditioned these roles are.

During the 1850s, Orlando has a brief but intense affair with an adventurer. She tells her lover that, if she were a man, she might not choose to die in battle for an uncertain cause, might find the price of death too high for freedom. "Would I then be a real man?" she asks. The lover replies that, were he a woman, he might not choose to live through and sacrifice everything for his children. He might choose instead to travel and go abroad rather than have a family. "Would I then be a real woman?" he asks. The film asks about the basis of male and female identity and tries to uncover a human identity deeper than gender. When Orlando wakes up and discovers that he is now a woman, he looks into the mirror, sees a woman's nude body, and says, "the same person, no difference at all, just a different sex."

The Piano and *Orlando,* though popular, are philosophically and aesthetically distinct from male-directed productions. In the unique terms of their narrative and images, and in the political and philosophical perspectives brought to gender, its social definition and impact on sexuality, speech, and art, each film offers the pleasures of distinctive female voices in cinema. Each film illustrates the importance of alternative female or feminist perspectives in film and forms of filmmaking.

Strengths of the Feminist Model

Feminist criticism has made a major contribution to the understanding of how gender perspectives and gender biases influence film images about the world and the way narratives are organized to emphasize male characters and experiences at the expense of strong female characters. To a large extent, this bias in favor of male experience results from the extraordinary power male filmmakers have long enjoyed relative to the much smaller number of women directors in charge of major productions. Because of this power, men have constructed images of women in films, and, for a feminist, these images necessarily say more about men than about women. Accordingly, feminist criticism emphasizes the importance of women directors getting an artistic voice in the world of cinema as a means of balancing the voices that male directors have long commanded.

Weaknesses of the Feminist Model

Gender is one of the many screens through which human experience is filtered, and, although it has a profound impact on the terms by which people live their lives, it is not the only means for ordering one's experience of the world or organizing the design of films. Sophisticated feminist criticism understands when best to apply accounts emphasizing gender differences and in what degree. The feminist sensibility behind *Orlando* or *The Piano* is more profound and enters more deeply into the design of those films than does the fact that *Blue Steel* or *Point Break* are directed by a woman. In the latter case, the weight of genre and traditional commercial formulas tend to minimize the distinctive contributions that a female director can make. As with all models of criticism, the feminist critic must develop a sensitive understanding of which material will most benefit from her (or his) distinctive tools of analysis.

☐ COGNITIVE MODELS

Cognitive film theory studies the ways viewers perceive and interpret visual and auditory information in film and how specific formal features may cue or invite particular kinds of interpretations. Cognitive film theory focuses on (1) the viewer's perception of visual and auditory information and (2) the ways that viewers organize and categorize these perceptions in order to derive meaning from a film. With its emphasis on perceptually-based interpretation and understanding, cognitive film theory derives many of its principles and assumptions from research in perceptual psychology, computer science, and communications. The cognitive film theorist is not as concerned with an interpretation of the content of a specific film but rather with understanding how viewers process audiovisual information and extract meaning from films in general.

Elements of Cognitive Models

For cognitive film theorists, the interpretation of visual and auditory information by film viewers involves two components: perceptual and interpretive processing. **Perceptual processing** refers to the sensory information that viewers take in. In the case of film, this involves the senses of sight and hearing. Viewers perceive in film an ordered series of images and an organized and carefully designed series of sounds. By controlling audiovisual design, filmmakers impose order upon the sights and sounds of their films. They may use, for example, the codes of continuity editing to build scenes and construct a narrative. One convention of continuity editing is cross-cutting, used to suggest that two or more events are occurring simultaneously.

Understood in terms of perceptual processing, a viewer watching a cross-cut sequence sees a succession of shots flashing by on screen as an alternating series of events. Understood in terms of interpretive processing, the viewer draws an inference from the alternating series of recurring images. That inference is a presumption of simultaneous action, the assumption that the narrative lines presented in the cross-cut sequence are occurring at the same moment of time. **Interpretive processing,** therefore, refers to the way that a viewer organizes sensory information to impose a higher-order level of meaning upon it. Interpretive processing is the cognitive or active interpretational response to sensory information. In the case of cross-cutting, the viewer not merely sees an alternating series of images but imposes a particular meaning upon that series, namely, an inference of simultaneity. The distinction between perceptual and interpretive processing emphasizes the viewer's contribution to the creation of meaning in cinema. These terms highlight the difference between the actual audiovisual information on screen and what a viewer attributes to that information.

Cognitive film theory studies the ways that specific audiovisual designs in cinema communicate information to the viewer who responds with an active interpretation. Another example should help clarify this. A basic code of continuity editing is the eye-

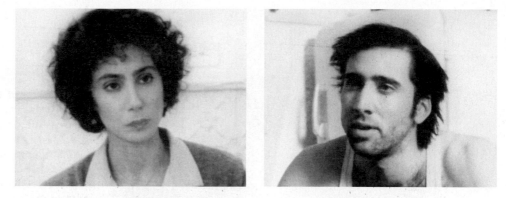

Moonstruck (MGM/United Artists, 1987)
Cognitive theory stresses how viewers perceive and interpret audiovisual information. Viewers give that information a higher-order level of meaning and structure then the images and sounds themselves convey. These two shots from *Moonstruck* illustrate the eyeline match. In terms of perceptual information, all a viewer sees are separate images of Cher and Nicholas Cage looking in different directions. But viewers organize the shots by inferring, across the cut, that the performers are looking at each other. This level of information is not in the images themselves. It is supplied by the viewer. Frame enlargement.

line match. In terms of perceptual processing, a viewer watching a sequence cut using the eyeline match sees a series of close-ups or medium shots of actors oriented so that the directions of their gazes are in complimentary directions—one looks screen left, the other looks screen right. From the interpretive perspective, cinema viewers respond to this editing code by inferring a relation of proximity and communication between the characters. The viewer *infers* that characters presented using the eyeline match are communicating with one another and/or are near each other.

Schemas

Attention to interpretive processing enables cognitive film theorists to examine the ways that a viewer's responses to film are guided by a series of *schemas* or frameworks of interpretation. A fundamental assumption of cognitive film theory is that viewers' responses to film are not strictly sensory driven, that is, they are not entirely explainable as immediate responses to the visual and auditory information contained in the film. Viewers bring to this information a large set of schemas, or frameworks of interpretation, that they have developed through personal experience in the world and as members of given cultures and societies.

By applying schemas to the images and narrative of a film, a viewer is able to process and interpret the information in that film in an efficient and rapid fashion. To viewers familiar with science fiction movies, that is, viewers whose experience in this genre has enabled them to develop an extensive set of interpretational schemas, a bright light on a character's face coupled with an awestruck expression instantly evokes the idea of an alien presence. Viewers familiar with Westerns will have schemas attuned to that genre. They know that a cowboy walking into a saloon will order whiskey, but seated around a campfire will prefer coffee. The more audience

The Silence of the Lambs
(Orion Pictures, 1991)
The cross-dressing villain in *The Silence of the Lambs* breaks cultural rules regarding proper gender behavior. The filmmakers count on this violation of a viewer's culturally influenced schemas to generate strong disgust and condemnation of the character. Frame enlargement.

knowledge a filmmaker can assume, the more efficient is story presentation. Less needs to be explained.

Filmmakers often count on the existence of particular interpretational schemas in their target audience and design their films to exploit these schemas. The gender-bending villain in *The Silence of the Lambs,* who cross-dresses and makes himself up to look like a woman, triggers viewers' cultural schemas regarding the acceptable range of gender displays and sexual behavior. The villain's flagrant violation of conventional schemas regarding proper gender display provokes, as the filmmakers intended, anxiety and disapproval from many audience members.

Why Film Is Comprehensible

In addition to studying the ways that audiences apply schemas to interpret visual and narrative information, cognitive film theory investigates the more general question of what makes film so comprehensible, accessible, and enjoyable to audiences worldwide. The answers provided by cognitive theory emphasize the correspondences that exist between film and a viewer's real-world perceptual and social experience. For the cognitive theorist, film is comprehensible, accessible, and enjoyable to audiences because it builds on an elaborate series of close similarities between the means used to represent a world on screen and the spectator's own familiar habits of perception and social understanding.

The viewer sees a three-dimensional world on the flat surface of the screen because the photographic images reproduce important real-world sources of information about spatial depth, about the location and distribution of objects in space. Just as this information tells viewers where objects are located in the real, three-dimensional world, it provides the same information in the represented reality of a screen world. Second, the codes of continuity editing used to build scenes create a consistent projective geometry within the represented three-dimensional world on screen that is analogous to the viewer's own visual and physical experience. Through-

Notorious
(RKO, 1946)
The three-dimensional information contained in this shot from Hitchcock's *Notorious* includes the relative sizes of the men, the converging parallel lines on the floor, and the diminishing size and spacing of the floor tiles. These cues establish the illusion of depth and distance in the image. Frame enlargement.

out a scene edited on continuity principles, the screen coordinates of up, down, front, back, right, and left remain constant, regardless of changes in camera position and angle.

Third, continuity editing establishes, for the viewer, easy narrative comprehension because the judicious use of long shot and close-up clarifies important narrative information and emphasizes characters' emotions. Viewers see everything they need to know and are given all the information they need in order to process the narrative. Fourth, in the film image, the viewer reads and understands the significance of characters' facial and gestural expressions, just as the viewer does with real people in daily life. Viewers are extremely good at decoding the meanings expressed on people's faces and through gestures, and they use these skills when watching a movie. Actors are professionals trained to mimic the range of gestural and facial cues significant in their culture to evoke the emotions typically associated with those expressions and gestures.

Pointing to these complex correspondences between the information contained in film images and the viewer's own real-world perceptual habits, cognitive film theorists persuasively explain why films are so easily understood by large numbers of people.

Social Correspondences

A second set of correspondences connects the screen world to viewers' experiential skills and knowledge. Viewers apply to the screen world assumptions and judgments about people and proper role-based behavior derived from social experience. These assumptions coexist with, and are modified by, other assumptions about behavior that the viewer derives from narrative formula and genre. Characters in a horror film behave like viewers expect characters in a horror film to behave, but these behaviors must also correlate with dimensions of human experience the viewer finds credible.

Research involving preschool children and adolescents indicates that a close relationship prevails between a child's developing stock of moral and ethical concepts and his or her abilities to use these concepts to interpret character behavior in movies. Very young children are likely to judge a character as good or bad depending on whether the character looks attractive or ugly. Older children override such appearance stereotyping with more complex evaluations based on the moral or ethical content of the character's behavior.

Person perception, then, is a process that commonly underlies nonfilmic interpersonal and social experience and the inferences and evaluations viewers make about characters in movie narratives. Filmmakers draw from this important source of correspondence in creative ways. The presentation of Hannibal Lecter in *The Silence of the Lambs*, the film's stress on his wit, intelligence, and compassion for the heroine Clarice Starling, as well as his sadistic cruelty, complicates the viewer's desire to establish a stable moral and ethical evaluation of that character.

Strengths of the Cognitive Model

The strengths of cognitive film theory are threefold. First, this model, unlike many of the others, is research based. The assumptions and principles of the theory are supported by empirical data that enable the theorist to establish a close connection between the features of films and the experiences of actual viewers. As a result, the assumptions and principles of cognitive theory are directly testable, and, accordingly, they assume a great deal of explanatory power.

Second, because of its empirical dimension, cognitive theory provides a strong foundation for understanding how viewers make sense of film images and narratives. Rather than relying on the development of a critical interpretation that may or may not be applicable to real viewers, the cognitive theorist studies the perceptions and interpretations of actual viewers and is able to clarify the bases that make film an intelligible medium for its audience.

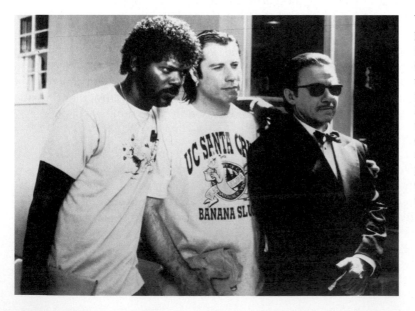

Pulp Fiction
(Miramax, 1994)
Cognitive theory helps explain why and how viewers readily understand cinema, but it is limited in its ability to explore the emotional appeals of cinema. Fans of *Pulp Fiction* respond emotionally to its pleasures and in ways that cognitive theory cannot fully explain.

Third, by providing explanations for the intelligibility of motion pictures, cognitive film theory provides an understanding of why the cinema has become so popular across cultures. Cinema provides viewers with an easily understood spectacle, and this helps ensure its enormous popularity throughout the world. If the motion picture medium was difficult to understand, it never would have become so popular.

Weaknesses of the Cognitive Model

The primary weakness of cognitive film theory is its relative lack of attention to the emotional components of the viewer's experience. Cognitive film theory is extremely good at analyzing how viewers perceive and interpret audiovisual cues in film narratives, but it has not proved as good at analyzing the complexities of a viewer's emotional responses. Interest in cognitive theory by film scholars, however, is a recent phenomenon, and it may be that cognitive theory will yet have something to contribute in this area. At present, however, psychoanalytic models have more to say about the emotional components of film viewing.

A second weakness of cognitive theory should also be noted. It has relatively little to say about the transformative functions of cinema, the way films go beyond and imaginatively transform the boundaries of the viewer's experience. Films are not mere copies or mirrors of that experience, but they reorganize and reconfigure it in complex ways. Moreover, the determinants of meaning in film are manifold. How a filmmaker manipulates structure, what a viewer brings to a film, and the visual and narrative traditions and genres in which a given film is located—all these are part of the elaborate mixture that produces meaning in film. Like all of the models of film theory, cognitive theory answers some questions and ignores others. The theorist must know when best to apply it and how.

SUMMARY

Because cinema is such a rich and powerful medium of communication, because it affects viewers' lives and the way they think about the world in so many ways, it is important to reach an understanding of what the medium itself *is*, independently of its existence in any given film. Film theories are systematic attempts to think about and explain the nature of cinema, how it works as a medium and how it embodies meaning for viewers.

Because the cinema is multidimensional, no one theory has all the answers. Each theory is best suited to answering certain kinds of questions. Realist theory emphasizes the cinema's recording and documenting functions and the ability of filmmakers to use photographic images and naturalistic sounds to capture social realities existing before the camera. Theories of realism tend to define a threshold beyond which the cinema's transformation of social realities is regarded as fictitious, duplicitous, stylized, or distorted. To this extent, realist theories stress the ethical contract that exists between filmmaker and audience.

Realist models try to establish difficult distinctions between the cinema's recording and documenting functions and its transformative abilities. It is often difficult, though, to know where these distinctions lie. Every camera position implies a viewpoint, and some degree of stylistic transformation of the raw material before the camera is inevitable. It is the job of realist theories to say how much transformation is too much.

Auteur theory stresses the human qualities of cinema and emphasizes that mechanically produced sights and sounds can be organized by artists into an aesthetically satisfying design. Auteurism insists that this mechanical, twentieth-century medium is capable, in the right hands, of producing art.

Psychoanalytic theory emphasizes the enormous potential of cinema to provoke emotional responses in its viewers that may be unconscious, primitive, nonrational, and even contrary to the behaviors polite society demands. Psychoanalytic theory is drawn to explain the highly charged poetic and emotional power of certain images and why they seem to exert such a hold over viewers.

As a medium seen by millions, cinema inevitably has a social impact, and its images and stories construct politically and socially charged views of the world. Ideological film theory uncovers the often subtle terms by which cinema codes its views of reality and, by revealing them, can give viewers control over them.

Feminist film theory reveals the gender biases long at work inside the views of social reality offered by films made by men within an industry where power is still largely wielded by men. Images of women in film have been defined by male filmmakers, and feminist theory looks for the alternative artistic and social voices of female filmmakers. Feminist film theory reminds viewers that gender is one of the most powerful screens through which film images and stories pass and that male filmmakers may tend to organize those images and stories differently than female filmmakers do.

Cognitive theories try to provide answers to some of the most basic questions about cinema. Why is it intelligible to viewers? Why are many films so easily understood? How can a filmmaker facilitate an audience's understanding of shots, scenes, and stories? How do viewers base their interpretations of films on analogies with their own perceptual and social experience? Cognitive theory points to the ways in which cinema works as a medium of communication.

All of these theoretical models are important because motion pictures are never just one thing. Films offer portraits of the world that can seem realistic but that code and transform sociopolitical content into an emotionally powerful experience. Each theory provides a different point of entry for analyzing a film's design and its effects on viewers.

Film viewers should always keep in mind the extraordinary richness of the motion picture medium. It is what makes cinema such a challenging medium to study and one that is so powerful to experience. Hopefully, these chapters indicate something of that richness. Equipped with this knowledge, you can embark on an exciting journey. A world of cinema—films from different decades, countries, and genres—awaits exploration. Let intelligence and curiosity be your guides, and enjoy an incredible diversity of film experiences. It is easy to love the cinema. It gives so much back in return.

SUGGESTED READINGS

Dudley Andrew, *The Major Film Theories* (New York: Oxford University Press, 1976).
Andre Bazin, *What Is Cinema?*, 2 vols., ed. and trans. Hugh Gray (Berkeley and Los Angeles: University of California Press, 1971).

David Bordwell and Noel Carroll, ed., *Post-Theory: Reconstructing Film Studies* (Madison: University of Wisconsin Press, 1996).

Diane Carson, Linda Dittmar, and Janice Welsch, eds., *Multiple Voices in Feminist Film Criticism* (Minneapolis, MN: University of Minnesota Press, 1994).

Molly Haskell, *From Reverence to Rape: The Treatment of Women in the Movies* (New York: Holt, Rinehart, and Winston, 1974).

E. Ann Kaplan, ed., *Psychoanalysis and Cinema* (New York: Routledge, 1990).

Annette Kuhn, *Women's Pictures: Feminism and Cinema* (London: Routledge and Kegan Paul, 1982).

Gerald Mast, Marshall Cohen, and Leo Braudy, eds., *Film Theory and Criticism: Introductory Readings,* fourth edition (New York: Oxford University Press, 1991).

Stephen Prince, *Visions of Empire: Political Imagery in Contemporary American Film* (New York: Praeger, 1992).

Glossary

Additive Color Mixing   System used for creating color on television where red, blue, and green lights are mixed together to create all other hues.

Aerial Perspective   Visual depth cue in which the effects of the atmosphere make very distant objects appear bluish and hazy.

Ambient Sound   Background sound characteristic of an environment or location. For a film like *The Last of the Mohicans,* set in a forest, ambient sounds include the rustle of branches and the cries of distant birds.

Ancillary Market   All nontheatrical markets from which a film distributor derives revenue. These include home video, cable television, and foreign markets.

Angle of View   Designates the amount of area recorded by a given lens. Telephoto lenses have a much smaller angle of view than wide-angle lenses.

Antinarrative   A narrative style that tends, paradoxically, toward eliminating narrative by employing lots of digression, avoiding a clear hierarchy of narrative events, and by suppressing the causal connections among events.

Aspect Ratio   Term designating the dimensions of the film frame or screen image. Aspect ratio is typically expressed in units of width to height.

Associational Montage   A style of editing that draws an explicit comparison between two or more images, as when Charles Chaplin compares workers and sheep in a pair of shots at the beginning of *Modern Times.*

Attributional Errors   Mistakes of interpretation arising when a critic erroneously decides that some

effect in a film has a meaning expressly intended by its creators or incorrectly assigns the creative responsibility for an effect to the wrong member of the production crew. Uncovering these errors typically requires documentation of a film's production history.

Auteur   A director whose work is characterized by a distinctive audiovisual design and recurring set of thematic issues. Auteurism is a model of film theory and criticism which searches for film authors or auteurs.

Auteurist Film Theory   A model of film theory that studies the work of a film auteur, or author. Directors are generally considered to be the prime auteurs in cinema. Auteurist theory studies the films of a cinema auteur as works of personal expression.

Back Light   Light illuminating the space between performers and the rear wall of a set. Along with key and fill lights, back light is one of the three principle sources of illumination in a scene.

Beta Movement   Designates a perceptual illusion in which the human eye responds to apparent movement as if it were real. Because of this illusion, viewers think they see real motion on a film or television screen when true movement does not actually occur.

Blockbuster   A hugely profitable film usually featuring a fantasy theme and a narrative heavily dependent on special effects.

Boom (or Crane) Shot   A type of moving camera shot in which the camera moves up or down through space. Also known as a crane shot, it takes its name from the apparatus—boom or crane—on which the camera is mounted.

Camera Position   The distance between the camera and the subject it is photographing. Camera positions are usually classified as variations of three basic set-ups: the long shot, the medium shot, and the close-up.

Canted Angle   A camera angle in which the camera itself leans toward screen right or screen left producing an imbalanced, off-center look to the image. Filmmakers often use canted angles to capture a character's subjective feelings of stress or disorientation.

Character Star   A star who plays different character personalities from film to film. Meryl Streep and Robert De Niro are character stars.

Cinematic Self-Reflexivity   A basic mode of screen reality in which the filmmaker establishes a self-referential audiovisual design. A self-reflexive film calls attention to its own artificially constructed nature.

Cinematography   The planning and execution of light and color design, camera position, and angle by the cinematographer in collaboration with the director.

Close-Up   One of the basic camera positions. The camera is set up in close proximity to an actor's face or other significant dramatic object which fills the frame. Close-ups tend to isolate objects or faces from their immediate surrounds.

Cognitive Film Theory   A model of film theory which examines how the viewer perceptually processes audiovisual information in cinema and cognitively interprets this information.

Composition   The arrangement of characters and objects within the frame. Through composition filmmakers arrange the visual space on screen into an artistic design.

Continuity Editing   As its name implies, continuity editing maximizes principles of continuity from shot to shot so that the action seems to flow smoothly across shot and scene transitions. Continuity editing facilitates narrative comprehension by the viewer.

Contrast   The differences of light intensity across a scene. A high-contrast scene features brightly illuminated and deeply shadowed areas.

Convention   A familiar, customary way of representing characters, story situations, or images. Conventions result from agreements between filmmakers and viewers to accept certain representations as valid.

Costumes   The clothing worn by performers in a film. Costumes help establish locale and period as well as a given film's color design.

Coverage   Shots an editor uses to bridge continuity problems in the editing of a scene. By cutting to coverage, rather than relying on the master shot, an editor can finesse many problems of scene construction and can help visually shape acting performances.

Criticism   The activity of searching for meaning in an artwork. The critic seeks to develop an original interpretation by uncovering novel meanings inside a film.

Cross-Cutting   Method of editing used to establish simultaneous, ongoing lines of action in a film narrative. By rapidly cutting back and forth between two or more lines of action, the editor establishes that they are happening simultaneously. By decreasing the length of the shots, editors can accelerate the pace of the editing and imply an approaching climax.

Cue Sheet   A break-down of a scene's action listing and timing all sections requiring musical cues.

Cut   Type of visual transition created in editing in which one shot is instantaneously replaced on screen by another. Because the change is instantaneous, the cut itself is invisible. The viewer sees only the change from one shot to the next.

Deduction   The method by which the critic works, using the general goals of the criticism to guide the search for supporting evidence.

Deep-Focus Cinematography   A style of cinematography which establishes great depth of field within shots. Gregg Toland's cinematography for Orson Welles' *Citizen Kane* is a classic example of deep-focus composition.

Depth of Field   The area of distance or separation between sharply focused foreground and background objects. Depth of field is determined by the focal length of a lens. Wide-angle lenses produce deep focus or great depth of field, whereas telephoto lenses have a shallow depth of field.

Description   A stage in creating criticism wherein the critic fully describes those relevant features of narrative or audiovisual design on which the critical interpretation will be based.

Design Concept   The underlying creative concept that organizes the way in which sets and costumes are built, dressed, and photographed on a given production.

Deviant Plot Structure   A narrative whose design and organization fails to conform with viewers' expectations regarding what is proper or permissible.

Dialogue Cutting Point   The place in a passage of spoken dialogue where an image or sound edit occurs.

Digressive Subplots   Elements in the narrative in which the viewer's attention is distracted from the main chain of events to focus on a minor character or secondary episode. Digressive subplots add texture and atmosphere to the story.

Direct Sound   Authentic sound which is captured and recorded directly on location. Direct sound also designates an absence of reflected components in the final recording.

Director   Member of the production crew who works closely with the cinematographer, editor, production designer, and sound designer to determine a film's organizing, creative structure. The director is generally the key member of the production team controlling and synthesizing the contributions of other team members. On budgetary issues, however, the director is answerable to the producer who has the highest administrative authority on a production.

Dissolve   A type of visual transition between shots or scenes created by the editor. Unlike the cut, the dissolve is a gradual screen transition with distinct optical characteristics. The editor overlaps the end of one shot with the beginning of the next shot to produce a brief superimposition.

Diversification   A corporate structure in which a company conducts business operations across a range of associated markets and product categories.

Documentary   A type of film dealing with a person, situation, or state of affairs that exists independently of the film. Documentaries can include a poetic, stylized audiovisual design, but they typically exclude the use of overt fictional elements.

Documentary Realism   A subcategory of the realist mode of screen reality. The documentary realist filmmaker employs the camera as a recording instrument to capture events or situations that are transpiring independently of the filmmaker. Documentary realism is also a stylistic construction because the filmmaker's audiovisual design imposes a stylistic organization upon the event unfolding before the camera.

Dolly   Type of moveable platform on which the camera is placed to execute a tracking shot. Tracking shots are sometimes called dollies or dolly shots.

Editing   The work of joining together shots to assemble the finished film. Editors select the best shots from the large amount of footage the director and cinematographer have provided and assemble these in the proper narrative order.

Editor   Member of the production crew who, in consultation with the director, designs the order and arrangement of shots as they will appear in the finished film and splices them together to create the final cut.

Emulsion   The light-sensitive surface of the film. Light sensitivity varies among film stocks. Fast films feature emulsions that are highly light sensitive, requiring very little light for a good exposure. Slow films feature emulsions that are less light sensitive, requiring more light on the scene or set for proper exposure.

Errors of Continuity   Disruptions in the appropriate flow of action or in the proper relation of camera perspectives from shot to shot. These errors may include the failure to match action across shots or to maintain consistent screen direction.

Establishing Shot   A type of long shot used to establish the setting or location of a scene. In classical continuity editing, establishing shots occur at the beginning of a scene and help contextualize subsequent close-ups and other partial views of the action.

Explicit Causality   The tight chaining of narrative events into a strong causal sequence in which early events directly and clearly cause subsequent events. Characteristic of Hollywood filmmaking.

Expressionism   A basic mode of screen reality in which filmmakers impose explicit audiovisual distortions on image and soundtrack to express extreme or aberrant emotions or perceptions.

Extras   Incidental characters in a film, often part of the background of a shot or scene.

Explicit Causality   Plot structure in which an event follows another as links in a chain. This causes characters to act in goal-directed ways.

Eyeline Match   Matching of eyelines between two or more characters, engaged in conversation or looking at each other in a scene, to establish relations of proximity and continuity. The directions in which the performers look from shot to shot are complimentary. That is, if performer A looks screen right in the first shot, performer B will look screen left in the next shot.

Fade A visual transition between shots or scenes created by the editor. Unlike the cut, the fade creates a gradual transition with distinct visual characteristics. A fade is visible on screen as a brief interval with no picture. The editor fades one shot to black and then, after a pause, fades in the next shot. Editors often use fades to indicate a substantial change of time or place in the narrative.

Fall-Off The area in a shot where light falls off into shadow. Fast fall-off occurs in a high-contrast image where the rate of change between the illuminated and shadowed areas is very quick.

Familiar Object Size A visual depth cue in which the viewer interprets the size of familiar objects as an indication of their distance.

Fantasy A basic mode of screen reality in which settings and subjects, characters and narrative time are far removed from the conditions of the viewer's ordinary life. Fantasy characters may have superpowers or advanced technology that lends them extraordinary abilities.

Feature Film A film typically running between 90 and 120 minutes.

Feminist Film Theory A model of film theory which examines the images of women in films created by men and the ways in which female directors represent women. Feminist theory examines the impact of gender on cinematic representation.

Fictional Documentary Realism The style of a fiction film employing the techniques of documentary realism to create the illusion that it is a documentary. The appearance of documentary realism is entirely fictionalized.

Fill Light Light placed opposite key light and used to soften shadows it casts. Along with key and back lights, fill light is one of the three principle sources of illumination in a scene.

Film Noir Term designating a cycle of crime and detective films popular in the American cinema of the 1940s. Low key lighting was the major stylistic characteristic of this cycle.

Final Cut The finished edit of a film. The form in which a film is released to and seen by audiences.

Flashing Technique used to de-saturate color and contrast from a shot and to create a misty, slightly hazy effect. Film stock is flashed by exposing it to a small amount of light prior to developing.

Flicker Fusion Along with persistence of vision and beta movement, this is one of the perceptual foundations on which the illusion of cinema rests. Because of the speed at which they are projected, the human eye cannot distinguish the individual still frames of a motion picture. Their rapid projection creates flicker fusion, the viewer's inability to perceive the pulsing flashes of light emitted by the projector. These flashes and the still pictures they illuminate blend together into the illusion of movement.

Focal Length The distance between the optical center of the lens and the film inside the camera. Lenses of different focal lengths will "see" the action in front of the camera very differently. See Wide-Angle, Telephoto, Normal, and Zoom Lenses.

Foley Technique The creation of sound effects by live performance in a sound recording studio. Foley performers enact sound effects in sync with a scene's action.

Forced Perspective A visual technique used to simulate great distances in matte paintings or miniature models. The convergence of parallel lines is accelerated in the represented rear portions of a matte or miniature. This enables the special effects artist to suggest great distances on a small scale.

Frame The borders of a projected image or the individual still photograph on a strip of film. Frame dimensions are measured by aspect ratio.

Framework of Interpretation The intellectual, social, or cultural frames of reference that a critic applies to a film in order to create a novel interpretation. It is the general intellectual framework within which an interpretation is produced.

General-Interest Journal-Based Criticism A mode of criticism that falls between newspaper/television reviews and the highly technical, scholarly criticism. In this mode, the critic can offer a more detailed and sophisticated discussion of a film's structure and meanings than can newspaper/television reviewers.

Genre   A type or category of film such as a Western, musical, gangster film, or horror film that follow a set of visual and narrative patterns that are unique within the genre.

Gradients of Density   Visual depth cue in which the textural density of an object increases as it becomes more distant from the viewer.

Gray Scale   A scale used for black and white cinematography which measures color intensity or brightness. Black and white film and the black and white video camera can differentiate colors only if they vary in degrees of brightness. The gray scale tells filmmakers which colors will separate naturally in black and white.

Gross   The total box-office revenue generated by a film before expenses are deducted.

Hard Light   Light which is not scattered or diffused by filters or reflecting screens. Hard light can establish high contrast.

High Angle   Camera angle usually above the eye level of performers in a scene.

High Key Lighting   A lighting design which minimizes contrast and fall-off by creating a bright, even level of illumination throughout a scene.

Historical Realism   A sub-category of the realist mode of screen reality. Historical realist films aim to recreate in close detail the manners, mores, settings, and costumes of a distant historical period.

Homage   A reference in a film to another film or filmmaker. The climatic gun battle on the train station steps in Brian DePalma's *The Untouchables* (1987) is an homage to Sergei Eisenstein's *The Battleship Potemkin* (1925) which features the famous massacre on the Odessa steps.

Hue   One of the basic attributes of color. Hue designates the color itself. Red, blue, and green are primary hues. They are not mixtures of any other color.

Identification   A stage in creating criticism wherein the critic selectively identifies those aspects of the film relevant for the critical argument being developed. Selective identification enables the critic to simplify and reduce the wealth of material in the film that he or she confronts.

Ideological Film Theory   A model of film theory which examines the representation of social and political issues in film.

Ideology   A system of social or political beliefs characteristic of a society or social community. Ideological film theory examines the ways in which films represent and express various ideologies.

Implicit Causality   The loose sequencing of narrative events. Narrative causality is minimized, and the viewer's sense of the direction in which the story is moving is weaker than it is in films that feature explicit causality.

Implied Author   The artistic perspective implied and embodied by a film's overall audiovisual design.

Integration   The ability of corporate film producers to generate revenue across a wide variety of media and markets. Some products include toys, games, and clothing.

Intensity   A basic attribute of color. Intensity measures the brightness of a hue.

Internal Structural Time   The dynamic tempo of a film, established by its internal structure (camera positions, editing, color and lighting design, soundtrack). Perceiving this internal tempo, viewers label films as fast or slow moving, yet internal structural time never unfolds at a constant rate. It is a dynamic rhythm. Filmmakers vary the tempo of internal structural time to maintain viewer interest.

Interpretation   The goal of criticism. By examining a film's structure and implied meanings, a critic assigns meaning to a scene or film that it does not immediately denote.

Interpretive Processing   The viewer's attribution of meaning to audiovisual information, as distinct from perceptual processing which is the purely perceptual response to this information. Film viewing involves both components. Understood in terms of perceptual processing, a viewer watching a cross-cut sequence sees a succession of shots flashing by on screen as an alternating series. Via interpretive processing, the viewer attributes a representation of simultaneous action to the alternating series. This attribution is not a meaning contained within the images themselves. It is the viewer's contribution.

Interpretive Reorganization   The critic's reshaping of a film's narrative and images to draw out implicit meanings. By strategically emphasizing selected details, criticism reorganizes a film's design so as to establish a new interpretation.

Iris   A type of optical transition between shots or scenes created by the editor. Irises are no longer used in contemporary films but were extremely common during the silent era. An iris was visible on screen as a circular pattern closing down over or opening in on a shot.

Jump Cut   Method of editing which produces discontinuity by leaving out portions of the action.

Key Light   The main source of illumination in a scene usually directed on the face of the performer. Along with fill and back lights, it is one of the three principal sources of illumination in a scene.

Latent Meaning   Meanings that are indirect or implied by a film's narrative and audiovisual design. They are not direct, immediately obvious or explicit.

Leitmotif   A recurring musical passage used to characterize a scene, character, or situation in a film narrative.

Letterbox   Method of formatting wide-screen motion pictures for video release. Frame bars mask the top and bottom of the television monitor, producing a wider-ratio picture area in the center of the screen. While the video image's aspect ratio on the television monitor closely matches the original theatrical aspect ratio, the trade-off is a small and extremely narrow image.

Linear Perspective   A visual depth cue in which parallel lines seem to converge as they recede into the distance.

Long Shot   One of the basic camera positions. Designates a camera set-up that is distant from the subject of the shot. Filmmakers usually use this shot to stress environment or setting.

Long Take   A shot of long duration, as distinct from a long shot which designates a camera position.

Low Angle   Camera angle usually below the eye level of performers in a scene.

Low-Key Lighting   A lighting design which maximizes contrast and fall-off by lighting only selected areas of the scene for proper exposure and leaving all other areas under-exposed.

Master Shot   A camera position used by filmmakers to record the entire action of a scene from beginning to end. Filmmakers then re-create portions of the scene for close-ups and medium shots. Editors cut these into the master shot to create the changing optical viewpoints of an edited scene. When used to establish the overall layout of a scene or location, the master shot can also double as an establishing shot.

Matched Cut   A cut joining two shots whose compositional elements strongly match. Matched cutting establishes strong continuity of action.

Matte   A painted landscape or location which is composited into the live action components of a shot. Mattes were traditionally done as paintings on glass, but many contemporary films use digital mattes created on a computer.

Medium Shot   One of the basic camera positions. Designates a camera set-up ranging from full to half-figure shots of the performer.

Melodrama   The predominant dramatic style of popular cinema, emphasizing clear moral distinctions between hero and villain, exaggerated emotions, and a narrative style in which the twists and turns of the plot determine character behavior.

Method Acting   An approach to screen performance in which the actor seeks to portray a character by using personal experience and emotion as a foundation for the portrayal.

Miniature   A small-scale model representing a portion of a much larger location or building.

Mise-en-scene   All of the elements placed before the camera to help create a film's total visual design. These elements principally include cinematography, production design, and performance style.

Montage   Used loosely, montage simply means editing. In a strict sense, however, montage designates scenes whose emotional impact and visual design are achieved primarily through the editing of many brief shots. The shower scene from Hitchcock's *Psycho* is a classic example of montage editing.

Motion Parallax   Also known as motion perspective. Changes in the apparent positioning and/or speed of near and distant objects as the viewer or the camera moves through space.

Motion Perspective   The change in visual perspective produced by the camera's movement through space. The visual positions of objects undergo systematic changes as the camera moves in relation to them. Camera movement will produce motion perspective but a zoom shot will not.

Narrative Causality   A basic principle of plot construction. A plot is not a random collection of events. Causality is the glue that holds the various events and episodes in the story together. One event causes another, subsequent event. Causality may be either explicit or implicit.

Neorealism   Filmmaking style that developed in postwar Italian cinema. The neorealist director aimed to truthfully portray Italian social reality by avoiding the gloss and glitter of expensive studio productions, emphasizing instead location filmmaking, a mixture of non- and semiprofessional actors, and simple, straightforward visual technique.

New Wave   A new stylistic direction or design appearing within a national cinema in the films of a group of (usually young) directors who are impatient with existing styles and are very intent on creating alternatives.

Newspaper Review   Mode of film criticism aimed at a general audience and that performs an explicit consumer function, telling readers whether or not they should see the film under review. Film reviews presented as part of a television news or review program also belong to this mode.

Nonsynchronous Sound   Sound which is not connected to a source visible on screen.

Normal Lens   A lens of moderate focal length which does not distort object size and depth of field. The normal lens records perspective much as the human eye does.

Off-Screen Sound (space)   A type of nonsynchronous sound in which the sound-producing source remains off-screen. Off-screen sound extends the viewer's perception of a represented screen location into an indefinite area of off-screen space.

180-Degree Rule   The foundation for establishing continuity of screen direction. The left and right coordinates of screen action remain consistent as long as all camera positions stay on the same side of the line of action. Crossing the line entails a change of screen direction.

Open Narrative   A narrative that is not brought to a definite conclusion but suggests, instead, events that are ongoing and extend beyond the end point of the film.

Ordinary Fictional Realism   A subcategory of the realist mode of screen reality. Ordinary fictional realist films feature a naturalistic visual design, a linear narrative, and plausible character behavior as the basis for establishing a realist style.

Overlap   A visual depth cue in which near objects, along the same line of sight, will occlude or block more distant objects.

Pan   Type of camera movement in which the camera pivots from side to side on a fixed tripod or base. Pans produce lateral optical movement on screen and are often used to follow the action of a scene or to anticipate the movements of performers.

Pan-and-Scan   Method of formatting wide-screen motion pictures for video release. Only a portion of the original wide-screen image is transferred to video. A full-size image appears on the video monitor, but it represents only a portion of the original wide-screen frame.

Parallel Action   Loosely designates the use of editing to establish multiple, ongoing plot lines and simultaneous lines of action. Editors generally use the technique of cross-cutting to establish parallel action.

Perceptual Processing   The film viewer's perceptual response to audiovisual information, as distinct from interpretive processing which is the active interpretation of that information. Film viewing involves both components. The viewer sees color, depth, and movement (perceptual processing) in cinema and may attribute particular meanings to those perceptions (interpretive processing). Understood in terms of perceptual processing, a viewer watching a cross-cut sequence sees a succession of shots flashing by on screen as an alternating series. Via interpretive processing, the viewer attributes a representation of simultaneous action to the alternating series. This attribution is not a meaning contained within the images themselves. It is the viewer's contribution.

Perceptual Realism   The ability of picture and sound in cinema to correspond with the ways viewers perceive space and sound in the real, three-dimensional world.

Performance Style   The actor's contribution to the audiovisual and narrative design of a film.

Persistence of Vision   Characteristic of the human eye in which the retina briefly retains the impression of an image after its source has been removed. Because of persistence of vision, viewers do not see the alternating periods of light and dark through which they sit in a theater auditorium.

Personality Star   A star such as John Wayne or Julia Roberts who tends to play the same personality type from film to film.

Phi Phenomena   Term that designates the many different conditions under which the human eye can be fooled into seeing the illusion of movement where no true movement exists. Beta movement is one of the phi phenomena.

Pictorial Lighting Design   A lighting design which does not aim to simulate the effects of an on-screen light source. Instead, the design moves in a purely pictorial direction to create mood and atmosphere.

Pixel   With reference to computer-generated effects, a pixel is the smallest unit of a picture capable of being digitally manipulated. The sharpness or resolution of an image is a function of the number of pixels it contains. High-end computer monitors, used in sophisticated film effects work, may have 2,000 pixels per screen line.

Plot   The order and arrangement of story events as they appear in a given film.

Point of View   The perspective from which narrative events are related. Point of view in cinema is typically a disembodied third-person perspective, although filmmakers routinely manipulate audiovisual design to suggest what individual characters are thinking or feeling. Point of view in cinema can assume a first-person perspective through the use of voice-over narration or subjective shots in which the camera views a scene as if through the eyes of a character.

Polyvalence   The attribute of having more than one meaning. Motion pictures are polyvalent because they possess multiple layers of meaning.

Post-dubbing   Practice of recording sound effects and dialogue after principal filming has been completed. In the case of post-dubbing dialogue, the technical challenge is to closely match the re-recorded dialogue with the performer's lip movements in the shot.

Practical (light)   A light source visible on a set and used for exposure.

Primary Color   A hue which is pure and which is not produced by mixing together combinations of any other hues.

Producer   Production administrator who hires a director and supervises a film's production to ensure that it comes in under budget and on schedule.

While directors work under a producer, in practice producers generally allow directors considerable creative freedom.

Product Placement   The appearance of products on screen as part of a film scene. These appearances are advertisements for which the merchandiser pays a fee to a product placement agency. Film production companies derive revenue from these fees.

Product Tie-Ins   Products marketed in conjunction with the release of a blockbuster film. For example, a *Jurassic Park* video game. These products often bear the logo or likeness of characters in the movie.

Production Design   The planning and creation of sets, costumes, mattes, and miniatures according to an overall concept designed by the production designer in collaboration with the director.

Production Values   Those elements of the film that show the money invested in its production. These typically include set designs, costumes, locations, and special effects.

Psychoanalytic Film Theory   A model of film theory which examines the unconscious, sometimes irrational, emotional and psychological relationship between viewers and films or between characters within films.

Rack Focusing   Changing focus within a shot as required by camera or character movement.

Real Author   The actual flesh-and-blood author of a film, as distinct from the implied author which is the artistic perspective implied and embodied by a film's overall audiovisual design.

Realism   A basic mode of screen reality. Ordinary fictional realism, historical realism, and documentary realism are subcategories of the realist mode.

Realistic Lighting Design   A lighting design which simulates the effects of a light source visible on screen.

Realistic Sound   Sound on screen which authentically captures the properties of its source. In practice this is a very elastic concept because many sounds which may seem to the viewer to be realistic are, in fact, highly artificial and may feature separately-recorded components layered overtop one another.

Realist Film Theory   A model of film theory that seeks to explain how filmmakers may capture, with minimal distortion, the essential features of real-world situations and events, or, in the case of fictionalized events, give them the appearance of real-world status.

Rear Projection   Technique for simulating location cinematography by projecting photographic images of a landscape onto and from behind a screen. Actors are photographed standing in front of the screen as if they were part of the represented location.

Reflected Sound   Sound which is reflected off surfaces in a physical environment before being captured by the microphone. By manipulating characteristics of sound reflection, sound designers can capture the physical attributes of an environment.

Rhetoric   The use of language to persuade and influence others. Film criticism is a rhetorical activity.

Room Tone   A type of ambient sound characterizing the acoustical properties of a room. Even an empty room will emit room tone.

Rough Cut   The film editor's initial assembly of shots in a scene or film before tightening, polishing, and perfecting the editing.

Running Time   The amount of real time it takes a viewer to watch a film from beginning to end. Most commercial films run between 90 and 120 minutes.

Saturation   A basic characteristic of color. Saturation measures color strength. Saturation is a function of how much white light is mixed into the color. The more white light that is present, the less saturated the color will seem to be.

Schema   A framework of perception or interpretation used by viewers to organize visual and narrative information. Through the use of establishing shots, continuity editing helps viewers create schemas to assist in the visual interpretation of represented screen events.

Scholarly Criticism   A mode of criticism aimed at a specialized audience of scholars, employing a technical, demanding vocabulary, and exploring the significance of given films in relation to issues of theory or film history.

Screen Reality   The represented reality depicted by a fictional film. Screen reality is established by the principles of time, space, character behavior, and audiovisual design as these are organized in a given film.

Selection and Omission of Detail   A basic principle of plot construction. As a plot is constructed, some events are deliberately included while others are deliberately left out and may only be implied.

Sequence Shot   A long take whose duration extends for an entire scene or sequence. Such a scene or sequence is accordingly composed of only one shot and features no editing.

Sets   The controlled physical environment in which filming occurs. Sets may be created by blocking and lighting an area of ground outdoors or by building and designing a physical environment indoors.

Shading   Visual depth cue in which gradations and patterns of light and shadow reveal texture and volume in a three-dimensional world and can be used to create a 3D impression on a flat theater or television screen.

Shot   The basic unit of film structure, corresponding to the amount of footage exposed in the camera from the time it is turned on until it is turned off. Shots are visible on screen as the intervals between cuts, fades, or dissolves.

Shot-Reverse-Shot Cutting   A type of continuity editing generally used for conversation scenes. The cutting alternates between opposing over-the-shoulder camera set-ups showing each character speaking in turn.

Shutter   Device inside the camera which regulates the light reaching the film. It is like an on/off switch inside the projector that regulates the light reaching the screen to produce beta movement and critical fusion frequency.

Sign   In communication theory, that which embodies or expresses meaning.

Soft Light   Light which is diffused or scattered by filters or reflecting screens. Soft light creates a low-contrast image.

Sound Bridge   Sound used to connect, or bridge, two or more shots. Sound bridges establish continuity of place, action, or time.

Sound Design (Designer)   The expressive use of sound throughout film in relation to its images and the contents of its narrative. Working in conjunction with the director, the sound designer supervises the work of other sound personnel.

Sound Hierarchy   The relative priority given to dialogue, effects, and music in a given scene. In most cases, dialogue is considered the most important of these sounds and rests atop the sound hierarchy.

Sound Montage   A type of sound editing in which the audio-environment of a scene is created by mixing together many discreet sound effects and sources.

Sound Perspective   The use of sound to augment visual perspective. Often, but not always, sound perspective correlates with visual perspective. In a long shot reflected sound may prevail, whereas in a close-up direct sound may prevail.

Speech   Dialogue spoken by performers representing characters in a narrative.

Spotting   A collaborative process between the director and composer during which they spot or identify passages in the film that require musical scoring.

Star   The highest profile performer in a film narrative. Stars draw audiences to theaters and establish intense personal relationships with their publics.

Star Persona   The relatively fixed screen personality of a star.

Story   The sequence of events constructed by a narrative film using a plot. The plot arranges story events into a given sequence. A film's plot imposes shape and organization upon its story information. A story is the comprehensive set of events referred to in a film's narrative.

Story Time   The amount of time covered by the narrative. This may vary considerably from film to film. The narrative of *2001: A Space Odyssey* begins during a period of primitive pre-human ancestry and extends into the era of space travel, while the narrative of *High Noon* spans, roughly, ninety minutes, closely approximating that film's running time.

Structure   The audiovisual design of a film. The elements of structure include the camera, lights and color, production design, performance style, editing, sound, and narrative.

Subjective Shot   Also known as a point-of-view shot. The camera's position and angle represent the exact viewpoint of a character in the narrative.

Subtractive Color Mixing   System used to create color in film in which magenta, cyan, and yellow filters are used in the color film strip to produce all other hues.

Supervising Art Director   Head of the art department who oversees all the films in production.

Supporting Player   A performer in a secondary role who does not receive either the billing or the pay of a major star. Many performers establish themselves first as supporting players before emerging as stars.

Surprise   A narrative technique used to jolt or startle the viewer. Creating surprise depends on withholding crucial narrative information from viewers whereas creating suspense depends on providing viewers with necessary information. Showing the audience the bomb under the table before it goes off will create suspense. Not showing the bomb before it goes off will create surprise.

Surrealism   An attempt to access the subconscious and irrational mind by creating art whose content and style is fantastic and dreamlike.

Suspense   A narrative technique used to create tension and anxiety in the film viewer. Creating suspense depends on revealing rather than withholding crucial narrative information. Showing the audience the bomb under the table before it goes off will create suspense. Not showing the bomb before it goes off will create surprise. Unlike suspense, surprise depends on withholding information from the audience.

Synchronous Sound   Sound which is connected to a source visible on screen.

Synthetic Sound   Artificially-designed sound which does not match any existing source. The sounds of the light sabers in the *Star Wars* films are examples of synthetic sound.

Technical Acting   An approach to acting in which the performer thinks through the requisite gestures and emotions and then exhibits them. In contrast to method acting, the technical actor does not look to personal experience as a base for understanding the character.

Telephoto Lens   A lens of long focal length which distorts object size and depth of field. Telephoto lenses magnify the size of distant objects and by doing so compress depth of field and make them appear closer than they are.

Temp Track   A temporary musical track usually derived from an existing film which a director uses early in production to show the composer the type of musical composition he or she wants.

Temporal Ambiguity   An uncertain, indefinite time structure in the narrative of a film. A film like *Hiroshima, Mon Amour* mixes past and present so completely that they are not clearly or easily separable.

Theory A philosophical or aesthetic model which seeks to explain the fundamental characteristics of a medium such as film. Film theory examines questions about the nature of cinema and how it expresses meaning.

Tilt Type of camera movement in which the camera pivots up and down on a fixed tripod or base. Tilts produce vertical movement on screen and are often used to follow action and reveal detail.

Tracking Camera movement in which the camera physically moves parallel to the ground to follow action or to reveal significant narrative information. Tracking shots can be executed by physically pushing the camera along tracks previously mounted on the ground, by attaching the camera to a moving vehicle such as a car, or by using a hand-held steadycam mount, in which case the camera operator runs or walks alongside the action. Tracking shots are sometimes called dolly shots, after the "dolly" or moveable platform on which the camera is sometimes mounted.

Typage The manipulation of a screen character's visual or physical characteristics to suggest psychological or social themes or ideas.

Unit Art Director In the classical Hollywood studio system in the 1930s and 1940s, the unit art director oversaw the creation of sets and costumes for a given production. The unit art director worked under a studio's supervising art director who supervised set and costume design on all of the studio's productions.

Visual Depth Cues Informational sources contained in light that convey information about shape, location, size, distance, speed, and other aspects of the visible three-dimensional world. Because the camera, like the human eye, records these sources of information, photographic images create a powerful impression of three-dimensionality. By manipulating audio-visual design, filmmakers control these depth cues to create the illusion of a 3D world on screen.

Voice The expressive manner in which a narrative is presented. In first-person narratives, voice may be associated with the persona of the narrator. Voice, in cinema, though, is almost always third-person and is conveyed through the elements of audiovisual structure. Voice is usually an attribute of the implied, rather than the real, author.

Voice-Over Narration Dialogue spoken by an off-screen narrator. This narrator may be a character reflecting in voice-over on story events from some later point in the narrative or, as sometimes occurs in documentary films, the narrator may exist independently of characters in the story.

Voyeurism A basic pleasure offered by cinema, derived from looking at the characters and situations on screen.

Wavelength The characteristic of light that corresponds to color. Colors are visible when white light is broken down into component wavelengths.

Wide-Angle Lens Lens of short focal length which distorts object size and depth of field. A wide-angle lens exaggerates depth of field by increasing the size of near objects and minimizing the size of distant objects. Because they can focus on near and far objects, wide-angle lenses possess great depth of field.

Widescreen Ratios Any of a large number of aspect ratios that exceed the nearly-square, 1.33:1 ratio of classical Hollywood film. Widescreen films must be reformatted for video release using methods of letterboxing or panning-and-scanning.

Wipe A type of optical transition between scenes created by the editor. Wipes are rare in contemporary film but were commonly used during the classical Hollywood period of the 1930s and 1940s. A wipe is visible on screen as a bar or line traveling across the frame, "pushing" one shot off and "pulling" the next shot into place.

Zoom Lens A lens capable of shifting from short (wide-angle) to long (telephoto) focal lengths. Using a zoom to change focal lengths within a shot produces the impression of camera movement, making it seem as if the camera is moving closer to or farther from its subject.

Index

A Nous La Liberté, 162
Abyss, The, 77
acting, 85–102
additive color, 47
Adventures of Robin Hood, The, 129, 269
African Queen, The, 89
Age of Innocence, The, 28, 44, 71, 220, 230
Aguirre, the Wrath of God, 312
Aiello, Danny, 88
Aldrich, Robert, 64
Alexander Nevsky, 97, 159–160
Alice in the Cities, 313
Alice's Restaurant, 133
Alien, 10, 45
Allen, Dede, 131, 132, 310
Allen, Robert, 187
Allen, Woody, 45, 53, 108, 110, 193, 196–197,
  199, 217, 236, 338
Altman, Robert, 4, 23, 45, 60, 157–159, 160,
  322–323
Always, 265
Amarcord, 295
ambient sound, 156, 157
American Gigolo, 67, 95
American Graffiti, 234
American in Paris, An, 57, 250, 253
ancillary markets, 257–258
And the Ship Sails On, 295
Andersson, Bibi, 286–288
Angels with Dirty Faces, 89, 171
angle of view, 21
Annie Hall, 45, 111–112, 193–195, 196, 199,
  217–218, 236, 338

Another Woman, 197
antinarrative, 313
Antonioni, Michelangelo, 281–285, 289, 292, 294,
  298–300, 315
Apocalypse Now, 5, 10, 45, 51–54, 107, 153–154,
  162, 167–168, 172, 173
Archer, Anne, 361
associational montage, 143–149
Astaire, Fred, 249
Astruc, Alexandre, 303, 305
attributional errors, 321, 333–338
auteurism, 280–81, 304
auteurist film theory, 347–351
Autumn Afternoon, An, 21

back light, 56
Back to the Future, 355
Bad Sleep Well, The, 268
Bailey, John, 67
Baldwin, William, 49, 99
Ballad of Cable Hogue, The, 142
Ballhaus, Michael, 50, 51, 79
Bananas, 196
Bancroft, Anne, 144
Bandwagon, The, 58, 250
Barbaro, Umberto, 299
Barbieri, Gato, 324
Barfly, 130
Barnes, Paul, 223
Barry, John, 182
Basic Instinct, 210, 270
Batman, 3, 37, 180, 182, 232–233, 235, 257–258
Batman Returns, 232

Battle of Algiers, The, 357

Battleship Potemkin, The, 378

Bazin, Andre, 343–346

Bed and Board, 307

Beetlejuice, 232

Bergman, Ingmar, 207, 281, 285–289, 292, 296, 298, 315, 347

Bergman, Ingrid, 18, 57, 89, 123, 229

Berkeley, Busby, 249

Bernstein, Elmer, 180–181

Bertolucci, Bernardo, 63, 66, 199–200, 322, 324–325

beta movement, 39

Beverly Hills Cop, 266

Bigelow, Kathryn, 363

Bill and Ted's Excellent Adventure, 174

Birds, The, 19, 181

Birth of a Nation, The, 187–189

Bitter Tears of Petra von Kant, The, 311

Björnstrand, Gunnar, 286

Black Cat, The, 227

Blade Runner, 81–82, 166–167

blockbuster, 258, 266–267

Blonde Venus, 351

Blow Up, 284

Blue Angel, The, 165

Blue Steel, 363, 365

Blue Velvet, 290, 293

Boat, The, 17

Bogart, Humphrey, 87, 88, 89, 122, 247, 268

Bonnie and Clyde, 131–132, 133, 134, 310

boom, 25, 27, 41

Booth, Wayne, 206–207

Born on the Fourth of July, 78–79, 323, 359

Bourne, Mel, 45

Boxcar Bertha, 230

Bram Stoker's Dracula, 50–51, 53, 72–74, 79–80, 81–84, 256

Branagh, Kenneth, 65, 171, 326

Brando, Marlon, 52, 85, 86, 91, 93, 133, 171, 199, 322–324

Breakfast at Tiffany's, 181

Breathless, 268, 304–305, 308, 315

Brecht, Bertolt, 238

Brennan, Walter, 88

Bresson, Robert, 94–95, 166–167

Breton, André, 289

Bride Wore Black, The, 268, 307

Bridges, Jeff, 272–273

Bridges of Madison County, The, 4, 8

Bring Me the Head of Alfredo Garcia, 142

British Sounds, 308

Broken Blossoms, 189

Buffalo Bill and the Indians, 159

Bugsy, 64

Bullets over Broadway, 197

Bullitt, 23, 180

Bullock, Sandra, 273

Bunuel, Luis, 281, 289–293, 295–296, 298, 315, 353

Burks, Robert, 35

Burn!, 357

Burr, Raymond, 113

Burton, Tim, 232, 235, 281

Burtt, Ben, 234

Butcher, The, 309

Cabinet of Dr. Caligari, The, 97, 98, 225

Cage, Nicholas, 367

Cagney, James, 87, 92, 171, 247

Cahiers du Cinema, 304, 343

Caine Mutiny, The, 89

California Split, 157

Cambern, Donn, 334–335

camera angle, 15–21, 41

camera lens, 21–25

camera movement, 25–31

camera position, 9–15

Cameron, James, 63

Campion, Jane, 364

Cape Fear, 228, 230

Capra, Frank, 281

Carné, Marcel, 325

Caron, Leslie, 57

Carpenter, John, 134

Carrey, Jim, 77

Casablanca, 89, 122–127, 130, 269, 351

Casanova, 295

Casino, 230

Casque d'Or, 325

Caucasian Chalk Circle, The, 238

causality, 200–205

Center for the Study of Commercialism, The, 260

Chabrol, Claude, 268, 304, 309

Chandler, Raymond, 209

Chaney, Lon, Jr., 250

Chaplin, Charles, 4, 9, 13–14, 87, 88, 95, 110, 141, 143, 162, 326–327, 374
character stars, 90
Chase, Borden, 198
Chase, The, 133
Chatman, Seymour, 210–211
Cher, 367
Chorus Line, A, 242, 248
Chung Kuo cina, 285
Cinecitta, 299
Cinema Journal, 326
cinematic self-reflexivity, 236–242
cinematography, 45, 49–67
Circus, The, 110
Citizen Kane, 5, 15, 99, 148–149, 170–171, 178–179, 327–328, 345–346, 375
City Lights, 13–14, 95
City of Hope, 202
City of Women, 295
Clair, René, 161
Cleo From Five to Seven, 309
Cliffhanger, 76, 257
Clift, Montgomery, 198, 219
Clive, Colin, 227
Close Encounters of the Third Kind, 264–265
Close, Glenn, 363
close-up, 9, 41
Clowns, The, 295
Cobweb, The, 181
Cocktail, 130
cognitive film theory, 366–371
color cinematography, 60–63
Color of Money, The, 91
Color Purple, The, 265
Columbo, 265
Come Back to the Five and Dime, Jimmie Dean, Jimmie Dean, 159
compositing, 74, 84
composition, 8
Conan the Barbarian, 358
Conformist, The, 66–67, 323, 325
continuity editing, 121–131, 366, 368
continuity of lighting, 58–60
contrast, 54
conventions, 63
Conversation, The, 53
Convoy, 142
Cool Hand Luke, 91

Cooper, James Fenimore, 243
Copland, Aaron, 176, 177, 178, 180
Coppola, Francis Ford, 50, 51, 61, 71–72, 73, 112, 246, 256, 281, 313, 347
Corman, Roger, 230
Costner, Kevin, 5, 96–97, 130, 181, 191, 321, 355
costume design, 72–73
costumes, 71
Cotton Club, The, 53
Cotton, Joseph, 14, 18, 170
coverage, 85
crane shots, 25, 41
Crenna, Richard, 360
Crimes and Misdemeanors, 197
Crisis, 285
Criss Cross, 168
criticism, 318
Cross of Iron, 142
cross-cutting, 121, 366
Crow, The, 37
Cruise, Tom, 256, 359
Cry in the Dark, A, 90
cue sheet, 174
Cukor, George, 12
Culkin, Macaulay, 266
Curtiz, Michael, 269, 351
cut, 106
Czapsky, Stefan, 233

Dali, Salvador, 290, 353
Dances With Wolves, 5, 112, 156, 182, 321–322
Daniel, 109
Daviau, Allen, 45, 56, 64
Davis, Bette, 88, 89
Day for Night, 307
Day-Lewis, Daniel, 163
Dead Again, 65–66, 326–328
Dead of Winter, 133
Dead Poets Society, 163, 270
Dean, James, 91, 93
Death of a Salesman, 310
Deathtrap, 109
deduction, 329–331
deep-focus cinematography, 344
Delerue, Georges, 174
Delinquents, The, 158
Dementia 13, 53
De Niro, Robert, 90, 91, 230, 375

DePalma, Brian, 28, 53, 246, 378
depth of field, 21, 49
description, 329–333
design concept, 80
deviant plot structure, 198
Devil Is a Woman, The, 351
Dial M for Murder, 327
dialogue cutting point, 172
Diary of Anna Magdalena Bach, The, 311
Dick Tracy, 99
Dickerson, Ernest, 61, 62, 338
Die Hard, 5
Die Hard with a Vengeance, 5
Dietrich, Marlene, 351–352, 363
direct sound, 156
Discreet Charm of the Bourgeoisie, The, 292–293
dissolve, 106
diversification, 258
Do the Right Thing, 75–76, 78, 240, 242, 338
documentaries, 221
documentary realism, 221–225
dolly shot, 25, 27, 41
Don't Drink the Water, 196
Double Indemnity, 168
Douglas, Michael, 361
Dr. Zhivago, 181
Dracula, 250
Dreyer, Carl, 281
Driller Killer, 346
Driving Miss Daisy, 216, 217
Drunken Angel, 178, 296
Duel, 265
Dunaway, Faye, 131
Duras, Marguerite, 306
Dustmen, 281
Duvall, Robert, 88

E.T., 44, 55, 177, 258, 263–266
Eastwood, Clint, 96, 219
Easy Rider, 26, 27, 47, 132, 134, 148–149, 181, 310, 334–335, 357
editing, 105–149
Edward Scissorhands, 182, 232, 233, 235
8½, 294
84 Charlie MoPic, 209
Eisenstein, Sergei, 96, 143, 159, 160, 281, 378
El Dorado, 245
Elfman, Danny, 180–182
Empire of the Sun, 265

Empire Strikes Back, The, 234
emulsion, 21
Enoch Arden, 188–189
Equus, 109
Eraserhead, 293
errors of continuity, 129
establishing shot, 9
Even Dwarfs Started Small, 312
Every Man for Himself and God Against All, 312
explicit causality, 201–202
expressionism, 18, 33, 34, 73, 97, 225–229, 231, 269
Exterminating Angel, The, 292
extras, 87
eyeline match, 123, 366–367

Face to Face, 289
fade, 106
fall-off, 54
Fame, 242, 248
Family Plot, 19
Fanny and Alexander, 289
fantasy, 231–235
Fassbinder, Rainer Werner, 311–312, 313–314, 315
Fatal Attraction, 361–363
Fear Eats the Soul, 311
Fearless, 56
feature films, 4
Fellini, Federico, 281, 294–296, 298–299, 315, 347
feminist film theory, 362–366
Ferzetti, Gabriel, 96
Field of Dreams, 97, 182, 355
fill light, 56
film noir, 56, 64, 66, 168
Film Quarterly, 326
final cut, 106
Finian's Rainbow, 53
Firm, The, 256
First Blood, 211
Fischer, Gunnar, 286–287
Fistful of Dollars, A, 296
flashing, 61
Flatliners, 89
Fleming, Victor, 71
Fly, The, 250
Flynn, Errol, 129
focal length, 21
Foley technique, 173
Fonda, Peter, 27

Fool for Love, 159
forced perspective, 83
Ford, Harrison, 121, 270
Ford, John, 88, 142, 201, 230, 268–269, 281, 304, 347
Forrest Gump, 76, 181, 266
Fort Apache, 142, 268
Foster, Jodie, 101, 271
Four Friends, 133
400 Blows, The, 306–307
Fourth Man, The, 270–271
Fox and His Friends, 311
Fox, Michael J., 355
frame, 8, 38
frameworks of interpretation, 333
Frankenheimer, John, 108
Frankenstein, 98, 226, 250
Freeman, Morgan, 130, 216
French Connection, The, 209–210, 212
French New Wave, 280, 299, 303–310, 347
Frenzy, 19, 327
Freud, Sigmund, 239, 351, 353
Freund, Carl, 31, 269
Friday the 13th, 252, 346
Fugitive Kind, The, 109
Fugitive, The, 121
Furst, Anton, 233

Galileo, 238
Gallipoli, 269
gangster film, 245–248
Ganz, Bruno, 314
Gardener Gets Watered, The, 186
Gardens of Stone, 53
Garland, Judy, 46, 86, 90, 249
Gaslight, 327–328
general-interest journal-based criticism, 322–325
genres, 242–252
George, Susan, 20
Gere, Richard, 67, 130, 271
Ghost, 260–261
Ghostbusters, 47
Gibson, Mel, 260, 269
Gielgud, John, 171
Ginger and Fred, 295
Glass, Philip, 223
Glory, 182
Go-Between, The, 46
Goalie's Anxiety at the Penalty Kick, The, 313–314

Godard, Jean-Luc, 30, 204, 238, 241, 268, 304, 308, 315, 325
Godfather, The, 46, 53, 61, 88, 112, 246, 248
Godfather Part II, The, 53, 61
Godfather Part III, The, 53
Gold Rush, The, 9
Golden Egg, The, 274
Goldsmith, Jerry, 176
Gone With The Wind, 27, 53, 71
Goodfellas, 28, 29, 80, 81, 91, 230
Graduate, The, 91, 144–149, 165–166, 181
Grant, Cary, 18, 19, 57, 228
gray scale, 47
Great Ecstasy of Sculptor Steiner, The, 312
Great Train Robbery, The, 26
Greenberg, Adam, 46, 63
Griffith, D. W., 188–190
gross, 256
Guilty as Sin, 109
Gunfighter, The, 245

Hail Mary, 308
Halloween, 250, 252
Hammett, 313
Hand, The, 358
Hanks, Tom, 76, 266, 357
Hannah and Her Sisters, 197
hard light, 54–55
Hawks, Howard, 88, 177, 198–199, 200, 304
Hayasaka, Fumio, 178
Health, 159
Heart of Darkness, 327
Heart of Glass, 312, 313–314
Heaven's Gate, 61
Heiress, The, 176
Hemingway, Ernest, 206–207
Hepburn, Katharine, 88, 89
Herlth, Robert, 31
Hero, 91
Herrmann, Bernard, 35, 178–179, 181
Herzog, Werner, 313–314
High Noon, 5, 181, 268, 383
High Sierra, 66, 247–248
high-key lighting, 56
Hiroshima, Mon Amour, 305–306, 383
historical realism, 220–221
Hitchcock, Alfred, 4, 14–15, 16–17, 18–19, 32–36, 40, 41, 48, 57, 113, 135, 149, 158, 207, 227, 229, 231, 236, 268–269, 281, 300, 302, 304,

309, 327–329, 344, 346–347, 348–349, 350, 369, 379

Hoffman, Dustin, 20, 90, 91, 144, 165, 335
homage, 95, 268
Home Alone, 266
Home Alone 2, 256
Honkytonk Man, 219
Hook, 265
Hopkins, Anthony, 101, 353
Hopper, Dennis, 27
Horner, James, 182
horror film, the, 250–252
Hour of the Wolf, 289
Hud, 91
hue, 46
Huillet, Danièle, 311
Humoresque, 327
Hunter, Holly, 364
Husbands and Wives, 197
Hustler, The, 91

I Vitelloni, 294
identification, 329–333
ideological film theory, 354–362
ideology, 354
Ikiru, 296
Il Grido, 281
implicit causality, 202
implied author, 206–208
Indecent Proposal, 45
Indiana Jones and the Last Crusade, 234, 264
Indiana Jones and the Temple of Doom, 234, 265
Industrial Light and Magic, 234
integration, 257
intensity, 46
Interiors, 196
internal structural time, 5
interpretaton, 332–333
interpretive processing, 366
interpretive reorganization, 333
Intolerance, 188–189
Invasion of the Body Snatchers, 20, 24, 332–333, 338
iris, 108, 110
Islands in the Stream, 206
Ivory, James, 220

Jackson, Samuel L., 195
Jancsó, Miklós, 11
Jannings, Emil, 165, 269

Jaws, 2, 234, 259, 261, 266, 344
JFK, 97, 192–193, 359
Josephson, Erland, 286
Journey into Fear, 327
Judith of Bethulia, 189
Juliet of the Spirits, 294–295
jump-cut, 131, 305
Jurassic Park, 2, 9, 36, 76, 84, 234, 256, 258–259, 262–266, 381
Just Before Nightfall, 309

Kael, Pauline, 322–325, 328
Kagemusha, 268–269, 296–297
Kaminski, Janusz, 221
Karloff, Boris, 250
Keaton, Diane, 111, 193
Kelly, Gene, 57
Kelly, Grace, 19
key light, 56
Killer Elite, The, 142
Killers, The, 168
King Lear, 296, 308
King of Comedy, The, 230
Kings of the Road, 313
Kinski, Klaus, 312
Kiss Me Deadly, 64, 65
Kluge, Alexander, 310
Kovacs, Laszlo, 47
Kovic, Ron, 359
Krabbe, Tim, 273–274
Kubrick, Stanley, 4, 5, 309
Kurosawa, Akira, 23, 28, 95, 96, 110, 178, 218, 268–269, 281, 295–298, 315, 347
Kyo, Machiko, 95

L.A. Story, 134–135, 141, 149
L'Atalante, 324–325
L'avventura, 281–282, 285
L'eclisse, 282–284, 285
La Bête Humaine, 324
La Chienne, 324
La Dolce Vita, 294
La Notte, 283
La Strada, 294
Lacan, Jacques, 351
Ladd, Alan, 208, 245
Lady in the Lake, 209
Lady Vanishes, The, 18
Lang, Fritz, 166, 226, 269, 281

Last Laugh, The, 31
Last of the Mohicans, The, 58–59, 163, 165, 374
Last Tango in Paris, 45, 48, 63, 91, 199–200, 210, 322, 328
Last Wave, The, 269
Last Year at Marienbad, 203–204, 205, 308
latent meaning, 332
Laughton, Charles, 55
Laura, 181
Lawrence of Arabia, 230
Le Gai Savoir, 204–205, 308, 315
Leaud, Jean-Pierre, 306–307
Lee, Brandon, 37
Lee, Spike, 46, 61, 62, 75, 76, 80, 240, 241, 338
Left-Handed Gun, The, 133
Leigh, Janet, 135, 330
Leone, Sergio, 96, 179
Leonetti, Matthew, 65, 66
Les Biches, 309
letterbox, 5
Levine, Ted, 153
Levinson, Barry, 64
Light Sleeper, 95
Lighting Over Water, 313
Lindblom, Gunnel, 286
Lion King, The, 212
Little Big Man, 133
Little Caesar, 245, 246
Lloyd, Walt, 60
Lonesome Dove, 88
long shot, 9, 41
long take, 148, 296, 344
Long Day's Journey into Night, 109
Long Goodbye, The, 159
Longtime Companion, 357
Lorenzo's Oil, 270
Lorre, Peter, 126
Losey, Joseph, 46
Lost Honor of Katherina Blum, The, 311
Love and Death, 196
Love at Twenty, 307
Love on the Run, 307
low-key lighting, 56
Lubitsch, Ernst, 269
Lucas, George, 53, 158, 191, 236, 259
Lugosi, Bela, 250
Lumet, Sidney, 107, 108–109
Lumière, Auguste, 186
Lumière, Louis, 186

Lundgren, Dolph, 96
Lynch, David, 290, 293
Lyne, Adrian, 45

M, 166, 269
M*A*S*H, 158
MacBeth, 296
Mad Magazine, 258
Mad Max, 270
Magic Flute, The, 289
Magnani, Anna, 301
Magnificent Seven, The, 180–181, 271, 296
Mainwaring, Daniel, 338
Malcolm X, 46, 61–62, 72
Malle, Louis, 309
Man Who Knew Too Much, The, 18, 19, 32–36, 181
Man with One Red Shoe, The, 271
Man with the Golden Arm, The, 181
Manhattan, 45, 197
Marathon Man, 24
Marcus Welby, 265
Marnie, 19, 181
Martin, Steve, 134
Masina, Giulietta, 294
Mask, The, 13, 15, 77
Masks, 309
Mason, James, 12, 327
master shot, 85, 123
Mastrantonio, Mary Elizabeth, 77
Mastroianni, Marcello, 294
matched cut, 123
mattes, 71
Mayer, Carl, 269
McCabe and Mrs. Miller, 23, 45, 157, 159
McCarthy, Kevin, 20, 24, 333
McCrea, Joel, 16
McQueen, Steve, 23, 54, 180, 242
Mean Streets, 230
medium shot, 9, 41
Meeker, Ralph, 65
Meet Me in St. Louis, 250
melodrama, 312
Menzies, William Cameron, 71
Merritt, Russell, 187
method acting, 91–93
Metropolis, 225–226, 269
Michi, Maria, 325
Mickey One, 133
Midnight Cowboy, 91

Midnight Express, 358
Midsummer Night's Sex Comedy, A, 197
Mifune, Toshiro, 95
Miller, George, 270, 315
miniatures, 71, 72
Minnelli, Vincente, 249–250
mise-en-scene, 44, 45
Mississippi Mermaid, 307
Missouri Breaks, The, 133
Mitchum, Robert, 55, 99, 169, 245
Mo' Better Blues, 62, 174
Modern Times, 141, 143, 162, 374
Mondshein, Andrew, 107
Monroe, Marilyn, 351, 363
Monsieur Verdoux, 328
montage, 112
Moonstruck, 367
Moore, Demi, 261
Moore, Michael, 192
Morning After, The, 109
Morocco, 351
Morricone, Ennio, 179
Morris, Errol, 222, 223
motion parallax, 23
motion perspective, 23, 27
Mr. Deeds Goes to Town, 88
Mulligan, Robert, 108
Murch, Walter, 153, 154, 161, 168, 173, 234
Murder on the Orient Express, 109
Murmur of the Heart, 309
Murnau, F. W., 28, 30, 31, 34, 231, 269, 281
Murphy, Eddie, 266
music, 173–182
musical, the, 248–250
My Night at Maud's, 309
Myers, Mike, 237
Mystic Pizza, 89

Nashville, 157, 159
Natural Born Killers, 17, 20, 181, 359
Nazarin, 291
neo-realism, 281, 294, 299–303, 310, 315
new wave, 299
New German Cinema, 299, 310–314
New Jack City, 246
New York, New York, 230
Newman, Paul, 91, 93
newspaper and television reviewing, 321–322
newsreels, 169

Nichols, Mike, 165
Nicholson, Jack, 285
Night Gallery, 265
Night Moves, 133
Night of the Hunter, The, 45, 55, 98
Nightmare Before Christmas, The, 232
Nightmare on Elm Street, 252
1941, 265
Nobody's Fool, 91
nonsynchronous sound, 157, 163–164, 166, 172
normal lens, 21
North by Northwest, 19, 181, 348
Nosferatu, 97, 98, 225–226, 231
Not Reconciled, 311
Notorious, 18, 57, 227–228, 229, 350, 369
Novak, Kim, 46
Numero Deux, 308
Nykvist, Sven, 286–287

Oberhausen Film Festival, 310
Of Mice and Men, 176
off-screen sound space, 157, 166–167
Oldman, Gary, 51
Olivier, Laurence, 24, 171
Olmi, Ermanno, 299
On the Waterfront, 85–86
Once Upon a Time in the West, 5, 96, 179
One From the Heart, 53
180-degree rule, 126–129
One Sings the Other Doesn't, 309
open narrative, 307
Open City, 300–303, 324–325
Opera, 238
Ophuls, Max, 325
ordinary fictional realism, 216–220
Orlando, 154, 364–366
Orphans of the Storm, 189
Ossessione, 299, 324–325
Osterman Weekend, The, 142
Our Town, 176
Out of Africa, 46, 91, 128–129, 182
Out of the Past, 168, 169
Out One Specter, 309
Ozu, Yasujiro, 18, 21

pan, 25–27, 41
panned-and-scanned, 5
parallel action, 121
Passenger, The, 285

Passion of Anna, The, 289
Pat Garrett and Billy the Kid, 142, 143
Paull, Lawrence, G., 81, 82, 166
Peck, Gregory, 245
Peckinpah, Sam, 16, 17, 133, 135, 136, 142, 148, 322–323, 335
Peggy Sue Got Married, 53
Penn, Arthur, 131, 132, 133, 310
People of the Po, 281
perceptual processing, 366
perceptual realism, 347
Perfect Couple, A, 159
performance styles, 45
Perkins, Tony, 207, 228, 349
persistence of vision, 38
Persona, 287–289
personality stars, 90
Peterson, Wolfgang, 17
phi phenomena, 39
Philadelphia, 357
Piano, The, 364–365
Pickpocket, 94, 95, 166
Picnic at Hanging Rock, 269
pictorial lighting design, 50–54
pixels, 74
Planet of the Apes, 176
Platoon, 174, 358
Play It Again Sam, 196
Player, The, 159
Playtime, 162–163, 345–346
plot, 193–206
Point Break, 363–365
point-of-view, 206, 208–209
polyvalence, 319
Pontecorvo, Gillo, 357
Popeye, 159
post-dubbing, 162
Postcards from the Edge, 90
postmodernism, 326, 328
Potemkin, 96, 97
Potter, Sally, 154, 364
practical, 49
Pratt, Roger, 233
Pretty Woman, 89, 90, 130, 260–261
primary color, 47
Prince of the City, 108, 109
product placement, 260–262
product tie-ins, 259
production design, 45, 70, 71–85

production values, 35
Providence, 309
Psycho, 16–17, 19, 135, 141, 181, 207, 227, 228, 265, 327, 329, 344, 379
psychoanalytic film theory, 351–354
Public Enemy, The, 245
Pulp Fiction, 195–196, 197–198, 370
Purple Rose of Cairo, The, 197

Q & A, 109
Quintet, 159

rack focusing, 34
Radio Days, 197
Raging Bull, 230
Ragtime, 174
Raiders of the Lost Ark, 234, 264–265
Rain Man, 91
Rains, Claude, 129
Raksin, David, 181
Rambo III, 360–361
Rambo: First Blood Part II, 319–320, 355
Ran, 296
Rashomon, 95, 96, 218, 296
Rathbone, Basil, 129
Ray, Nicholas, 313
Ready-to-Wear, 159
real author, 206
realism, 216–225
realist film theory, 343–347
realistic lighting design, 49–50
realistic sound, 153
rear projection, 51
Rear Window, 19
Rebecca, 18, 327–328
Red Psalm, 11
Red River, 88, 177, 198–199, 200, 219
Reeves, Keanu, 51
reflected sound, 156
Reifenstahl, Leni, 191
Reiner, Rob, 224–225
Remains of the Day, The, 220
Remington, Frederic, 243
Renoir, Jean, 324–325, 345
Resnais, Alain, 203, 305, 315
Return of Martin Guerre, The, 271
Return of the Jedi, 153, 234
rhetoric, 320
Richardson, Ralph, 171

Ride the High Country, 46, 142
Rio Bravo, 88
Rite of Spring, The, 322, 324
River Wild, The, 91
Rivette, Jacques, 309
Road Warrior, The, 270
Roaring Twenties, The, 89
Robbe-Grillet, Alain, 308
Roberts, Julia, 89, 90, 130, 261
Robin Hood: Prince of Thieves, 129, 130, 182
Robinson, Edward G., 246
Robocop, 270, 357
Rocky, 31
Rocky IV, 96, 97, 356
Roger and Me, 192–193, 222
Rogers, Ginger, 249
Rohmer, Eric, 309
room tone, 157
Rope, 149, 346
Rosenblum, Ralph, 111, 338
Rosenman, Leonard, 181
Rossellini, Roberto, 300–303, 324
Rosza, Miklos, 175
rough cut, 106
Rumble Fish, 53
running time, 4
Running on Empty, 107, 108, 109

Salvador, 358
Sand Pebbles, The, 242
Sanjuro, 268
saturation, 46
Saturday Night Live, 236
Satyricon, 295
Sauve Qui Peut LaVie, 308
Sayles, John, 202
Scarface, 245, 246, 358
Scarfiotti, Ferdinando, 66, 67
Scarlet Express, The, 351
Scenes from a Marriage, 289
Schaffner, Franklin, 108
Scheider, Roy, 24
schema, 118, 367
Schindler's List, 46, 220, 221, 264–265, 335
Schlesinger, John, 24
Schlondorff, Volker, 310–311
Schneider, Maria, 325
scholarly criticism, 325–329
Schrader, Paul, 67

Schwarzenegger, Arnold, 54, 63, 212, 270, 351
Scorsese, Martin, 28, 29, 44, 53, 71, 80, 81, 220, 228, 230, 281, 323, 347
Scott, George C., 206
Scott, Randolph, 16
screen reality, 215
Screen, 326
Seagull, The, 109
Searchers, The, 142, 201–202, 205, 244, 268
Second Awakening of Christa Klages, The, 311
Seigfried, 226
Selznick, David O., 350
Senso, 325
sequence shot, 148
Serpico, 109
sets, 71
Seven Samurai, 28, 271, 296–298
Seventh Seal, The, 285–286
Seventh Veil, The, 327
Shadow of a Doubt, 14–15, 18
Shame, 289
Shane, 46, 155, 208–209, 245
Shanghai Express, 351
She Wore a Yellow Ribbon, 268
She's Gotta Have It, 80–81, 240
Sheen, Martin, 10, 52, 107, 167
Shining, The, 309
Shoot the Piano Player, 307
Shootist, The, 93–94
Short Cuts, 60, 159
shot, 11
shot-reverse-shot series, 125, 165
shutter, 38
Sid Caesar Show, The, 196
Siegel, Don, 94, 332, 338
Signoret, Simone, 325
signs, 319
Silence of the Lambs, 101, 153, 352–353, 368–369
Silence, The, 287
Simon, Michel, 324
Singin' in the Rain, 57, 250, 253
Sinise, Gary, 76
Sirk, Douglas, 311, 315
60 Minutes, 223
Sjöstrom, Victor, 286
Sleeper, 196
Sleepless in Seattle, 256
Sliver, 46, 49–50, 58, 59–60, 61, 99
Sluizer, George, 141, 272, 277

Smiles of a Summer Night, 285
soft light, 54–55
Soldier of Orange, 270
Sommersby, 271
Sophie's Choice, 90
Sorrow and the Pity, The, 194
sound bridges, 157, 164–166, 172
sound design, 153–168
sound designer, 153
sound effects, 172–173
sound hierarchy, 157
sound montage, 157, 167–168
sound perspective, 157, 160–163
Speech, 168
Speed, 76
Spielberg, Steven, 44, 45, 46, 55, 84, 106, 128,
    153, 158, 181, 207, 220, 230, 234, 256, 259,
    263, 264–265, 281, 335, 344
Spinotti, Dante, 58
spotting, 174
Stagecoach, 88, 142, 269
Stallone, Sylvester, 76, 96, 211, 257, 260, 270, 319,
    351–352, 358
star persona, 88
Star Is Born, A, 12–13, 46, 87, 249
Star Wars, 174, 181, 191, 231, 234, 235–236,
    258–259, 266, 336, 383
Stardust Memories, 197
stars, 87
State of Things, The, 313
Steadicam, 31
Steiger, Rod, 85, 86
Stevens, George, 155, 208
Stewart, James, 18, 19, 48, 113, 227, 350
Stolen Kisses, 307
Stone, Oliver, 17, 20, 78, 106, 191–192, 358–359
Stone, Sharon, 49, 99
Storaro, Vittorio, 46, 51, 52, 63, 66, 324
story, 193–196
story time, 5
Story of a Love Affair, 281
Story of Adele H., The, 307
Stranger, The, 327
Strangers on a Train, 19, 348
Strasberg, Lee, 91
Straub, Jean-Marie, 311
Stravinsky, Igor, 322, 324
Straw Dogs, 17, 20, 142, 335
Stray Dog, 296

Streamers, 159
Streep, Meryl, 90–91, 375
Streisand, Barbra, 90
Strike, 143
Struggle, The, 189
sub-plots, 205–206
subjective shot, 34, 47, 208
subtractive color, 47
Sunrise, 28–29
Sunset Boulevard, 169
supervising art director, 71
supporting players, 87
surprise, 33
surrealism, 289
suspense, 33
Sutherland, Kiefer, 141, 272–273
Swayze, Patrick, 261
synchronous sound, 157, 163–164
synthetic sound, 153

Take the Money and Run, 196
Talk Radio, 359
Tandy, Jessica, 216
Tarantino, Quentin, 195, 197
Target, 133
Tati, Jacques, 162, 345–346
Taxi Driver, 28, 91, 230
technical acting, 91–93
Technicolor, 46
telephoto lens, 21, 22, 23, 24, 36, 41, 298
temp track, 174
temporal ambiguity, 305
Terminator, The, 46, 54, 63
Terminator 2, 77, 78, 258–260, 266
That Obscure Object of Desire, 293
Thieves Like Us, 159
Thin Blue Line, The, 222–224
Thing, The, 134, 250
Thirty-Nine Steps, The, 18, 348
This Is Spinal Tap, 224–225
Thomas, Henry, 177
Thomas, Wynn, 61, 75, 76, 80, 338
Thompson, Emma, 65, 326
Three Men and a Baby, 271
Threepenny Opera, The, 238
Throne of Blood, 28, 110, 296–297
Through a Glass Darkly, 287
THX-1138
tilt, 25–27, 41

Time-Warner, 259
Tin Drum, The, 310
Tiomkin, Dimitri, 177
To Catch a Thief, 19
To Kill a Mockingbird, 88
Toland, Gregg, 375
Tomasini, George, 113, 135
Toolbox Murders, The, 346
Top Gun, 356
Topaz, 19
Torn Curtain, 19, 181
Total Recall, 260–262, 270, 360
Touch of Evil, 24
Tout va bien, 308
tracking shot, 25, 27, 41
Travis, Nancy, 272–273
Travolta, John, 195, 197
Treasure of the Sierra Madre, The, 89
Tree of Wooden Clogs, The, 299
Triumph of the Will, 191–192
Trouble with Harry, The, 181
True Heart Susie, 189
True Lies, 75, 212
Truffaut, Francois, 267, 304, 306
Tucker, 53
Turturro, John, 241
Twilight Zone—The Movie, 270
2001: A Space Odessey, 5, 383
typage, 96

Ullman, Liv, 286–287
Un Chien Andalou, 290–291, 353
Under Fire, 176
Under Siege, 256
Under the Roofs of Paris, 161–162
Unforgiven, 4
unit art director, 71
Untouchables, The, 28, 97, 378

Vagabond, 309
Van Peebles, Mario, 246
Vanished World, A, 221
Vanishing, The, 141, 271, 272–278
Varda, Agnes, 309, 311
Variety, 256–257
Veidt, Conrad, 269
Verdict, The, 91
Verhoeven, Paul, 270–271, 277, 315

Vertigo, 18, 19, 40, 41, 46, 181, 227–228, 229, 350
Vigo, Jean, 324–325
Viridiana, 291
Visconti, Luchino, 299, 324
Vishniac, Roman, 221
Vitti, Monica, 283
voice, 205–208
voice-over narration, 111, 168–171
von Sternberg, Josef, 325, 351–352
von Trotta, Margarethe, 311
von Sydow, Max, 286
voyeurism, 351

Wagner, Richard, 179
Wall Street, 359
War and Peace, 4
War is Over, The, 309
Warner Communications Inc., 258
Warshow, Robert, 243
Washington, Denzel, 62
wavelength, 46
Way Down East, 189
Wayne, John, 88, 90, 93, 198, 201, 219, 244
Wayne's World, 236–238
Webb, James, 159
Wedding, A, 159
Weekend, 30–31, 238–240, 242, 308
Weir, Peter, 56, 163, 269, 315
Welch, Bo, 233
Welles, Orson, 5, 15, 24, 148, 170, 179, 281, 302, 327–328, 345, 375
Wenders, Wim, 313–314, 315
Wertheimer, Max, 39
Western, the, 243–245, 355
Wexler, Haskell, 27
White Heat, 92, 247–248
White Hunter, Black Heart, 219
White Sheik, The, 294
Wide Angle, 326
wide-angle lens, 21, 22, 24, 25, 36, 41
widescreen, 5
Wild Bunch, The, 135, 136–140, 141, 142, 357, 360
Wild Child, The, 307
Wild One, The, 171
Wild Strawberries, 286
Wilder, Billy, 169

Williams, John, 177, 181
Williams, Robin, 270
Williams, Treat, 108
Willis, Bruce, 195
Willis, Gordon, 46, 61, 63
Wind from the East, 308
Wings of Desire, 313–314
Winter Light, 287
wipes, 108
Witches of Eastwick, The, 270
Witness, 270
Wiz, The, 109
Wizard of Oz, The, 87
Wood, Robin, 250
Woolf, Virginia, 364–365
Wright, Teresa, 14
Wrong Man, The, 181, 348
Wrong Move, The, 313

Yankee Doodle Dandy, 269
Year of the Dragon, 358
Yesterday Girl, 310
Yojimbo, 268, 296
Young Torless, 310

Zabriskie Point, 285
Zavattini, Cesare, 299
Zea, Kristi, 81
Zelig, 197
Zinnemann, Fred, 5
Zinner, Peter, 111, 248
Zoetrope Studios, 53
zoom lens, 22, 23, 41
Zsigmond, Vilmos, 23, 45, 49, 59, 61